Joel Whitburn's
2003 MUSIC YEARBOOK

Chart Data Compiled From *Billboard's* 2003 Charts.

ISBN 0-89820-159-4

Record Research Inc.
P.O. Box 200
Menomonee Falls, Wisconsin   53052-0200
U.S.A.

Phone: (262) 251-5408
Fax: (262) 251-9452
E-Mail: books@recordresearch.com
Web Site: www.recordresearch.com

CONTENTS

4

2003

INTERNATIONAL HEADLINES — chronologically: The first reports of a new, unnamed disease emerge from Asia in February. Within weeks, cases of Severe Acute Respiratory Syndrome (SARS) spread to more than 25 countries in North America, South America, Europe and Asia. More than 8,000 people are infected and nearly 800 die of the illness.➜➜In March, U.S. and British forces invade Iraq in the war against terrorism and quickly seize huge areas of land. By early April, the forces take control of Baghdad and drive the former Iraqi leadership into hiding. The United States declares major combat over in May; however, fierce resistance fighting continues for the rest of the year. Ex-Iraqi President Saddam Hussein is captured by forces and taken into custody in December.➜➜A 6.4 magnitude earthquake hits Turkey, killing 150 and injuring over a thousand.➜➜An arsonist throws a flaming milk carton aboard a crowded subway train in Daegu, South Korea; the resulting fire kills 120 passengers.

NATIONAL HEADLINES — chronologically: The Columbia space shuttle mission comes to a tragic end when the craft disintegrates into fiery debris over Texas, killing all seven astronauts aboard.➜➜Nearly 100 people perish as a flash fire sweeps through a nightclub in West Warwick, Rhode Island. The band Great White was on stage when pyrotechnics ignited the wood structure.➜➜After missing for nearly four months, the bodies of Laci Peterson and her unborn baby are discovered in San Francisco Bay. Laci's husband, Scott Peterson, is arrested and charged with her murder.➜➜The biggest electrical blackout in history envelopes much of the northeastern U.S., including New York City where thousands of workers take to the streets with little incident.➜➜Unpopular California Governor Gray Davis is recalled by the state's voters. Over 100 candidates seek the office, including the eventual winner, bodybuilder-turned action film star Arnold Schwarzenegger.➜➜Wildfires rage through Southern California, causing 22 deaths and $75 million in property damage.

SPORTS: The Tampa Bay Buccaneers crush the Oakland Raiders 48-21 in Super Bowl XXXVII.➜➜The Syracuse Orangemen capture the school's first-ever NCAA men's basketball title in a thrilling 81-78 win over the Kansas Jayhawks.➜➜The New Jersey Devils beat the Anaheim Mighty Ducks four games to three to win the Stanley Cup.➜➜Led by MVP Tim Duncan, the San Antonio Spurs easily handle the New Jersey Nets for the NBA title, four games to two.➜➜In a heartbreaking postseason, both the Boston Red Sox and the Chicago Cubs continue to suffer the effects of their respective curses as fan interference helps the Florida Marlins beat the Cubs on their way to their second World Series title over the heavily favored New York Yankees, four games to two.➔➔Among the sports legends to pass away in 2003 are gold medal U.S. Olympic hockey coach Herb Brooks (age 66), baseball's Warren Spahn and football's Otto Graham (both age 82).

MOVIES: The year's top moneymakers include *The Lord of the Rings: The Return of the King*, *Finding Nemo*, *Pirates of the Caribbean: The Curse of the Black Pearl*, *The Matrix Reloaded* and *Bruce Almighty*. *The Lord of the Rings: The Return of the King* wins a record-tying 11 Academy Awards, including Best Picture and Best Director (Peter Jackson). *Mystic River* wins the Best Actor Oscar for Sean Penn and the Best Supporting Actor Oscar for Tim Robbins. Charlize Theron wins the Best Actress Oscar for her role in *Monster*, while Renee Zellweger takes home Best Supporting Actress honors for *Cold Mountain*.

TELEVISION: Millions of viewers tune in to watch Clay Aiken and Ruben Studdard battle for the title on *American Idol* (which Studdard eventually won). Other reality shows such as *Survivor* and *The Bachelor* also pull in strong ratings. Other Nielsen ratings winners include *CSI*, *Friends*, *ER*, *Will & Grace* and *Everybody Loves Raymond*.

THE SINGLES

There are two annual sections in this yearbook, a *Pop Annual* and a *Country Annual*. Each section lists in rank order, according to chart performance, all titles that reached their peak position on **The Billboard Hot 100** and **Hot Country Singles & Tracks**, respectively, during 2003. The ranking is based on peak position according to the following criteria:

1) All titles peaking at #1 are listed first, then titles that peaked at #2 are grouped together and shown secondly, then the #3s, etc., all the way through position #100 (#60 for *Country Annual*).

2) Ties among each highest position grouping are broken in the following order:
   a) Total weeks title held its peak position
   b) Total weeks charted in the Top 10
   c) Total weeks charted in the Top 40
   d) Total weeks charted

If there are still ties among titles, a computerized inverse point system is used to calculate a point total for each title based on its weekly chart positions. For each week a title appears on the charts, it is given points based on its chart position for that week (For example, #1 = 100 points, #2 = 99 points, etc.). These points are added together to create a raw point total for each title, which is used to break any remaining ties.

EXPLANATION OF HEADINGS AND SYMBOLS

PEAK POSITION: Title's highest charted position (large bold number)

PEAK DATE: Date title reached its peak position

WEEKS:
- **CH** - Total weeks charted
- **40** - Total weeks charted in the Top 40
- **10** - Total weeks charted in the Top 10
- **PK** - Total weeks title held its peak position

7

RANK: Rank position for the year

GOLD:
- ● RIAA-certified gold single (500,000 units sold)
- ▲ RIAA-certified platinum single (one million units sold — additional million units sold are indicated by a numeral following the symbol)

TIME: Playing time of each title (Pop Annual section only)

DEBUT:
- ❶ Artist's first appearance on chart
- ✦ Artist's first and only appearance on chart

Letter(s) in brackets indicates:
- C - Comedy Recording
- F - Foreign Language Recording
- I - Instrumental Recording
- L - Live Recording
- N - Novelty Recording
- R - Re-entry, reissue, remix, or re-recording of a previous hit by that artist (on the same chart)
- X - Christmas Recording

WEEKLY CHART POSITIONS OF TOP 5

Listed below each Top 5 title are its week-by-week positions as the title climbed, peaked, faded, and fell off the chart. The entire chart life of each Top 5 title is available at a glance.

Lists alphabetically, by artist name, in seven separate sections, all the titles that debuted on *Billboard's Hot 100*, *Bubbling Under The Hot 100*, *Country*, *R&B/Hip-Hop*, *Adult Contemporary*, *Dance Club Play*, *Mainstream Rock Tracks*, and *Modern Rock Tracks* charts from January 4, 2003 through December 27, 2003. The *Hot 100* and *R&B* sections include data from their Sales and Airplay charts; the Country section includes data from its Sales chart.

All #1 titles are identified by a special #1 symbol (❶). All Top 10 hits are shaded and all peak positions and titles are shown in bold (dark) typeface.

EXPLANATION OF COLUMNAR HEADINGS

DEBUT DATE: Date title first charted

PEAK POS: Title's highest charted position (highlighted in bold type). A superscript 'S' next to the peak position identifies Sales chart hits that did not make the *Hot 100*, *Hot R&B/Hip-Hop Singles & Tracks* or *Hot Country Singles & Tracks*. (All Airplay chart hits made these charts.)

WKS CHR: Total weeks charted

GLD: ● RIAA-certified gold single (500,000 units sold)

▲ RIAA-certified platinum single (one million units sold — additional million units sold are indicated by a numeral following the symbol)

CNT: Sequential count of an artist's *Hot 100* (pop) hits — count is continued from our *Top Pop Singles 1955-2002* book (count appears in *Hot 100* section only)

SALES/AIR: The peak positions of all titles that hit the *Sales* (noted with an **S:**) and/or *Airplay* (**A:**) charts appear in this column. (In the Country Singles section only a "Sales" column heading is needed.)

LABEL & NUMBER: Original single label and number ("album cut" is listed in this column for airplay hits never released as commercial singles)

OTHER DATA AND SYMBOLS

¹: A superior number next to a title that peaked at #1 or #2 indicates the total weeks the title held that position

+: Indicates title peaked in 2004

★: Artist's first appearance on chart (symbol not used in *Bubbling Under The Hot 100* section)

↑: Indicates the highest position and/or weeks charted data are subject to change since the title was still charted as of the 4/3/04 cut-off date

/ : Divides a double-hit single. Complete chart data (debut date, peak position, etc.) is shown for both songs of a double-hit single.

(T): 12″ vinyl single

(M): CD maxi-single

(D): DVD single

Letter(s) in brackets indicates:
- **C** - Comedy Recording
- **F** - Foreign Language Recording
- **I** - Instrumental Recording
- **L** - Live Recording
- **N** - Novelty Recording
- **R** - Re-entry, reissue, remix or re-recording of a previously charted title by that artist
- **X** - Christmas Recording

Biographical information appears for nearly every new artist. If a new artist made the *Hot 100* or *Bubbling Under Hot 100* chart, and also made one or more of the other singles charts, their biographical information appears in the *Hot 100* and *Bubbling Under Hot 100* sections only.

TOP 20 ARTISTS

This section lists the *Top 20 Artists* of 2003, in rank order, for each "Singles" chart category. The rankings are compiled from only those titles which **peaked** on the charts in 2003. Since the ranking includes all titles which peaked in 2003, some titles which debuted in late 2002 are included, but are not listed in the 2003 artist sections. Those titles in the 2003 artist sections that have a "+" after their debut date do not qualify for points in 2003 as they peaked in 2004. For example, "Beautiful" by Christina Aguilera debuted in 2002, but peaked at #2 for 1 week in 2003 on the *Hot 100* chart. "Me, Myself And I" by Beyoncé peaked in 2004 so does not qualify for 2003 points.

★ Indicates those top artists who debuted on that particular chart during 2003.

POINT SYSTEM

Points are awarded according to the following formula:

1. Each artist's charted titles are given points based on their highest charted position:

   #1 = 100 points for its first week at #1, plus 10 points
   for each additional week at #1

   #2 = 90 points for its first week at #2, plus 5 points
   for each additional week at #2

   #3 = 80 points for its first week at #3, plus 3 points
   for each additional week at #3

#4-5	= 70		#41-50	= 35
#6-10	= 60		#51-60	= 30
#11-15	= 55		#61-70	= 25
#16-20	= 50		#71-80	= 20
#21-30	= 45		#81-90	= 15
#31-40	= 40		#91-100	= 10

2. Titles that hit exclusively on the *Airplay* and *Sales* charts are given points based on their highest charted position:

#1-10 = 25 points	#31-40 = 10
#11-20 = 20	#41-75 = 5
#21-30 = 15	

3. Total weeks charted are added in.

Ties are broken in this order: most charted hits, most charted Top 40 hits, most charted Top 10 hits, most weeks at #1; and, finally, most #1 hits.

When two or more artists combine for a hit, such as "It's Five O'Clock Somewhere" by Alan Jackson & Jimmy Buffett, the full point value is given to both artists. A duo, such as Brooks & Dunn, is considered a regular recording team, and the points are not shared by either artist individually.

NEW: FEATURING / INTRODUCING

An artist listed on a recording as "Featuring," "With," "Introducing," etc. is now awarded 30% of the total points rather than 100%. For example, in the case of "Love @ 1st Sight" by Mary J. Blige featuring Method Man, Blige (the primary artist) will get 100% of the points and Method Man will get 30%. If two artists are "featured" they will split the 30% equally (15% each). If three artists are featured, they will each get 10%, and so on. The primary artist will always get 100% of the points. Occasionally an artist will release two versions of the same song with a different "featuring" artist on each version. For example, *Billboard* listed the Hot 100 hit "Into You" as by FABOLOUS Featuring Ashanti or Tamia. In this case Ashanti and Tamia will each get 30% of the points, rather than splitting it equally.

TOP HITS

Following is the chronology used in ranking each year's hits:

1) The title's peak position

    All titles peaking at #1 are listed first, then titles that peaked at #2 are grouped together and shown secondly, then the #3s, etc. Ties among each highest position grouping are broken down in this order:

2) Total weeks title held its peak position

3) Total weeks charted in Top 10

4) Total weeks charted in Top 40

5) Total weeks charted

If there are still ties, a computerized inverse point system is used to calculate a point total for each hit based on its weekly chart positions. Each week that a title appears on a chart, it is given points based on its chart position for that week. The maximum points awarded is based on the size of the chart. On a weekly top 100 chart, such as the *Hot 100*, the point scaling is as follows: #1 = 100 points, #2 = 99 points, etc. The maximum points a #1 hit receives on a top 75 chart is 75 points, and so on. These points are added together to create a raw point total for each title, which is used to break any remaining ties.

POP ANNUAL

The Pop Annual section lists, by rank, every title that *peaked* on **The Billboard Hot 100** weekly singles chart in 2003.

HOT 100

The *Hot 100* section lists, by artist, every title that *debuted* on **The Billboard Hot 100** weekly singles chart in 2003. The *Hot 100* section also lists every title that debuted on *Billboard's* weekly **Hot 100 Airplay** and **Hot 100 Singles Sales** charts. Sales hits that did not make the *Hot 100* are identified by a superscript 'S' next to their position in the PEAK POS column. (All *Hot 100 Airplay* hits from 2003 made the *Hot 100*.)

PEAK DATE	WEEKS CH	40	10	PK	RANK	GOLD	Title / PEAK POSITION	Time	DEBUT	Artist

1

PEAK DATE	CH	40	10	PK	RANK	GOLD	Title / PEAK POSITION	Time	DEBUT	Artist
3/8	30	26	17	9	1		**In Da Club** 67,55,27,15,11,4,2,2,**1,1,1,1,1,1,1,1**,2,4,6,8,9,13,18,20,25,31,35,44,46	3:45		50 Cent
12/13	25	23	17	9	2	▲	**Hey Ya!** 57,41,25,15,13,5,3,2,**1,1,1,1,1,1,1,1,1**,3,5,5,6,10,12,16,22... {still charted as of the 4/3/04 cut-off date}	4:09		OutKast
10/4	29	26	15	9	3		**Baby Boy** 57,29,12,9,4,2,2,**1,1,1,1,1,1,1,1,1**,3,5,11,12,13,14,14,17,22,37,38,43,47	4:03		Beyoncé
7/12	27	24	16	8	4		**Crazy In Love** 58,27,13,8,7,6,3,**1,1,1,1,1,1,1**,2,3,7,8,11,14,19,23,26,26,44,46	3:54		Beyoncé
5/31	23	20	13	4	5		**21 Questions** 74,47,21,15,10,5,5,4,2,2,**1,1,1**,3,5,5,11,16,22,35,38,49	3:44		50 Cent
9/6	30	27	12	4	6		**Shake Ya Tailfeather** 66,44,35,34,25,18,12,12,4,3,**1,1,1**,2,2,2,3,5,8,14,14,19,25,27,35,40,41,40,38	4:52		Nelly/P. Diddy/Murphy Lee
2/8	21	20	12	4	7		**All I Have** 25,15,15,12,10,5,**1,1,1**,2,2,2,3,5,9,12,18,26,31,49	4:14		Jennifer Lopez
5/10	32	27	17	3	8		**Get Busy** 82,65,46,34,19,16,6,3,3,3,2,**1,1**,2,2,2,2,4,6,6,8,15,20,20,26,33,38,38,43,50	3:33		Sean Paul
6/28	16	7	4	2	9	▲	**This Is The Night** **1,1**,3,8,17,23,40,46,58,65,80,87,89,96,98,97	3:27	❶	Clay Aiken
12/6	28	25	16	1	10		**Stand Up** 84,59,38,21,15,9,6,4,2,2,2,2,**1**,2,3,4,5,5,5,6,12,15,23,29,31,34,44	3:33		Ludacris
2/1	22	19	11	1	11		**Bump, Bump, Bump** 67,45,22,12,7,7,5,4,2,**1**,2,3,4,4,6,11,13,17,22,27,38,49	4:47		B2K & P. Diddy

2

PEAK DATE	CH	40	10	PK	RANK	GOLD	Title / PEAK POSITION	Time	DEBUT	Artist
8/9	33	28	17	5	12		**Right Thurr** 97,93,79,74,45,31,21,15,9,4,4,3,**2,2,2,2**,3,2,3,3,3,4,4,7,8,13,15,15,31,28,25,29,35	3:36	❶	Chingy
3/29	42	32	15	5	13		**Ignition** 92,87,79,66,57,51,35,32,32,43,38,21,17,13,13,12,12,6,3,**2,2,2,2**,3,3,3,3,5,6,7,9,13,16,21,28,33,40,44,50,50	3:38		R. Kelly
7/12	24	21	12	3	14		**Magic Stick** 75,46,29,19,13,10,8,5,3,5,4,**2,2,2**,4,4,7,13,18,21,30,31,39,50	3:31		Lil' Kim
6/28	10	5	2	2	15	●	**Flying Without Wings** **2,2**,13,18,38,55,70,71,85,91	3:40	❶	Ruben Studdard
10/25	45	36	16	1	16		**Get Low** 98,97,89,85,80,71,60,49,40,32,30,26,19,16,10,11,8,6,6,5,6,4,4,3,3,**2**,3,4,6,7,10,11,12,14,15,18,13,13,15,21,31,35,34,36,49	5:27		Lil Jon & The East Side Boyz
2/1	27	24	12	1	17		**Beautiful** 62,39,22,11,10,6,6,7,6,4,**2**,3,5,7,8,10,12,12,15,16,19,21,25,27,37,44,49	3:58		Christina Aguilera
2/15	20	17	10	1	18		**Mesmerize** 67,25,21,18,12,8,5,**2**,3,3,3,4,6,10,14,19,26,42,63	4:37		Ja Rule
8/2	21	18	9	1	19		**Rock Wit U (Awww Baby)** 56,35,25,21,17,15,10,9,7,4,3,3,**2**,3,5,12,15,19,31,41,46	3:33		Ashanti

3

PEAK DATE	CH	40	10	PK	RANK	GOLD	Title / PEAK POSITION	Time	DEBUT	Artist
12/27	22	16	9	5	20		**Milkshake** 95,91,80,70,57,53,36,25,13,12,4,4,**3,3,3,3,3**,5,7,14,27,35	3:05		Kelis
1/4	20	18	10	4	21		**Air Force Ones** 69,40,23,12,10,7,4,5,**3,3,3,3**,7,10,12,15,19,23,31,41	4:31		Nelly
5/31	24	22	11	3	22		**I Know What You Want** 57,39,30,18,14,11,11,8,7,6,6,4,**3,3,3**,4,7,9,11,14,18,28,39,48	4:53		Busta Rhymes & Mariah Carey
11/8	21	18	10	3	23		**Holidae In** 73,61,31,21,18,9,7,**3,3,3**,4,5,6,8,9,14,16,15,21,33,42	4:30		Chingy
4/5	30	28	13	1	24		**Miss You** 55,38,31,24,15,11,11,14,11,10,7,8,8,5,4,4,5,4,**3**,5,6,9,12,15,15,18,24,39,40,50	4:00		Aaliyah
8/23	25	21	12	1	25		**P.I.M.P.** 70,60,51,48,30,28,18,17,13,7,7,4,**3**,4,4,8,8,6,7,7,10,11,15,20,37	4:09		50 Cent
2/1	20	17	9	1	26		**Cry Me A River** 44,29,17,17,15,8,**3**,6,7,5,6,5,5,10,14,15,23,27,42,58	4:48		Justin Timberlake
8/16	20	16	7	1	27		**Never Leave You - Uh Oooh, Uh Oooh!** 61,54,41,29,24,17,15,10,5,5,6,**3**,5,10,12,11,17,26,36,47	3:03	✦	Lumidee

4

PEAK DATE	CH	40	10	PK	RANK	GOLD	Title / PEAK POSITION	Time	DEBUT	Artist
4/5	34	28	10	3	28	●	**Picture** 91,71,57,46,34,24,24,24,19,16,15,11,11,11,10,6,5,**4,4,4**,7,9,11,10,10,13,14,18,21,32,38,44,50	4:13		Kid Rock
11/1	32	25	10	3	29		**Damn!** 85,73,59,49,35,21,11,11,9,6,5,5,**4,6,4**,4,7,9,11,12,13,15,15,16,20,28,28,36,39,48,46,50	4:58		Youngbloodz
5/31	23	19	9	3	30		**Can't Let You Go** 73,52,36,29,19,17,15,10,8,7,5,5,**4,4,4**,5,12,13,16,19,24,43,48	3:43		Fabolous
2/1	27	24	10	2	31	▲	**I'm With You** 63,35,26,16,12,12,11,7,**4,4**,6,6,7,9,9,8,9,11,12,16,22,23,25,32,35,46,50	3:44		Avril Lavigne

PEAK DATE	WEEKS				RANK	GOLD	Title / PEAK POSITION	Time	DEBUT	Artist
	CH	40	10	PK						
4/26	45	37	10	1	32		**When I'm Gone** 67,65,61,52,49,38,36,36,32,30,29,24,18,17,14,15,14,14,12,7,6,5,**4,6**,8,9,9,9,10,12,13,17,18,19,25,26,29,31,32,35, 39,40,41,45,47	4:20		3 Doors Down
9/20	26	24	10	1	33		**Into You** 67,40,34,30,22,20,15,14,11,9,6,5,5,6,4,5,6,8,9,12,19,19,20,33,40,49	4:21		Fabolous
5/3	8	2	1	1	34	●	**God Bless The U.S.A.** **4**,19,53,71,92,84,100,94	3:02	❶	American Idol Finalists

5

PEAK DATE	WEEKS				RANK	GOLD	Title / PEAK POSITION	Time	DEBUT	Artist
11/8	32	29	17	3	35		**Here Without You** .... 64,53,46,40,25,17,13,8,6,6,**5,5**,6,6,6,7,**5**,7,8,8,7,10,11,9,10,13,17,21,21,24,27,29... {still charted as of the 4/3/04 cut-off date}	3:52		3 Doors Down
9/20	23	16	9	3	36		**Frontin'** 89,76,76,61,56,41,29,20,15,13,7,7,7,**7,5**,7,**5,5**,7,13,16,30,46	3:56	❶	Pharrell
7/19	54	42	17	2	37		**Unwell** 59,49,44,39,34,27,25,20,18,14,12,12,10,8,10,10,7,**5,6**,6,**6,5**,6,9,8,8,10,10,10,10,11,15,15,14,16,17,20,28,32,40,46,48, 49,37,30,34,38,41,40,36,43,42,45,49,50	3:48		Matchbox Twenty
6/7	32	28	12	1	38		**Bring Me To Life** 64,54,43,39,26,25,15,14,10,8,8,6,**5**,6,6,8,8,8,7,7,11,16,17,18,20,22,28,28,33,35,38,42	3:58	❶	Evanescence
5/10	22	19	7	1	39		**Rock Your Body** 61,37,28,21,13,11,10,**5**,7,7,7,7,9,12,14,21,20,31,37,39,43,49	4:28		Justin Timberlake

6

PEAK DATE	WEEKS				RANK	GOLD	Title / PEAK POSITION	Time	DEBUT	Artist
12/20	27	22	10	5	40		**Walked Outta Heaven**	4:30		Jagged Edge
4/26	20	17	4	1	41		**Beautiful**	4:02		Snoop Dogg

7

PEAK DATE	WEEKS				RANK	GOLD	Title / PEAK POSITION	Time	DEBUT	Artist
12/6	33	27	11	4	42		**Suga Suga** .... {still charted as of the 4/3/04 cut-off date}	3:59	✦	Baby Bash
3/8	29	22	9	3	43		**Landslide**	3:44		Dixie Chicks
3/29	25	20	4	1	44		**How You Gonna Act Like That**	3:53		Tyrese
11/8	20	12	4	1	45		**Rain On Me**	4:58		Ashanti

8

PEAK DATE	WEEKS				RANK	GOLD	Title / PEAK POSITION	Time	DEBUT	Artist
8/9	25	22	9	3	46		**Where Is The Love?**	4:28		Black Eyed Peas
3/8	20	14	6	3	47		**Gossip Folks**	3:53		Missy Elliott
8/2	20	14	5	1	48		**In Those Jeans**	4:27		Ginuwine
10/25	35	29	4	1	49		**Why Don't You & I**	3:48		Santana
4/12	19	13	3	1	50		**Excuse Me Miss**	4:18		Jay-Z

9

PEAK DATE	WEEKS				RANK	GOLD	Title / PEAK POSITION	Time	DEBUT	Artist
7/19	20	17	3	2	51		**Miss Independent**	3:33		Kelly Clarkson
12/20	27	21	4	1	52		**Step In The Name Of Love**	4:55		R. Kelly
8/2	35	28	1	1	53		**Drift Away** ....[R]	3:41		Uncle Kracker
1/4	27	18	1	1	54		**Love Of My Life** (An Ode To Hip Hop)	3:45		Erykah Badu

10

PEAK DATE	WEEKS				RANK	GOLD	Title / PEAK POSITION	Time	DEBUT	Artist
7/12	22	17	1	1	55		**So Gone**	3:22		Monica
12/27	18	11	1	1	56		**Change Clothes**	4:17		Jay-Z

11

PEAK DATE	WEEKS				RANK	GOLD	Title / PEAK POSITION	Time	DEBUT	Artist
5/31	31	21		3	57		**No Letting Go**	3:20	✦	Wayne Wonder

12

PEAK DATE	WEEKS				RANK	GOLD	Title / PEAK POSITION	Time	DEBUT	Artist
9/13	20	15		3	58		**Can't Hold Us Down**	4:15		Christina Aguilera
5/10	20	13		1	59		**I Can**	4:13		Nas

13

PEAK DATE	WEEKS				RANK	GOLD	Title / PEAK POSITION	Time	DEBUT	Artist
9/6	20	13		4	60		**My Love Is Like...WO**	3:31		Mya
12/6	18	10		2	61		**Stunt 101**	3:53	❶	G-Unit
10/4	20	14		1	62		**Thoia Thoing**	3:43		R. Kelly
3/1	20	14		1	63		**Wanksta**	3:39	❶	50 Cent
8/30	20	11		1	64		**Like Glue**	3:53		Sean Paul

14

PEAK DATE	WEEKS				RANK	GOLD	Title / PEAK POSITION	Time	DEBUT	Artist
10/18	20	11		1	65		**Can't Stop, Won't Stop**	3:42	❶	Young Gunz
5/10	18	10		1	66		**Sing For The Moment**	4:47		Eminem
9/20	17	9		1	67		**Let's Get Down**	4:16		Bow Wow

15

PEAK DATE	WEEKS				RANK	GOLD	Title / PEAK POSITION	Time	DEBUT	Artist
9/13	28	14		2	68		**The Remedy (I Won't Worry)**	4:13	✦	Jason Mraz
5/31	20	14		1	69		**If You're Not The One**	4:01		Daniel Bedingfield

PEAK DATE	CH	40	10	PK	RANK	GOLD	Title	PEAK POSITION	Time	DEBUT	Artist
3/15	16	10		1	70		Superman		4:44		Eminem
							16				
11/15	43	17		3	71		Headstrong		3:57	❶	Trapt
8/16	20	16		3	72		Are You Happy Now?		3:48		Michelle Branch
6/7	17	9		3	73		Snake		4:40		R. Kelly
							17				
11/29	20	13		4	74		Wat Da Hook Gon Be		3:44		Murphy Lee
9/6	20	15		2	75		It's Five O'Clock Somewhere		3:50		Alan Jackson & Jimmy Buffett
4/26	20	12		2	76		Hell Yeah		3:38		Ginuwine
4/19	20	11		1	77		The Jump Off		3:58		Lil' Kim
							18				
11/1	22	14		3	78		Harder To Breathe		2:52	❶	Maroon5
1/11	29	25		1	79		Your Body Is A Wonderland		3:44		John Mayer
3/15	20	9		1	80		Sick Of Being Lonely		3:34	✦	Field Mob
							19				
6/21	20	12		3	81		Don't Wanna Try		4:04	❶	Frankie J.
9/13	29	18		2	82		Calling All Angels		3:40		Train
12/20	20	11		1	83		Runnin (Dying To Live)		3:48		Tupac
							20				
1/4	20	13		4	84	●	Family Portrait		3:49		P!nk
5/24	20	11		4	85		Fighter		4:06		Christina Aguilera
3/15	20	9		2	86		All The Things She Said		3:26		t.A.T.u.
9/20	18	8		2	87		The Boys Of Summer		4:01	✦	The Ataris
9/6	23	16		1	88		Forever And For Always		4:02		Shania Twain
5/3	20	15		1	89		Angel		3:36		Amanda Perez
7/26	20	12		1	90		Intuition		3:47		Jewel
6/21	20	11		1	91		Put That Woman First		4:06		Jaheim
2/15	20	7		1	92		Lifestyles Of The Rich And Famous		3:10	❶	Good Charlotte
							21				
11/15	17	8		2	93		Stacy's Mom		3:15		Fountains Of Wayne
							22				
9/27	20	10		2	94		What Was I Thinkin'		3:43	✦	Dierks Bentley
6/28	20	12		1	95		Beer For My Horses		3:20		Toby Keith w/Willie Nelson
4/12	20	10		1	96		Have You Forgotten?		3:57		Darryl Worley
8/23	19	10		1	97		I Want You		3:28	❶	Thalia
8/9	13	6		1	98		Love @ 1st Sight		4:40		Mary J. Blige
							23				
11/15	21	11		5	99		Bright Lights		3:54		Matchbox Twenty
1/18	20	14		4	100		19 Somethin'		3:16		Mark Wills
6/21	22	13		2	101		My Front Porch Looking In		3:20		Lonestar
							24				
11/8	28	18		3	102		So Far Away		4:00		Staind
12/20	20	11		2	103		Perfect		4:40		Simple Plan
6/14	20	9		1	104		Say Yes		3:58	✦	Floetry
							25				
1/11	17	9		3	105		I Should Be...		4:57		Dru Hill
8/9	20	9		1	106		Red Dirt Road		3:57		Brooks & Dunn
3/15	20	6		1	107		Man To Man		3:36		Gary Allan
3/22	10	5		1	108		Travelin' Soldier		5:34		Dixie Chicks
							26				
6/21	20	6		3	109		Never Scared		5:15	❶	Bone Crusher
11/15	20	9		1	110		I Love This Bar		4:01		Toby Keith
							27				
10/4	20	8		2	111		Real Good Man		4:10		Tim McGraw
11/1	15	6		2	112		Pass That Dutch		3:39		Missy Elliott
5/10	20	9		1	113		She's My Kind Of Rain		4:07		Tim McGraw
3/29	20	8		1	114		Brokenheartsville		3:50		Joe Nichols

2003

PEAK DATE	WEEKS				RANK	GOLD	Title	PEAK POSITION	Time	DEBUT	Artist
	CH	40	10	PK							
2/22	20	7		1	115		I Just Wanna Be Mad		3:22		Terri Clark
9/27	17	6		1	116		Señorita		4:35		Justin Timberlake
1/11	16	4		1	117		Satisfaction		4:02		Eve

28

PEAK DATE	CH	40	10	PK	RANK	GOLD	Title		Time	DEBUT	Artist
8/9	20	8		4	118		No Shoes, No Shirt, No Problems		2:53		Kenny Chesney
4/26	20	8		2	119		Big Star		3:35		Kenny Chesney
3/8	16	6		2	120		Tell Me (What's Goin' On)		4:11		Smilez & Southstar
1/18	20	9		1	121		Fabulous		3:47		Jaheim
2/22	20	7		1	122		The Baby		3:54		Blake Shelton

29

PEAK DATE	CH	40	10	PK	RANK	GOLD	Title		Time	DEBUT	Artist
5/17	22	10		3	123		Clocks		4:10		Coldplay
12/27	20	10		1	124		There Goes My Life		5:02		Kenny Chesney
4/26	20	8		1	125		That'd Be Alright		3:36		Alan Jackson
10/4	20	5		1	126		Help Pour Out The Rain (Lacey's Song)		3:45	❶	Buddy Jewell
10/18	12	3		1	127		Ooh!		3:10		Mary J. Blige

30

PEAK DATE	CH	40	10	PK	RANK	GOLD	Title		Time	DEBUT	Artist
12/13	20	7		2	128		(there's gotta be) More To Life		3:18		Stacie Orrico
4/26	13	3		2	129		Girlfriend		3:26		B2K
3/15	31	6		1	130		Don't Know Why		3:01	❶	Norah Jones
11/15	20	6		1	131		Who Wouldn't Wanna Be Me		3:38		Keith Urban
6/21	20	3		1	132		Love You Out Loud		3:05		Rascal Flatts

31

PEAK DATE	CH	40	10	PK	RANK	GOLD	Title		Time	DEBUT	Artist
5/17	20	10		2	133		Like A Stone		4:54		Audioslave
8/16	20	6		1	134		Celebrity		3:40		Brad Paisley
6/7	20	5		1	135		Three Wooden Crosses		3:18		Randy Travis
5/31	20	4		1	136		I Believe		3:33		Diamond Rio

32

PEAK DATE	CH	40	10	PK	RANK	GOLD	Title		Time	DEBUT	Artist
5/24	16	5		4	137		I'm Glad		3:42		Jennifer Lopez
5/3	20	9		2	138		Somewhere I Belong		3:34		Linkin Park
9/20	20	7		2	139		Come Over		3:54		Aaliyah
12/20	20	6		2	140		Why Can't I?		3:24		Liz Phair
10/18	20	5		2	141		Tough Little Boys		3:53		Gary Allan
6/21	20	6		1	142		Stay Gone		3:45	❶	Jimmy Wayne
2/1	13	6		1	143		Made You Look		3:21		Nas
7/12	11	2		1	144		Act A Fool		4:30		Ludacris

33

PEAK DATE	CH	40	10	PK	RANK	GOLD	Title		Time	DEBUT	Artist
10/18	20	5		2	145		Bigger Than My Body		4:24		John Mayer
1/11	20	4		1	146		Do That...		5:10		Baby
5/17	12	2		1	147		Beware Of The Boys (Mundian To Bach Ke)		3:56	✦	Pan'jabi MC

34

PEAK DATE	CH	40	10	PK	RANK	GOLD	Title		Time	DEBUT	Artist
2/1	20	4		2	148		Fall Into Me		2:36		Emerson Drive
11/29	20	3		2	149		I Melt		3:53		Rascal Flatts

35

PEAK DATE	CH	40	10	PK	RANK	GOLD	Title		Time	DEBUT	Artist
3/1	17	4		3	150		Blowin' Me Up (With Her Love)		4:18	❶	JC Chasez
11/29	13	4		1	151		Me Against The Music		3:44		Britney Spears
2/1	20	1		1	152		Something		3:40	❶	Lasgo

36

PEAK DATE	CH	40	10	PK	RANK	GOLD	Title		Time	DEBUT	Artist
2/1	15	3		1	153		Paradise		4:02		LL Cool J
12/13	18	2		1	154		Breathe		3:30		Michelle Branch

37

PEAK DATE	CH	40	10	PK	RANK	GOLD	Title		Time	DEBUT	Artist
6/14	20	3		2	155		4 Ever		4:28		Lil' Mo
4/26	8	1		1	156		American Life		4:27		Madonna

38

PEAK DATE	CH	40	10	PK	RANK	GOLD	Title		Time	DEBUT	Artist
2/15	17	3		2	157		You Can't Hide Beautiful		3:28	✦	Aaron Lines
5/24	19	2		2	158		Raining On Sunday		3:50		Keith Urban
9/27	20	4		1	159		Dance With My Father		4:20		Luther Vandross
12/20	19	2		1	160		Cowboys Like Us		3:35		George Strait
6/28	19	1		1	161		Pump It Up		4:00		Joe Budden

PEAK DATE	CH	40	10	PK	RANK	GOLD	Title	PEAK POSITION	Time	DEBUT	Artist
8/9	10	1		1	162		Did My Time		4:04		Korn

39

PEAK DATE	CH	40	10	PK	RANK	GOLD	Title	PEAK POSITION	Time	DEBUT	Artist
11/29	20	2		2	163		Wave On Wave		3:59	✦	Pat Green
10/25	20	2		1	164		This One's For The Girls		4:00		Martina McBride
11/1	20	1		1	165		Clubbin		4:03		Marques (MH) Houston
3/29	19	1		1	166		Emotional Rollercoaster		3:12	✦	Vivian Green

41

PEAK DATE	CH	40	10	PK	RANK	GOLD	Title	PEAK POSITION	Time	DEBUT	Artist
6/7	20			1	167		What A Beautiful Day		3:42		Chris Cagle

42

PEAK DATE	CH	40	10	PK	RANK	GOLD	Title	PEAK POSITION	Time	DEBUT	Artist
7/5	20			1	168		Big Yellow Taxi		3:40		Counting Crows
10/25	20			1	169		So Yesterday		3:31	❶	Hilary Duff

43

PEAK DATE	CH	40	10	PK	RANK	GOLD	Title	PEAK POSITION	Time	DEBUT	Artist
4/19	11			2	170		The Anthem		2:55		Good Charlotte

44

PEAK DATE	CH	40	10	PK	RANK	GOLD	Title	PEAK POSITION	Time	DEBUT	Artist
6/7	16			2	171		In Love Wit Chu		4:11		Da Brat
11/29	10			1	172		Clap Back		4:12		Ja Rule

45

PEAK DATE	CH	40	10	PK	RANK	GOLD	Title	PEAK POSITION	Time	DEBUT	Artist
3/8	11			3	173		What Happened To That Boy		4:29		Baby
12/13	20			1	174		Hell Yeah		4:01		Montgomery Gentry
8/9	19			1	175		Addicted		3:52		Simple Plan
3/29	13			1	176		I Drove All Night		3:56		Celine Dion

46

PEAK DATE	CH	40	10	PK	RANK	GOLD	Title	PEAK POSITION	Time	DEBUT	Artist
1/11	20			3	177		Make It Clap		3:41		Busta Rhymes

47

PEAK DATE	CH	40	10	PK	RANK	GOLD	Title	PEAK POSITION	Time	DEBUT	Artist
7/5	20			3	178		Speed		3:59		Montgomery Gentry
4/19	19			2	179		Concrete Angel		3:45		Martina McBride

48

PEAK DATE	CH	40	10	PK	RANK	GOLD	Title	PEAK POSITION	Time	DEBUT	Artist
7/26	20			2	180		Like A Pimp		4:14		David Banner
9/6	20			1	181		Faint		2:42		Linkin Park
12/13	20			1	182		More & More		3:41		Joe
9/13	13			1	183		Girls And Boys		3:01		Good Charlotte

49

PEAK DATE	CH	40	10	PK	RANK	GOLD	Title	PEAK POSITION	Time	DEBUT	Artist
5/31	20			3	184		What Would You Do?		3:49		The Isley Brothers

50

PEAK DATE	CH	40	10	PK	RANK	GOLD	Title	PEAK POSITION	Time	DEBUT	Artist
11/8	9			2	185		Bad Boy This Bad Boy That		3:17	✦	Bad Boy's Da Band

51

PEAK DATE	CH	40	10	PK	RANK	GOLD	Title	PEAK POSITION	Time	DEBUT	Artist
3/15	12			3	186		I'd Do Anything		3:16	❶	Simple Plan
2/15	20			1	187		Always		3:51	✦	Saliva
3/1	20			1	188		No One Knows		4:14	✦	Queens Of The Stone Age

52

PEAK DATE	CH	40	10	PK	RANK	GOLD	Title	PEAK POSITION	Time	DEBUT	Artist
6/14	11			2	189		Stuck		3:40	❶	Stacie Orrico
8/30	13			1	190		Then They Do		4:11		Trace Adkins

53

PEAK DATE	CH	40	10	PK	RANK	GOLD	Title	PEAK POSITION	Time	DEBUT	Artist
12/27	17			2	191		forthenight		3:49		Musiq
4/5	4			2	192		Damaged		3:50		TLC
12/20	15			1	193		Chicks Dig It		3:29		Chris Cagle

54

PEAK DATE	CH	40	10	PK	RANK	GOLD	Title	PEAK POSITION	Time	DEBUT	Artist
10/18	11			1	194		Got Some Teeth		3:46	❶	Obie Trice

55

PEAK DATE	CH	40	10	PK	RANK	GOLD	Title	PEAK POSITION	Time	DEBUT	Artist
12/27	0			3	195		(I Hate) Everything About You		3:48	✦	Three Days Grace
10/4	13			2	196		A Few Questions		3:43		Clay Walker
7/19	20			1	197		I Wish I Wasn't		4:14		Heather Headley

2003

PEAK DATE	CH	40	10	PK	RANK	GOLD	Title	PEAK POSITION	Time	DEBUT	Artist
							56				
1/4	20			1	198		The Red		3:58	✦	Chevelle
							57				
3/15	20			2	199		Can't Stop		4:27		Red Hot Chili Peppers
8/30	14			1	200		Signs Of Love Makin'		4:05		Tyrese
8/23	11			1	201		99.9% Sure (I've Never Been Here Before)		3:12		Brian McComas
2/22	10			1	202		I Wish You'd Stay		3:57		Brad Paisley
							58				
8/30	10			3	203		Light Your A** On Fire		3:40		Busta Rhymes
3/8	9			2	204		Laundromat		4:25		Nivea
10/11	11			1	205		Low		3:25		Kelly Clarkson
4/19	7			1	206		Pimp Juice		4:52		Nelly
							59				
10/18	20			2	207		Heaven		3:44		Live
6/14	14			2	208		Almost Home		4:49	✦	Craig Morgan
7/19	12			1	209		The Love Song		4:00	✦	Jeff Bates
							60				
7/19	11			2	210		Swing, Swing		3:25	✦	The All-American Rejects
3/8	9			2	211		A.D.I.D.A.S.		3:27	❶	Killer Mike
7/5	5			2	212		Feel Good Time		3:42		P!nk
4/5	16			1	213		X Gon' Give It To Ya		3:36		DMX
							61				
1/25	20			2	214		Fine Again		4:02	✦	Seether
11/8	18			2	215		Weak And Powerless		3:11	✦	A Perfect Circle
12/6	11			2	216		Walking In Memphis		3:46		Lonestar
							62				
3/29	6			2	217		Running		4:01		No Doubt
							63				
3/15	7			2	218		That Girl		3:34	❶	Marques Houston
3/8	10			1	219		Up!		2:52		Shania Twain
							64				
4/19	9			2	220		Girl All The Bad Guys Want		3:15	✦	Bowling For Soup
5/10	6			2	221 ●		Losing Grip		3:53		Avril Lavigne
							65				
4/19	20			3	222		Times Like These		4:16		Foo Fighters
2/1	15			2	223		Come Close To Me		4:18		Common
8/2	20			1	224		Send The Pain Below		4:10		Chevelle
11/22	9			1	225		Party To Damascus		4:03		Wyclef Jean
							66				
3/22	5			2	226		Rock You Baby		3:39		Toby Keith
5/24	10			1	227		Price To Play		3:35		Staind
2/1	5			1	228		Unusually Unusual		3:31		Lonestar
							67				
9/20	20			2	229		Show Me How To Live		4:35		Audioslave
10/25	15			2	230		Walk A Little Straighter		3:38	✦	Billy Currington
							68				
10/25	4			2	231		Trouble		3:11		P!nk
9/27	8			1	232		Where The Hood At		3:39		DMX
							69				
11/22	20			3	233		Still Frame		4:01		Trapt
4/12	20			2	234		Still Ballin		2:50		2Pac
8/23	14			1	235		Hole In The World		4:43		Eagles
7/19	7			1	236		Tell Me Something Bad About Tulsa		3:12		George Strait
							70				
8/23	20			1	237		Breathe		3:47		Blu Cantrell

PEAK DATE	WEEKS				R A N K	G O L D	Title	PEAK POSITION	Time	D E B U T	Artist
	CH	40	10	PK							
11/15	9			1	238		Hot & Wet		3:41		112
7/26	8			1	239		What The World Needs		3:34		Wynonna
							71				
11/1	18			2	240		I Can Only Imagine		4:03	✦	Mercyme
							{still charted as of the 4/3/04 cut-off date}				
							72				
12/20	16			2	241		Away From Me		3:56		Puddle Of Mudd
7/26	9			2	242		Just Because		3:50	✦	Jane's Addiction
2/1	19			1	243		One Of Those Days		3:56		Whitney Houston
8/23	5			1	244		She Only Smokes When She Drinks		3:18		Joe Nichols
							73				
4/19	8			1	245		Straight Out Of Line		3:53	✦	Godsmack
							74				
3/1	4			2	246		Chrome		3:22		Trace Adkins
5/31	8			1	247		Tal Vez ....[F]		4:40		Ricky Martin
							75				
8/30	6			2	248		Na Na Na		4:48		112
12/6	18			1	249		Knock Knock		3:31		Monica
							76				
2/1	20			3	250		Can't Stop Loving You		4:11		Phil Collins
10/18	8			3	251		If I Can't		3:16		50 Cent
5/24	20			2	252		Seven Nation Army		3:51	✦	The White Stripes
3/8	10			2	253		Beautiful Goodbye		3:37	✦	Jennifer Hanson
							77				
5/31	13			4	254		I Love You		5:07		Dru Hill
5/10	5			2	255		P***ycat		3:35		Missy "Misdemeanor" Elliott
4/26	10			1	256		Get By		3:47		Talib Kweli
7/19	5			1	257		The Truth About Men ....[N]		2:56		Tracy Byrd
							78				
12/6	16			2	258		Love You More		4:01		Ginuwine
10/11	15			2	259		24's		4:20		T.I.
2/8	10			2	260		Breathe		7:48	✦	Télépopmusik
4/5	6			1	261		Don't Dream It's Over		3:39		Sixpence None The Richer
							79				
10/18	20			2	262		Amazing		3:43	✦	Josh Kelley
							80				
4/19	3			2	263		Soldier's Heart		4:36		R. Kelly
5/17	11			1	264		Peacekeeper		4:07		Fleetwood Mac
							81				
10/11	10			1	265		Lovin' All Night		3:23		Patty Loveless
1/18	9			1	266		Through The Rain		4:51		Mariah Carey
							82				
10/25	8			2	267		Roc Ya Body "Mic Check 1, 2"		3:24	✦	M.V.P. (Most Valuable Playas)
12/13	15			1	268		Another Postcard		3:22		Barenaked Ladies
10/18	11			1	269		Danger		4:24		Erykah Badu
							83				
2/22	14			4	270		B R Right		4:57		Trina
8/16	18			3	271		Officially Missing You		4:01		Tamia
12/13	5			1	272		One More Chance		3:46		Michael Jackson
							84				
5/17	12			2	273 ●		Try It On My Own		4:28		Whitney Houston

2003

PEAK DATE	CH	40	10	PK	RANK	GOLD	Title	PEAK POSITION	Time	DEBUT	Artist
							85				
2/1	5			2	274		Take You Home		3:52		Angie Martinez
							86				
10/11	13			2	275		Pon De River, Pon De Bank		4:00	❶	Elephant Man
3/22	8			2	276		All I Need		4:00		Fat Joe
3/1	6			2	277		Ma, I Don't Love Her		3:57		Clipse
							87				
10/11	10			5	278		Naggin		4:18		Ying Yang Twins
1/4	9			2	279		Thug Holiday		4:23		Trick Daddy
11/29	6			2	280		Take Me Away		3:28	✦	Fefe Dobson
7/12	20			1	281		Stupid Girl		3:10	✦	Cold
							88				
6/7	6			2	282		How You Want That		3:40		Loon
3/22	2			2	283		The Wreckoning		3:09	✦	Boomkat
							89				
11/22	8			1	284		Waiting For You		3:38		Seal
							90				
5/17	3			2	285		Step Daddy		3:50	✦	Hitman Sammy Sam
1/25	13			1	286		He Is		3:46	❶	Heather Headley
							91				
1/4	8			1	287		Come Into My World		4:02		Kylie Minogue
12/13	6			1	288		I Can't Take You Anywhere		3:16		Scotty Emerick w/Toby Keith
5/17	4			1	289		Roll Wit M.V.P. (We Be Like! The La La Song)........		3:55	❶	Stagga Lee
							92				
8/23	3			2	290		Feelin' Freaky		3:35		Nick Cannon
							93				
11/29	12			1	291		Find A Way		4:11	✦	Dwele
9/27	3			1	292		Rest In Pieces		3:42		Saliva
							94				
3/22	6			1	293		Choppa Style		4:29	✦	Choppa
9/27	2			1	294		Rubberneckin'............................[R]		3:26		Elvis Presley
							95				
8/23	2			2	295		Cop That Sh#!...............................		3:33		Timbaland & Magoo
9/20	8			1	296		Crazy		4:52	✦	Javier
6/7	3			1	297		Flipside......................................		3:50		Freeway
							96				
4/12	5			3	298		No One's Gonna Change You................		4:15	✦	Reina
9/6	4			1	299		Roun' The Globe.............................		3:59		Nappy Roots
11/29	3			1	300		I Need You Now ....[L]		7:00	✦	Smokie Norful
							97				
3/15	5			3	301		Can't Nobody................................		4:04		Kelly Rowland
11/29	5			1	302		Never (Past Tense).........................		3:40	✦	The Roc Project
11/15	3			1	303		This Is How We Do		4:19		Big Tymers
3/8	2			1	304		What We Do..................................		3:45		Freeway
10/4	1			1	305		Sympathy For The Devil		4:04		The Rolling Stones
							98				
9/13	3			3	306		Somnambulist		4:38	✦	BT
							99				
6/7	2			2	307		Make Me A Song............................		3:14	❶	Kiley Dean
3/15	1			1	308		Break You Off		3:36		The Roots
4/19	1			1	309		Yeah Yeah U Know It.........................		4:09		Keith Murray

DEBUT DATE	PEAK POS	WKS CHR	G L D	ARTIST / Title	Sales/Air	Label & Number
				AALIYAH		
6/14/03	32	20		17 Come Over...A:29		album cut
				from the album *I Care 4 U* on Blackground 060082		
				ADAGIO ★		
				R&B vocal group from Chicago, Illinois: Rocky, Jesse Richardson, Chip t.d. and Marceló.		
2/15/03	51 S	1		1 Wednesday		Satin Horse 4934
				ADKINS, Trace		
3/1/03	74	4		6 Chrome...A:73		album cut
				from the album *Chrome* on Capitol 30618		
7/19/03	52	13		7 Then They Do A:48		album cut
				from the album *Greatest Hits Collection, Volume I* on Capitol 81512		
				AGUILERA, Christina		
4/12/03	20	20		12 Fighter..A:19		album cut
8/2/03	12	20		13 Can't Hold Us Down...A:12		RCA 54526 (T)
				CHRISTINA AGUILERA featuring Lil' Kim		
11/29/03+	33	16		14 The Voice Within...A:35		album cut
				all of above from the album *Stripped* on RCA 68037		
				AIKEN, Clay ★		
				Born on 11/30/78 in Chapel Hill, North Carolina. White male vocalist. Finished in second place on the second season of TV's *American Idol* in 2003. Also see American Idol Finalists.		
6/28/03	❶²	16	▲	1 This Is The Night	S:❶¹¹	RCA 51785
				co-written by Aldo Nova; the *Hot 100 Sales* chart also showed the B-side ("Bridge Over Troubled Water")		
11/22/03+	37	20		2 Invisible A:41		album cut
				from the album *Measure Of A Man* on RCA 54638		
				AJ ★		
				Born Anthony England in Chicago, Illinois; later based in San Diego, California. Male rapper.		
8/23/03	32 S	10		1 I Like		Ripe 9194
				ALL-AMERICAN REJECTS, The ★		
				Punk-rock group from Stillwater, Oklahoma: Tyson Ritter (vocals, bass), Mike Kennerty and Nick Wheeler (guitars), and Chris Gaylor (drums).		
6/21/03	60	11		1 Swing, Swing..A:59		album cut
				from the album *The All-American Rejects* on Doghouse 450407		
				ALLAN, Gary		
1/4/03	25	20		4 Man To Man A:23		album cut
				from the album *Alright Guy* on MCA Nashville 70201		
8/23/03	32	20		5 Tough Little Boys A:28		album cut
				from the album *See If I Care* on MCA Nashville 000111		
				AMERICAN IDOL FINALISTS ★		
				Group of contestants from season two of the TV talent show *American Idol*: Clay Aiken, Kimberly Caldwell, Corey Clark, Julia Demato, Joshua Gracin, Kimberley Locke, Carmen Rasmusen, Rickey Smith, Ruben Studdard and Trenyce.		
5/3/03	4	8	●	1 God Bless The U.S.A.	S:❶⁸	RCA 51780
				#16 hit for Lee Greenwood in 2001 (first hit #7 Country in 1984)		
5/17/03	4 S	24		2 What The World Needs Now Is Love		RCA 52557
				#7 hit for Jackie DeShannon in 1965		
				AMERICAN JUNIORS ★		
				Group of pre-teen contestants from the first season of the TV talent show *American Juniors*: Morgan Blake, Lucy Hale, Chantel Kohl, Chauncey Matthews, Jordan McCoy, A.J. Melendez, Katelyn Tarver, Taylor Thompson, Tori Thompson and Danielle White.		
8/30/03	6 S	21		1 One Step Closer		19/Jive 55896
				co-written by Cathy Dennis		
				AMOS, Tori		
4/26/03	9 S	6		10 A Sorta Fairytale		Epic 79804 (D)
				ANDREW W.K. ★		
				Born Andrew Wilkes Krier in 1979 in California; raised in Detroit, Michigan. Hard-rock singer/songwriter.		
8/2/03	26 S	4		1 Tear It Up		Island 000938
				includes a bonus DVD of video footage		
				ARENA, Tina		
8/23/03	97	5		2 Never (Past Tense) S:59		Tommy Boy 2401 (M)
				THE ROC PROJECT FEAT. TINA ARENA		
				samples "Terror" by Fused		
				ASHANTI		
5/10/03	2¹	21		8 Rock Wit U (Awww Baby)	A:2 / S:36	Murder Inc. 000540 (T)
6/14/03	4	26		9 Into You	A:4 / S:71	Desert Storm 67452 (T)
				FABOLOUS Featuring Ashanti or Tamia		
				the version with Ashanti is from the Fabolous album *Street Dreams* on Desert Storm 62791		
8/30/03	7	20		10 Rain On Me	A:7	Murder Inc. 001107 (T)
				samples "The Look Of Love" by Isaac Hayes		

DEBUT DATE	PEAK POS	WKS CHR	G L D	ARTIST Title	Sales/Air	Label & Number

ATARIS, The ★
Punk-rock group from Los Angeles, California: Kris Roe (vocals, guitar), John Collura (guitar),
Mike Davenport (bass) and Chris Knapp (drums).

| 7/26/03 | 20 | 18 | | 1 The Boys Of Summer ....A:22 | | album cut |

#5 hit for Don Henley in 1985; from the album *So Long, Astoria* on Columbia 86184

ATKINS, Rodney ★
Born on 3/28/69 in Knoxville, Tennessee. Country singer/songwriter.

| 10/4/03+ | 57 | 19 | | 1 Honesty (Write Me A List) ....A:56 / S:61 | | Curb 73149 |

ATL ★
Male R&B vocal group from Atlanta, Georgia: Danger, Tre, Will and L-Rock.

| 9/20/03 | 11ˢ | 28 | | 1 Calling All Girls .... | | Noontime/Epic 76999 |

written and produced by R. Kelly

AUDIO ADRENALINE ★
Christian pop-rock group from Grayson, Kentucky: Mark Stuart (vocals), Tyler Burkum (guitar),
Bob Herdman (keyboards), Will McGinniss (bass) and Ben Cissel (drums).

| 6/21/03 | 67ˢ | 2 | | 1 Dirty .... | | ForeFront 52062 |

AUDIOSLAVE

| 3/1/03 | 31 | 20 | | 2 Like A Stone ....A:28 | | album cut |
| 8/16/03 | 67 | 20 | | 3 Show Me How To Live ....A:64 | | album cut |

above 2 from the album *Audioslave* on Epic 86968

AVANT

| 10/4/03+ | 13 | 26 | | 6 Read Your Mind ....S:2 / A:13 | | Geffen 001449 |

BABY

| 2/15/03 | 45 | 11 | | 2 What Happened To That Boy ....A:43 | | album cut |

BABY A.K.A. The Birdman featuring Clipse
from the album *Birdman* on Cash Money 060076

| 2/22/03 | 17 | 20 | | 3 Hell Yeah ....A:17 / S:25 | | Epic 76881 |

GINUWINE (feat. Baby)
written and produced by R. Kelly

| 7/5/03 | 14 | 17 | | 4 Let's Get Down ....S:4 / A:12 | | Columbia 79928 |

BOW WOW (Feat. Baby)

BABY BASH ★
Born Ronald Bryant in Vallejo, California; raised in Houston, Texas. Latin male rapper.

| 8/23/03 | 7 | 33↑ | | 1 Suga Suga...A:7 / S:8 | | Universal 001055 |

BABY BASH Feat. Frankie J

BAD BOY'S DA BAND ★
Rap group assembled by P. Diddy for the reality TV series *Making The Band 2*: Dylan John, Sara Stokes, Lloyd
"Ness" Mathis, Frederick Watson, Lynese "Babs" Wiley and Rodney "Young City" Hill.

| 10/25/03 | 50 | 9 | | 1 Bad Boy This Bad Boy That..A:46 | | album cut |

produced by P. Diddy; from the album *Too Hot For T.V.* on Bad Boy 001118

BADU, Erykah

| 4/5/03 | 22ˢ | 16 | | 8 Come Close Remix (Closer)................................... | | MCA 000575 |

COMMON Feat. Erykah Badu, Pharrell From The Neptunes, and Q-Tip
remix of Common's #65 hit from 2002

| 8/23/03 | 82 | 11 | | 9 Danger ....S:62 | | Motown 001052 (T) |
| 11/15/03 | 43ˢ | 1 | | 10 I C U (Doin' It) .... | | Violator 57358 (T) |

VIOLATOR FEATURING A TRIBE CALLED QUEST AND ERYKAH BADU
samples "High On Sunshine" by the Commodores and "Wild Thang" by 2 Much

BANNER, David ★
Born in Mississippi. Male rapper.

| 4/26/03 | 48 | 20 | | 1 Like A Pimp ....S:40 / A:45 | | SRC 000402 (T) |

DAVID BANNER feat. Lil' Flip
samples "Take It Off" by UGK

BARENAKED LADIES

| 10/18/03 | 82 | 15 | | 7 Another Postcard..S:41 | | Reprise 16537 |

song shown on the charts as "Another Postcard (Chimps)"

BATES, Jeff ★
Born on 9/19/63 in Bunker Hill, Mississippi. Country singer/songwriter/guitarist.

| 5/24/03 | 59 | 12 | | 1 The Love Song ....A:54 | | album cut |

from the album *Rainbow Man* on RCA 67071

BEDINGFIELD, Daniel

| 4/5/03 | 15 | 20 | | 2 If You're Not The One ....S:2 / A:18 | | Island 000267 |

BELLE AND SEBASTIAN

| 12/6/03 | 64ˢ | 1 | | 4 Step Into My Office, Baby.............................. | | Rough Trade 83231 |

BENSON, Rhian ★
Born in Ghana, West Africa (mother from Wales; father from West Africa); raised in New Dehli, India.
Female R&B singer/songwriter.

| 9/27/03 | 45ˢ | 2 | | 1 Say How I Feel .... | | DKG 6110 |

DEBUT DATE	PEAK POS	WKS CHR	G L D	ARTIST Title	Sales/Air	Label & Number

BENTLEY, Dierks ★
Born on 11/20/75 in Phoenix, Arizona. Country singer/songwriter/guitarist.

| 6/21/03 | 22 | 20 | | 1 What Was I Thinkin' ....S:9 / A:22 | | Capitol 77963 |

BEYONCÉ ★
Born Beyoncé Knowles on 9/4/81 in Houston, Texas. R&B singer/songwriter/actress. Member of Destiny's Child. Acted in the movies *Austin Powers In Goldmember* and *The Fighting Temptations*.

| 5/24/03 | ❶⁸ | 27 | | 1 Crazy In Love ....A:❶⁸ / S:11 | | Columbia 79949 (D) |

BEYONCÉ (Featuring Jay-Z)
samples "Are You My Woman? (Tell Me So)" by The Chi-Lites

| 8/16/03 | ❶⁹ | 29 | | 2 Baby Boy ....A:❶⁹ | | Columbia 76867 (T) |

BEYONCÉ feat. Sean Paul
Sean Paul is featured on the CD promo single (he does NOT appear on the commercial 12" single)

| 11/15/03+ | 4 | 21↑ | | 3 Me, Myself And I ....S:❶³ / A:4 | | Columbia 76911 |
| 11/15/03 | 58ˢ | 2 | | 4 Summertime .... | | Columbia 76915 (T) |

BEYONCÉ featuring P. Diddy
from the movie *The Fighting Temptations* starring Beyoncé and Cuba Gooding Jr.

BIG ADVICE ★
Funk group formed in Los Angeles, California: Ahaguna G. Sun (vocals), Juan Nelson (vocals, bass), Werner Schuchner (guitar), Wayne Bergeron, Larry Lunetta, Nicholas Lane and Brandon Fields (horns), Lenny Castro (percussion), Clarence Allen (keyboards) and Paul Allen (drums).

| 12/13/03 | 32ˢ | 2 | | 1 Hearts On Fire .... [L] | | Electric Monkey 1010 (D) |

BIG C

| 3/8/03 | 28ˢ | 11 | | 2 Hell Is A Flame .... | | Southpaw 18299 |

includes vocals by The Open Door Youth Choir

BIG TYMERS

| 11/1/03 | 97 | 3 | | 4 This Is How We Do...S:65 | | Cash Money 001361 (T) |
| 12/27/03+ | 85 | 9 | | 5 Gangsta Girl ....S:55 | | Cash Money 001355 (T) |

BIG TYMERS featuring R. Kelly
written and produced by R. Kelly

BLACK EYED PEAS

| 6/14/03 | 8 | 25 | | 2 Where Is The Love? ....A:9 | | A&M 000714 (T) |

Justin Timberlake (guest vocal)

BLIGE, Mary J.

| 7/5/03 | 22 | 13 | | 27 Love @ 1st Sight...............................S:5 / A:22 | | Geffen 000954 |

MARY J. BLIGE featuring Method Man
samples "Hot Sex" by A Tribe Called Quest

| 9/6/03 | 29 | 12 | | 28 Ooh! ....A:27 | | album cut |

samples "Singing This Song For My Mother" by Hamilton Bohannon; above 2 produced by P. Diddy

| 12/13/03+ | 41 | 10 | | 29 Not Today ....A:39 | | album cut |

MARY J. BLIGE featuring Eve
produced by Dr. Dre; featured in the movie *Barbershop 2: Back In Business* starring Ice Cube; above 2 from the album *Love & Life* on Geffen 000956

BONE CRUSHER ★
Born Wayne Hardnett on 8/23/71 in Atlanta, Georgia. Male rapper.

| 4/5/03 | 26 | 20 | | 1 Never Scared ....A:24 / S:26 | | Break-Em-Off 50870 (T) |

BONE CRUSHER Featuring Killer Mike & T.I.
first released as a promotional CD maxi-single in very limited quantities with no bar-code on the actual product (label assigned it a number of 777); the 12" above is the widely available release

BONE THUGS-N-HARMONY

| 4/26/03 | 10ˢ | 11 | | 12 All Life Long .... | | D3 9915 |

MO THUGS

BOOMKAT ★
Pop duo from Tuscon, Arizona: brother-and sister Kellin and Taryn Manning. Taryn acted in such movies as *Crossroads* and *8 Mile*.

| 3/22/03 | 88 | 2 | | 1 The Wreckoning ....S:9 | | DreamWorks 450779 |

BOWIE, David

| 12/27/03+ | 66ˢ | 2 | | 31 Peace On Earth/Little Drummer Boy .... [X-R] | | Oglio 85001 (M) |

DAVID BOWIE & BING CROSBY
hit the *Hot 100 Sales* charts in 2000 (#58), 2001 (#75) and 2002 (#43)

BOWLING FOR SOUP ★
Punk-rock group from Wichita Falls, Texas: Jaret Reddick (vocals, guitar), Chris Burney (guitar), Erik Chandler (bass) and Gary Wiseman (drums).

| 3/29/03 | 64 | 9 | | 1 Girl All The Bad Guys Want ....A:65 | | album cut |

from the album *Drunk Enough To Dance* on Ffroe 41819

BOW WOW see LIL' BOW WOW

BRANCH, Michelle

| 5/31/03 | 16 | 20 | | 5 Are You Happy Now?.............................A:16 / S:54 | | album cut |

single available only as a paid download; from the album *Hotel Paper* on Maverick 48426

| 11/8/03 | 36 | 18 | | 6 Breathe ....S:24 / A:40 | | Maverick 42689 (M) |

BRIGHTMAN, Sarah

| 11/22/03 | 27ˢ | 9 | | 2 Harem (Cancao do Mar)...................................... | | Angel 53240 (M) |

adapted from the song "Cancao do Mar" first recorded by female Portugese singer Dulce Pontes in 1996

DEBUT DATE	PEAK POS	WKS CHR	G L D	ARTIST Title	Sales/Air	Label & Number

BROOKS & DUNN

DEBUT DATE	PEAK POS	WKS CHR	G L D	ARTIST Title	Sales/Air	Label & Number
5/31/03	25	20		13 Red Dirt Road	A:24	album cut
11/8/03+	39	20		14 You Can't Take The Honky Tonk Out Of The Girl	A:37	album cut

above 2 from the album *Red Dirt Road* on Arista Nashville 67070

BROWN, Foxy

| 4/12/03 | 52 S | 2 | | 7 I Need A Man | | Def Jam 000251 (T) |

FOXY BROWN feat. The Letter M.

BT ★
Born Brian Transeau on 10/4/70 in Washington DC. Electronic keyboardist/producer.

| 9/13/03 | 98 | 3 | | 1 Somnambulist | S:34 | Nettwerk 33190 (M) |

a Somnambulist is a sleep walker; song also known as "Simply Being Loved"

B2K

| 3/8/03 | 30 | 13 | | 5 Girlfriend | S:19 / A:31 | Epic 76877 |
| 8/16/03 | 92 | 3 | | 6 Feelin' Freaky | S:74 | Nick/Jive 53700 (D) |

NICK CANNON Featuring B2K
above 2 written and produced by R. Kelly

| 12/20/03+ | 59 | 8 | | 7 Badaboom | A:55 | Epic 76716 (T) |

B2K featuring Fabolous
from the movie *You Got Served* starring B2K

BUDDEN, Joe ★
Born in 1980 in Jersey City, New Jersey. Male rapper.

| 1/18/03 | 58 S | 3 | | 1 Focus | | Def Jam 063782 (T) |

JOE BUDDEN feat. LL Cool J
Dutchess (additional vocals)

| 2/22/03 | 52 S | 1 | | 2 Drop Drop | | Def Jam 077017 (T) |
| 4/19/03 | 38 | 19 | | 3 Pump It Up | S:23 / A:39 | Def Jam 000395 (T) |

samples "Soul Vibrations" by Kool & The Gang

| 8/2/03 | 51 S | 3 | | 4 Fire (Yes, Yes Y'all) | | Def Jam 000844 (T) |

JOE BUDDEN feat. Busta Rhymes
contains interpolations of "Super Rappin'" by Grandmaster Flash and "Whores In This House" by Al McLaren

| 9/6/03 | 39 | 20 | | 5 Clubbin | A:37 | album cut |

MARQUES HOUSTON Featuring Joe Budden & Pied Piper
written and produced by R. Kelly; from Houston's album *MH* on T.U.G. 62935

BUFFETT, Jimmy

| 6/28/03 | 17 | 20 | | 11 It's Five O'Clock Somewhere | A:14 | album cut |

ALAN JACKSON & JIMMY BUFFETT
from Jackson's album *Greatest Hits Volume II and Some Other Stuff* on Arista Nashville 53097

BUSTA RHYMES

| 3/8/03 | 3 | 24 | | 17 I Know What You Want | A:3 / S:15 | J Records 21258 (T) |

BUSTA RHYMES AND MARIAH CAREY (feat. The Flipmode Squad)

| 8/2/03 | 51 S | 3 | | 18 Fire (Yes, Yes Y'all) | | Def Jam 000844 (T) |

JOE BUDDEN feat. Busta Rhymes
contains interpolations of "Super Rappin'" by Grandmaster Flash and "Whores In This House" by Al McLaren

| 8/9/03 | 58 | 10 | | 19 Light Your A** On Fire | S:32 / A:59 | Star Trak 54245 (T) |

BUSTA RHYMES Featuring Pharrell

| 11/29/03 | 56 S | 1 | | 20 Get Low Remix | | BME 2394 (T) |

LIL JON & THE EAST SIDE BOYZ Feat. Elephant Man, Busta Rhymes & Ying Yang Twins

BYRD, Tracy

| 7/5/03 | 77 | 5 | | 8 The Truth About Men | A:73 [N] | album cut |

Andy Griggs, Montgomery Gentry and Blake Shelton (guest vocals)

| 11/29/03+ | 60 | 16 | | 9 Drinkin' Bone | A:59 | album cut |

above 2 from the album *The Truth About Men* on RCA 67073

CAGLE, Chris

| 3/29/03 | 41 | 20 | | 4 What A Beautiful Day | A:38 | album cut |
| 11/1/03 | 53 | 15 | | 5 Chicks Dig It | A:50 | album cut |

above 2 from the album *Chris Cagle* on Capitol 40516

CAM'RON

| 4/5/03+ | 70 S | 4 | | 8 Dipset Anthem | | Roc-A-Fella 077995 (T) |

DIPLOMATS feat. Cam'Ron and Juelz Santana
samples "One In A Million" by Sam Dees

| 4/26/03 | 16 | 17 | | 9 Snake | A:15 / S:21 | Jive 40108 (T) |

R. KELLY featuring Cam'ron and Big Tigger

CANNON, Nick ★
Born on 10/17/80 in San Diego, California. R&B singer/actor. Regular on TV's *All That* (1998-2001). Starred in the movie *Drumline*.

| 3/22/03 | 22 S | 15 | | 1 Your Pops Don't Like Me (i really don't like this dude) | | Nick/Jive 49513 |

samples "Big Ole Butt" by LL Cool J and "More Bounce To The Ounce" by Zapp

| 8/16/03 | 92 | 3 | | 2 Feelin' Freaky | S:74 | Nick/Jive 53700 (D) |

NICK CANNON Featuring B2K

DEBUT DATE	PEAK POS	WKS CHR	G L D	ARTIST Title	Sales/Air	Label & Number
				CANNON, Nick — Cont'd		
11/15/03+	24	20		3 Gigolo	A:22 / S:70	Nick/Jive 56646 (T)
				NICK CANNON featuring R. Kelly		
				above 2 written and produced by R. Kelly		
				CANTRELL, Blu		
3/1/03	70	20		2 Breathe	S:10 / A:72	Arista 50984
				BLU CANTRELL (Featuring Sean Paul)		
				samples "What's The Difference" by Dr. Dre		
				CAPONE-N-NOREAGA ★		
				Rap duo from Queens, New York: Kiam "Capone" Holley and Victor "Noreaga" Santiago.		
4/5/03	55^S	1		1 Stompdash*toutu (Vendetta)..................................		Def Jam 000160 (T)
				CNN Featuring M.O.P.		
				samples "You've Got The Papers (I've Got The Man)" by Ann Peebles; from the movie		
				Cradle 2 The Grave starring Jet Li and DMX		
				CAREY, Mariah		
3/8/03	3	24		38 I Know What You Want	A:3 / S:15	J Records 21258 (T)
				BUSTA RHYMES AND MARIAH CAREY (feat. The Flipmode Squad)		
				CARIBBEAN PULSE ★		
				Reggae group from Belize: brothers William (guitar) and Jason (bass) Smith, Ezzy Judah (male vocals, percussion) and LaNiece McKay (female vocals). Featured vocalist Damian "Jr. Gong" Marley is the son of Bob Marley.		
2/8/03	13^S	12		1 Jah is My Rock		Irie 1102
				CARIBBEAN PULSE Featuring Damian "Jr. Gong" Marley		
				CARLTON, Vanessa		
3/29/03	42	20		3 Big Yellow Taxi	A:41	album cut
				COUNTING CROWS Featuring Vanessa Carlton		
				#24 hit for Joni Mitchell in 1975; from the album Hard Candy on Geffen 493356		
				CASH, Johnny		
12/6/03+	10^S	18↑	▲2	49 Hurt		American 077084 (D)
				#54 Hot 100 Airplay hit for Nine Inch Nails in 1995		
				CASSIDY ★		
				Born Barry Reese in 1983 in Philadelphia, Pennsylvania. Male rapper.		
12/20/03+	4	16↑		1 Hotel	A:4 / S:10	J Records 56053 (T)
				CASSIDY feat. R. Kelly		
				samples "Rapper's Delight" by Sugarhill Gang		
				CHASEZ, JC ★		
				Born Joshua Chasez on 8/8/76 in Washington DC. Pop singer/songwriter. Member of *NSYNC.		
1/4/03	35	17		1 Blowin' Me Up (With Her Love)................................	S:6 / A:39	Fox/Jive 40070
				samples "Money (Dollar Bill Y'all)" by Coolio; from the movie Drumline starring Nick Cannon		
				CHECKER, Chubby		
11/29/03	29^S	7		36 Limbo Rock..	[R]	TEEC 1024
				CHUBBY C & OD Featuring Inner Circle		
				new version of Chubby's #2 hit from 1962; project assembled by producer Gary Lefkowith; OD includes musicians Jermaine Brown and Hovannes Dilakian		
				CHER		
2/22/03	7^S	11		36 When The Money's Gone		Warner 42496 (M)
				CHESNEY, Kenny		
2/22/03	28	20		12 Big Star..	A:25	album cut
6/28/03	28	20		13 No Shoes, No Shirt, No Problems	A:24	album cut
				above 2 from the album No Shoes, No Shirt, No Problems on BNA 67038		
11/8/03	29	20		14 There Goes My Life..	A:28	album cut
				from the album When The Sun Goes Down on BNA 56609		
				CHEVELLE		
5/10/03	65	20		2 Send The Pain Below	A:60	album cut
				from the album Wonder What's Next on Epic 86157		
				CHINGY ★		
				Born Howard Bailey on 3/9/80 in St. Louis, Missouri. Male rapper.		
5/17/03	2^5	33		1 Right Thurr	A:2 / S:3	Disturb. Tha P. 77995
9/20/03	3	21		2 Holidae In	A:3 / S:42	Disturb. Tha P. 52816 (T)
				CHINGY featuring Ludacris & Snoop Dogg		
				!!! (CHK CHK CHK) ★		
				Punk-disco group from Sacramento, California: Nic Offer (vocals), Mario Andreoni and Tyler Pope (guitars), Dan Gorman (trumpet), Allan Wilson (sax), Jason Racine (percussion), Justin Van Der Volgen (bass) and John Pugh (drums).		
6/21/03	33^S	5		1 Me And Giuliani Down By The School Yard		Touch And Go 247 (M)
				CHOPPA ★		
				Born Darwin Turner in New Orleans, Louisiana. Male rapper.		
3/8/03	94	6		1 Choppa Style..	S:62	New No Limit 019400 (T)
				CHOPPA Featuring Master P		
				C-LANAE ★		
				Born in Minneapolis, Minnesota. Female R&B singer. Pronounced: see-la-nay.		
2/8/03	10^S	12		1 Incomplete		Wright Enterprises 60402
				Eric Radford (male vocal)		

DEBUT DATE	PEAK POS	WKS CHR	G L D	ARTIST / Title	Sales/Air	Label & Number
				CLARK, Terri		
12/13/03+	38	17↑	6	I Wanna Do It All A:37		album cut
				from the album *Pain To Kill* on on Mercury 170325		
				CLARKSON, Kelly		
5/17/03	9	20	2	Miss Independent	A:10	album cut
				co-written by Christina Aguilera		
9/20/03	58	11	3	Low...A:60		album cut
				above 2 from the album *Thankful* on RCA 68159		
				CLEAR ★		
				Studio group assembled by producer J. Quinn "General" Patton and featuring bassist Andreas Geck.		
12/6/03	38^S	1	1	Hold You Close		Raw Naked 60712
				CLIPSE		
2/15/03	45	11	4	What Happened To That Boy...A:43		album cut
				BABY A.K.A. The Birdman featuring Clipse		
				from the album *Birdman* on Cash Money 060076		
2/15/03	86	6	5	Ma, I Don't Love Her S:26		Star Trak 51319
				CLIPSE featuring Faith Evans		
5/17/03	56^S	3	6	Hot Damn		Star Trak 51930 (T)
				CLIPSE Featuring Ab-Liva & Rosco P. Coldchain		
				COLD ★		
				Hard-rock group from Jacksonville, Florida: Ronald "Scooter" Ward (vocals, guitar), Stephen "Kelly" Hayes (guitar), Terry Balsamo (guitar), Jeremy Marshall (bass) and Sam McCandless (drums).		
4/19/03	87	20	1	Stupid Girl...S:7		Flip 000240
				COLDPLAY		
2/1/03	29	22	2	Clocks...S:13 / A:29		Capitol 52608
				COLLINS, Phil		
2/1/03	76	20	28	Can't Stop Loving You A:75		album cut
				from the album *Testify* on Atlantic 83563		
				COMMON		
4/5/03	22^S	16	6	Come Close Remix (Closer) .... [R]		MCA 000575
				COMMON Feat. Erykah Badu, Pharrell From The Neptunes, and Q-Tip		
				remix of Common's #65 hit from 2002		
				COOLER KIDS ★		
				Dance duo: female singer Sisely and male DJ Kaz Gamble.		
5/17/03	45^S	9	1	All Around The World (Punk Debutante)		DreamWorks 000273
				COUNTING CROWS		
3/29/03	42	20	9	Big Yellow Taxi A:41		album cut
				COUNTING CROWS Featuring Vanessa Carlton		
				#24 hit for Joni Mitchell in 1975; from the album *Hard Candy* on Geffen 493356		
				CROSBY, Bing		
12/27/03+	66^S	2	25	Peace On Earth/Little Drummer Boy............................ [X]		Oglio 85001 (M)
				DAVID BOWIE & BING CROSBY		
				hit the *Hot 100 Sales* charts in 2000 (#58), 2001 (#75) and 2002 (#66)		
				CROW, Sheryl		
10/25/03+	14↑	24↑	13	The First Cut Is The Deepest A:14		album cut
				written by Cat Stevens; #21 hit for Rod Stewart in 1977; from the album *The Very Best Of Sheryl Crow* on A&M 152102		
				CURRINGTON, Billy ★		
				Born on 11/19/73 in Savannah, Georgia; raised in Rincon, Georgia. Country singer/songwriter/guitarist.		
8/23/03	67	15	1	Walk A Little Straighter..................................S:29 / A:67		Mercury 000972
				CURSIVE ★		
				Alternative-rock group from Omaha, Nebraska: Tim Kasher (vocals, guitar), Ted Stevens (guitar), Gretta Cohn (cello), Matt Maginn (bass) and Clint Schnase (drums).		
2/1/03	18^S	4	1	Art Is Hard...		Saddle Creek 10049
				DA BRAT		
4/26/03	44	16	14	In Love Wit Chu..S:8 / A:51		So So Def 52308
				DA BRAT Featuring Cherish		
				DAVIS, Alana		
2/15/03	30^S	3	2	Carry On..		Columbia 79852
				song featured in the Sony Electronics TV commercial "The Trip"; first recorded by Crosby, Stills, Nash & Young in 1970		
				DAY, Spencer ★		
				Born in 1979 in San Francisco, California. White male singer. Was a runner-up in the "adult singer" category on TV's *Star Search*.		
3/22/03	18^S	6	1	What A Wonderful World..		Columbia 79867
				#32 hit for Louis Armstrong in 1988; released on the same single with "There's A Winner In You" by Tiffany Evans		

DEBUT DATE	PEAK POS	WKS CHR	G L D	ARTIST Title	Sales/Air	Label & Number
				DEAN, Kiley ★		
				Born Kiley Dean Bowlin in 1982 in Alma, Arkansas; raised in Orlando, Florida. Female singer.		
6/7/03	99	2		1 Make Me A Song	S:45	Beatclub 000460
11/22/03	64^S	12		2 Who Will I Run To		Beatclub 001652
				DEF SQUAD — see MURRAY, Keith		
				DELERIUM		
6/7/03	57^S	2		3 After All		Nettwerk 33191
				DELERIUM featuring Jaël (of Lunik)		
				DIAMOND RIO		
3/22/03	31	20		6 I Believe	A:27	album cut
				from the album *Completely* on Arista Nashville 67046		
				DIDO		
9/20/03+	18	29↑		3 White Flag	S:19 / A:19	Arista 58336 (**D**)
				DION, Celine		
2/15/03	45	13		21 I Drove All Night	S:26 / A:46	Epic 79931
				#6 hit for Cyndi Lauper in 1989		
				DIPLOMATS, The		
4/5/03+	70^S	4		2 Dipset Anthem		Roc-A-Fella 077995 (**T**)
				DIPLOMATS feat. Cam'Ron and Juelz Santana		
				samples "One In A Million" by Sam Dees		
				DIXIE CHICKS		
2/1/03	25	10		15 Travelin' Soldier	A:23	album cut
				from the album *Home* on Monument 86840		
				DMX		
2/8/03	60	16		15 X Gon' Give It To Ya	S:23 / A:58	Def Jam 063776 (**T**)
				from the movie *Cradle 2 The Grave* starring Jet Li and DMX		
8/23/03	68	8		16 Where The Hood At	S:60 / A:66	Def Jam 001048 (**T**)
				contains an interpolation of "Young, Gifted And Black" by Big Daddy Kane		
11/15/03	73^S	1		17 Get It On The Floor		Def Jam 001440 (**T**)
				DMX featuring Swizz Beatz		
				DOBSON, Fefe ★		
				Born in Toronto, Ontario, Canada. Black female rock singer/songwriter.		
11/15/03	87	6		1 Take Me Away	S:8	Island 001184
				D.O.C., The ★		
				Born Tracy Curry in Dallas, Texas. Male rapper.		
3/1/03	48^S	2		1 The ?hit		Silverback 2114
				MC Ren, Ice Cube, Snoop Dogg and 6 Two (guest vocals)		
				DONNAS, The ★		
				Female punk-rock group from Palo Alto, California: Brett "Donna A." Anderson (vocals), Allison "Donna R." Robertson (guitar), Maya "Donna F." Ford (bass) and Torry "Donna C." Castellano (drums).		
6/21/03	65^S	3		1 Who Invited You		Atlantic 88117
				DOUBLE DOZE ★		
12/6/03	30^S	2		1 Make Room		Realistic South 16074
				DREAM STREET		
1/4/03	11^S	10		3 With All My Heart		Columbia 79823
				DRU HILL		
5/3/03	77	13		13 I Love You	S:31	Def Soul 000785
				DUARTE, Ryan ★		
				R&B singer/songwriter.		
12/27/03+	81	13↑		1 You	S:37	Marque 001814
				DUFF, Hilary ★		
				Born on 9/28/87 in Houston, Texas. Actress/singer. Plays the title character in both the TV series and the movie *Lizzie McGuire*.		
8/16/03	42	20		1 So Yesterday	S:**①**² / A:56	Buena Vista 161014
				DUKES, Skent ★		
				Born in Cleveland, Ohio. Male rapper.		
9/27/03	34^S	5		1 Grind Right		Wise Owl 94752
				SKENT DUKES featuring Sly Fam		
				DUPRI, Jermaine		
10/11/03	17	20		7 Wat Da Hook Gon Be	A:16 / S:49	Fo' Reel 001451 (**T**)
				MURPHY LEE Featuring Jermaine Dupri		
12/13/03+	76	9		8 Pop That Booty		T.U.G. 67501 (**T**)
				MARQUES HOUSTON (Featuring Jermaine "JD" Dupri)		
				DWELE ★		
				Born Andwele Gardner in Detroit, Michigan. Male R&B singer/songwriter/producer.		
9/20/03	93	12		1 Find A Way		Virgin 38865 (**T**)

DEBUT DATE	PEAK POS	WKS CHR	G L D	ARTIST Title	Sales/Air	Label & Number
8/2/03	69	14		**EAGLES** 23 Hole In The World..................................S:3		ERC II 3322 (D)
				includes a bonus audio CD of the song		
				EALEY, Theodis ★ Born in Natchez, Mississippi; later based in Atlanta, Georgia. Blues singer/guitarist.		
12/27/03+	5ˢ	14↑		1 Stand Up In It.......................................		Ifgam 212 (M)
				EAMON ★ Born Eamon Doyle in 1984 in Staten Island, New York. Male R&B singer/songwriter.		
12/6/03+	16	18↑		1 F**k It (I Don't Want You Back) ....S:❶⁹ / A:19		Jive 56647
				EARTHQUAKE INSTITUTE, The ★ Male hip-hop duo from Los Angeles, California: Alex Flores and Luis Ontiveras.		
4/19/03	22ˢ	7		1 Super B-Boy Pimpin'		Richter Scale 60502
				EDER, Linda ★ Born on 2/3/61 in Tuscon, Arizona; raised in Brainerd, Minnesota. Singer/actress. Starred in the Broadway show *Jekyll & Hyde*.		
8/23/03	70ˢ	1		1 I Am What I Am...		Atlantic 88183 (M)
				from the Broadway show *La Cage Aux Folles*; #102 hit for Gloria Gaynor in 1983		
				ELECTRIC SIX ★ Eclectic-rock group from Detroit, Michigan: Dick Valentine (vocals), The Rock And Roll Indian (guitar), Surge Joebot (guitar), Tait Nucleus (keyboards), Disco (bass) and M. (drums). Band members insist these are their real names.		
2/22/03	69ˢ	1		1 Danger! High Voltage		XL 41157 (M)
				ELEPHANT MAN ★ Born O'Neil Bryant in Kingston, Jamaica. Dancehall reggae singer.		
7/19/03	86	13		1 Pon De River, Pon De Bank		VP 6404 (T)
11/29/03	56ˢ	1		2 Get Low Remix		BME 2394 (T)
				LIL JON & THE EAST SIDE BOYZ Feat. Elephant Man, Busta Rhymes & Ying Yang Twins		
				ELLIOTT, Missy "Misdemeanor"		
4/26/03	62ˢ	2		23 Back In The Day		Goldmind 67387 (T)
				MISSY ELLIOTT (Featuring Jay-Z) samples "I Don't Know What This World Is Coming To" by The Soul Children		
5/10/03	77	5		24 P***ycat...A:74		Goldmind 67340 (T)
				Tweet (additional vocals); B-side of her 2002 hit "Work It"		
8/23/03	95	2		25 Cop That Sh#! S:45		Blackground 001609 (T)
				TIMBALAND & MAGOO featuring Missy Elliott		
10/4/03	24ˢ	4		26 Honk Your Horn		Universal 019351
				DANI STEVENSON Featuring Missy Elliott		
10/18/03	27	15		27 Pass That Dutch ....S:14 / A:26		EastWest 67506 (T)
				MISSY ELLIOTT samples "Magic Mountain" by War and "Potholes In My Lawn" by De La Soul		
10/18/03	65	9		28 Party To Damascus ....S:45 / A:64		J Records 54960 (T)
				WYCLEF JEAN (feat. Missy Elliott)		
				EMERICK, Scotty ★ Born in 1974 in Vero Beach, Florida. Country singer/songwriter/guitarist.		
11/22/03	91	6		1 I Can't Take You Anywhere...............................S:26		DreamWorks 001581
				SCOTTY EMERICK with Toby Keith		
				EMINEM		
2/1/03	15	16		10 Superman A:15		album cut
				Dina Rae (female vocal)		
4/5/03	14	18		11 Sing For The Moment A:14		album cut
				samples "Dream On" by Aerosmith; above 2 from the album *The Eminem Show* on Aftermath 493290		
				ENGVALL, Bill		
11/29/03	8ˢ	7		2 Here's Your Sign Christmas [X-N]		Warner 16507
				#39 Country hit in 1998; released on the same single as "Redneck 12 Days Of Christmas" by Jeff Foxworthy		
				ENYA		
12/6/03	16ˢ	6		8 Oíche Chiún (Silent Night).....................[X-F-R]		Reprise 40660 (M)
				ERASURE		
2/1/03	10ˢ	12		8 Solsbury Hill		Mute 9200
				#68 hit for Peter Gabriel in 1977		
5/24/03	40ˢ	2		9 Make Me Smile (Come Up And See Me)............................		Mute 9208
				#96 hit for Steve Harley & Cockney Rebel in 1976		
11/22/03	68ˢ	1		10 Oh L'Amour...[R]		Mute 69234 (M)
				remix of their #3 Dance hit from 1986		
				EVANESCENCE ★ Rock group from Little Rock, Arkansas: Amy Lee (vocals), Ben Moody (guitar), Josh LeCompt (bass) and Rocky Gray (drums). Won the 2003 Best New Artist Grammy Award.		
3/15/03	5	32		1 Bring Me To Life A:5		album cut
				Paul McCoy (of rock group 12 Stones; guest vocal); from the movie *Daredevil* starring Ben Affleck (soundtrack on Wind-Up 13079); also from their album *Fallen* on Wind-Up 13063		

DEBUT DATE	PEAK POS	WKS CHR	G L D	ARTIST Title	Sales/Air	Label & Number

EVANS, Faith

| 2/15/03 | 86 | 6 | | 20 Ma, I Don't Love Her .... | S:26 | Star Trak 51319 |

CLIPSE featuring Faith Evans

EVANS, Tiffany ★

Born in 1993 in Ocean City, New Jersey. Pre-teen R&B singer. Won the "junior singer" category on TV's *Star Search*.

| 3/22/03 | 18^S | 6 | | 1 There's A Winner In You.. | | Columbia 79867 |

first recorded by Patti LaBelle in 1986; released on the same commercial single with "What A Wonderful World" by Spencer Day

EVE

| 12/13/03+ | 41 | 10 | | 12 Not Today .... | A:39 | album cut |

MARY J. BLIGE featuring Eve
produced by Dr. Dre; featured in the movie *Barbershop 2: Back In Business* starring Ice Cube; from Blige's album *Love & Life* on Geffen 000956

FABOLOUS

| 3/8/03 | 4 | 23 | | 7 Can't Let You Go | A:4 / S:42 | Desert Storm 67428 (T) |

FABOLOUS featuring Mike Shorey & Lil' Mo

| 3/22/03 | 37 | 20 | | 8 4 Ever... | S:33 / A:34 | Elektra 67379 (T) |

LIL' MO (Featuring Fabolous)

| 6/14/03 | 4 | 26 | | 9 Into You | A:4 / S:71 | Desert Storm 67452 (T) |

FABOLOUS Featuring Ashanti or Tamia
the version with Tamia is the 12" single above (samples "Fancy Dancer" by the Commodores); the version with Ashanti is from his album *Street Dreams* on Desert Storm 62791 (no sample)

| 12/20/03+ | 59 | 8 | | 10 Badaboom .... | A:55 | Epic 76716 (T) |

B2K featuring Fabolous
from the movie *You Got Served* starring B2K

FANNYPACK ★

Female dance vocal trio from Brooklyn, New York: Jessibel Suthiwong, Belinda Lovell and Cat Martell. Assembled by male producers Matt Goias and Keith "Fancy" Grady.

| 6/28/03 | 63^S | 4 | | 1 Cameltoe .... | [N] | Tommy Boy 2402 |

FANTASY ★

Female dance trio from Miami, Florida: Dee, Jaz and Lil J.

| 4/19/03 | 37^S | 4 | | 1 Again .... | | TVI/Orpheus 91010 |

FAT JOE

| 2/15/03 | 86 | 8 | | 9 All I Need .... | S:48 | Atlantic 88013 (T) |

FAT JOE (featuring Tony Sunshine & Armageddon)
samples "Wish That You Were Mine" by The Manhattans; contains an interpolation of "Can You Stand The Rain" by New Edition

| 6/14/03 | 22 | 19 | | 10 I Want You .... | A:23 | Virgin 47305 (T) |

THALIA featuring Fat Joe
samples "A Little Bit Of Love" by Brenda Russell

50 CENT

| 1/11/03 | ❶⁹ | 30 | | 2 In Da Club .... | A:❶⁹ / S:4 | Shady 497856 (T) |
| 3/22/03 | ❶⁴ | 23 | | 3 21 Questions .... | A:❶⁵ / S:13 | Shady 080739 (T) |

50 CENT Feat. Nate Dogg
samples "It's Only Love Doing Its Thing" by Barry White

| 4/26/03 | 2³ | 24 | | 4 Magic Stick .... | A:❶¹ | album cut |

LIL' KIM (feat. 50 Cent)
samples "The Thrill Is Gone" by B.B. King; from Lil' Kim's album *La Bella Mafia* on Queen Bee 83572

| 5/31/03 | 3 | 25 | | 5 P.I.M.P. .... | A:3 / S:30 | Shady 000888 (T) |
| 10/4/03 | 76 | 8 | | 6 If I Can't... | A:72 | album cut |

from the album *Get Rich Or Die Tryin'* on Shady 493544

FLEETWOOD MAC

| 3/29/03 | 80 | 11 | | 26 Peacekeeper... | S:11 | album cut |

single available only as a paid download; from the album *Say You Will* on Reprise 48394

FLIPMODE SQUAD — see BUSTA RHYMES

FLOETRY ★

Female R&B vocal duo: Marsha Ambrosius (born in London, England) and Natalie Stewart (born in Atlanta, Georgia).

| 3/29/03 | 24 | 20 | | 1 Say Yes.. | A:21 | album cut |

from the album *Floetic* on DreamWorks 450313

FOO FIGHTERS

| 3/8/03 | 65 | 20 | | 9 Times Like These .... | A:64 | album cut |

from the album *One By One* on Roswell 68008

| 7/19/03 | 10^S | 10 | | 10 Low | | Roswell 53912 (D) |

FORD, Willa

| 12/6/03 | 45^S | 10 | | 2 A Toast To Men .... | | Lava 88242 |

WILLA FORD Featuring May

FOUNTAINS OF WAYNE

| 10/11/03 | 21 | 17 | | 2 Stacy's Mom .... | A:25 | album cut |

from the album *Welcome Interstate Managers* on S-Curve 90875

DEBUT DATE	PEAK POS	WKS CHR	G L D	ARTIST Title / Sales/Air	Label & Number
				FOXWORTHY, Jeff	
11/29/03	8^S	7	4	Redneck 12 Days Of Christmas [X-N]	Warner 16507
				#18 Country hit in 1995; released on the same single as "Here's Your Sign Christmas" by Bill Engvall	
				FOXX, Jamie	
12/6/03+	❶¹	18↑	2	Slow Jamz A:❶² / S:17	Atlantic 88288 (T)
				TWISTA Featuring Kanye West & Jamie Foxx	
				samples "A House Is Not A Home" by Luther Vandross	
				FRANKIE J ★	
				Born Francis Jay Bautista in Tijuana, Mexico; raised in San Diego, California. Latino singer/songwriter/producer.	
4/12/03	19	20	1	Don't Wanna Try .... S:7 / A:22	Columbia 79872
8/23/03	7	33↑	2	Suga Suga A:7 / S:8	Universal 001055
				BABY BASH Feat. Frankie J	
				FREEWAY	
2/8/03	97	2	3	What We Do S:24	Roc-A-Fella 063846 (T)
				FREEWAY feat. Jay-Z and Beanie Sigel	
				samples "I Just Can't See Myself Without You" by Creative Source	
6/7/03	95	3	4	Flipside S:43	Roc-A-Fella 000428 (T)
				FREEWAY feat. Peedi Crakk	
				GAHAN, Dave ★	
				Born on 5/9/62 in Epping, Essex, England. Lead singer of Depeche Mode.	
6/14/03	30^S	2	1	Dirty Sticky Floors	Mute/Reprise 42620
9/6/03	61^S	2	2	I Need You	Mute/Reprise 42643 (M)
				GANG STARR	
4/26/03	31^S	6	4	Nice Girl, Wrong Place	Virgin 38859 (T)
				GANG STARR feat / Boy Big	
				samples "Kung Fu" by Curtis Mayfield	
10/25/03	61^S	1	5	The Ownerz...	Virgin 38874 (T)
				GEARING, Ashley ★	
				Born in 1991 in Springfield, Massachusetts. Pre-teen country singer.	
8/2/03	27^S	17	1	Can You Hear Me When I Talk To You?	Lyric Street 164075
				GHOSTLAND ★	
				Electronic trio from London, England: Justin Adams (guitar), Caroline Dale (cello) and John Reynolds (producer).	
4/12/03	67^S	1	1	Guide Me God...	Tommy Boy 2396 (M)
				GHOSTLAND Featuring Sinéad O'Connor & Natacha Atlas	
				GINUWINE	
2/22/03	17	20	15	Hell Yeah... A:17 / S:25	Epic 76881
				GINUWINE (feat. Baby)	
				written and produced by R. Kelly	
6/14/03	8	20	16	In Those Jeans A:7	album cut
				from the album The Senior on Epic 86960	
11/1/03	78	16	17	Love You More	Epic 76890 (T)
				GIVE UP THE GHOST ★	
				Punk-rock group from Boston, Massachusetts: Wes Eisold (vocals), Tim Cossar and Brian Massek (guitars), Matt Woods (bass) and Nate Helm (drums).	
9/20/03	72^S	1	1	Love American	Bridge Nine 38
				GODSMACK ★	
				Hard-rock group formed in Boston, Massachusetts: Salvatore "Sully" Erna (vocals), Tony Rombola (guitar), Robbie Merrill (bass) and Tommy Stewart (drums).	
4/19/03	73	8	1	Straight Out Of Line... A:71	album cut
				from the album Faceless on Republic 067854	
				GOLDFRAPP ★	
				Eclectic-pop duo from Bath, England: singer/songwriter/keyboardist Alison Goldfrapp and songwriter Will Gregory.	
5/10/03	64^S	1	1	Train	Mute 9207
				GOOD CHARLOTTE	
3/29/03	43	11	2	The Anthem... S:22 / A:45	Daylight 79932
7/26/03	48	13	3	Girls And Boys... A:53	album cut
				from the album The Young And The Hopeless on Epic/Daylight 86486	
				GORE, Martin L. ★	
				Born on 7/23/61 in Basildon, Essex, England. Member of Depeche Mode.	
5/10/03	55^S	2	1	Stardust	Mute/Reprise 42617 (M)
				first recorded by David Essex in 1974	
				GRAFIC INTERNATIONAL ★	
				Born Cleveland Fuller in Nashville, Tennessee. Male rapper.	
5/24/03	25^S	11	1	Respect My Pimpin'	Graft 650000
				GRAY, Dobie	
3/29/03	9	35	9	Drift Away A:9 [R]	album cut
				UNCLE KRACKER Featuring Dobie Gray	
				new version of Gray's #5 hit in 1973; from the album No Stranger To Shame on Lava 83542	

DEBUT DATE	PEAK POS	WKS CHR	G L D	ARTIST Title	Sales/Air	Label & Number
				GREEN, Al		
1/25/03	73^S	2		21 Love Iz		J Records 21256 (T)
				ERICK SERMON Featuring Al Green		
				samples "Love & Happiness" by Al Green and "Here We Go" by Run-D.M.C.		
11/22/03	67^S	2		22 I Can't Stop		Blue Note 53284
				GREEN, Pat ★		
				Born on 4/5/72 in San Antonio, Texas; raised in Waco, Texas. Male country singer/songwriter/guitarist.		
8/30/03	39	20		1 Wave On Wave A:36		album cut
				from the album *Wave On Wave* on Republic 000562		
				GREEN, Vivian ★		
				Born in 1979 in Philadelphia, Pennsylvania. R&B singer/songwriter.		
2/15/03	39	19		1 Emotional Rollercoaster ....S:5 / A:45		Columbia 79858
				G-UNIT ★		
				Male rap trio from Jamaica, Queens, New York: Curtis "50 Cent" Jackson, Christopher Lloyd "Banks" and David "Young Buck" Brown.		
11/1/03	13	18		1 Stunt 101 ....A:13 / S:27		G-Unit 001601 (T)
				G-WIZ ★		
				Born Glenn Browder in Louisville, Kentucky; raised in Indianapolis, Indiana. Male rapper.		
1/18/03	27^S	17		1 Just Like You...		Compound 691007
				GWYNN, Nee-Nee ★		
				Born in 1985 in San Diego, California. Teen R&B singer. Daughter of baseball great Tony Gwynn and Base Hit Records founder Alicia Gwynn.		
2/22/03	16^S	19		1 No Means No		Base Hit 83022
				NEE-NEE GWYNN Featuring: Baby Diva		
				Tony Gwynn (backing vocals)		
				GYRLZ SOCIETY ★		
				Interracial female vocal group formed in Minneapolis, Minnesota: Amy Correa, Katy Scanlan, Tynisha Soares and Melissa Tessmer.		
5/10/03	54^S	1		1 Respect Me		MCA 155933
				HAHZ THE RIPPA ★		
				Born Hahz McMillan in Pensacola, Florida. Male rapper.		
1/25/03	7^S	14		1 Everybody's Gotta Live		Body Head 6035
				samples "Everybody's Gotta Live" by Love		
				HALL, Ellis ★		
				Born in Oakland, California. Male R&B singer/songwriter/multi-instrumentalist. Briefly lead singer for Tower Of Power in the 1970s.		
9/27/03	32^S	5		1 Gotta Get The Money		Crossover 70027
				HANSON, Jennifer ★		
				Born in Whittier, California; raised in La Habra, California. Country singer/songwriter.		
1/18/03	76	10		1 Beautiful Goodbye...S:31		Capitol 77816
				HEADLEY, Heather		
5/3/03	55	20		2 I Wish I Wasn't...A:51		album cut
				from the album *This Is Who I Am* on RCA 69376		
				HENNESSY, Carly ★		
				Born in 1984 in Dublin, Ireland. Female singer/songwriter.		
3/8/03	45^S	1		1 Beautiful You..		MCA 155885
				co-written by actress Danielle Brisebois (played "Stephanie" on TV's *All In The Family*)		
				HILL, Faith		
6/28/03	29^S	11		15 You're Still Here		Warner 16647
				HITMAN SAMMY SAM ★		
				Born Sammy King in Atlanta, Georgia. Male rapper.		
5/17/03	90	3		1 Step Daddy S:22		Universal 000676
				samples "Double Dutch Bus" by Frankie Smith; a children's chorus sings "Itsy Bitsy Spider"		
				HOUSTON, Marques ★		
				Born on 8/4/81 in Los Angeles, California. R&B singer. Member of Immature.		
3/8/03	63	7		1 That Girl A:61		album cut
9/6/03	39	20		2 Clubbin A:37		album cut
				MARQUES HOUSTON Featuring Joe Budden & Pied Piper		
				written and produced by R. Kelly; above 2 from the album *MH* on T.U.G. 000046		
12/13/03+	76	9		3 Pop That Booty		T.U.G. 67501 (T)
				MARQUES HOUSTON (Featuring Jermaine "JD" Dupri)		
				HOUSTON, Whitney		
4/26/03	84	12	●	42 Try It On My Own S:24		Arista 51156 (D)
				ICED EARTH ★		
				Hard-rock group from Indiana: Tim Owens (vocals), Jon Schaffer (guitar), James MacDonough (bass) and Richard Christy (drums).		
11/15/03	13^S	10		1 The Reckoning (Don't Tread On Me)		SPV 74983

DEBUT DATE	PEAK POS	WKS CHR	G L D	ARTIST Title	Sales/Air	Label & Number
				IN-GRID ★		
				Born Ingrid Alberini on 9/11/80 in Italy. Female dance singer/songwriter.		
12/6/03+	40^S	14↑		1 **You Promised Me**		Benz Street 75434
				INNER CIRCLE		
11/29/03	29^S	7		6 **Limbo Rock**		TEEC 1024
				CHUBBY C & OD Featuring Inner Circle		
				new version of Chubby's #2 Pop hit from 1962; project assembled by producer Gary Lefkowith; OD includes musicains Jermaine Brown and Hovannes Dilakian		
				ISLEY BROTHERS, The		
4/5/03	49	20		47 **What Would You Do?** A:46		album cut
				THE ISLEY BROTHERS Featuring RONALD ISLEY AKA MR. BIGGS		
				written and produced by R. Kelly; from the album *Body Kiss* on DreamWorks 450409		
				JACKSON, Alan		
2/8/03	29	20		17 **That'd Be Alright** A:28		album cut
				from the album *Drive* on Arista Nashville 67039		
6/28/03	17	20		18 **It's Five O'Clock Somewhere** A:14		album cut
				ALAN JACKSON & JIMMY BUFFETT		
12/13/03+	29	17↑		19 **Remember When** A:27		album cut
				above 2 from the album *Greatest Hits Volume II and Some Other Stuff* on Arista Nashville 53097		
				JACKSON, Michael		
12/6/03	83	5		47 **One More Chance** S:2		Epic 76802 (**M**)
				written and co-produced by R. Kelly		
				JADAKISS		
8/30/03	43^S	8		6 **Let's Get It**		RapRock/Pyramid 10422
				SMOOT featuring Jadakiss & Swizz Beatz		
				JAGGED EDGE		
9/6/03	6	27		13 Walked Outta Heaven	S:2 / A:6	So So Def 76974
12/6/03+	42	11		14 **My Baby** A:40		Columbia 76779 (**T**)
				BOW WOW Featuring Jagged Edge		
				JAHEIM		
3/22/03	20	20		5 **Put That Woman First** A:19		album cut
				samples "I Forgot To Be Your Lover" by William Bell; from the album *Still Ghetto* on Divine Mill 48214		
				JANE'S ADDICTION ★		
				Rock group from Los Angeles, California: Perry Farrell (vocals), Dave Navarro (guitar), Chris Chaney (bass) and Stephen Perkins (drums). Farrell and Perkins were also members of Porno For Pyros. Navarro was a member of Red Hot Chili Peppers; married actress Carmen Electra on 11/22/2003.		
7/26/03	72	9		1 **Just Because** A:68		album cut
				from the album *Strays* on Capitol 90186		
				JA RULE		
10/25/03	44	10		15 **Clap Back** ....S:30 / A:44		Murder Inc. 001584 (**T**)
				JAVIER ★		
				Born Javier Colon in 1978 in Hartford, Connecticut. R&B singer/songwriter/guitarist.		
8/16/03	95	8		1 **Crazy** S:69		Capitol 52413
				JAY-EL ★		
				Born in Middletown, Connecticut; later based in Atlanta, Georgia. Male R&B singer.		
6/14/03	56^S	4		1 **Be About Yours**		Powersource 91012 (**M**)
				JAY-Z		
2/8/03	97	2		36 **What We Do** S:24		Roc-A-Fella 063846 (**T**)
				FREEWAY feat. Jay-Z and Beanie Sigel		
				samples "I Just Can't See Myself Without You" by Creative Source		
2/15/03	8	19		37 **Excuse Me Miss** ....A:8 / S:14		Roc-A-Fella 063717 (**T**)
4/12/03	33	12		38 **Beware Of The Boys** (Mundian To Bach Ke) ....S:7 / A:36		Sequence 8012 (**M**)
				PAN'JABI MC Featuring JAY-Z		
				Indian vocals by Labh Janjua; samples the theme from TV's *Knight Rider*		
4/26/03	62^S	2		39 **Back In The Day**		Goldmind 67387 (**T**)
				MISSY ELLIOTT (Featuring Jay-Z)		
				samples "I Don't Know What This World Is Coming To" by The Soul Children		
5/10/03	18^S	11		40 **Stop**		Roc-A-Fella 000398 (**T**)
5/24/03	❶^8	27		41 Crazy In Love	A:❶^8 / S:11	Columbia 79949 (**D**)
				BEYONCÉ (Featuring Jay-Z)		
				samples "Are You My Woman (Tell Me So)" by The Chi-Lites		
6/14/03	5	23		42 **Frontin'**	A:5 / S:7	Star Trak 58647
				PHARRELL Featuring Jay-Z		
11/15/03	10	18		43 Change Clothes	A:12 / S:14	Roc-A-Fella 001651 (**T**)
				Danne Doty (additional vocals)		
				JEAN, Wyclef		
10/18/03	65	9		12 **Party To Damascus** ....S:45 / A:64		J Records 54960 (**T**)
				WYCLEF JEAN (feat. Missy Elliott)		

DEBUT DATE	PEAK POS	WKS CHR	G L D	ARTIST Title	Sales/Air	Label & Number
				JEDI MIND TRICKS ★		
				Male rap duo from Brooklyn, New York: Vinnie Paz (rapper) and Stoupe (producer).		
3/1/03	58^S	5		1 Animal Rap		Babygrande 0102 (M)
				JEDI MIND TRICKS feat Kool G Rap		
				JET ★		
				Rock group from Melbourne, Australia: brothers Nick (guitar) and Chris (drums) Cester, Cameron Muncey (vocals, guitar) and Mark Wilson (bass).		
12/20/03+	32↑	16↑		1 Are You Gonna Be My Girl............................	A:33	album cut
				from the album Get Born on Elektra 62892		
				JEWEL		
5/10/03	20	20		9 Intuition..	S:3 / A:22	Atlantic 88108
11/1/03	16^S	12		10 Stand		Atlantic 88233
				JEWELL, Buddy ★		
				Born on 4/2/61 in Lepanto, Arkansas. Country singer/songwriter. Winner on the first season of TV's Nashville Star talent show in 2003.		
6/21/03	29	20		1 Help Pour Out The Rain (Lacey's Song)...............	S:3 / A:27	Columbia 79885
				produced by Clint Black		
				JOE		
11/22/03	48	20		13 More & More	A:45	album cut
				written and produced by R. Kelly; from the album And Then... on Jive 53707		
				JOHNSON, Syleena		
4/19/03	8^S	14		2 Guess What (Guess Again) Remix		Jive 40099
				SYLEENA JOHNSON featuring R. Kelly		
				remix of Johnson's original version titled "Guess What" ("Bubbled Under" at #104); the Hot 100 Sales chart also showed the B-side ("Faithful To You")		
				JOLLY.GREEN ★		
				Male rapper.		
3/15/03	24^S	15		1 .Yall Don't Know..		Zoe Pound 5601
				JONELL		
2/22/03	49^S	1		2 So Whassup		Def Soul 063781 (T)
				JONELL feat. Redman		
				JONES, Norah		
12/20/03	2^{1S}	16↑		2 Turn Me On		Blue Note 53475
				first recorded by Nina Simone in 1967		
				JONES, Roy Jr.		
4/26/03	11^S	9		2 Who Run This		Body Head 274771
				ROY JONES, JR. Featuring Pastor Troy, Lil John And The Eastside Boyz		
				JUSTIN, Dean ★		
				Born in Minnesota. Country singer/guitarist.		
7/19/03	29^S	11		1 Carry The Flag...		SLR 0006
				KARDINAL OFFISHALL ★		
				Born Jason Harrow in Toronto, Ontario, Canada. Male rapper/producer.		
5/3/03	68^S	1		1 Belly Dancer		MCA 113949 (T)
				KARDINAL OFFISHALL Featuring Pharrell Williams		
				KEITH, Toby		
3/15/03	66	5		12 Rock You Baby	A:63	album cut
5/3/03	22	20		13 Beer For My Horses..	A:18	album cut
				TOBY KEITH with Willie Nelson		
				above 2 from Keith's album Unleashed on DreamWorks 450254		
9/6/03	26	20		14 I Love This Bar	A:21	album cut
				from the album Shock'n Y'all on DreamWorks 450435		
11/22/03	91	6		15 I Can't Take You Anywhere..................................	S:26	DreamWorks 001581
				SCOTTY EMERICK with Toby Keith		
12/27/03+	28	15↑		16 American Soldier	A:28	album cut
				from the album Shock'n Y'all on DreamWorks 450435		
				KELIS		
1/25/03	85	5		4 Take You Home..	S:66	Elektra 67351 (T)
				ANGIE MARTINEZ Featuring Kelis		
5/17/03	88	6		5 How You Want That	S:31	Bad Boy 000430 (T)
				LOON Featuring Kelis		
				samples "Saturday Night" by Schooly D		
10/4/03	3	22		6 Milkshake	A:3 / S:8	Star Trak 58648 (D)
				KELLEY, Josh ★		
				Born in Augusta, Georgia. Pop singer/songwriter/guitarist.		
8/9/03	79	20		1 Amazing		Hollywood 164074

DEBUT DATE	PEAK POS	WKS CHR	G L D	ARTIST Title	Sales/Air	Label & Number
				KELLY, R.		
4/19/03	8ˢ	14		31 Guess What (Guess Again) Remix		Jive 40099
				SYLEENA JOHNSON featuring R. Kelly		
				remix of Johnson's original version titled "Guess What" ("Bubbled Under" at #104)		
4/19/03	80	3		32 Soldier's Heart...	S:18	Jive 40029
4/26/03	16	17		33 Snake..	A:15 / S:21	Jive 40108 (T)
				R. KELLY featuring Cam'ron and Big Tigger		
5/3/03	41ˢ	10		34 Rich Man		R Records 91008
				RUSSELL Feat. R. Kelly		
				written and produced by R. Kelly		
7/19/03	13	20		35 Thoia Thoing...	A:12 / S:30	Jive 54283 (T)
8/23/03	9	27		36 Step In The Name Of Love	A:8 / S:67	Jive 55572 (T)
11/15/03+	24	20		37 Gigolo...	A:22 / S:70	Nick/Jive 56646 (T)
				NICK CANNON featuring R. Kelly		
12/20/03+	4	16↑		38 Hotel	A:4 / S:10	J Records 56053 (T)
				CASSIDY feat. R. Kelly		
				samples "Rapper's Delight" by Sugarhill Gang		
12/27/03+	85	9		39 Gangsta Girl...	S:55	Cash Money 001355 (T)
				BIG TYMERS featuring R. Kelly		
				written and produced by R. Kelly		
				KEYS, Alicia		
11/15/03+	3	20		5 You Don't Know My Name	A:3	J Records 56599 (T)
				samples "Let Me Prove My Love To You" by The Main Ingredient		
				KILLER MIKE ★		
				Born Michael Render in Atlanta, Georgia. Male rapper. Discovered by OutKast.		
2/15/03	60	9		1 A.D.I.D.A.S...	A:59	album cut
				KILLER MIKE Featuring Big Boi		
				A.D.I.D.A.S.: All Day I Dream About Sex; from the album *Monster* on Columbia 86862		
2/22/03	74ˢ	1		2 AKshon (Yeah!)		Aquemini 79784 (M)
4/5/03	26	20		3 Never Scared	A:24 / S:26	Break-Em-Off 50870 (T)
				BONE CRUSHER Featuring Killer Mike & T.I.		
				first released as a promotional CD maxi-single in very limited quantities with no bar-code on the actual product (label assigned it a number of 777); the 12" above is the widely available release		
				KOOL G RAP		
3/1/03	58ˢ	5		3 Animal Rap		Babygrande 0102 (M)
				JEDI MIND TRICKS feat Kool G Rap		
				KORN		
8/9/03	38	10		2 Did My Time	S:2	Epic/Immortal 79977
				from the move *Lara Croft Tomb Raider: The Cradle Of Life* starring Angelina Jolie (not on soundtrack album)		
				KRISTINE W		
2/22/03	39ˢ	3		4 Some Lovin'..		Tommy Boy 2393 (M)
				MURK vs KRISTINE W		
12/27/03	60ˢ	1		5 Fly Again..		Tommy Boy 2423 (M)
				KROEGER, Chad		
7/26/03	8	35		2 Why Don't You & I	A:8	album cut
				SANTANA Featuring Alex Band or Chad Kroeger		
				the Chad Kroeger (of Nickelback) version is from Santana's album *Shaman* on Arista 14737; the Alex Band (of The Calling) version is available as a promo single only (Arista 53233)		
				KWELI, Talib		
3/29/03	77	10		9 Get By	S:47	Rawkus 113938 (T)
				samples "Sinnerman" by Nina Simone		
				LA BOUCHE		
2/1/03	49ˢ	11		5 In Your Life		Logic 98813
				dedicated to the memory of member Melanie Thornton (died in a plane crash on 11/24/2001, age 34)		
				LABRADO, Darrell		
6/7/03	22ˢ	5		2 I Want My Island Girl.......................................		Aloha 7029 (M)
				LAMAR, Nathaniel ★		
				Born in Los Angeles, California. R&B singer/songwriter/actor. Played "Kyle Stokes" on the TV soap *Days Of Our Lives*.		
8/23/03	31ˢ	10		1 Soul Shake..		Jenstar 1387
				LASGO		
12/27/03+	83	14		2 Alone...	S:72	Robbins 72074 (M)
				LATIF ★		
				Born Corey Williams in 1983 in Philadelphia, Pennsylvania. R&B singer/songwriter.		
6/7/03	46ˢ	15		1 I Don't Wanna Hurt You		Motown 000439
				samples "Time Will Reveal" by DeBarge		
				LAVIGNE, Avril		
4/26/03	64	6	●	4 Losing Grip	S:19 / A:67	Arista 51025 (D)

DEBUT DATE	PEAK POS	WKS CHR	G L D	ARTIST Title	Sales/Air	Label & Number
				LEE, Murphy ★		
				Born Tohri Harper in St. Louis, Missouri. Male rapper. Member of St. Lunatics.		
6/28/03	❶⁴	30		1 Shake Ya Tailfeather	A:❶⁴	album cut
				NELLY/P. DIDDY/MURPHY LEE		
				from the movie *Bad Boys II* starring Will Smith and Martin Lawrence (soundtrack on Bad Boy 000716)		
10/11/03	17	20		2 Wat Da Hook Gon Be	A:16 / S:49	Fo' Reel 001451 (T)
				MURPHY LEE Featuring Jermaine Dupri		
				LENNOX, Annie		
9/27/03	17ˢ	9		7 Pavement Cracks		J Records 55884 (M)
				LEXX ★		
				Born Alexander Garcia on 1/25/77 in Oakland, California. Latino rapper.		
2/15/03	13ˢ	10		1 How I Feel		Takeover 600001
				LEXX featuring Lil' Flip		
				LIL BOW WOW		
7/5/03	14	17		7 Let's Get Down	S:4 / A:12	Columbia 79928
				BOW WOW (Feat. Baby)		
12/6/03+	42	11		8 My Baby	A:40	Columbia 76779 (T)
				BOW WOW Featuring Jagged Edge		
				LIL' FLIP ★		
				Born Wesley Weston in Houston, Texas. Male rapper.		
2/15/03	13ˢ	10		1 How I Feel		Takeover 600001
				LEXX featuring Lil' Flip		
4/26/03	48	20		2 Like A Pimp	S:40 / A:45	SRC 000402 (T)
				DAVID BANNER feat. Lil' Flip		
				samples "Take It Off" by UGK		
9/27/03	25ˢ	5		3 What Cha Gone Do		Ball Hawg 60652
				PLAYBOY SHANE Featuring Lil Flip		
				LIL JON & THE EAST SIDE BOYZ		
4/26/03	11ˢ	9		3 Who Run This		Body Head 274771
				ROY JONES, JR. Featuring Pastor Troy, Lil John And The Eastside Boyz		
5/3/03	2¹	45		4 Get Low	A:2 / S:21	BME 2377 (T)
				LIL JON & THE EAST SIDE BOYZ Featuring Ying Yang Twins		
8/9/03	4	32		5 Damn!	A:4 / S:40	So So Def 52215 (T)
				YOUNGBLOODZ Featuring Lil' Jon		
11/15/03+	9	21↑		6 Salt Shaker	A:8 / S:14	Collipark 2485 (T)
				YING YANG TWINS Feat. LIL JON & The EAST SIDE BOYZ		
11/22/03+	84	20		7 Shake That Monkey		$hort 55065 (T)
				TOO $hort feat Lil Jon & The Eastside Boyz		
11/29/03	56ˢ	1		8 Get Low Remix	[R]	BME 2394 (T)
				LIL JON & THE EAST SIDE BOYZ Feat. Elephant Man, Busta Rhymes & Ying Yang Twins		
				LIL' KIM		
2/8/03	17	20		16 The Jump Off	S:11 / A:16	Queen Bee 88036 (T)
				LIL' KIM (featuring Mr. Cheeks)		
				samples "Jeeps, Lex Coups, Bimaz & Benz" by Lost Boyz		
4/26/03	2³	24		17 Magic Stick	A:❶¹	album cut
				LIL' KIM (feat. 50 Cent)		
				samples "The Thrill Is Gone" by B.B. King; from the album *La Bella Mafia* on Queen Bee 83572		
8/2/03	12	20		18 Can't Hold Us Down	A:12	RCA 54526 (T)
				CHRISTINA AGUILERA featuring Lil' Kim		
11/1/03	48ˢ	10		19 Thug Luv		Queen Bee 88246
				LIL' KIM (feat. Twista)		
				LIL' MO		
3/8/03	4	23		7 Can't Let You Go	A:4 / S:42	Desert Storm 67428 (T)
				FABOLOUS featuring Mike Shorey & Lil' Mo		
3/22/03	37	20		8 4 Ever	S:33 / A:34	Elektra 67379 (T)
				LIL' MO (Featuring Fabolous)		
				LIL SCRAPPY ★		
				Born Darryl Richards in Atlanta, Georgia. Male rapper.		
12/13/03+	18ˢ	15↑		1 Head Bussa		BME 16506
				LIL' ZANE		
8/30/03	44ˢ	6		4 Tonite, I'm Yours		Priority 52480
				ZANE featuring Tank		
				LINKIN PARK		
3/15/03	32	20		5 Somewhere I Belong	A:29	album cut
7/26/03	48	20		6 Faint	A:48	album cut
11/8/03+	11	22↑		7 Numb	A:11	album cut
				above 3 from the album *Meteora* on Warner 48186		
				LIVE		
8/30/03	59	20		10 Heaven	A:56	album cut
				from the album *Birds Of Pray* on Radioactive 000374		

DEBUT DATE	PEAK POS	WKS CHR	G L D	ARTIST Title	Sales/Air	Label & Number
				LL COOL J		
1/18/03	58^S	3		25 Focus		Def Jam 063782 (**T**)
				JOE BUDDEN feat. LL Cool J		
				Dutchess (additional vocals)		
				LONESTAR		
1/25/03	66	5		10 Unusually Unusual	A:66	album cut
				from the album *I'm Already There* on BNA 67011		
4/19/03	23	22		11 My Front Porch Looking In	A:19	album cut
11/8/03	61	11		12 Walking In Memphis	A:59	album cut
				#13 hit for Marc Cohn in 1991; above 2 from the album *From There To Here: Greatest Hits* on BNA 67076		
				LOON		
5/17/03	88	6		4 How You Want That	S:31	Bad Boy 000430 (**T**)
				LOON Featuring Kelis		
				samples "Saturday Night" by Schooly D		
				LOPEZ, Jennifer		
5/3/03	32	16		11 I'm Glad	S:12 / A:33	Epic 79868
				samples "P.S.K. What Does It Mean?" by Schooly D		
				LOS LONELY BOYS ★		
				Rock trio of brothers from Texas: Henry (guitar), Joey "JoJo" (bass) and Ringo (drums) Garza. All share vocals.		
7/19/03	71^S	1		1 Real Emotions		Pedernales 803042
				LOVELESS, Patty		
8/23/03	81	10		3 Lovin' All Night		Epic 79954
				#10 Country hit for Rodney Crowell in 1992		
				LOY, Rachel ★		
				Born in 1984 in Austin, Texas. Singer/songwriter/guitarist.		
5/10/03	47^S	2		1 The Same Man		Epic 79887
				LUDACRIS		
1/11/03	83	14		13 B R Right	S:65	Slip-N-Slide 85395 (**T**)
				TRINA Featuring Ludacris		
6/7/03	32	11		14 Act A Fool	A:30 / S:31	Def Jam S. 000539 (**T**)
				from the movie *2 Fast 2 Furious* starring Paul Walker and Tyrese		
9/6/03	❶^1	28		15 Stand Up	A:❶^1 / S:24	Def Jam S. 001183 (**T**)
				LUDACRIS featuring Shawnna		
9/20/03	3	21		16 Holidae In	A:3 / S:42	Disturb. Tha P. 52816 (**T**)
				CHINGY featuring Ludacris & Snoop Dogg		
10/18/03	70	9		17 Hot & Wet	S:62 / A:70	Bad Boy 001150 (**T**)
				112 Featuring Ludacris		
				LUMIDEE ★		
				Born Lumidee Cedeno in Harlem, New York (Puerto Rican parents). Female singer/rapper/songwriter.		
5/31/03	3	20		1 Never Leave You - Uh Oooh, Uh Oooh!	A:3 / S:17	Universal 000652 (**T**)
				samples "Diwali (Rhythm)" by Steven Marsden		
				MADONNA		
4/5/03	37	8		50 American Life	S:2 / A:61	Maverick 16658
7/26/03	4^S	22		51 Hollywood		Maverick 42638 (**M**)
10/25/03	35	13		52 Me Against The Music	S:3 / A:38	Jive 58215 (**M**)
				BRITNEY SPEARS featuring Madonna		
12/27/03	❶^{1S}	15↑		53 Nothing Fails		Maverick 42682 (**M**)
				MANSON, Marilyn ★		
				Born Brian Warner on 1/5/69 in Canton, Ohio. Hard-rock singer/songwriter. Noted for his controversial stage performances. His band includes: Scott "Daisy Berkowitz" Putesky (guitar), Steve "Madonna Wayne Gacy" Bier (keyboards), Jeordi "Twiggy Ramirez" White (bass) and Ken "Ginger Fish" Wilson (drums).		
5/10/03	5^S	5		1 mOBSCENE		Nothing 000372
				MAROON5 ★		
				Alternative pop-rock group from Los Angeles, California: Adam Levine (vocals, guitar), James Valentine (guitar), Jesse Carmichael (keyboards), Mickey Madden (bass) and Ryan Dusick (drums).		
8/23/03	18	22		1 Harder To Breathe	A:18	album cut
				from the album *Songs About Jane* on Octone 50001		
				MARTIN, Ricky		
5/31/03	74	8		12 Tal Vez	A:73 [F]	album cut
				title is Spanish for "Perhaps"; from the album *Almas Del Silencio* on Sony Discos 70439		
				MARTINEZ, Angie		
1/25/03	85	5		4 Take You Home	S:66	Elektra 67351 (**T**)
				ANGIE MARTINEZ Featuring Kelis		
				MASTER P		
3/8/03	94	6		18 Choppa Style	S:62	New No Limit 019400 (**T**)
				CHOPPA Featuring Master P		

DEBUT DATE	PEAK POS	WKS CHR	G L D	ARTIST Title	Sales/Air	Label & Number
				MATCHBOX TWENTY		
3/22/03	5	54		9 Unwell	A:4	album cut
9/27/03	23	21		10 Bright Lights	A:22	album cut
				above 2 from the album *More Than You Think You Are* on Atlantic 83612		
12/13/03	22ˢ	5		11 A New York Christmas	[X]	Atlantic 88251
				ROB THOMAS		
				MAYER, John		
8/30/03	33	20		3 Bigger Than My Body	A:38	album cut
				from the album *Heavier Things* on Aware 86185		
				McBRIDE, Martina		
3/15/03	47	19		11 Concrete Angel	A:43	album cut
				from the album *Greatest Hits* on RCA 67012		
8/9/03	39	20		12 This One's For The Girls	A:37	album cut
				backing vocalists include Faith Hill, Carolyn Dawn Johnson and McBride's daughters Delaney and Emma; from the album *Martina* on RCA 54207		
				McCOMAS, Brian		
7/12/03	57	11		2 99.9% Sure (I've Never Been Here Before)	A:54	album cut
				from the album *Brian McComas* on Lyric Street 165025		
				McGRAW, Tim		
3/1/03	27	20		22 She's My Kind Of Rain	A:25	album cut
7/12/03	27	20		23 Real Good Man	A:23	album cut
12/13/03+	32	17↑		24 Watch The Wind Blow By	A:32	album cut
				above 3 from the album *Tim McGraw And The Dancehall Doctors* on Curb 78746		
				McLACHLAN, Sarah		
10/25/03+	41	21		10 Fallen	S:6 / A:40	Arista 60143
				MERCYME ★		
				Christian pop group from Lakeland, Florida: Bart Millard (vocals), Mike Scheuchzer (guitar), Nathan Cochran (bass) and Robby Shaffer (drums).		
10/11/03	71	18↑		1 I Can Only Imagine	S:❶¹⁰	INO/Curb 73150
				METHOD MAN		
7/5/03	22	13		17 Love @ 1st Sight	S:5 / A:22	Geffen 000954
				MARY J. BLIGE featuring Method Man samples "Hot Sex" by A Tribe Called Quest		
				MR. CHEEKS		
2/8/03	17	20		3 The Jump Off	S:11 / A:16	Queen Bee 88036 (T)
				LIL' KIM (featuring Mr. Cheeks) samples "Jeeps, Lex Coups, Bimaz & Benz" by Lost Boyz		
5/17/03	42ˢ	3		4 Crush On You		Universal 000448 (T)
				MR. CHEEKS featuring Mario Winans		
				MR. LIF ★		
				Born Jeffrey Haynes in Boston, Massachusetts. Male rapper.		
3/15/03	72ˢ	1		1 Live From The Plantation		Definitive Jux 45 (T)
				12" single is a limited edition picture disc; produced by El-P		
				MONICA		
4/26/03	10	22		12 So Gone	A:8 / S:41	J Records 21260 (T)
				samples "You Are Number One" by The Whispers		
9/27/03	75	18		13 Knock Knock	S:65	J Records 57593 (D)
				samples "It's A Terrible Thing To Waste Your Love" by The Masqueraders; above 2 co-written and produced by Missy Elliott		
				MONTGOMERY GENTRY		
3/22/03	47	20		7 Speed	S:14 / A:46	Columbia 79864
11/1/03	45	20		8 Hell Yeah	A:42	album cut
				from the album *My Town* on Columbia 86520		
				M.O.P.		
4/5/03	55ˢ	1		3 Stompdash*toutu (Vendetta)		Def Jam 000160 (T)
				CNN Featuring M.O.P. samples "You've Got The Papers (I've Got The Man)" by Ann Peebles; from the movie *Cradle 2 The Grave* starring Jet Li and DMX		
				MORGAN, Craig ★		
				Born Craig Morgan Greer in Kingston Springs, Tennessee. Country singer/songwriter.		
5/31/03	59	14		1 Almost Home	A:55	album cut
				from the album *I Love It* on Broken Bow 77567		
				MOSLEY, Lou		
4/19/03	15ˢ	16		2 If You Let Me		Jenstar 1383
				Vanessa Holmes (backing vocals); first recorded by the Four Tops in 1972		
				MOSS-SCOTT, Brandy		
3/8/03	16ˢ	23		4 Starting With Me		Heavenly Tunes 2005
				MRAZ, Jason ★		
				Born on 10/20/72 in Mechanicsville, Virginia. Singer/songwriter/guitarist.		
5/3/03	15	28		1 The Remedy (I Won't Worry)	A:15	album cut
				from the album *Waiting For My Rocket To Come* on Elektra 62829		

DEBUT DATE	PEAK POS	WKS CHR	G L D	ARTIST Title	Sales/Air	Label & Number
				MUDVAYNE		
8/2/03	17^S	5		2 Not Falling		Epic 55758 (**D**)
				MURK ★		
				Techno-dance duo from New York: producers Oscar Gaetan and Ralph Falcon. Former members of Funky Green Dogs.		
2/22/03	39^S	3		1 Some Lovin'		Tommy Boy 2393 (**M**)
				MURK vs KRISTINE W		
				MURRAY, Keith		
4/19/03	99	1		7 Yeah Yeah U Know It S:33		Def Jam 000787
				KEITH MURRAY feat. Def Squad		
6/7/03	47^S	4		8 Candi Bar		Def Jam 000563 (**T**)
				Patti Austin (female vocal); samples "Havana Candy" by Patti Austin		
				MURS ★		
				Born in Los Angeles, California. Male rapper.		
3/1/03	64^S	1		1 God's Work		Definive Jux 47 (**T**)
				MUSIQ		
3/15/03	99	1		6 Break You Off S:36		MCA 113971 (**T**)
				THE ROOTS featuring Musiq		
6/7/03	37^S	11	●	7 Nothing At All		Arista 51159 (**D**)
				SANTANA featuring Musiq		
				co-written by Rob Thomas (of Matchbox Twenty)		
11/8/03	53	17		8 forthenight...A:51		Def Soul 001649 (**T**)
				M.V.P. (MOST VALUABLE PLAYAS) ★		
				Rap-dance group formed by producer Robert Clivilles (of C & C Music Factory). Members include female singer Jasmine "Mimi" Ray and male singer Victor "Vice Versa" Matos.		
10/18/03	82	8		1 Roc Ya Body "Mic Check 1, 2"..........................		Casablanca 001366 (**T**)
				M.V.P. (MOST VALUABLE PLAYAS) Featuring Stagga-Lee		
				MYA		
6/28/03	13	20		11 My Love Is Like...WO ....S:5 / A:14		A&M 000768
				co-written and produced by Missy Elliott		
11/29/03+	51	12		12 Fallen...S:10 / A:56		A&M 001681
				samples "Saudade Vem Corrondo" by Stan Getz & Luiz Bonfa		
				MY RUIN ★		
				Goth-rock group formed in Los Angeles, California: Tairrie B. (vocals), Mick Murphy (guitar), Meghan Mattex (bass) and Yael (drums). Murphy is the lone male member.		
9/20/03	60^S	2		1 The Shape Of Things To Come... .... [EP]		Century Media 81212
				this is actually a 5 song EP preview of their full length album *The Horror of Beauty*; songs: 2 versions of "Made To Measure," "Grotesque," "Unmanageable" and "Sex Junkie"		
				NAPPY ROOTS		
8/30/03	96	4		3 Roun' The Globe		Atlantic 88228 (**T**)
				NAS		
3/1/03	12	20		17 I Can..A:11 / S:31		Columbia 79941
				backing vocals by a children's chorus; melody is Beethoven's "Fur Elise"		
				NATE DOGG		
3/22/03	❶⁴	23		13 21 Questions ....A:❶⁵ / S:13		Shady 080739 (**T**)
				50 CENT Feat. Nate Dogg		
				samples "It's Only Love Doing Its Thing" by Barry White		
12/6/03+	33	18↑		14 Gangsta Nation ....S:32 / A:34		Hoo-Bangin' 53289 (**T**)
				WESTSIDE CONNECTION Featuring Nate Dogg		
				NATURAL		
11/1/03+	3^S	6	●	2 What If		Trans Continental 90712
				NELLY		
4/12/03	58	7		10 Pimp Juice ....S:41 / A:59		Universal 000239 (**T**)
				samples "Love Comes In All Colors/Tellin' Lies" by The Staple Singers		
6/28/03	❶⁴	30		11 Shake Ya Tailfeather ....A:❶⁴		album cut
				NELLY/P. DIDDY/MURPHY LEE		
				from the movie *Bad Boys II* starring Will Smith and Martin Lawrence (soundtrack on Bad Boy 000716)		
				NELSON, Willie		
5/3/03	22	20		12 Beer For My Horses..A:18		album cut
				TOBY KEITH with Willie Nelson		
				from Keith's album *Unleashed* on DreamWorks 450254		
				NEW FOUND GLORY		
6/21/03	34^S	5		2 Head On Collision		Drive-Thru 000522
				NICHOLS, Joe		
1/25/03	27	20		2 Brokenheartsville............................A:26 / S:48		Universal South 000782
8/16/03	72	5		3 She Only Smokes When She Drinks.............A:66		album cut
				from the album *Man With A Memory* on Universal South 170285		

DEBUT DATE	PEAK POS	WKS CHR	G L D	ARTIST Title	Sales/Air	Label & Number

NICKELBACK

| 8/23/03+ | 7 | 33↑ | 3 | Someday | A:7 | album cut |

from the album *Long Road* on Roadrunner 618390

NIVEA

| 2/22/03 | 58 | 9 | 3 | Laundromat | A:56 | album cut |

written and produced by R. Kelly; from the album *Nivea* on Jive 41746

NO DOUBT

| 3/29/03 | 62 | 6 | 8 | Running | A:68 | album cut |

from the album *Rock Steady* on Interscope 493158

| 11/1/03+ | 10 | 23↑ | 9 | It's My Life | A:10 | album cut |

#31 hit for Talk Talk in 1984; from the album *The Singles 1992-2003* on Interscope 000149

NORFUL, Smokie ★
Born William Norful in Pine Bluff, Arkansas. Gospel singer/songwriter/organist.

| 11/29/03 | 96 | 3 | 1 | I Need You Now | S:21 [L] | EMI Gospel 77947 |

NOTORIOUS B.I.G., The

| 10/18/03 | 19 | 20 | 22 | Runnin (Dying To Live) | A:17 / S:24 | Amaru 001670 (T) |

TUPAC Featuring The Notorious B.I.G.
new mix (produced by Eminem) of their #81 hit in 1997

O'CONNOR, Sinéad

| 2/1/03 | 53[S] | 3 | 3 | Troy (The Phoenix From The Flame) | | Radikal 99155 (M) |

issued on 2 separate CDs: 99155 (8 versions) and 99158 (Remixes: 8 versions);
original version released on her 1988 album *The Lion And The Cobra*

| 4/12/03 | 67[S] | 1 | 4 | Guide Me God | | Tommy Boy 2396 (M) |

GHOSTLAND Featuring Sinéad O'Connor & Natacha Atlas

OFFSPRING, The

| 12/20/03+ | 64 | 15 | 11 | Hit That | A:62 | album cut |

from the album *Splinter* on Columbia 89026

112

| 8/9/03 | 75 | 6 | 17 | Na Na Na | S:16 / A:75 | Bad Boy 000940 |

112 featuring Super Cat

| 10/18/03 | 70 | 9 | 18 | Hot & Wet | S:62 / A:70 | Bad Boy 001150 (T) |

112 Featuring Ludacris

ONO, Yoko

| 4/12/03 | 25[S] | 10 | 2 | Walking On Thin Ice | [R] | Mindtrain 82669 (M) |

ONO
new mix of her #58 hit from 1981 (remixed by the Pet Shop Boys)

ORRICO, Stacie ★
Born on 3/3/86 in Seattle, Washington. Christian pop singer/songwriter.

| 5/17/03 | 52 | 11 | 1 | Stuck | S:13 / A:61 | Virgin/ForeFront 38869 |
| 9/20/03 | 30 | 20 | 2 | (there's gotta be) More To Life | S:15 / A:32 | Virgin/ForeFront 52925 |

OTTO, James ★
Born on the Ft. Louis Army Base in Washington state. Country singer/songwriter/guitarist.

| 11/15/03 | 61[S] | 1 | 1 | Days Of Our Lives | | Mercury 001500 |

OUTKAST

| 2/15/03 | 60 | 9 | 13 | A.D.I.D.A.S. | A:59 | album cut |

KILLER MIKE Featuring Big Boi
A.D.I.D.A.S.: All Day I Dream About Sex; from Killer Mike's album *Monster* on Columbia 86862

| 8/2/03 | 61[S] | 3 | 14 | GhettoMusick | | Arista 54249 (T) |

samples "Love, Want And Need You" by Patti LaBelle

| 10/18/03 | ❶[9] | 25↑ | ▲ 15 | Hey Ya! / | A:❶[9] | |
| 9/27/03+ | ❶[1] | 28↑ | 16 | The Way You Move | A:2 / S:3 | Arista 54962 (D) |

OUTKAST Featuring Sleepy Brown

PAISLEY, Brad

| 1/18/03 | 57 | 10 | 8 | I Wish You'd Stay | A:57 | album cut |

from the album *Part II* on Arista Nashville 67008

| 6/14/03 | 31 | 20 | 9 | Celebrity | A:28 | album cut |
| 12/20/03+ | 35 | 16↑ | 10 | Little Moments | A:35 | album cut |

above 2 from the album *Mud On The Tires* on Arista Nashville 50605

PAN'JABI MC ★
Born Rajinder Rai in 1975 in Coventry, England (Indian parents). Male DJ. Employs the "Bhangra" style
of East Indian chants and beats combined with Western dance music.

| 4/12/03 | 33 | 12 | 1 | Beware Of The Boys (Mundian To Bach Ke) | S:7 / A:36 | Sequence 8012 (M) |

PAN'JABI MC Featuring JAY-Z
Indian vocals by Labh Janjua; samples the theme from TV's *Knight Rider*

PASTOR TROY

| 4/26/03 | 11[S] | 9 | 2 | Who Run This | | Body Head 274771 |

ROY JONES, JR. Featuring Pastor Troy, Lil John And The Eastside Boyz

DEBUT DATE	PEAK POS	WKS CHR	G L D	ARTIST Title	Sales/Air	Label & Number
				PAUL, Sean		
2/22/03	❶³	32	6	Get Busy	A:❶³ / S:12	VP/Atlantic 88020 (T)
3/1/03	70	20	7	Breathe	S:10 / A:72	Arista 50984
				BLU CANTRELL (Featuring Sean Paul) samples "What's The Difference" by Dr. Dre		
6/7/03	13	20	8	Like Glue	A:13 / S:60	VP/Atlantic 88145 (T)
8/16/03	❶⁹	29	9	Baby Boy	A:❶⁹	Columbia 76867 (T)
				BEYONCÉ feat. Sean Paul Sean Paul is featured on the CD promo single (does NOT appear on the commerical 12" single)		
				PEARL JAM		
3/1/03	4ˢ	14	19	Save You		Epic 79844
				PEREZ, Amanda		
2/1/03	20	20	2	Angel	S:6 / A:20	Virgin 47265
				PERFECT CIRCLE, A ★ Rock duo from Hollywood, California: Maynard James Keenan (vocals) and Billy Howerdel (guitar). Keenan is also lead singer of Tool.		
9/27/03	61	18	1	Weak And Powerless	S:28 / A:60	Virgin 38888
				PHAIR, Liz		
9/20/03	32	20	2	Why Can't I?	A:34	album cut
				from the album *Liz Phair* on Capitol 83928		
				PHARRELL Born Pharrell Williams on 4/5/73 in Virginia Beach, Virginia. Male rapper/producer. Member of prolific production trio The Neptunes (recorded as N*E*R*D).		
2/8/03	6	20	1	Beautiful	A:6 / S:14	Priority 77887 (T)
				SNOOP DOGG featuring Pharrell, Uncle Charlie Wilson		
4/5/03	22ˢ	16	2	Come Close Remix (Closer)		MCA 000575
				COMMON Feat. Erykah Badu, Pharrell From The Neptunes, and Q-Tip remix of Common's #65 hit from 2002		
5/3/03	68ˢ	1	3	Belly Dancer		MCA 113949 (T)
				KARDINAL OFFISHALL Featuring Pharrell Williams		
6/14/03	5	23	4	Frontin'	A:5 / S:7	Star Trak 58647
				PHARRELL Featuring Jay-Z		
8/9/03	58	10	5	Light Your A** On Fire	S:32 / A:59	Star Trak 54245 (T)
				BUSTA RHYMES Featuring Pharrell		
				P!NK		
6/28/03	60	5	10	Feel Good Time	A:62	album cut
				P!NK Featuring William Orbit samples "Fresh Garbage" by Spirit; from the movie *Charlie's Angels: Full Throttle* starring Cameron Diaz, Drew Barrymore and Lucy Liu (soundtrack on Columbia 90132)		
10/18/03	68	4	11	Trouble	S:6 / A:73	Arista 58646
				PLAYBOY SHANE ★ Born in 1978 in Arkansas. Male rapper. Vice President of Ball Hawg record label.		
9/27/03	25ˢ	5	1	What Cha Gone Do		Ball Hawg 60652
				PLAYBOY SHANE Featuring Lil Flip		
				POSTAL SERVICE, The ★ Pop-rock duo from Bellingham, Washington: Benjamin Gibbard and James Tamborello.		
2/8/03	21ˢ	20↑	1	Such Great Heights		Sub Pop 608
7/26/03	26ˢ	18↑	2	The District Sleeps Alone Tonight		Sub Pop 614
				POWELL, Jesse		
8/30/03	51ˢ	4	3	By The Way		D3/Riviera 9922
				PRESLEY, Elvis		
9/27/03	94	2	154	Rubberneckin'	S:❶² [R]	RCA 54218
				remix (by Paul Oakenfold) of Presley's original 1969 recording; featured in a TV commercial for the Toyota Solara		
				PUDDLE OF MUDD		
11/22/03	72	16	5	Away From Me	A:71	album cut
				from the album *Life On Display* on Flawless 000108		
				PUFF DADDY		
6/28/03	❶⁴	30	30	Shake Ya Tailfeather	A:❶⁴	album cut
				NELLY/P. DIDDY/MURPHY LEE from the movie *Bad Boys II* starring Will Smith and Martin Lawrence (soundtrack on Bad Boy 000716)		
11/15/03	58ˢ	2	31	Summertime		Columbia 76915 (T)
				BEYONCÉ featuring P. Diddy from the movie *The Fighting Temptations* starring Beyoncé and Cuba Gooding Jr.		
				Q-TIP		
4/5/03	22ˢ	16	6	Come Close Remix (Closer)		MCA 000575
				COMMON Feat. Erykah Badu, Pharrell From The Neptunes, and Q-Tip remix of Common's #65 hit from 2002		

DEBUT DATE	PEAK POS	WKS CHR	G L D	ARTIST / Title	Sales/Air	Label & Number
				RADIOHEAD		
9/6/03	8ˢ	19		6 Go To Sleep		Capitol 52953
				RAMSEY, Tarralyn ★		
				Born on 1/1/80 in Melbourne, Florida. Female R&B singer. Winner of VH-1's *Born To Diva* talent show.		
12/27/03	31ˢ	15↑		1 Up Against All Odds		Casablanca 001813
				RASCAL FLATTS		
4/5/03	30	20		6 Love You Out Loud	A:28	album cut
8/23/03	34	20		7 I Melt	A:33	album cut
				above 2 from the album *Melt* on Lyric Street 165031		
				RAYNE, Tha' ★		
				Female R&B vocal trio from New York.		
11/8/03	73ˢ	1		1 Didn't You Know		Arista 56688
				RED HOT CHILI PEPPERS		
2/8/03	57	20		13 Can't Stop	A:54	album cut
				from the album *By The Way* on Warner 48140		
				REDMAN		
2/22/03	49ˢ	1		18 So Whassup		Def Soul 063781 (T)
				JONELL feat. Redman		
				REINA ★		
				Born in the Bronx, New York. Latin dance singer. Name is Spanish for "Queen."		
4/12/03	96	5		1 No One's Gonna Change You	S:45	Robbins 72081 (M)
				REVENUE ★		
				Born in New Orleans, Louisiana; raised in Las Vegas, Nevada. Male rapper.		
2/8/03	12ˢ	13		1 Up In Da Club 2Nite		Stack A Grip 10002
				RJD2		
3/22/03	55ˢ	1		2 The Horror		Definitive Jux 46 (T)
				ROCK, Pete, & C.L. Smooth		
4/26/03	64ˢ	1		3 Shine On Me!		St. Nick 0001 (T)
				ROC PROJECT, The ★		
				Dance studio production of Ray "Roc" Checo.		
8/23/03	97	5		1 Never (Past Tense)	S:59	Tommy Boy 2401 (M)
				THE ROC PROJECT FEAT. TINA ARENA		
				samples "Terror" by Fused		
				ROEZ BOYZ ★		
				Male rap duo from Los Angeles, California: Eric "OE" Wilson and Jahmal "Kash" House.		
4/26/03	33ˢ	13		1 63/64		Green Teeth 0452
				Envyi (backing vocals)		
				ROLLING STONES, The		
10/4/03	97	1		58 Sympathy For The Devil..	S:❶¹	Abkco 9666 (M)
				their original 1968 recording remixed by The Neptunes (single also includes remixes by Fatboy Slim and Full Phatt as well as the original version)		
				ROOTS, The		
3/15/03	99	1		4 Break You Off..	S:36	MCA 113971 (T)
				THE ROOTS featuring Musiq		
				ROWLAND, Kelly		
3/8/03	97	5		3 Can't Nobody..		Music World 79839 (T)
				RUSSELL ★		
				Born in Chicago, Illinois. R&B singer.		
5/3/03	41ˢ	10		1 Rich Man		R Records 91008
				RUSSELL Feat. R. Kelly		
				written and produced by R. Kelly		
				SALIVA		
9/27/03	93	3		2 Rest In Pieces	S:40	Island 001191
				co-written by Nikki Sixx (of Mötley Crüe)		
				SANTANA		
6/7/03	37ˢ	11	●	24 Nothing At All		Arista 51159 (D)
				SANTANA featuring Musiq		
				co-written by Rob Thomas (of Matchbox Twenty)		
7/26/03	8	35		25 Why Don't You & I	A:8	album cut
				SANTANA Featuring Alex Band or Chad Kroeger		
				the Chad Kroeger (of Nickelback) version is from Santana's album *Shaman* on Arista 14737; the Alex Band (of The Calling) version is available as a promo single only (Arista 53233)		
				SANTANA, Juelz — see DIPLOMATS		
				SARAI ★		
				Born Sarai Howard in 1982 in Kingston, New York. White female rapper/songwriter.		
3/8/03	18ˢ	11		1 Pack Ya Bags		Epic 79841

DEBUT DATE	PEAK POS	WKS CHR	G L D	ARTIST Title	Sales/Air	Label & Number
				SEAL		
9/6/03	40^S	6		7 Get It Together		Warner 42645 (**M**)
10/18/03	89	8		8 Waiting For You	S:27	Warner 16574
				SEDUCTION		
7/19/03	29^S	15		6 All Night Long		Jenstar 1384
				SEDUCTION with Saddler		
				SERMON, Erick		
1/25/03	73^S	2		11 Love Iz		J Records 21256 (**T**)
				ERICK SERMON Featuring Al Green		
				samples "Love & Happiness" by Al Green and "Here We Go" by Run-D.M.C.		
				SHINS, The ★		
				Pop-rock group from Albuquerque, New Mexico: James Mercer (vocals, guitar), Marty Crandall (keyboards), Neal Langford (bass) and Jesse Sandoval (drums).		
10/11/03	14^S	5		1 So Says I		Sub Pop 621
				SHOTGUN THE REPRESENTER ★		
				Born in Savannah, Georgia. Male rapper.		
6/28/03	36^S	8		1 Chow Chow Chow		Black 5 0005
				SIGEL, Beanie		
2/8/03	97	2		5 What We Do	S:24	Roc-A-Fella 063846 (**T**)
				FREEWAY feat. Jay-Z and Beanie Sigel		
				samples "I Just Can't See Myself Without You" by Creative Source		
				SIGUR RÓS ★		
				Eclectic-ethereal group from Reykjavik, Iceland: Jon Thor Birgisson (vocals, guitar), Kjarten Sveinsson (keyboards), Georg Holm (bass) and Orri Pall Dyrason (drums). Group name translates to "Victory Rose."		
5/31/03	11^S	25		1 Untitled #1		Fat Cat/MCA 000270
				first issued as a 3" mini CD in a mini digipak sleeve, sealed within a standard clear plastic blister (Phat Cat/MCA 000272); later issued as a standard 2-disc CD/DVD set (Phat Cat/MCA 000270)		
				SIMPLE PLAN ★		
				Punk-rock group from Montreal, Quebec, Canada: Pierre Bouvier (vocals), Jeff Stinco (guitar), Seb Lefebvre (guitar), David Desrosiers (bass) and Chuck Comeau (drums).		
2/15/03	51	12		1 I'd Do Anything	A:57	album cut
6/28/03	45	19		2 Addicted	A:46	album cut
11/1/03	24	20		3 Perfect	A:25	album cut
				above 3 from the album No Pads, No Helmets...Just Balls on Lava 83534		
				SIMPSON, Jessica		
8/9/03+	6^S	35↑		5 Sweetest Sin		Columbia 79946
12/27/03+	14	15↑		6 With You	A:15 / S:17	Columbia 76710 (**D**)
				SIR IVAN ★		
				Born in San Francisco, California. Electronic musician/producer.		
5/10/03	48^S	2↑		1 San Francisco		Jellybean 08654
				#4 hit for Scott McKenzie in 1967		
				SIXPENCE NONE THE RICHER		
3/22/03	78	6		5 Don't Dream It's Over	S:54	Squint/Curb 886260
				#2 hit for Crowded House in 1987		
				SMILEZ & SOUTHSTAR		
1/4/03	28	16		2 Tell Me (What's Goin' On)	A:29	album cut
				samples "Stop, Look, Listen (To Your Heart)" by The Stylistics; from the album Crash The Party on Artist Direct 01030		
				SMOOT ★		
				Born Jeffrey Huntley in Atlanta, Georgia. Male rapper.		
8/30/03	43^S	8		1 Let's Get It		RapRock/Pyramid 10422
				SMOOT featuring Jadakiss & Swizz Beatz		
				SNOOP DOGG		
2/8/03	6	20		23 Beautiful	A:6 / S:14	Priority 77887 (**T**)
				SNOOP DOGG featuring Pharrell, Uncle Charlie Wilson		
9/20/03	3	21		24 Holidae In	A:3 / S:42	Disturb. Tha P. 52816 (**T**)
				CHINGY featuring Ludacris & Snoop Dogg		
				SOLANGE ⋏		
				Born Solange Knowles on 6/24/86 in Houston, Texas. Female R&B singer. Sister of Beyoncé Knowles of Destiny's Child.		
1/4/03	9^S	12		1 Feelin' You		Music World 79831 (**M**)
				SPARXXX, Bubba		
6/21/03	10^S	27		2 Jimmy Mathis		Beatclub 000746
				samples "Stone Fox Chase" by Area Code 615		
				SPEARS, Britney		
10/25/03	35	13		10 Me Against The Music	S:3 / A:38	Jive 58215 (**M**)
				BRITNEY SPEARS featuring Madonna		

DEBUT DATE	PEAK POS	WKS CHR	G L D	ARTIST / Title	Sales/Air	Label & Number
				SPECIAL GOODNESS, The ★		
				Pop-rock duo from Los Angeles, California: Patrick Wilson and Atom Willard. Wilson is also the drummer of Weezer.		
3/1/03	19^S	4		1 Life Goes By		n.o.s. 6210
				STAGGA LEE ★		
				Born Eric Newman in the Bronx, New York; raised in Yonkers, New York. White male rapper.		
5/3/03	91	4		1 Roll Wit M.V.P. (We Be Like! The La La Song)	S:25	Artist Direct 01128
10/18/03	82	8		2 Roc Ya Body "Mic Check 1, 2"		Casablanca 001366 (T)
				M.V.P. (MOST VALUABLE PLAYAS) Featuring Stagga-Lee		
				STAIND		
4/26/03	66	10		5 Price To Play	A:64	album cut
8/2/03	24	28		6 So Far Away	A:22	album cut
				above 2 from the album *14 Shades Of Grey* on Flip 62882		
				STAKEY, Renée ★		
				Born on 1/20/70 in Southampton, Long Island, New York. White female dance singer.		
3/8/03	72^S	1		1 Rainy Day		Robbins 72084 (M)
				STEELY DAN		
6/7/03	17^S	1		16 Blues Beach		album cut
				single available only as a paid download; from the album *Everything Must Go* on Reprise 48435		
				STEVENSON, Dani ★		
				Born in Atlanta, Georgia; raised in Harlem, New York. Female hip-hop singer/songwriter.		
10/4/03	24^S	4		1 Honk Your Horn		Universal 019351
				DANI STEVENSON Featuring Missy Elliott		
				STRAIT, George		
6/21/03	69	7		18 Tell Me Something Bad About Tulsa	A:64	album cut
10/4/03	38	19		19 Cowboys Like Us	A:37	album cut
				above 2 from the album *Honkytonkville* on MCA Nashville 000114		
				STUDDARD, Ruben ★		
				Born on 7/14/78 in Birmingham, Alabama. Black male vocalist. Winner on the second season of TV's *American Idol* in 2003.		
6/28/03	2²	10	●	1 Flying Without Wings	S:2	J Records 51786
				first recorded by Westlife in 2000; the *Hot 100 Sales* chart also showed the B-side ("Superstar" - Bubbled Under #112)		
				SUGABABES ★		
				Female pop vocal trio from England: Keisha Buchanan, Rosa Buena and Heidi Range.		
10/11/03	34^S	3		1 Round Round		Universal 063850
				SUPER CAT		
8/9/03	75	6		3 Na Na Na	S:16 / A:75	Bad Boy 000940
				112 featuring Super Cat		
				SURVIVALIST		
12/6/03+	23^S	15		2 Immaculate		Slave 97341
				SURVIVALIST featuring Kumandae		
				SWIZZ BEATZ — see DMX / SMOOT		
				TAMIA		
6/14/03	4	26		9 Into You	A:4 / S:71	Desert Storm 67452 (T)
				FABOLOUS Featuring Ashanti or Tamia		
				the version with Ashanti is from his album *Street Dreams* on Desert Storm 62791; the version with Tamia is available as a promo single only		
8/2/03	83	18		10 Officially Missing You	S:22	Elektra 67436 (M)
				TANK		
8/30/03	44^S	6		2 Tonite, I'm Yours		Priority 52480
				ZANE featuring Tank		
				t.A.T.u. ★		
				Female teen dance-rock duo from Moscow, Russia: Julia Volkova and Lena Katina.		
1/4/03	20	20		1 All The Things She Said	S:3 / A:21	Interscope 019354
				THALIA ★		
				Born Ariadna Thalia Sodi Miranda on 8/26/71 in Mexico City, Mexico. Female Latin singer. Married record executive Tommy Mottola (former husband of Mariah Carey) on 12/2/2000.		
6/14/03	22	19		1 I Want You	A:23	Virgin 47305 (T)
				THALIA featuring Fat Joe		
				samples "A Little Bit Of Love" by Brenda Russell		
12/20/03	51^S	2		2 Baby, I'm In Love		Virgin 53630
				THREE DAYS GRACE ★		
				Hard-rock trio from Norwood, Ontario, Canada: Adam Gontier (vocals, guitar), Brad Walst (bass) and Neil Sanderson (drums).		
11/29/03	55	19↑		1 (I Hate) Everything About You	A:52	album cut
				from the album *Three Days Grace* on Jive 53479		

DEBUT DATE	PEAK POS	WKS CHR	G L D	ARTIST Title	Sales/Air	Label & Number
				3 DOORS DOWN		
8/30/03	5	32↑		5 Here Without You	A:5	album cut
				from the album *Away From The Sun* on Republic 066165		
				T.I. ★		
				Born Clifford Harris on 9/25/80 in Atlanta, Georgia. Male rapper.		
4/5/03	26	20		1 Never Scared	A:24 / S:26	Break-Em-Off 50870 (T)
				BONE CRUSHER Featuring Killer Mike & T.I.		
				first released as a promotional CD maxi-single in very limited quantities with no bar-code on the actual product (label assigned it a number of 777); the 12" above is the widely available release		
8/2/03	78	15		2 24's		Atlantic 88124 (T)
				TIMBALAND AND MAGOO		
8/23/03	95	2		8 Cop That Sh#!	S:45	Blackground 001609 (T)
				TIMBALAND & MAGOO featuring Missy Elliott		
				TIMBERLAKE, Justin		
3/22/03	5	22		3 Rock Your Body	A:6	album cut
8/2/03	27	17		4 Señorita	A:29	album cut
				Pharrell (additional vocals); above 2 from the album *Justified* on Jive 41823		
				TLC		
3/29/03	53	4		17 Damaged	A:54	album cut
				from the album *3D* on Arista 14780		
5/10/03	18ˢ	11	●	18 Hands Up		Arista 51157 (D)
				TOO $HORT		
11/22/03+	84	20		16 Shake That Monkey		$hort 55065 (T)
				TOO $hort feat Lil Jon & The Eastside Boyz		
				TRAIN		
5/24/03	19	29		3 Calling All Angels	A:19	album cut
				from the album *My Private Nation* on Columbia 86593		
				TRAPT ★		
				Rock group from Los Gatos, California: Chris Brown (vocals, guitar), Simon Ormandy (guitar), Peter Charell (bass) and Aaron Montgomery (drums).		
4/5/03	16	43		1 Headstrong	A:17	album cut
11/15/03	69	20		2 Still Frame	A:67	album cut
				above 2 from the album *Trapt* on Warner 48296		
				TRAVIS, Randy		
4/5/03	31	20		7 Three Wooden Crosses	A:28	album cut
				from the album *Rise And Shine* on Warner 886236		
				TRIBE CALLED QUEST, A		
11/15/03	43ˢ	1		7 I C U (Doin' It)		Violator 57358 (T)
				VIOLATOR FEATURING A TRIBE CALLED QUEST AND ERYKAH BADU		
				samples "High On Sunshine" by the Commordores and "Wild Thang" by 2 Much		
				TRICE, Obie ★		
				Born on 11/14/79 in Detroit, Michigan. Male rapper.		
9/6/03	54	11		1 Got Some Teeth	S:47 / A:53	Shady 001116 (T)
				co-written and produced by Eminem		
				TRICK DADDY		
4/5/03	69	20		7 Still Ballin	A:66	album cut
				2PAC Featuring Trick Daddy		
				from the album *Better Dayz* on Amaru 497070		
				TRILLVILLE ★		
				Male rap trio from Atlanta, Georgia: Dirty Mouth, Don P and Lil LA.		
12/20/03+	77	16↑		1 Neva Eva	S:8	BME 16505
				TRINA		
1/11/03	83	14		5 B R Right	S:65	Slip-N-Slide 85395 (T)
				TRINA Featuring Ludacris		
				TURNER, Josh ★		
				Born in 1977 in Hannah, South Carolina. Country singer/songwriter/guitarist.		
12/13/03+	72	18↑		1 Long Black Train	S:21 / A:72	MCA Nashville 000976
				TWAIN, Shania		
2/1/03	63	10		15 Up!	A:62	album cut
5/24/03	20	23		16 Forever And For Always	A:17	album cut
12/6/03+	56	13		17 She's Not Just A Pretty Face	A:56	album cut
				above 3 from the album *Up!* on Mercury 170314		
				TWISTA		
11/1/03	48ˢ	10		8 Thug Luv		Queen Bee 88246
				LIL' KIM (feat. Twista)		
12/6/03+	❶¹	18↑		9 Slow Jamz	A:❶² / S:17	Atlantic 88288 (T)
				TWISTA Featuring Kanye West & Jamie Foxx		
				samples "A House Is Not A Home" by Luther Vandross		

DEBUT DATE	PEAK POS	WKS CHR	G L D	ARTIST Title	Sales/Air	Label & Number
				2PAC		
4/5/03	69	20	20	Still Ballin	A:66	album cut
				2PAC Featuring Trick Daddy		
				from the album *Better Dayz* on Amaru 497070		
10/18/03	19	20	21	Runnin (Dying To Live).............................	A:17 / S:24 [R]	Amaru 001670 (**T**)
				TUPAC Featuring The Notorious B.I.G.		
				new mix (produced by Eminem) of their #81 hit in 1997		
				TYRESE		
1/4/03	7	25	9	How You Gonna Act Like That /	A:6 / S:61	
7/26/03	57	14	10	Signs Of Love Makin'..................................	A:54	J Records 52518 (**D**)
				UNCLE KRACKER		
3/29/03	9	35	3	Drift Away	A:9 [R]	album cut
				UNCLE KRACKER (Featuring Dobie Gray)		
				new version of Gray's #5 hit in 1973 (including new vocals by Gray); from Uncle Kracker's album *No Stranger To Shame* on Lava 83542		
				UNION TURNPIKE ★		
				Studio group assembled by producer Chris Davis.		
2/15/03	63^S	1	1	Oh!..		Epic 79827
				samples "The Stroke" by Billy Squier and "Jam Master Jay" by Run-D.M.C.; featured in the Fox-TV series *Fastlane*		
				URBAN, Keith		
3/15/03	38	19	5	Raining On Sunday......................................	A:36	album cut
8/16/03	30	20	6	Who Wouldn't Wanna Be Me	A:27	album cut
				above 2 from the album *Golden Road* on Capitol 32936		
				VANDROSS, Luther		
6/28/03	38	20	26	Dance With My Father..................................	S:24 / A:35	J Records 57595 (**D**)
				written by Vandross and Richard Marx; backing vocalists include Cissy Houston		
				VAN DYK, Paul		
5/10/03	37^S	7	2	Nothing But You..	[I]	Mute 9204 (**M**)
				PAUL VAN DYK Feat. Hemstock & Jennings		
10/18/03	63^S	4	3	Time Of Our Lives		Mute 9225 (**M**)
				PAUL VAN DYK Featuring Vega 4		
				VIOLATOR		
11/15/03	43^S	1	2	I C U (Doin' It)		Violator 57358 (**T**)
				VIOLATOR FEATURING A TRIBE CALLED QUEST AND ERYKAH BADU		
				samples "High On Sunshine" by the Commodores and "Wild Thang" by 2 Much		
				WALKER, Clay		
8/9/03	55	13	7	A Few Questions......................................	A:54	album cut
				from the album *A Few Questions* on RCA 67068		
				WAYNE, Jimmy ★		
				Born on 10/23/72 in Bessemer City, North Carolina; raised in Gastonia, North Carolina. Country singer/songwriter.		
4/26/03	32	20	1	Stay Gone..	S:12 / A:33	DreamWorks 000345
				"45": DreamWorks 50789; B-side: "Blue and Brown"		
				WEST, Kanye ★		
				Born in 1977 in Chicago, Illinois. Male rapper/songwriter/producer.		
11/29/03+	15	19↑	1	Through The Wire......................................	A:13 / S:29	Roc-A-Fella 001441 (**T**)
				samples "Through The Fire" by Chaka Khan		
12/6/03+	❶¹	18↑	2	Slow Jamz	A:❶² / S:17	Atlantic 88288 (**T**)
				TWISTA Featuring Kanye West & Jamie Foxx		
				samples "A House Is Not A Home" by Luther Vandross		
				WESTSIDE CONNECTION		
12/6/03+	33	18↑	3	Gangsta Nation..	S:32 / A:34	Hoo-Bangin' 53289 (**T**)
				WESTSIDE CONNECTION Featuring Nate Dogg		
				WHITE STRIPES, The ★		
				Rock duo from Detroit, Michigan: Jack White (vocals, guitar; born John Gillis) and Meg White (drums).		
5/24/03	76	20	1	Seven Nation Army	A:75	album cut
				from the album *Elephant* on Third Man 27148		
				WILSON, Charlie		
2/8/03	6	20	3	Beautiful	A:6 / S:14	Priority 77887 (**T**)
				SNOOP DOGG featuring Pharrell, Uncle Charlie Wilson		
				WINANS, Mario		
5/17/03	42^S	3	3	Crush On You..		Universal 000448 (**T**)
				MR. CHEEKS Featuring Mario Winans		

DEBUT DATE	PEAK POS	WKS CHR	G L D	ARTIST Title	Sales/Air	Label & Number
				WONDER, Wayne ★		
				Born VonWayne Charles in Jamaica. Reggae singer.		
1/11/03	**11**	31		1 **No Letting Go**...A:11 / S:49		VP/Atlantic 88254
				WORLEY, Darryl		
3/15/03	**22**	20		4 **Have You Forgotten?** A:21		album cut
				from the album *Have You Forgotten* on DreamWorks 000064		
				WYNONNA		
7/5/03	**70**	8		7 **What The World Needs**..................................A:67		album cut
				from the album *What The World Needs Now Is Love* on Curb 78811		
				YING YANG TWINS		
5/3/03	**2**[1]	45		3 Get Low A:2 / S:21		BME 2377 (**T**)
				LIL JON & THE EAST SIDE BOYZ Featuring Ying Yang Twins		
9/27/03	87	10		4 **Naggin**		Collipark 2481 (**T**)
11/15/03+	**9**	21↑		5 Salt Shaker A:8 / S:14		Collipark 2485 (**T**)
				YING YANG TWINS Feat. LIL JON & The EAST SIDE BOYZ		
11/29/03	**56**[S]	1		6 **Get Low Remix**		BME 2394 (**T**)
				LIL JON & THE EAST SIDE BOYZ Feat. Elephant Man, Busta Rhymes & Ying Yang Twins		
				YOUNGBLOODZ		
8/9/03	**4**	32		2 Damn! A:4 / S:40		So So Def 52215 (**T**)
				YOUNGBLOODZ Featuring Lil' Jon		
				YOUNG GUNZ ★		
				Male rap duo: Chris and Neef.		
8/9/03	**14**	20		1 **Can't Stop, Won't Stop** A:13		album cut
				samples "Overweight Lovers In The House" by Heavy D and "Super Rappin'" by Grandmaster Flash; from the various artists album *The Chain Gang Vol. II* on Roc-A-Fella 000971		
				ZION ★		
				Born in Miami, Florida; later based in California. Female R&B singer. Started own Zion record label.		
5/31/03	**23**[S]	10		1 **Blowin' Me Up (Callin' Me)**......................................		Zion 6055

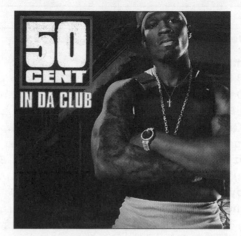

1. **50 CENT**
608

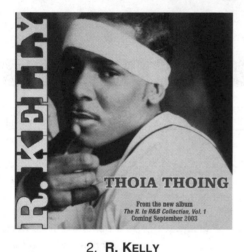

2. **R. KELLY**
423

3. **BEYONCÉ** ★
413

4.	306	NELLY		13.	238	LUDACRIS
5.	303	SEAN PAUL		14.	236	LIL' KIM
6.	295	P. DIDDY		15.	230	MURPHY LEE ★
7.	278	FABOLOUS		16.	225 +	OUTKAST
8.	276	JAY-Z		17.	217 +	3 DOORS DOWN
9.	262	CHRISTINA AGUILERA		18.	215	MATCHBOX TWENTY
10.	254	JUSTIN TIMBERLAKE		19.	208	BUSTA RHYMES
11.	253	ASHANTI		20.	207	JENNIFER LOPEZ
12.	250	CHINGY ★				

+ Subject to change since a title that peaked in 2003 by this artist is still charted as of the 4/3/04 cut-off date.

#1 "HOT 100"

	Date Hit #1	Wks @ #1	Title	Artist
1.	1/4	12	**Lose Yourself**.. *Eminem* (includes 8 weeks at #1 in 2002)	
2.	2/1	1	**Bump, Bump, Bump** .... *B2K & P. Diddy*	
3.	2/8	4	**All I Have**.......................... *Jennifer Lopez Featuring LL Cool J*	
4.	3/8	9	**In Da Club** ....*50 Cent*	
5.	5/10	3	**Get Busy** .... *Sean Paul*	
6.	5/31	4	**21 Questions**.................................... *50 Cent Feat. Nate Dogg*	
7.	6/28	2	**This Is The Night** ....*Clay Aiken*	
8.	7/12	8	**Crazy In Love**.............................. *Beyoncé (Featuring Jay-Z)*	
9.	9/6	4	**Shake Ya Tailfeather** .... *Nelly/P. Diddy/Murphy Lee*	
10.	10/4	9	**Baby Boy**.............................. *Beyoncé (Featuring Sean Paul)*	
11.	12/6	1	**Stand Up** .... *Ludacris featuring Shawnna*	
12.	12/13	9	**Hey Ya!**.. *OutKast* (includes 6 weeks at #1 in 2004)	

#1 "HOT 100" AIRPLAY

	Date Hit #1	Wks @ #1	Title	Artist
1.	1/4	11	**Lose Yourself**.. *Eminem* (includes 8 weeks at #1 in 2002)	
2.	1/25	2	**Bump, Bump, Bump** .... *B2K & P. Diddy*	
3.	2/8	4	**All I Have**.......................... *Jennifer Lopez Featuring LL Cool J*	
4.	3/8	9	**In Da Club** ....*50 Cent*	
5.	5/10	3	**Get Busy** .... *Sean Paul*	
6.	5/31	5	**21 Questions**.................................... *50 Cent Feat. Nate Dogg*	
7.	7/5	1	**Magic Stick** .... *Lil' Kim Featuring 50 Cent*	
8.	7/12	8	**Crazy In Love**.............................. *Beyoncé (Featuring Jay-Z)*	
9.	9/6	4	**Shake Ya Tailfeather** .... *Nelly/P. Diddy/Murphy Lee*	
10.	10/4	9	**Baby Boy**.............................. *Beyoncé (Featuring Sean Paul)*	
11.	12/6	1	**Stand Up** .... *Ludacris featuring Shawnna*	
12.	12/13	9	**Hey Ya!**.. *OutKast* (includes 6 weeks at #1 in 2004)	

#1 "HOT 100" SINGLES SALES

	Date Hit #1	Wks @ #1	Title	Artist
1.	1/4	11	Die Another Day (includes 8 weeks at #1 in 2002)	Madonna
2.	1/25	12↕	Picture	Kid Rock Featuring Allison Moorer
3.	2/22	2	Through The Rain	Mariah Carey
4.	5/3	8	God Bless The U.S.A.	American Idol Finalists
5.	6/28	11↕	This Is The Night/Bridge Over Troubled Water	Clay Aiken
6.	8/30	2	So Yesterday	Hilary Duff
7.	9/27	2↕	Rubberneckin'	Elvis Presley
8.	10/4	1	Sympathy For The Devil	The Rolling Stones
9.	10/18	10	I Can Only Imagine	Mercyme
10.	12/27	1	Nothing Fails	Madonna

#1 HOT DIGITAL TRACKS *

	Date Hit #1	Wks @ #1	Title	Artist
1.	7/19	6↕	Crazy In Love	Beyoncé (Featuring Jay-Z)
2.	8/9	1	In Between Days	Ben Folds
3.	8/16	1	Love Of Strings	Moby
4.	8/30	2	Bigger Than My Body (Album Version)	John Mayer
5.	9/27	1	Where Is The Love? (Radio Edit)	Black Eyed Peas
6.	10/4	1	Hurt (Quiet)	Johnny Cash
7.	10/11	1	Fallen (Album Mix)	Sarah McLachlan
8.	10/18	19↕	Hey Ya! (Radio Mix) (includes 8 weeks at #1 in 2004)	OutKast

* Chart first published in *Billboard* on 7/19/03.

BUBBLING UNDER THE HOT 100

This section lists, by artist, every title that debuted on *Billboard's* weekly **Bubbling Under The Hot 100** chart (a 25-position listing) in 2003, with the exception of those titles that charted on the *Hot 100*.

❂: Indicates the artist has never appeared on the *Hot 100*, *Bubbling Under The Hot 100*, or *Hot 100 Airplay* charts.

DEBUT DATE	PEAK POS	WKS CHR	ARTIST Title	Label & Number
			AFI ○	
			Hard-rock group from San Francisco, California: Davey "Havok" Marchard (vocals), Jade Puget (guitar), Hunter Burgan (bass) and Adam Carson (drums). AFI: A Fire Inside.	
4/5/03	114	6	Girl's Not Grey	album cut
			from the album *Sing The Sorrow* on DreamWorks 50380	
			ANDREWS, Jessica	
4/12/03	108	8	There's More To Me Than You	album cut
			from the album *Now* on DreamWorks 450356	
			AUSTIN, Sherrié	
11/1/03	113	7	Streets Of Heaven	album cut
			from the album *Streets Of Heaven* on Broken Bow 75872	
			BERMUDEZ, Obie ○	
			Born in Aibonito, Puerto Rico; raised in Vineland, New Jersey. Latin pop singer/songwriter.	
9/6/03	120	8	Antes .... [F]	album cut
			title is Spanish for "Before"	
12/27/03+	118	6	Me Cansé De Ti .... [F]	album cut
			title is Spanish for "I'm Tired Of You"; above 2 from the album *Confesiones* on EMI Latin 84647	
			BEYONCÉ	
8/23/03	108	8	Summertime	Columbia 76915 (T)
			BEYONCÉ featuring P. Diddy	
			from the movie *The Fighting Temptations* starring Beyoncé and Cuba Gooding Jr.	
			BLINK-182	
11/1/03	102	15	Feeling This	album cut
			from the album *Blink-182* on Geffen 001334	
			BON JOVI	
2/15/03	106	10	Misunderstood	album cut
			from the album *Bounce* on Island 063055	
			BUSTA RHYMES — see EMINEM	
			CARLTON, Vanessa	
1/4/03	101	9	Pretty Baby	album cut
			from the album *Be Not Nobody* on A&M 493307	
			CARTER, Deana	
2/15/03	102	10	There's No Limit	album cut
			from the album *I'm Just A Girl* on Arista Nashville 67054	
			CHAYANNE	
9/6/03	120	2	Un Siglo Sin Ti .... [F]	album cut
			title is Spanish for "A Century Without You"; from the album *Sincero* on Sony Discos 70627	
			CHEVELLE	
12/20/03+	120	3	Closure	album cut
			from the album *Wonder What's Next* on Epic 86157	
			CLARKSON, Kelly	
12/27/03+	101	10	The Trouble With Love Is	album cut
			from the album *Thankful* on RCA 68159	
			CONJUNTO PRIMAVERA ○	
			Latin group from Chihuahua, Mexico: Tony Melendez (vocals), Rolando Perez (guitar), Felix Contreras (keyboards), Juan Dominguez (sax), Oscar Ochoa (bass) and Adan Huerta (drums).	
3/22/03	111	8	Una Vez Mas .... [F]	album cut
			title is Spanish for "Once Again"; from the album *Perdoname Mi Amor* on Fonovisa 86237	
			DAVID, Craig	
2/15/03	119	2	Hidden Agenda	album cut
			from the album *Slicker Than Your Average* on Wildstar 80027	
			DEFTONES	
5/17/03	120	6	Minerva	album cut
			from the album *Deftones* on Maverick 48350	
			DF DUB ○	
			Born William Green in Detroit, Michigan. White rapper. Worked as DJ "Billy The Kid" on WILD-FM in Dallas, Texas.	
2/22/03	120	4	Country Girl	album cut
			from the album *Country Girl* on 3Sixty 89089	
			DIAMOND RIO	
11/8/03	107	8	Wrinkles	album cut
			from the album *Completely* on Arista Nashville 67046	

DEBUG DATE	PEAK POS	WKS CHR	ARTIST Title	Label & Number
			DION, Celine	
5/17/03	104	24	Have You Ever Been In Love	album cut
			from the album One Heart on Epic 87185	
			DISTURBED	
3/22/03	110	4	Remember	album cut
9/27/03	121	5	Liberate	album cut
			above 2 from the album Believe on Reprise 48320	
			DR. DRE — see FAT JOE	
			EMERSON DRIVE	
9/6/03	124	1	Only God (Could Stop Me Loving You).....................	album cut
			from the album Emerson Drive on DreamWorks 450272	
			EMINEM	
5/17/03	111	6	Hail Mary	AP 105 (**T**)
			EMINEM, 50 CENT & BUSTA RHYMES	
			ESTEFAN, Gloria	
9/6/03	110	11	Wrapped...	album cut
			from the album Unwrapped on Epic 86790	
			EVANESCENCE	
9/6/03	104	9	Going Under	album cut
			from the album Fallen on Wind-Up 13063	
			EVANS, Sara	
6/7/03	103	13	Backseat Of A Greyhound Bus...............................	album cut
			from the album Restless on RCA 67074	
			FAT JOE	
9/20/03	122	1	Girl I'm A Bad Boy..	album cut
			FAT JOE & P. DIDDY Feat. Dre	
			from the movie Bad Boys II starring Will Smith and Martin Lawrence (soundtrack on Bad Boy 000716)	
			50 CENT	
1/4/03	106	19	Realest N*ggas	album cut
			NOTORIOUS B.I.G. & 50 CENT	
			from the movie Bad Boys II starring Will Smith and Martin Lawrence (soundtrack on Bad Boy 00716)	
5/17/03	111	6	Hail Mary	AP 105 (**T**)
			EMINEM, 50 CENT & BUSTA RHYMES	
7/19/03	101	12	What Up Gangsta	album cut
			from the album Get Rich Or Die Tryin' on Shady 493544	
			FLOETRY	
10/11/03	114	4	Getting Late	album cut
			from the album Floetic on DreamWorks 450313	
			FURTADO, Nelly	
7/19/03	116	5	Fotografía .... [**F**]	album cut
			JUANES with Nelly Furtado	
			title is Spanish for "Photograph"; from the album Un Dia Normal on Surco 017532	
11/1/03	109	7	Powerless (Say What You Want)	album cut
			from the album Folklore on DreamWorks 001007	
			GILL, Vince	
1/18/03	105	9	Next Big Thing..	album cut
			from the album Next Big Thing on MCA Nashville 170286	
			GODSMACK	
9/13/03	113	9	Serenity..	album cut
			from the album Faceless on Republic 067854	
			GOO GOO DOLLS	
4/26/03	115	11	Sympathy	album cut
			from the album Gutterflower on Warner 48206	
			GROBAN, Josh	
1/4/03	109	1	O Holy Night.. [**X**]	album cut
			from the album Josh Groban In Concert on 143 Records 48413	
			HILL, Faith	
2/1/03	120	6	When The Lights Go Down	album cut
7/5/03	124	2	One	album cut
			above 2 from the album Cry on Warner 48001	

DEBUT DATE	PEAK POS	WKS CHR	ARTIST Title	Label & Number

IGLESIAS, Enrique

2/22/03	121	1	Quizás .... [F] album cut
			title is Spanish for "Perhaps"
5/24/03	102	4	Para Qué La Vida .... [F] album cut
			title is Spanish for "So That The Life"; above 2 from the album *Quizás* on Universal latino 064385
11/15/03	101	10	Addicted .... album cut
			from the album *Seven* on Interscope 001711

INDIA ○
Born Linda Caballero in Puerto Rico; raised in the Bronx, New York. Latin dance singer/songwriter.

| 2/8/03 | 123 | 4 | Seduce Me Now .... Sony Discos 8655 (M) |

INTOCABLE ○
Latin group from Zapata, Texas: Ricardo Munoz, Daniel Sanchez, Rene Martinez, Felix Salinas, Sergio Serna and Juan Hernandez. Group name is Spanish for Untouchable.

| 1/4/03 | 118 | 3 | Sueña .... [F] album cut |
| | | | title Is Spanish for "It Sounds"; from the album *Sueños* on EMI Latin 537745 |

ISLEY BROTHERS, The

10/25/03	112	6	Busted .... album cut
			THE ISLEY BROTHERS Featuring RONALD ISLEY AKA MR. BIGGS and JS
			written and produced by R. Kelly; from the album *Body Kiss* on DreamWorks 450409

JAY-Z

| 6/28/03 | 112 | 9 | La-La-La (Excuse Me Again) .... album cut |
| | | | from the movie *Bad Boys II* starring Will Smith and Martin Lawrence (soundtrack on Bad Boy 000716) |

JOHNSON, Syleena

| 1/25/03 | 104 | 13 | Guess What .... album cut |
| | | | written and produced by R. Kelly; from the album *Chapter 2: The Voice* on Jive 41815 |

JS ○
R&B vocal duo from Los Angeles, California: sisters Kim and Kandy Johnson. JS: Johnson Sisters.

8/23/03	124	2	Ice Cream .... album cut
			from the album *Ice Cream* on DreamWorks 450332
10/25/03	112	6	Busted .... album cut
			THE ISLEY BROTHERS Featuring RONALD ISLEY AKA MR. BIGGS and JS
			above 2 written and produced by R. Kelly; from the album *Body Kiss* on DreamWorks 450409

JUANES

7/19/03	116	5	Fotografía .... [F] album cut
			JUANES with Nelly Furtado
			title is Spanish for "Photograph"; from the album *Un Dia Normal* on Surco 017532

KELLY, R.

| 5/17/03 | 103 | 19 | I'll Never Leave .... album cut |
| | | | from the album *Chocolate Factory* on Jive 41812 |

KEM ○
Born Kem Owens in Nashville, Tennessee; later based in Detroit, Michigan. Male R&B singer/songwriter.

| 8/2/03 | 106 | 25 | Love Calls .... album cut |
| | | | from the album *Kemistry* on Motown 067516 |

KORN

| 12/6/03 | 119 | 3 | Right Now .... album cut |
| | | | from the album *Take A Look In The Mirror* on Immortal 90335 |

LEVERT, Gerald

| 11/22/03 | 103 | 14 | U Got That Love (Call It A Night) .... album cut |
| | | | from the album *Stroke Of Genius* on Elektra 62903 |

LOON

11/1/03	103	13	Down For Me .... album cut
			LOON Feat. Mario Winans
			from the album *Loon* on Bad Boy 000892

MANÁ ○
Latin rock group from Mexico: Fher Olvera (vocals), Sergio Vallin (guitar), Juan Calleros (bass) and Alex Gonzalez (drums).

| 7/5/03 | 120 | 1 | Mariposa Traicionera .... [F] album cut |
| | | | title is Spanish for "Treacherous Butterfly"; from the album *Revolución De Amor* on Warner Latina 48566 |

MARTIN, Ricky

| 8/9/03 | 122 | 1 | Jaleo .... [F] album cut |
| | | | title is Spanish for "Commotion"; from the album *Almas Del Silencio* on Sony Discos 70439 |

BUBBLING UNDER THE HOT 100

DEBUT DATE	PEAK POS	WKS CHR	ARTIST / Title	Label & Number
			MATTHEWS, Dave, Band	
1/4/03	**119**	4	Grey Street.. *from the album* Busted Stuff *on RCA 68117*	album cut
			MAYER, John	
4/5/03	**102**	19	Why Georgia.. *from the album* Room For Squares *on Aware 85293*	album cut
			McENTIRE, Reba	
9/20/03	**103**	10	I'm Gonna Take That Mountain... *from the album* Room To Breathe *on MCA Nashville 00451*	album cut
			McKNIGHT, Brian	
4/5/03	**106**	7	Shoulda, Woulda, Coulda.. *from the album* U Turn *on Motown 067315*	album cut
			MESSINA, Jo Dee	
4/26/03	**114**	8	Was That My Life.. *from the album* Greatest Hits *on Curb 78790*	album cut
			METALLICA	
6/14/03	**107**	5	St. Anger... *from the album* St. Anger *on Elektra 62853*	album cut
			MIGUEL, Luis	
10/25/03	**119**	3	Te Necesito.. [F] *title is Spanish for "Need You"; from the album* 33 *on Warner Latina 60873*	album cut
			NELLY	
11/8/03	**103**	3	Iz U... *from the album* Da Derrty Versions - The Reinvention *on Fo' Reel 001665*	album cut
			NOTORIOUS B.I.G., The	
1/4/03	**106**	19	Realest N*ggas... **NOTORIOUS B.I.G. & 50 CENT** *from the movie* Bad Boys II *starring Will Smith and Martin Lawrence (soundtrack on Bad Boy 000716)*	album cut
			P!NK	
12/27/03+	**103**	6	God Is A DJ.. *from the album* Try This *on Arista 52139*	album cut
			PIRES, Alexandre ✪	
			Born on 1/8/76 in Uberlandia, Brazil. Latin ballad singer.	
4/5/03	**114**	8	Amame... [F] *from the album* Estrella Guia *on RCA 50632*	album cut
			P.O.D.	
12/6/03	**117**	3	Will You... *from the album* Payable On Death *on Atlantic 83676*	album cut
			PRESLEY, Lisa Marie ✪	
			Born on 2/1/68 in Memphis, Tennessee. Pop-dance singer. Daughter of Priscilla and Elvis Presley. Married to Michael Jackson from 1994-96. Married actor Nicolas Cage on 8/10/2002 (since seperated).	
4/26/03	**114**	5	Lights Out.. *from the album* To Whom It May Concern *on Capitol 96668*	album cut
			PUFF DADDY	
8/23/03	**108**	8	Summertime .... **BEYONCÉ featuring P. Diddy** *from the movie* The Fighting Temptations *starring Beyoncé and Cuba Gooding Jr.*	Columbia 76915 (**T**)
9/20/03	**122**	1	Girl I'm A Bad Boy.. **FAT JOE & P. DIDDY Feat. Dre** *from the movie* Bad Boys II *starring Will Smith and Martin Lawrence (soundtrack on Bad Boy 000716)*	album cut
			QUEENS OF THE STONE AGE	
6/28/03	**116**	6	Go With The Flow.. *from the album* Songs For The Deaf *on Interscope 493425*	album cut
			RED HOT CHILI PEPPERS	
11/29/03	**112**	8	Fortune Faded.. *from the album* Greatest Hits *on Warner 48545*	album cut
			RUSHLOW	
9/27/03	**106**	11	I Can't Be Your Friend .... *from the album* Right Now *on Lyric Street 165039*	album cut

DEBUT DATE	PEAK POS	WKS CHR	ARTIST Title	Label & Number
			SARAI	
7/12/03	**101**	10	Ladies.. album cut	
			from the album *The Original* on Sweat 85859	
			SEETHER	
6/21/03	**122**	2	Driven Under.. album cut	
			from the album *Disclaimer* on Wind-Up 13068	
			SIMPLY RED	
11/15/03	**122**	2	Sunrise.. album cut	
			samples "I Can't Go For That (No Can Do)" by Daryl Hall & John Oates; from the album *Home* on simplyred.com 0001	
			SIN BANDERA ○	
			Latin pop duo: Leonel Garcia (from Mexico) and Noel Scha (from Argentina).	
11/22/03	**114**	8	Mientes Tan Bien .... [F] album cut	
			title is Spanish for "Minds So Well"; from the album *De Viaje* on Sony Discos 70633	
			SMILE EMPTY SOUL ○	
			Hard-rock trio from Los Angeles, California: Sean Danielsen (vocals, guitar), Ryan Martin (bass) and Derek Gledhill (drums).	
8/16/03	**107**	10	Bottom Of A Bottle.. album cut	
			from the album *Smile Empty Soul* on Throback 83639	
			SOCIALBURN ○	
			Rock group from Blountstown, Florida: Neil Alday (vocals, guitar), Chris Cobb (guitar), Dusty Price (bass) and Brandon Bittner (drums).	
3/29/03	**123**	1	Down.. album cut	
			from the album *Where You Are* on Elektra 62790	
			SOLÍS, Marco Antonio	
7/5/03	**121**	2	Tu Amor O Tu Desprecio .... [F] album cut	
			title is Spanish for "From Love To Contempt"; from the album *Tu Amor O Tu Desprecio* on Fonovisa 350840	
			SORAYA ○	
			Born in Columbia and raised in America. Female dance singer/songwriter.	
8/2/03	**125**	1	Casi .... [F] album cut	
			from the album *Soraya* on EMI Latin 81120	
			SPARXXX, Bubba	
9/13/03	**101**	12	Deliverance.. album cut	
			from the album *Deliverance* on Beat Club 001147	
			STONE TEMPLE PILOTS	
11/29/03	**118**	4	All In The Suit That You Wear.. album cut	
			from the album *Thank You* on Atlantic 83586	
			STUDDARD, Ruben	
7/5/03	**112**	10	Superstar .... J Records 51786	
			#2 Pop hit for the Carpenters in 1971; B-side of "Flying Without Wings" (#2-Pop)	
			TAÑÓN, Olga	
2/1/03	**121**	1	Asi Es La Vida .... [F] album cut	
			title is Spanish for "This Is The Life"; from the album *Sobrevivir* on Warner Latina 49393	
			THIRD EYE BLIND	
5/31/03	**116**	5	Blinded (When I See You) .... album cut	
			from the album *Out Of The Vein* on Elektra 62888	
			311	
8/2/03	**118**	6	Creatures (For A While)... album cut	
			from the album *Evolver* on Volcano 53714	
			213 ○	
			All-star rap trio: Snoop Dogg, Nate Dogg and Warren G.	
9/20/03	**102**	9	Fly.. album cut	
			VASSAR, Phil	
3/15/03	**109**	6	This Is God .... album cut	
			from the album *American Child* on Arista Nashville 67077	
			WINANS, Mario — see LOON	
			WOODWARD, Lucy ○	
			Born in 1978 in England; raised in New York. Pop singer/songwriter.	
3/29/03	**112**	2	Dumb Girls.. album cut	

COUNTRY SINGLES

COUNTRY ANNUAL

The Country Annual section lists, by rank, every title that *peaked* on the
Hot Country Singles & Tracks weekly singles chart in 2003 (a top 60 listing).

HOT COUNTRY SINGLES & TRACKS

The Country artist section lists, by artist, every title that *debuted* on the
Hot Country Singles & Tracks weekly singles chart in 2003. It also lists every title
that debuted on *Billboard's* weekly **Top Country Singles Sales** chart.

PEAK DATE	WEEKS CH	40	10	PK	RANK	Title / PEAK POSITION	DEBUT	Artist

1

PEAK DATE	CH	40	10	PK	RANK	Title / PEAK POSITION	D	Artist
8/9	27	27	17	8	1	It's Five O'Clock Somewhere 31,20,14,7,7,6,2,1,**1**,**1**,**1**,**1**,**1**,2,1,3,6,8,8,11,12,11,13,14,19,20		Alan Jackson & Jimmy Buffett
12/20	20	19	14	7	2	There Goes My Life 46,28,21,15,9,8,7,4,1,**1**,**1**,**1**,**1**,**1**,2,3,6,12,13		Kenny Chesney
4/5	20	19	12	7	3	Have You Forgotten? 41,22,9,2,1,**1**,**1**,**1**,**1**,**1**,3,7,8,12,16,17,21,23,23		Darryl Worley
1/11	34	33	19	6	4	19 Somethin' 56,39,35,29,26,22,21,18,12,9,7,4,4,2,1,**1**,**1**,**1**,**1**,3,2,4,5,7,8,8,9,11,12,13,15,18,19		Mark Wills
6/14	39	27	15	6	5	Beer For My Horses 59,54,54,60,54,56,55,55,57,59,57,46,31,27,20,17,13,10,8,5,3,**1**,**1**,**1**,**1**,**1**,3,5,5,7,8,11,12,15,15,16,16,16		Toby Keith w/Willie Nelson
11/15	24	24	15	5	6	I Love This Bar 30,23,18,14,11,11,9,8,4,4,2,**1**,**1**,**1**,**1**,2,3,5,5,4,11,13,15		Toby Keith
2/22	24	23	13	3	7	The Baby 48,39,35,27,25,18,14,11,10,9,6,6,4,2,2,2,**1**,**1**,**1**,3,6,11,15,19		Blake Shelton
10/11	27	24	14	2	8	Real Good Man 60,60,48,35,29,24,22,20,19,15,12,9,8,9,7,7,5,4,4,4,3,4,**1**,**1**,5,7,12,16		Tim McGraw
5/31	34	32	13	2	9	I Believe 58,55,39,39,32,32,28,26,27,24,27,23,24,22,23,21,17,14,12,10,8,8,8,7,5,5,4,**1**,4,4,8,15,20		Diamond Rio
10/25	24	22	10	2	10	Tough Little Boys 45,42,36,29,25,23,21,20,16,16,15,12,8,7,5,5,2,**1**,**1**,3,5,6,11,15		Gary Allan
7/26	32	31	16	1	11	My Front Porch Looking In 48,35,31,27,22,15,14,12,12,9,9,8,6,2,2,2,2,2,2,**1**,4,6,6,9,10,14,13,16,14,14,17,20		Lonestar
9/27	35	30	14	1	12	What Was I Thinkin' 57,56,47,41,39,41,32,30,27,26,24,23,21,16,15,11,9,8,6,4,3,3,2,1,2,2,3,7,9,9,11,12,15,13,17	❶	Dierks Bentley
11/8	33	30	13	1	13	Who Wouldn't Wanna Be Me 58,60,47,37,30,28,26,23,21,18,16,15,15,13,10,10,8,6,7,5,2,2,**1**,2,3,5,8,12,15,18,19,18,19		Keith Urban
8/2	29	27	13	1	14	Red Dirt Road 57,41,37,29,24,22,15,14,11,9,6,4,4,4,2,**1**,2,4,4,6,8,7,11,13,13,14,16,17,19		Brooks & Dunn
3/29	32	29	12	1	15	Brokenheartsville 56,48,42,40,37,33,30,29,27,24,21,22,18,13,11,9,6,7,7,4,3,1,2,2,4,6,10,11,13,15,15,16,18		Joe Nichols
3/15	31	29	12	1	16	Man To Man 45,41,38,33,32,29,26,25,23,21,21,18,16,12,13,12,10,7,7,6,5,4,3,1,2,4,7,10,13,13,18		Gary Allan
5/24	34	25	11	1	17	Three Wooden Crosses 52,56,56,53,54,52,48,45,44,39,36,34,33,30,29,22,20,16,12,10,10,8,7,4,**1**,2,2,5,6,7,11,13,17,20		Randy Travis
3/22	25	13	7	1	18	Travelin' Soldier 59,58,58,58,60,57,59,59,54,57,48,43,39,34,34,25,21,15,10,7,6,2,2,**1**,3		Dixie Chicks

2

PEAK DATE	CH	40	10	PK	RANK	Title / PEAK POSITION	D	Artist
8/16	23	22	13	5	19	No Shoes, No Shirt, No Problems 57,40,28,24,22,16,12,10,8,7,6,3,**2**,**2**,**2**,**2**,3,5,8,11,15,19		Kenny Chesney
11/22	25	23	13	3	20	I Melt 54,43,33,26,22,21,20,18,16,16,12,10,10,8,9,6,5,4,3,**2**,**2**,**2**,3,7,17		Rascal Flatts
5/10	22	20	13	3	21	She's My Kind Of Rain 55,47,38,30,26,21,22,13,10,8,7,5,5,5,4,3,**2**,**2**,**2**,9,10,18		Tim McGraw
4/26	23	22	13	2	22	Big Star 51,35,33,26,22,17,12,10,9,4,5,3,3,3,**2**,**2**,3,3,10,10,15,19,19		Kenny Chesney
12/13	25	23	10	2	23	Cowboys Like Us 57,43,33,32,25,23,22,20,15,15,13,12,11,7,7,5,4,4,**2**,**3**,**2**,6,10,12,15		George Strait
2/22	34	32	14	1	24	I Just Wanna Be Mad 51,43,37,32,29,26,25,23,22,20,16,14,14,12,11,10,9,7,7,7,7,5,3,3,**2**,3,5,7,10,14,13,16,19		Terri Clark
4/19	24	22	11	1	25	That'd Be Alright 53,45,40,35,37,27,25,19,15,11,9,8,6,5,6,4,4,**2**,3,4,9,11,14,18		Alan Jackson

3

PEAK DATE	CH	40	10	PK	RANK	Title / PEAK POSITION	D	Artist
8/2	29	26	11	4	26	Celebrity 56,50,40,41,33,30,28,25,25,27,21,19,15,11,12,7,6,5,4,**3**,4,**3**,**3**,**3**,6,8,13,17,20		Brad Paisley
1/18	36	32	12	3	27	Fall Into Me 56,43,42,41,40,38,37,34,31,31,29,26,26,25,23,22,20,16,14,13,11,10,8,8,5,5,5,**3**,**3**,**3**,4,5,9,11,15,20		Emerson Drive
7/5	28	24	9	3	28	Stay Gone 58,53,46,43,37,36,30,28,25,24,18,16,14,14,12,11,11,9,7,5,4,**3**,**3**,**3**,5,8,12,17	❶	Jimmy Wayne
6/14	25	22	9	3	29	Love You Out Loud 59,53,42,34,29,29,25,25,20,17,12,13,12,11,11,10,8,7,6,4,**3**,**3**,**3**,10,16		Rascal Flatts
10/25	23	22	10	2	30	This One's For The Girls 49,39,29,27,24,22,18,15,14,14,14,10,11,6,6,7,6,4,**3**,**3**,5,6,15		Martina McBride
11/29	32	26	9	2	31	Wave On Wave 57,49,45,44,42,41,37,34,28,24,23,22,21,19,19,17,17,15,12,12,10,9,6,6,4,4,**3**,**3**,6,12,16,20		Pat Green
5/31	30	27	12	1	32	Raining On Sunday 57,53,43,37,37,31,28,28,28,26,22,21,19,18,14,13,12,10,9,7,7,6,4,6,5,**3**,7,8,15		Keith Urban

2003

PEAK DATE	WEEKS				RANK	Title	PEAK POSITION	DEBUT	Artist
	CH	40	10	PK					
10/4	24	23	9	1	33	Help Pour Out The Rain (Lacey's Song)		❶	Buddy Jewell
							44,37,32,28,29,25,25,25,22,18,15,13,12,12,8,7,5,5,4,**3**,4,7,10,15		

4

PEAK DATE	CH	40	10	PK	RANK	Title	PEAK POSITION	DEBUT	Artist
2/15	32	27	9	2	34	You Can't Hide Beautiful		❶	Aaron Lines
							58,54,45,41,39,43,37,37,34,32,30,29,26,25,23,22,19,18,17,17,13,11,10,8,6,5,**4**,**4**,5,6,8,13		
9/6	26	24	13	1	35	Forever And For Always			Shania Twain
							60,49,37,32,28,27,24,23,20,14,12,10,9,9,10,9,7,7,5,5,5,4,6,7,12,19		
5/31	32	28	9	1	36	What A Beautiful Day			Chris Cagle
							58,57,49,42,38,36,38,38,39,39,32,32,29,30,27,28,24,24,19,15,11,11,9,9,9,6,7,6,**4**,5,6,14		
12/20	26	24	6	1	37	Hell Yeah			Montgomery Gentry
							59,45,39,33,30,27,28,27,26,23,22,21,17,15,13,13,10,7,6,5,5,**4**,11,14,15,17		

5

PEAK DATE	CH	40	10	PK	RANK	Title	PEAK POSITION	DEBUT	Artist
6/28	33	27	7	3	38	Speed			Montgomery Gentry
							57,55,56,50,44,42,35,35,32,31,29,30,24,23,21,20,20,18,16,17,16,13,13,11,10,7,**5**,**5**,**5**,6,8,13,19		
4/26	26	24	7	2	39	Concrete Angel			Martina McBride
							52,43,37,35,35,34,32,32,31,31,25,23,23,21,16,11,11,9,6,6,6,**5**,**5**,8,15,20		
12/20	30	27	9	1	40	Chicks Dig It			Chris Cagle
							57,55,48,39,35,32,30,27,26,22,22,22,21,21,18,14,14,12,10,8,8,7,6,7,**5**,6,7,13,13		

6

PEAK DATE	CH	40	10	PK	RANK	Title	PEAK POSITION	DEBUT	Artist
1/4	25	19	7	1	41	A Lot Of Things Different			Kenny Chesney
7/5	37	21	4	1	42	Almost Home			Craig Morgan

7

PEAK DATE	CH	40	10	PK	RANK	Title	PEAK POSITION	DEBUT	Artist
2/15	30	28	6	1	43	I Wish You'd Stay			Brad Paisley

8

PEAK DATE	CH	40	10	PK	RANK	Title	PEAK POSITION	DEBUT	Artist
7/5	30	28	5	2	44	The Love Song		❶	Jeff Bates
12/20	20	18	5	2	45	Walking In Memphis			Lonestar
11/8	30	25	3	1	46	Walk A Little Straighter		❶	Billy Currington

9

PEAK DATE	CH	40	10	PK	RANK	Title	PEAK POSITION	DEBUT	Artist
9/13	27	24	5	4	47	A Few Questions			Clay Walker
8/30	28	25	3	2	48	Then They Do			Trace Adkins

10

PEAK DATE	CH	40	10	PK	RANK	Title	PEAK POSITION	DEBUT	Artist
8/2	27	23	3	3	49	99.9% Sure (I've Never Been Here Before)			Brian McComas
3/1	25	23	1	1	50	Chrome			Trace Adkins

11

PEAK DATE	CH	40	10	PK	RANK	Title	PEAK POSITION	DEBUT	Artist
7/19	20	18		1	51	Tell Me Something Bad About Tulsa			George Strait

12

PEAK DATE	CH	40	10	PK	RANK	Title	PEAK POSITION	DEBUT	Artist
2/1	26	21		1	52	Unusually Unusual	[R]		Lonestar
3/8	20	16		1	53	Up!			Shania Twain

13

PEAK DATE	CH	40	10	PK	RANK	Title	PEAK POSITION	DEBUT	Artist
7/19	21	20		1	54	The Truth About Men	[N]		Tracy Byrd
3/29	20	14		1	55	Rock You Baby			Toby Keith

14

PEAK DATE	CH	40	10	PK	RANK	Title	PEAK POSITION	DEBUT	Artist
4/5	26	23		2	56	There's No Limit			Deana Carter
8/2	20	16		2	57	What The World Needs			Wynonna
11/1	21	15		1	58	I'm Gonna Take That Mountain			Reba McEntire

15

PEAK DATE	CH	40	10	PK	RANK	Title	PEAK POSITION	DEBUT	Artist
12/27	28	25		2	59	I Wish			Jo Dee Messina

16

PEAK DATE	CH	40	10	PK	RANK	Title	PEAK POSITION	DEBUT	Artist
11/8	30	24		2	60	I Can't Be Your Friend			Rushlow
12/6	22	21		2	61	Wrinkles			Diamond Rio
3/15	32	23		1	62	Beautiful Goodbye		❶	Jennifer Hanson
8/2	26	22		1	63	Backseat Of A Greyhound Bus			Sara Evans

17

PEAK DATE	CH	40	10	PK	RANK	Title	PEAK POSITION	DEBUT	Artist
8/23	20	16		3	64	She Only Smokes When She Drinks			Joe Nichols
4/12	19	16		2	65	This Is God			Phil Vassar
4/26	26	19		1	66	There's More To Me Than You			Jessica Andrews
3/1	20	18		1	67	Next Big Thing			Vince Gill

PEAK DATE	WEEKS CH	40	10	PK	RANK	Title	PEAK POSITION	DEBUT	Artist
						18			
9/27	20	16		3	68	Lovin' All Night			Patty Loveless
1/11	26	23		2	69	At The End Of The Day			Kellie Coffey
11/29	26	21		1	70	Streets Of Heaven			Sherrié Austin
						19			
1/11	24	20		2	71	On A Mission			Trick Pony
						21			
5/10	20	17		2	72	Was That My Life			Jo Dee Messina
4/26	33	14		1	73	Picture			Kid Rock
						23			
8/30	24	15		1	74	Only God (Could Stop Me Loving You)			Emerson Drive
						24			
12/13	23	18		2	75	I Can't Take You Anywhere			Scotty Emerick w/Toby Keith
8/30	21	14		2	76	Days Like This		❶	Rachel Proctor
11/8	20	18		1	77	Playboys Of The Southwestern World			Blake Shelton
5/3	15	12		1	78	Why Ain't I Running			Garth Brooks
						26			
6/7	20	16		3	79	One Last Time			Dusty Drake
4/26	20	15		2	80	Country Ain't Country			Travis Tritt
1/18	20	17		1	81	Family Tree			Darryl Worley
2/22	20	16		1	82	When The Lights Go Down			Faith Hill
						27			
6/7	20	12		1	83	Love's Got An Attitude (It Is What It Is)		❶	Amy Dalley
						28			
7/5	20	12		1	84	When You Think Of Me			Mark Wills
7/19	16	10		1	85	You're Still Here			Faith Hill
4/26	10	7		1	86	Hey Mr. President			The Warren Brothers
						29			
9/20	21	12		1	87	And The Crowd Goes Wild			Mark Wills
						30			
6/28	18	10		1	88	Three Mississippi			Terri Clark
						31			
10/11	19	13		1	89	Tennessee River Run			Darryl Worley
6/28	17	10		1	90	Someday			Vince Gill
4/5	20	9		1	91	Love Won't Let Me			Tammy Cochran
						32			
6/28	13	7		1	92	Heavy Liftin'			Blake Shelton
						33			
3/29	20	13		3	93	I Want My Money Back			Sammy Kershaw
						34			
8/16	16	6		1	94	Every Little Thing			Jamie O'Neal
						35			
3/29	19	8		2	95	Love Like There's No Tomorrow			Aaron Tippin
7/12	12	8		2	96	I'm Just A Girl			Deana Carter
						36			
11/8	20	6		2	97	Run, Run, Run		✦	Ryan Tyler
2/22	20	6		2	98	I Drove All Night			Pinmonkey
8/16	16	7		1	99	Can You Hear Me When I Talk To You?		✦	Ashley Gearing
						37			
3/22	14	7		3	100	Rock-A-Bye Heart			Steve Holy
11/8	15	3		1	101	Heaven Help Me			Wynonna
1/4	5	2		1	102	Let It Be Christmas [X]			Alan Jackson

PEAK DATE	WEEKS				RANK	Title	PEAK POSITION	DEBUT	Artist
	CH	40	10	PK					
						38			
1/25	16	1		1	103	Lately (Been Dreamin' 'Bout Babies)			Tracy Byrd
						39			
3/29	13	3		2	104	After All			Brett James
7/12	15	3		1	105	Love Changes Everything			Aaron Lines
10/11	11	1		1	106	I'm One Of You			Hank Williams, Jr.
						40			
12/20	17	3		3	107	Handprints On The Wall			Kenny Rogers
10/11	13	1		1	108	Half A Heart Tattoo			Jennifer Hanson
3/29	12	1		1	109	Half A Man			Anthony Smith
						41			
10/18	20			1	110	In My Dreams			Rick Trevino
7/19	15			1	111	It Doesn't Mean I Don't Love You		✦	McHayes
8/23	11			1	112	If There Ain't There Ought'a Be			Marty Stuart
8/2	8			1	113	Ultimate Love			Phil Vassar
						42			
6/14	12			2	114	This Far Gone			Jennifer Hanson
4/19	7			1	115	I Raq And Roll			Clint Black
						43			
8/23	10			2	116	What A Shame			Rebecca Lynn Howard
1/25	15			1	117	It'll Go Away			Kevin Denney
5/3	15			1	118	Suddenly			LeAnn Rimes
11/8	13			1	119	I Think You're Beautiful			Amy Dalley
						44			
12/20	16			2	120	A Year At A Time			Kevin Denney
12/6	11			1	121	Young Man's Town			Vince Gill
3/22	10			1	122	Whatever It Takes			Kellie Coffey
						45			
3/8	8			1	123	Country Thang			John Michael Montgomery
						46			
8/9	12			1	124	When You Come Around		✦	Deric Ruttan
3/8	12			1	125	The Lucky One	[R]		Alison Krauss
						47			
5/10	10			2	126	A Boy Like You			Trick Pony
2/15	9			2	127	We Shook Hands (Man To Man)		✦	Tebey
9/27	6			2	128	Rainbow Man			Jeff Bates
						48			
6/28	9			2	129	Godspeed (Sweet Dreams)			Dixie Chicks
10/11	14			1	130	Pray For The Fish			Randy Travis
3/8	10			1	131	I'm In Love With A Married Woman			Mark Chesnutt
9/27	9			1	132	I'll Be Around			Sawyer Brown
						49			
12/13	16			3	133	I Need A Vacation			Rebecca Lynn Howard
2/15	15			2	134	Tiny Dancer			Tim McGraw
3/22	9			1	135	Old Weakness (Coming On Strong)			Tanya Tucker
6/14	6			1	136	I'm Missing You			Kenny Rogers
8/9	5			1	137	Good Time			Jessica Andrews
1/11	2			1	138	Feliz Navidad	[X]		Clay Walker
						50			
8/2	10			1	139	I Can Only Imagine			Jeff Carson
5/10	9			1	140	One Of Those Days			Brad Martin
8/30	6			1	141	Smaller Pieces			Dusty Drake
8/9	4			1	142	Lonesome, On'ry And Mean			Travis Tritt

PEAK DATE	CH	40	10	PK	RANK	Title	PEAK POSITION	DEBUT	Artist

51

PEAK DATE	CH	40	10	PK	RANK	Title	DEBUT	Artist
10/11	10			3	143	Sell A Lot Of Beer		The Warren Brothers
2/22	6			1	144	Southern Boy		Charlie Daniels Band with Travis Tritt

52

11/29	16			3	145	I'm In Love With You		Billy Dean
2/22	6			3	146	Snowfall On The Sand		Steve Wariner
3/22	9			1	147	Scary Old World		Radney Foster
8/16	9			1	148	The Late Great Golden State		Dwight Yoakam
6/21	6			1	149	The Back Of Your Hand		Dwight Yoakam
6/14	5			1	150	Four-Wheel Drive		John Michael Montgomery

54

| 7/26 | 4 | | | 2 | 151 | Break The Record | | The Warren Brothers |
| 12/6 | 2 | | | 1 | 152 | Too Much Month (At The End Of The Money) | | Marty Stuart |

55

| 11/1 | 4 | | | 1 | 153 | Martie, Emily & Natalie [N] | | Cledus T. Judd |

56

10/11	6			1	154	She Is		Susan Ashton
2/22	1			1	155	Cryin' Steel	✦	Jerry Burkhart
3/8	1			1	156	Hurt		Johnny Cash
5/17	1			1	157	The Letter (Almost Home)		Clint Daniels

57

12/13	2			2	158	Coat Of Many Colors		Shania Twain w/Alison Krauss & Union Station
12/6	3			1	159	I Will Hold My Ground		Darryl Worley
5/10	2			1	160	In Your Love		Rhett Akins
1/4	2			1	161	Winter Wonderland [X]		Brooks & Dunn
1/11	1			1	162	Rockin' Little Christmas [X]		Brooks & Dunn
2/22	1			1	163	Angel	✦	Renee McCrary
12/20	1			1	164	Fridaynititus	✦	Brad Tyler

58

9/27	4			2	165	Strictly Business	✦	Brad Wolf
3/15	3			1	166	That Was Us		Chad Brock
8/16	3			1	167	I've Never Been Anywhere		Sammy Kershaw
1/11	1			1	168	Jingle Bells [X]		Alan Jackson
5/17	1			1	169	Walter		Charlie Robison
8/2	1			1	170	I'm Your Man		Steve Wariner
6/28	1			1	171	You Can't Take It With You When You Go	❶	Rhonda Vincent
11/29	1			1	172	There Is No War	❶	Donovan Chapman
12/20	1			1	173	Middle Age Crazy		T. Graham Brown
7/19	1			1	174	My Beautiful America [S]		Charlie Daniels Band

59

2/1	2			2	175	It Can All Be Gone	✦	Jamie Lee Thurston
2/22	1			1	176	Unkissed		Holly Lamar
3/1	1			1	177	Hey Love, No Fair		Leland Martin
12/6	1			1	178	Forrest County Line		4 Runner

60

3/1	1			1	179	One Mississippi	❶	Jill King
3/15	1			1	180	Don't Look Now [N]		Rodney Carrington
3/22	1			1	181	The Real Thing		George Strait
7/5	1			1	182	Back To Memphis		Billy Ray Cyrus
11/22	1			1	183	Everyday Girl	✦	Roxie Dean
12/20	1			1	184	I'll Be Home For Christmas [X]		Kenny Chesney
11/8	1			1	185	Earthbound		Rodney Crowell

DEBUT DATE	PEAK POS	WKS CHR	G L D	ARTIST / Title	Sales	Label & Number
				ADKINS, Trace		
3/15/03	9	28		Then They Do		album cut
				from the album *Greatest Hits Collection, Volume I* on Capitol 81512		
9/27/03+	5	28↑		Hot Mama		album cut
				from the album *Comin' On Strong* on Capitol 40517		
				AKINS, Rhett		
5/10/03	57	2		In Your Love		album cut
				from the album *Friday Night In Dixie* on Audium 8153		
				ALLAN, Gary		
6/28/03	❶²	24		Tough Little Boys		MCA Nashville 000946
11/22/03+	14↑	20↑		Songs About Rain		album cut
				from the album *See If I Care* on MCA Nashville 000111		
				ANDREWS, Jessica		
8/9/03	49	5		Good Time		album cut
				from the album *Now* on DreamWorks 450356		
				ASHTON, Susan		
9/20/03	56	6		She Is		Capitol 52936
				ATKINS, Rodney		
6/21/03+	4	33		Honesty (Write Me A List)	S:5	Curb 73149
				AUSTIN, Sherrié		
6/14/03	18	26		Streets Of Heaven		album cut
				from the album *Streets Of Heaven* on Broken Bow 75872		
				BATES, Jeff ★		
1/4/03	8	30		The Love Song		album cut
9/13/03	47	6		Rainbow Man		album cut
				above 2 from the album *Rainbow Man* on RCA 67071		
				BENTLEY, Dierks ★		
4/12/03	❶¹	35		What Was I Thinkin'	S:2	Capitol 77963
10/25/03+	18↑	24↑		My Last Name		album cut
				from the album *Dierks Bentley* on Capitol 39814		
				BIG & RICH ★		
				Duo from Texas: Big Kenny and John Rich (former member of Lonestar).		
12/27/03+	23↑	14↑		Wild West Show	S:❶¹	Warner 16515
				BLACK, Clint		
3/29/03	42	7		I Raq And Roll		album cut
				only available as a free download on Black's official website		
11/1/03+	16	22		Spend My Time		Equity 003
				BLUE COUNTY ★		
				Duo formed in Nashville, Tennessee: Aaron Benward (from Auburn, Indiana) and Scott Reeves (from Delight, Arkansas).		
10/18/03+	16↑	25↑		Good Little Girls		album cut
				from the album *Blue County* on Curb 78833		
				BROCK, Chad		
3/15/03	58	3		That Was Us		album cut
12/20/03+	48	7		You Are		album cut
				above 2 from the album *Free* on Broken Bow 75372		
				BROOKS, Garth		
3/8/03	24	15		Why Ain't I Running		album cut
				from the album *Scarecrow* on Capitol 31330		
				BROOKS & DUNN		
1/4/03	57	2		Winter Wonderland	[X]	album cut
1/11/03	57	1		Rockin' Little Christmas	[X]	album cut
				above 2 from the album *It Won't Be Christmas Without You* on Arista Nashville 67053		
4/19/03	❶¹	29		Red Dirt Road		album cut
9/20/03+	3	23		You Can't Take The Honky Tonk Out Of The Girl		album cut
				above 2 from the album *Red Dirt Road* on Arista Nashville 67070		
				BROWN, T. Graham		
12/20/03	58	1		Middle Age Crazy		album cut
				from the album *The Next Right Thing* on Intersound 5499		
				BUFFETT, Jimmy — see JACKSON, Alan		
				BURKHART, Jerry ★		
				Born in Waco, Texas. Singer/songwriter/guitarist. Owns an auto repair shop.		
2/22/03	56	1		Cryin' Steel		album cut
				from the album *Cryin' Country* on Cupit 7774		

COUNTRY SINGLES

DEBUT DATE	PEAK POS	WKS CHR	G L D	ARTIST / Title	Sales	Label & Number
				BYRD, Tracy		
3/15/03	13	21		The Truth About Men .... [N]		album cut
				Andy Griggs, Montgomery Gentry and Blake Shelton (guest vocals)		
8/9/03+	7	27		Drinkin' Bone		album cut
				above 2 from the album *The Truth About Men* on RCA 67073		
				CAGLE, Chris		
6/28/03	5	30		Chicks Dig It		album cut
				from the album *Chris Cagle* on Capitol 40516		
				CARRINGTON, Rodney		
3/15/03	60	1		Don't Look Now .... [N]		album cut
				from the album *Nut Sack* on Capitol 36579		
				CARSON, Jeff		
6/14/03	50	10		I Can Only Imagine..		album cut
				from the various artists album *God Bless The USA 2003* on Curb 78810		
				CARTER, Deana		
5/24/03	35	12		I'm Just A Girl..		album cut
				from the album *I'm Just A Girl* on Arista Nashville 67054		
				CASH, Johnny		
3/8/03	56	1	▲²	Hurt ....S:❶¹³		American 077084 (D)
				#54 *Hot 100 Airplay* hit for Nine Inch Nails in 1995		
				CHAPMAN, Donovan ★		
				Born in 1975 in Farmerville, Louisiana (white father; Hawaiian mother). Singer/songwriter/guitarist. Decorated member of the pararescue team of the U.S. Air Force.		
11/29/03	58	1		There Is No War..		album cut
				CHESNEY, Kenny		
1/18/03	2²	23		Big Star		album cut
5/24/03	2⁵	23		No Shoes, No Shirt, No Problems		album cut
				above 2 from the album *No Shoes, No Shirt, No Problems* on BNA 67038		
10/25/03	❶⁷	20		There Goes My Life		album cut
				from the album *When The Sun Goes Down* on BNA 56609		
12/13/03+	30	5		All I Want For Christmas Is A Real Good Tan .... [X]		album cut
12/20/03	60	1		I'll Be Home For Christmas.. [X]		album cut
12/27/03+	49	3		Jingle Bells.. [X]		album cut
				above 3 from the album *All I Want For Christmas Is A Real Good Tan* on BNA 51808		
				CHESNUTT, Mark		
2/15/03	48	10		I'm In Love With A Married Woman		album cut
				from the album *Mark Chesnutt* on Columbia 86540		
				CLARK, Terri		
3/22/03	30	18		Three Mississippi...		Mercury 172262
8/16/03+	3	30		I Wanna Do It All		Mercury 001257
				COFFEY, Kellie		
3/1/03	44	10		Whatever It Takes		album cut
				from the album *When You Lie Next To Me* on BNA 67040		
10/11/03+	24	22		Texas Plates		album cut
				from the album *Little More Me* on BNA 55846		
				CROW, Sheryl		
11/1/03+	35	20		The First Cut Is The Deepest		album cut
				written by Cat Stevens; #21 Pop hit for Rod Stewart in 1977; from the album *The Very Best Of Sheryl Crow* on A&M 152102		
				CROWELL, Rodney		
11/8/03	60	1		Earthbound..		album cut
				from the album *Fate's Right Hand* on DMZ/Epic 89082		
				CURRINGTON, Billy ★		
5/3/03	8	30		Walk A Little Straighter	S:3	Mercury 000972
				CYRUS, Billy Ray		
7/5/03	60	1		Back To Memphis		album cut
				from the album *Time Flies* on SMCMG 4114		
				DALLEY, Amy ★		
				Born in Kingsport, Tennessee. Singer/songwriter/guitarist.		
3/8/03	27	20		Love's Got An Attitude (It Is What It Is)		album cut
8/23/03	43	13		I Think You're Beautiful		album cut

DEBUT DATE	PEAK POS	WKS CHR	G L D	ARTIST Title	Sales	Label & Number
				DANIELS, Charlie		
1/25/03	51	6		Southern Boy		album cut
				THE CHARLIE DANIELS BAND with Travis Tritt		
				from the album *Redneck Fiddlin' Man* on Audium 8159		
7/19/03	58	1		My Beautiful America	[S]	album cut
				from the album *Freedom And Justice For All* on Audium 8188		
				DANIELS, Clint		
5/17/03	56	1		The Letter (Almost Home)		album cut
				DEAN, Billy		
9/27/03	52	16		I'm In Love With You		album cut
				DEAN, Roxie ★		
				Born on 3/23/74 in Baton Rouge, Louisiana. Singer/songwriter.		
11/22/03	60	1		Everyday Girl		DreamWorks 000404
				DENNEY, Kevin		
10/11/03	44	16		A Year At A Time		Lyric Street 64081
				DIAMOND RIO		
8/2/03	16	22		Wrinkles		album cut
				from the album *Completely* on Arista Nashville 67046		
				DIXIE CHICKS		
6/7/03	48	9		Godspeed (Sweet Dreams)		album cut
				#74 hit for Radney Foster in 1999; from the album *Home* on Monument 86840		
				DRAKE, Dusty		
3/22/03	26	20		One Last Time		Warner 16651
8/9/03	50	6		Smaller Pieces		album cut
				from the album *Dusty Drake* on Warner 48051		
				EMERICK, Scotty ★		
7/26/03	24	23		I Can't Take You Anywhere	S:2	DreamWorks 001581
				SCOTTY EMERICK with Toby Keith		
				EMERSON DRIVE		
4/5/03	23	24		Only God (Could Stop Me Loving You)		DreamWorks 450788
				ENGVALL, Bill		
11/29/03	❶[3S]	8		Here's Your Sign Christmas [X-N-R]		Warner 16507
				hit #39 in 1998 and #46 in 1999; released on the same single as "Redneck 12 Days Of Christmas" by Jeff Foxworthy		
				EVANS, Sara		
3/1/03	16	26		Backseat Of A Greyhound Bus		album cut
9/20/03+	2[1]↑	29↑		Perfect		album cut
				above 2 from the album *Restless* on RCA 67074		
				FOSTER, Radney		
2/15/03	52	9		Scary Old World		album cut
				RADNEY FOSTER Featuring Chely Wright or Georgia Middleman		
				version with Wright is on Foster's album *Another Way To Go* on Dualtone 1128; version with Middleman was realesed as a promotional single only		
				4 RUNNER		
12/6/03	59	1		Forrest County Line		album cut
				from the album *Getaway Car* on Fresh 146220		
				FOXWORTHY, Jeff		
11/29/03	❶[3S]	8		Redneck 12 Days Of Christmas [X-N-R]		Warner 16507
				hit #18 in 1995, #39 in 1996, #39 in 1997, #37 in 1998 and #35 in 1999; released on the same single as "Here's Your Sign Christmas" by Bill Engvall		
				GEARING, Ashley ★		
6/21/03	36	16		Can You Hear Me When I Talk To You?	S:3	Lyric Street 164075
				GILL, Vince		
3/29/03	31	17		Someday		album cut
				from the album *Next Big Thing* on MCA Nashville 170286		
10/11/03	44	11		Young Man's Town		MCA Nashville 001648
				GREEN, Pat		
5/31/03	3	32		Wave On Wave		album cut
12/27/03+	31↑	15↑		Guy Like Me		album cut
				above 2 from the album *Wave On Wave* on Republic 000562		
12/27/03+	43	3		Winter Wonderland	[X]	album cut
				from the various artists album *A Very Special Acoustic Christmas* on Lost Highway 001038		

DEBUT DATE	PEAK POS	WKS CHR	G L D	ARTIST / Title	Sales	Label & Number
				HANSON, Jennifer		
4/19/03	42	12		This Far Gone....................		album cut
8/2/03	40	13		Half A Heart Tattoo		album cut
				above 2 from the album Jennifer Hanson on Capitol 35247		
				HILL, Faith		
5/10/03	28	16		You're Still Here.............................	S:6	Warner 16647
				HOLY, Steve		
2/8/03	37	14		Rock-A-Bye Heart		album cut
				HOWARD, Rebecca Lynn		
7/26/03	43	10		What A Shame		MCA Nashville 001050
11/1/03	49	16		I Need A Vacation		MCA Nashville 001647
				ISAACS, Sonya		
11/15/03+	36	17		No Regrets Yet		album cut
				JACKSON, Alan		
1/11/03	58	1		Jingle Bells........................ [X]		album cut
				from the album Let It Be Christmas on Arista Nashville 67062		
6/21/03	❶8	27		It's Five O'Clock Somewhere		Arista Nashville 54205
				ALAN JACKSON & JIMMY BUFFETT		
11/8/03+	❶2	22↑		Remember When		
				from the album Greatest Hits Volume II and Some Other Stuff on Arista Nashville 53097		
				JAMES, Brett		
2/15/03	39	13		After All		album cut
				JEWELL, Buddy ★		
5/24/03	3	24		Help Pour Out The Rain (Lacey's Song)	S:❶2	Columbia 79885
11/1/03+	3↑	23↑		Sweet Southern Comfort		album cut
				from the album Buddy Jewell on Columbia 90131		
				JOHNSON, Carolyn Dawn		
11/29/03+	17↑	19↑		Simple Life		album cut
				from the album Dress Rehearsal on Arista 57500		
				JUDD, Cledus T.		
10/18/03	55	4		Martie, Emily & Natalie.................... [N]		album cut
				parody of "Celebrity" by Brad Paisley; from the album The Original Dixie Hick on Audium 8194		
				JUSTIN, Dean ★		
7/19/03	4S	11		Carry The Flag		SLR 0006
				KEITH, Toby		
1/18/03	13	20		Rock You Baby....................		DreamWorks 450785
7/26/03	24	23		I Can't Take You Anywhere	S:2	DreamWorks 001581
				SCOTTY EMERICK with Toby Keith		
8/30/03	❶5	24		I Love This Bar		DreamWorks 001238
11/22/03+	❶4	20↑		American Soldier		DreamWorks 002046
				KERSHAW, Sammy		
1/25/03	33	20		I Want My Money Back		album cut
8/16/03	58	3		I've Never Been Anywhere		album cut
				above 2 from the album I Want My Money Back on Audium 8167		
				KING, Jill ★		
				Born on 4/2/74 in Arab, Alabama. Singer/songwriter.		
3/1/03	60	1		One Mississippi....................		album cut
				from the album lillhilly on Blue Diamond 1513		
				KRAUSS, Alison, & Union Station		
3/8/03	46	12		The Lucky One .... [R]		album cut
				hit #53 in 2001; from the album New Favorite on Rounder 610495		
12/13/03	57	2		Coat Of Many Colors		album cut
				SHANIA TWAIN with Alison Krauss & Union Station		
				#4 hit for Dolly Parton in 1971; from the various artists album Just Because I'm A Woman: Songs Of Dolly Parton on Sugar Hill 3980		
				LAMAR, Holly		
2/22/03	59	1		Unkissed		album cut
				from the album Unkissed on Universal South 170293		

DEBUT DATE	PEAK POS	WKS CHR	G L D	ARTIST Title	Sales	Label & Number
				LAWRENCE, Tracy		
11/1/03+	15↑	23↑		Paint Me A Birmingham		album cut
				from the album *Strong* on DreamWorks 103212		
				LINES, Aaron		
4/19/03	39	15		Love Changes Everything		album cut
				from the album *Living Out Loud* on RCA 67057		
				LONESTAR		
3/15/03	❶¹	32		My Front Porch Looking In		album cut
8/16/03	8	20		Walking In Memphis		album cut
				#74 hit for Marc Cohn in 1991; above 2 from the album *From There To Here: Greatest Hits* on BNA 67076		
				LOVELESS, Patty		
6/14/03	18	20		Lovin' All Night..	S:10	Epic 79954
				#10 hit for Rodney Crowell in 1992		
11/8/03+	29	20		On Your Way Home		album cut
				from the album *On Your Way Home* on Epic 86620		
				MARTIN, Brad		
4/19/03	50	9		One Of Those Days		album cut
				MARTIN, Leland		
3/1/03	59	1		Hey Love, No Fair..		album cut
				from the album *Simply Traditional* on IGO 3841		
				McBRIDE, Martina		
6/21/03	3	23		This One's For The Girls		album cut
				backing vocalists include Faith Hill, Carolyn Dawn Johnson and McBride's daughters Delaney and Emma		
11/22/03+	4	20↑		In My Daughter's Eyes		album cut
				above 2 from the album *Martina* on RCA 54207		
				McCOMAS, Brian		
3/8/03	10	27		99.9% Sure (I've Never Been Here Before)		album cut
10/4/03+	26	27↑		You're In My Head		album cut
				above 2 from the album *Brian McComas* on Lyric Street 165025		
				McCRARY, Renee ★		
				Born in Baton Rouge, Louisiana. Singer/songwriter.		
2/22/03	57	1		Angel		album cut
				McENTIRE, Reba		
8/30/03	14	21		I'm Gonna Take That Mountain..............................		MCA Nashville 001404
				McGRAW, Tim		
5/17/03	❶²	27		Real Good Man		album cut
11/1/03+	❶²	23↑		Watch The Wind Blow By		album cut
				above 2 from the album *Tim McGraw And The Dancehall Doctors* on Curb 78746		
				McHAYES ★		
				Duo formed in Nashville, Tennessee: Mark McClurg and Wade Hayes.		
4/19/03	41	15		It Doesn't Mean I Don't Love You.......................	S:7	Universal South 000329
				MERCYME ★		
12/27/03+	52	15↑		I Can Only Imagine..		INO/Curb 73150
				MESSINA, Jo Dee		
1/18/03	21	20		Was That My Life..		album cut
7/26/03	15	28		I Wish		album cut
				above 2 from the album *Greatest Hits* on Curb 78790		
				MIDDLEMAN, Georgia — see FOSTER, Radney		
				MONTGOMERY, John Michael		
2/8/03	45	8		Country Thang		album cut
6/7/03	52	5		Four-Wheel Drive		album cut
				above 2 from the album *Pictures* on Warner 48341		
				MONTGOMERY GENTRY		
7/26/03	4	26		Hell Yeah		album cut
				from the album *My Town* on Columbia 86520		
				MORGAN, Craig		
8/16/03+	25	27		Every Friday Afternoon		album cut
				from the album *I Love It* on Broken Bow 77567		
				MORGAN, Lorrie		
10/11/03+	50	12		Do You Still Want To Buy Me That Drink (Frank).............		album cut
				from the album *Show Me How* on Image 0609		

COUNTRY SINGLES

DEBUT DATE	PEAK POS	WKS CHR	G L D	ARTIST / Title	Sales	Label & Number
				NICHOLS, Joe		
5/3/03	17	20		She Only Smokes When She Drinks		Universal South 000157
9/27/03+	18	25		Cool To Be A Fool		Universal South 001371
				O'NEAL, Jamie		
5/24/03	34	16		Every Little Thing		Mercury 000584
				OTTO, James		
10/4/03+	33	20		Days Of Our Lives	S:4	Mercury 001500
				PAISLEY, Brad		
3/22/03	3	29		Celebrity		album cut
9/6/03+	2[1]	31↑		Little Moments		album cut
				above 2 from the album *Mud On The Tires* on Arista Nashville 50605		
				PROCTOR, Rachel ★		
				Born in Charleston, West Virginia. Singer/songwriter.		
5/17/03	24	21		Days Like This		album cut
12/27/03+	43	11		Didn't I		album cut
				above 2 from the album *Days Like This* on BNA 51217		
				RASCAL FLATTS		
1/25/03	3	25		Love You Out Loud		album cut
7/12/03	2[3]	25		I Melt		album cut
				above 2 from the album *Melt* on Lyric Street 165031		
				RIMES, LeAnn		
3/8/03	43	15		Suddenly		album cut
				from the album *Twisted Angel* on Curb 78747		
12/13/03+	37	16		This Love		album cut
				from the album *Greatest Hits* on Curb 78829		
				ROBISON, Charlie		
5/17/03	58	1		Walter		album cut
				from the album *Live* on Columbia 86787		
				ROGERS, Kenny		
5/31/03	49	6		I'm Missing You		album cut
10/18/03	40	17		Handprints On The Wall		album cut
				above 2 from the album *Back To The Well* on DreamCatcher 8		
				RUSHLOW		
5/10/03	16	30		I Can't Be Your Friend		Lyric Street 64080
				RUTTAN, Deric ★		
				Born in Bracebridge, Ontario, Canada. Singer/songwriter/guitarist.		
6/14/03	46	12		When You Come Around		album cut
				SAWYER BROWN		
8/2/03	48	9		I'll Be Around		Lyric Street 64079
				SHELTON, Blake		
4/26/03	32	13		Heavy Liftin'		Warner 16650
7/12/03	24	20		Playboys Of The Southwestern World		Warner 16538
				SMITH, Anthony		
2/8/03	40	12		Half A Man		album cut
				from the album *If That Ain't Country* on Mercury 170292		
				STRAIT, George		
3/22/03	60	1		The Real Thing		album cut
				from the album *The Road Less Traveled* on MCA Nashville 170220		
4/12/03	11	20		Tell Me Something Bad About Tulsa		MCA Nashville 000586
8/9/03	2[2]	25		Cowboys Like Us		MCA Nashville 001250
				STUART, Marty		
7/12/03	41	11		If There Ain't There Ought'a Be		album cut
12/6/03	54	2		Too Much Month (At The End Of The Money)		album cut
				MARTY STUART and His Fabulous Superlatives (above 2)		
				#25 hit for Billy Hill in 1989; above 2 from the album *Country Music* on Columbia 87063		

DEBUT DATE	PEAK POS	WKS CHR	G L D	ARTIST / Title	Sales	Label & Number
				TEBEY ★		
				Born in 1983 in Burlington, Ontario, Canada (Canadian mother; African father). Male singer/songwriter. Name pronounced: Tay-Bay.		
1/18/03	47	9		We Shook Hands (Man To Man)		album cut
				THURSTON, Jamie Lee ★		
				Born in Montpeiler, Vermont; raised in Waterbury, Vermont. Male singer/songwriter/guitarist.		
2/1/03	59	2		It Can All Be Gone		album cut
				TRAVIS, Randy		
7/26/03	48	14		Pray For The Fish		album cut
				from the album *Rise And Shine* on Warner 886236		
				TREVINO, Rick		
6/21/03	41	20		In My Dreams		Warner 16641
				TRICK PONY		
4/5/03	47	10		A Boy Like You		album cut
				from the album *On A Mission* on Warner 48236		
				TRITT, Travis		
1/25/03	26	20		Country Ain't Country		album cut
				from the album *Strong Enough* on Columbia 86660		
1/25/03	51	6		Southern Boy		album cut
				THE CHARLIE DANIELS BAND with Travis Tritt		
				from the album *Redneck Fiddlin' Man* on Audium 8159		
8/9/03	50	4		Lonesome, On'ry And Mean		album cut
				first recorded by Waylon Jennings in 1972; from the various artists album *I've Always Been Crazy: A Tribute To Waylon Jennings* on RCA 67064		
				TUCKER, Tanya		
3/8/03	49	9		Old Weakness (Coming On Strong)		album cut
				from the album *Tanya* on Tuckertime 38827		
				TURNER, Josh		
5/31/03+	13	44		Long Black Train	S:2	MCA Nashville 000976
				TWAIN, Shania		
4/12/03	4	26		Forever And For Always		Mercury 001251
10/11/03+	9	20		She's Not Just A Pretty Face		Mercury 001646
12/13/03	57	2		Coat Of Many Colors		album cut
				SHANIA TWAIN with Alison Krauss & Union Station		
				#4 hit for Dolly Parton in 1971; from the various artists album *Just Because I'm A Woman: Songs Of Dolly Parton* on Sugar Hill 3980		
				TYLER, Brad ★		
12/20/03	57	1		Fridaynititus		album cut
				TYLER, Ryan ★		
				Born on 10/6/73 in Atlanta, Georgia; raised in Duluth, Georgia. Female singer.		
8/16/03	36	20		Run, Run, Run		album cut
				URBAN, Keith		
6/7/03	❶¹	33		Who Wouldn't Wanna Be Me		album cut
12/6/03+	6↑	18↑		You'll Think Of Me		album cut
				above 2 from the album *Golden Road* on Capitol 32936		
				VASSAR, Phil		
1/11/03	17	19		This Is God		album cut
7/5/03	41	8		Ultimate Love		album cut
				above 2 from the album *American Child* on Arista Nashville 67077		
				VINCENT, Rhonda ★		
				Born on 7/13/62 in Kirksville, Missouri. Bluegrass singer/songwriter/guitarist.		
6/28/03	58	1		You Can't Take It With You When You Go		album cut
				from the album *One Step Ahead* on Rounder 610497		
				WALKER, Clay		
1/4/03	49	2		Feliz Navidad	[X]	album cut
				from the album *Christmas* on Warner 48235		
4/26/03	9	27		A Few Questions		album cut
12/13/03+	25↑	17↑		I Can't Sleep		album cut
				above 2 from the album *A Few Questions* on RCA 67068		
				WARINER, Steve		
2/15/03	52	6		Snowfall On The Sand		album cut
8/2/03	58	1		I'm Your Man		album cut
				above 2 from the album *Steal Another Day* on Selectone 11955		

COUNTRY SINGLES

DEBUT DATE	PEAK POS	WKS CHR	G L D	ARTIST Title	Sales	Label & Number
				WARREN BROTHERS, The		
4/5/03	28	10		Hey Mr. President..		album cut
7/19/03	54	4		Break The Record		album cut
9/13/03	51	10		Sell A Lot Of Beer		album cut
				Tim McGraw (backing vocal)		
				WAYNE, Jimmy ★		
2/8/03	**3**	28		Stay Gone	S:2	DreamWorks 000345
8/23/03+	**6**	32		I Love You This Much /		
12/27/03+	40	3		Paper Angels	[X]	DreamWorks 001239
				WILLIAMS, Hank Jr.		
8/2/03	39	11		I'm One Of You		album cut
				from the album *I'm One Of You* on Curb 78830		
				WILLS, Mark		
3/1/03	28	20		When You Think Of Me..		Mercury 172267
7/26/03	29	21		And The Crowd Goes Wild		Mercury 001152
11/15/03+	40	17		That's A Woman		Mercury 001984
				WOLF, Brad ★		
				Born in Caryville, Tennessee. Singer/songwriter. Great-great-grandson of Fiddlin' John Carson.		
9/27/03	58	4		Strictly Business..		Warner 16570
				WORLEY, Darryl		
3/8/03	**❶**[7]	20		Have You Forgotten?		DreamWorks 000063
7/12/03	31	19		Tennessee River Run		album cut
11/22/03	57	3		I Will Hold My Ground...		album cut
				above 2 from the album *Have You Forgotten* on DreamWorks 000064		
				WRIGHT, Chely — see FOSTER, Radney		
				WYNONNA		
5/10/03	14	20		What The World Needs..		album cut
9/13/03	37	15		Heaven Help Me		album cut
				above 2 from the album *What The World Needs Now Is Love* on Curb 78811		
				YOAKAM, Dwight		
6/21/03	52	6		The Back Of Your Hand...		album cut
8/2/03	52	9		The Late Great Golden State.................................		album cut
				above 2 from the album *Population: Me* on Audium 8176		

1. KENNY CHESNEY
547

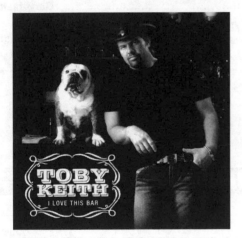

2. TOBY KEITH
448

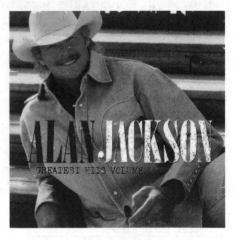

3. ALAN JACKSON
387

4.	337	DARRYL WORLEY	13.	216	DIAMOND RIO
5.	315	MARK WILLS	14.	208	BRAD PAISLEY
6.	309	TIM McGRAW	15.	203	SHANIA TWAIN
7.	293	LONESTAR	16.	202	MARTINA McBRIDE
8.	265	GARY ALLAN	17.	202	CHRIS CAGLE
9.	262	BLAKE SHELTON	18.	202	JOE NICHOLS
10.	243	KEITH URBAN	19.	199	MONTGOMERY GENTRY
11.	236	RASCAL FLATTS	20.	197	JIMMY BUFFETT
12.	226	GEORGE STRAIT			

#1 COUNTRY SINGLES

	Date Hit #1	Wks @ #1	Title	Artist
1.	1/4	2	She'll Leave You With A Smile.................................... (includes 1 week at #1 in 2002)	George Strait
2.	1/11	6	19 Somethin'..	Mark Wills
3.	2/22	3	The Baby	Blake Shelton
4.	3/15	1	Man To Man..	Gary Allan
5.	3/22	1	Travelin' Soldier	Dixie Chicks
6.	3/29	1	Brokenheartsville	Joe Nichols
7.	4/5	7	Have You Forgotten?	Darryl Worley
8.	5/24	1	Three Wooden Crosses	Randy Travis
9.	5/31	2	I Believe	Diamond Rio
10.	6/14	6	Beer For My Horses............................. Toby Keith with Willie Nelson	
11.	7/26	1	My Front Porch Looking In..	Lonestar
12.	8/2	1	Red Dirt Road	Brooks & Dunn
13.	8/9	8↕	It's Five O'Clock Somewhere .... Alan Jackson & Jimmy Buffett	
14.	9/27	1	What Was I Thinkin'...	Dierks Bentley
15.	10/11	2	Real Good Man	Tim McGraw
16.	10/25	2	Tough Little Boys	Gary Allan
17.	11/8	1	Who Wouldn't Wanna Be Me..	Keith Urban
18.	11/15	5	I Love This Bar..	Toby Keith
19.	12/20	7	There Goes My Life .... (includes 5 weeks at #1 in 2004)	Kenny Chesney

#1 COUNTRY SINGLES SALES

	Date Hit #1	Wks @ #1	Title	Artist
1.	1/4	52↕	Picture.. Kid Rock Featuring Allison Moorer (includes 5 weeks at #1 in 2002 and 1 week at #1 in 2004)	
2.	7/5	2	Help Pour Out The Rain (Lacey's Song)	Buddy Jewell
3.	12/6	13↕	Hurt .... (includes 12 weeks at #1 in 2004)	Johnny Cash
4.	12/13	3	Redneck 12 Days Of Christmas/Here's Your Sign Christmas ...Jeff Foxworthy/Bill Engvall	

R&B/ HIP-HOP SINGLES

This section lists, by artist, every title that debuted in 2003 on *Billboard's* weekly **Hot R&B/Hip-Hop Singles & Tracks** chart (a top 100 listing). It also lists every title that debuted on *Billboard's* weekly **Hot R&B/Hip-Hop Airplay** and **Hot R&B/Hip-Hop Singles Sales** charts. Sales hits that did not make the *Hot R&B/Hip-Hop Singles & Tracks* chart are identified by a superscript '**S**' next to their position in the PEAK POS column. (All *Hot R&B/Hip-Hop Airplay* hits from 2003 made the *Hot R&B/Hip-Hop Singles* chart.)

DEBUT DATE	PEAK POS	WKS CHR	G L D	ARTIST Title	Sales/Air	Label & Number
				AALIYAH		
4/19/03	9	41		Come Over	A:9	album cut
				from the album *I Care 4 U* on Blackground 060082		
9/27/03	70^S	1		Don't Know What To Tell Ya		Blackground 117511 (T)
				ADAGIO ★		
2/15/03	44^S	1		Wednesday		Satin Horse 4934
				ADAMS, Yolanda		
1/4/03	75	20		The Battle Is The Lord's	A:74	album cut
				from her 1997 album *Save The World* on Verity 43026		
				AJ ★		
8/23/03	91	8		I Like	S:4	Ripe 9194
				AKROBATIK ★		
				Born Jared Bridgeman in Boston, Massachusetts. Male rapper.		
2/1/03	48^S	1		Hypocrite		Coup D'etat 0006 (T)
				ALCHEMIST PRESENTS..., The		
6/21/03	59^S	1		The Midnight Creep		ALC 3020 (T)
				THE ALCHEMIST PRESENTS...1ST INFANTRY (Feat. Havoc and Twin)		
				AMERIE — see DJ KAYSLAY		
				AMG — see SHADE SHEIST		
				ANTHONY, Allen ★		
				Born in Oakland, California. R&B singer. Former member of the duo Christión.		
3/15/03	64	10		Alright	A:65	album cut
				FREEWAY Feat. Allen Anthony		
				from the album *Philadelphia Freeway* on Roc-A-Fella 586920		
5/17/03	42^S	4		Alright		Roc-A-Fella 039411 (T)
				APANI B ★		
				Born in Brooklyn, New York. Female rapper.		
9/6/03	55^S	1		Abracadabra		Q-Boro 002 (T)
				ASHANTI		
5/3/03	4	20		Rock Wit U (Awww Baby)	A:4 / S:6	Murder Inc. 000540 (T)
5/24/03	6	26		Into You	A:6 / S:15	Desert Storm 67452 (T)
				FABOLOUS Featuring Ashanti or Tamia		
				the version with Ashanti is from the Fabolous album *Street Dreams* on Desert Storm 62791		
7/26/03	2^1	29		Rain On Me	A:2 / S:36	Murder Inc. 001107 (T)
				samples "The Look Of Love" by Isaac Hayes		
				ATL ★		
8/23/03	48	15		Calling All Girls	S:2 / A:57	Noontime/Epic 76999
				written and produced by R. Kelly		
				AVANT		
8/9/03	5	35↑		Read Your Mind	S:❶^2 / A:5	Geffen 001449
				AX ★		
				Born Daryl Tell in Atlanta, Georgia. Male singer/songwriter. AX: Artist Xtraordinaire.		
7/5/03	88	7		Dream Eyes	S:26	1972 Ent. 40094
				AX Featuring Killer Mike		
				AZ		
4/12/03	59^S	2		Feel Good		Full Clip 4003 (T)
				BABY		
1/25/03	16	20		Hell Yeah	A:14 / S:17	Epic 76881
				GINUWINE (feat. Baby)		
				written and produced by R. Kelly		
3/15/03	53	14		Too Much For Me	A:53	album cut
				DJ KAYSLAY Featuring Nas, Foxy Brown, Baby and Amerie		
				from the album *The Streetsweeper: Vol. 1* on Columbia 87048		
6/21/03	12	20		Let's Get Down	S:2 / A:12	Columbia 79928
				BOW WOW Featuring Baby		
7/12/03	73^S	1		Baby You Can Do It		Cash Money 033811 (T)
				BABY Featuring Toni Braxton		
				BABY BASH ★		
8/23/03	54	20		Suga Suga	S:5 / A:50	Universal 001055
				BABY BASH Feat. Frankie J		
				BABY D ★		
				Born Dania Birks in 1984 in Atlanta, Georgia. Male rapper.		
11/8/03	88	6		It's Goin' Down		Big Oomp 76848 (T)
				BABY D (Featuring Bonecrusher & Dru)		

DEBUT DATE	PEAK POS	WKS CHR	G L D	ARTIST Title	Sales/Air	Label & Number
9/27/03	15	20		**BAD BOY'S DA BAND** ★ Bad Boy This Bad Boy That...A:16 album cut produced by P. Diddy; from the album *Too Hot For T.V.* on Bad Boy 001118		
				BADU, Erykah		
4/5/03	86	3		Come Close Remix (Closer)..................................S:15 MCA 000575 COMMON Feat. Erykah Badu, Pharrell From The Neptunes, and Q-Tip remix of Common's #21 hit from 2002		
8/16/03	27	20		Danger..S:20 / A:28 Motown 001052 **(T)**		
11/8/03	89	5		I C U (Doin' It)..S:20 Violator 57358 **(T)** VIOLATOR FEATURING A TRIBE CALLED QUEST AND ERYKAH BADU samples "High On Sunshine" by the Commodores and "Wild Thang" by 2 Much		
12/13/03+	62	17↑		Back In The Day (Puff).......................................A:62 album cut from the album *World Wide Underground* on Motown 000739		
				BANNER, David ★		
3/22/03	15	31		Like A Pimp.................................A:15 / S:18 SRC 000402 **(T)** DAVID BANNER feat. Lil' Flip samples "Take It Off" by UGK		
9/27/03	83	12		Cadillac On 22's...S:35 SRC 001189 **(T)**		
				BEATNUTS, The		
4/12/03	56^S	2		Ya Betta Believe It.. Landspeed 3018 **(T)**		
				BEENIE MAN		
12/27/03+	27↑	15↑		Dude...S:7 / A:27 Shocking Vibes 38890 BEENIE MAN featuring Ms Thing		
				BENSON, Rhian ★		
9/27/03	66	18		Say How I Feel..A:65 DKG 6110		
				BENZINO		
3/1/03	72^S	1		Would You .... Elektra 67371 **(T)**		
				BEYONCÉ ★		
3/22/03	67	7		In Da Club ....A:67 TKK 1512 **(T)**		
5/24/03	❶^3	25		Crazy In Love ....A:❶^4 / S:4 Columbia 79949 **(D)** BEYONCÉ (Featuring Jay-Z) samples "Are You My Woman? (Tell Me So)" by The Chi-Lites		
7/5/03	❶^5	33		Baby Boy ....A:❶^5 / S:30 Columbia 76867 **(T)** BEYONCÉ Featuring Sean Paul Sean Paul is featured on the CD promo single (he does NOT appear on the commerical 12" single)		
7/26/03	35	20		Summertime..................................S:15 / A:34 Columbia 76915 **(T)** BEYONCÉ featuring P. Diddy from the movie *The Fighting Temptations* starring Beyoncé and Cuba Gooding Jr.		
11/8/03+	2^1	22↑		Me, Myself And I ....S:2 / A:2 Columbia 76911		
				B.G.		
3/29/03	74	7		Hottest Of The Hot ....A:74 Choppa City 8650 **(T)**		
12/6/03+	15^S	6		Free .... South Flock 001 DA FLOCK Featuring BG		
				BIG ADVICE ★		
12/20/03	99	1		Hearts On Fire ....S:4 [L] Electric Monkey 1010 **(D)**		
				BIG C		
3/22/03	96	5		Hell Is A Flame..S:6 Southpaw 18299 includes vocals by The Open Door Youth Choir		
				BIG MOE		
9/20/03	69	20		Just A Dog...A:67 album cut from the album *Moe Life* on Wreckshop 4040		
				BIG NOYD — see MOBB DEEB		
				BIG TYMERS		
10/11/03	53	14		This Is How We Do ....S:11 / A:53 Cash Money 001361 **(T)**		
11/8/03+	38	19		Gangsta Girl ....S:7 / A:41 Cash Money 001355 **(T)** BIG TYMERS featuring R. Kelly written and produced by R. Kelly		
				BIZ MARKIE		
10/11/03	50^S	4		Let Me See U Bounce .... Tommy Boy 2424 **(T)** BIZ MARKIE feat. Elephant Man		
				BLACK EYED PEAS		
6/21/03	82	14		Where Is The Love? .... A&M 000714 **(T)** Justin Timberlake (guest vocal)		
				BLACK MOON		
10/18/03	64^S	1		Stay Real .... Duck Down 3004 **(T)**		
				BLAQ POET Born in Queens, New York. Male rapper.		
11/15/03	46^S	3		Poet Has Come .... Year Round 112 **(T)**		

DEBUT DATE	PEAK POS	WKS CHR	GLD	ARTIST / Title	Sales/Air	Label & Number
				BLAQUE		
6/21/03	70^S	3		Ugly		Elektra 67394 (T)
				BLAQUE Featuring Missy Elliott		
11/15/03	95	4		I'm Good		Elektra 67479 (T)
				BLIGE, Mary J.		
3/29/03	54	9		Hooked	A:54	album cut
				MARY J. BLIGE Featuring P. Diddy		
				produced by Dr. Dre; samples "In Da Club" by 50 Cent; available only as a computer download track		
6/28/03	10	21		Love @ 1st Sight	S:❶² / A:10	Geffen 000954
				MARY J. BLIGE featuring Method Man		
				samples "Hot Sex" by A Tribe Called Quest		
8/23/03	14	20		Ooh!	A:13	album cut
				samples "Singing This Song For My Mother" by Hamilton Bohannon; above 2 produced by P. Diddy		
11/22/03	21	17		Not Today	A:21	album cut
				MARY J. BLIGE featuring Eve		
				produced by Dr. Dre; featured in the movie *Barbershop 2: Back In Business* starring Ice Cube; above 2 from the album *Love & Life* on Geffen 000956		
				BONE CRUSHER ★		
1/4/03	8	35		Never Scared	S:5 / A:8	Break-Em-Off 50870 (T)
				BONE CRUSHER Featuring Killer Mike & T.I.		
				first released as a promotional CD maxi-single in very limited quantities with no bar-code on the actual product (label assigned it a number of 777); the 12" above is the widely available release		
11/8/03	88	6		It's Goin' Down		Big Oomp 76848 (T)
				BABY D (Featuring Bonecrusher & Dru)		
11/22/03	38^S	2		Fat Man Stomp		Break 'Em Off 57036 (T)
				BONE CRUSHER Featuring Cotton Mouth		
				BONE THUGS-N-HARMONY		
5/3/03	83	3		All Life Long	S:❶¹	D3 9915
				MO THUGS		
				BOOMKAT ★		
3/22/03+	33^S	8		The Wreckoning		DreamWorks 450779
				BRAND NUBIAN		
10/11/03	75^S	1		Walking On A Cloud		Spun 4 (T)
				BRAVEHEARTS ★		
				Male rap duo from Queens, New York: Jabari "Jungle" Jones and Mike "Wiz" Epps.		
11/22/03	48	20		Quick To Back Down	S:15 / A:51	Ill Will 76793 (T)
				BRAVEHEARTS featuring Nas and Lil Jon		
				BRAXTON, Toni — see BABY		
				BROTHER ALI ★		
				Born in Madison, Wisconsin; raised in Michigan and Minnesota. White male rapper.		
4/12/03	58^S	1		Room With A View		Rhymesayers 0028 (T)
				BROWN, Foxy		
3/15/03	53	14		Too Much For Me	A:53	album cut
				DJ KAYSLAY Featuring Nas, Foxy Brown, Baby and Amerie		
				from the album *The Streetsweeper: Vol. 1* on Columbia 87048		
4/5/03	62	14		I Need A Man	S:27 / A:60	Def Jam 000251 (T)
				FOXY BROWN feat. The Letter M.		
				BROWN, Kev ★		
				Born in Philadelphia, Pennsylvania. Male rapper/producer.		
8/9/03	72^S	2		Allways		Touch Of Jazz 10
9/6/03	71^S	1		Nitefall		Traffic 3040
				B2K		
2/8/03	19	20		Girlfriend	S:16 / A:17	Epic 76877
7/12/03	46	12		Feelin' Freaky	A:46 / S:48	Nick/Jive 53700 (D)
				NICK CANNON Featuring B2K		
8/16/03	47	12		What A Girl Wants	A:47	album cut
				from the album *B2K: The Remixes - Vol. 2* on Epic 86885; above 3 written and produced by R. Kelly		
12/13/03+	29	14		Badaboom	A:29 / S:40	Epic 76716 (T)
				B2K featuring Fabolous		
				from the movie *You Got Served* starring B2K		
				BUDDEN, Joe		
2/15/03	26^S	7		Drop Drop		Def Jam 077017 (T)
3/1/03	16	24		Pump It Up	S:5 / A:18	Def Jam 000395 (T)
				samples "Soul Vibrations" by Kool & The Gang		
7/5/03	48	20		Fire (Yes, Yes Y'all)	S:16 / A:47	Def Jam 000844 (T)
				JOE BUDDEN feat. Busta Rhymes		
				contains interpolations of "Super Rappin'" by Grandmaster Flash and "Whore's In This House" by Al McLaren		
8/2/03	12	31		Clubbin	A:12	album cut
				MARQUES HOUSTON Featuring Joe Budden & Pied Piper		
				written and produced by R. Kelly; from Houston's album *MH* on T.U.G. 62935		

R&B SINGLES

DEBUT DATE	PEAK POS	WKS CHR	G L D	ARTIST / Title	Sales/Air	Label & Number
				BUSTA RHYMES		
2/1/03	2[1]	29		I Know What You Want .... BUSTA RHYMES AND MARIAH CAREY (feat. The Flipmode Squad)	A:3 / S:4	J Records 21258 (T)
5/10/03	33	15		Hail Mary .... EMINEM, 50 CENT & BUSTA RHYMES	A:32	AP 105 (T)
7/5/03	23	20		Light Your A** On Fire .... BUSTA RHYMES Featuring Pharrell	S:5 / A:23	Star Trak 54245 (T)
7/5/03	48	20		Fire (Yes, Yes Y'all) .... JOE BUDDEN feat. Busta Rhymes contains interpolations of "Supper Rappin'" by Grandmaster Flash and "Whores In This House" by Al McLaren	S:16 / A:47	Def Jam 000844 (T)
7/12/03	34[S]	3		Call The Ambulance .... BUSTA RHYMES (feat. Rah Digga & M.O.P.)		J Records 53716 (T)
11/29/03	15[S]	1		Get Low Remix .... LIL JON & THE EAST SIDE BOYZ Featuring Elephant Man, Busta Rhymes & Ying Yang Twins		BME 2394 (T)
11/29/03+	92	8		Keep Doin' It .... VIOLATOR Featuring Mystikal, Dirtbag & Busta Rhymes	S:36	Violator 57615 (T)
				CADDILLAC TAH		
4/12/03	88	6		I Got'cha Ma .... CADDILLAC TAH Featuring Althea		Def Jam 000051 (T)
				CAM'RON		
2/22/03	68	8		Boy (I Need You) .... MARIAH CAREY Feat. Cam'ron samples "I'm Going Down" by Rose Royce	S:34 / A:72	Monarc 063794 (T)
3/15/03	9	21		Snake .... R. KELLY featuring Cam'ron and Big Tigger	S:❶[1] / A:10	Jive 40108 (T)
3/29/03	94	1		Built This City .... DIPLOMATS feat. Cam'ron, Jimmy Jones and Juelz Santana samples "We Built This City" by Starship	S:42	Roc-A-Fella 077007 (T)
4/5/03	64	11		Dipset Anthem .... DIPLOMATS feat. Cam'ron and Juelz Santana samples "One In A Million" by Sam Dees	S:24 / A:66	Roc-A-Fella 077995 (T)
8/2/03	70	10		Dipset (Santana's Town) .... JUELZ SANTANA Feat. Cam'ron samples "Anvil Chorus" by The Chicago Symphony and Chorus	S:35 / A:74	Roc-A-Fella 000807 (T)
				CANNON, Nick ★		
3/22/03	45[S]	12		Your Pops Don't Like Me (i really don't like this dude) .... samples "Big Ole Butt" by LL Cool J and "More Bounce To The Ounce" by Zapp		Nick/Jive 49513
7/12/03	46	12		Feelin' Freaky .... NICK CANNON Featuring B2K	A:46 / S:48	Nick/Jive 53700 (D)
10/11/03+	21	23		Gigolo .... NICK CANNON featuring R. Kelly above 2 written and produced by R. Kelly	S:14 / A:22	Nick/Jive 56646 (T)
				CAPONE-N-NOREAGA		
3/29/03	38[S]	4		Stompdash*toutu (Vendetta) .... CNN Featuring M.O.P. samples "You've Got The Papers (I've Got The Man)" by Ann Peebles; from the movie *Cradle 2 The Grave* starring Jet Li and DMX		Def Jam 000160 (T)
6/21/03	53[S]	1		Hood Money .... CNN (CAPONE-N-N.O.R.E.)		Def Jam 000630 (T)
10/18/03	85	9		Anything Goes .... CNN (CAPONE-N-N.O.R.E.), WAYNE WONDER and LEXXUS from the various artists album *Red Star Sounds Presents Def Jamaica* on Def Jam 001195	S:23	album cut
				CAREY, Mariah		
2/1/03	2[1]	29		I Know What You Want .... BUSTA RHYMES AND MARIAH CAREY (feat. The Flipmode Squad)	A:3 / S:4	J Records 21258 (T)
2/22/03	68	8		Boy (I Need You) .... MARIAH CAREY Feat. Cam'ron samples "I'm Going Down" by Rose Royce	S:34 / A:72	Monarc 063794 (T)
2/22/03	69	7		Through The Rain	S:❶[1]	Monarc 063904
12/20/03+	57	15		What Would You Do .... DAMIZZA PRESENTS: Shade Sheist, Nate Dogg & Mariah Carey	A:57	album cut
				CARIBBEAN PULSE ★		
2/8/03	87	8		Jah is My Rock .... CARIBBEAN PULSE Featuring Damian "Jr. Gong" Marley	S:4	Irie 1102
				CASE — see WC		
				CASSIDY ★		
10/18/03+	6	25↑		Hotel .... CASSIDY feat. R. Kelly samples "Rapper's Delight" by Sugarhill Gang	S:3 / A:6	J Records 56053 (T)

84

DEBUT DATE	PEAK POS	WKS CHR	G L D	ARTIST Title	Sales/Air	Label & Number
				CEE-LO		
5/17/03	77	7		All I Know S:65		MCA 113950 (T)
				FIELD MOB Featuring Cee-Lo & Jazze Pha		
11/22/03+	52	20		I'll Be Around ....S:15 / A:52		Arista 59811 (T)
				CEE-LO Featuring Timbaland		
				CHASEZ, JC ★		
3/15/03	15S	11		Blowin' Me Up (With Her Love)		Fox/Jive 40070
				samples "Money (Dollar Bill Y'all)" by Coolio; from the movie *Drumline* starring Nick Cannon		
				CHECKER, Chubby		
12/6/03	9S	7		Limbo Rock		TEEC 1024
				CHUBBY C & OD Featuring Inner Circle		
				new version of Chubby's #3 hit from 1962; project assembled by producer Gary Lefkowith; OD includes musicians Jermaine Brown and Hovannes Dilakian		
				CHERISH ★		
				Female R&B vocal group from Atlanta, Georgia: sisters Farrah, Neosha, Fallon and Felicia (Fallon and Felicia are twins).		
8/2/03	87	7		Miss P. S:49		Reprise 16579
				CHERISH Featuring Da Brat		
				CHINGY ★		
4/26/03	2[1]	43		Right Thurr	S:2 / A:3	Disturb. Tha P. 77995
9/6/03	2[1]	24		Holidae In	A:2 / S:6	Disturb. Tha P. 52816 (T)
				CHINGY featuring Ludacris & Snoop Dogg		
				C-LANAE ★		
2/8/03	90	5		Incomplete S:5		Wright Enterprises 60402
				Eric Radford (male vocal)		
				CLEAR ★		
12/6/03	25S	2		Hold You Close		Raw Naked 60712
				CLIPSE		
1/4/03	46S	6		Mr. Baller...		Game 2017 (T)
				ROYCE DA 5'9" Featuring Clipse		
1/4/03	98	2		Star S:7		Motown 019583
				702 Featuring Clipse		
1/11/03	58	20		Hot Damn ....S:23 / A:60		Star Trak 51930 (T)
				CLIPSE Featuring Ab-Liva & Rosco P. Coldchain		
				COLLARDGREENS ★		
				Born Adrian Taylor in 1981 in Columbia, South Carolina. Male rapper.		
11/29/03	42S	3		Hey You! Shorty What's Yo Name?		Chuck Nice 2
				COLLARDGREENS feat. Kayla		
				COMMON		
4/5/03	86	3		Come Close Remix (Closer)................................S:15 [R]		MCA 000575
				COMMON Featuring Erykah Badu, Pharrell & Q-Tip		
				remix of Common's #21 hit from 2002		
				COPYWRITE ★		
				Born in Columbus, Ohio. White male rapper.		
3/22/03	56S	1		Fire It Up		Eastern Conf. 01 (T)
				CRAIG-G ★		
				Born Craig Curry in 1972 in Queens, New York. Male rapper.		
3/1/03	65S	2		Let's Get Up		D&D 641252 (T)
				C-RAYZ WALZ		
7/19/03	69S	2		The Essence		Definitive Jux 62 (T)
				DA BRAT		
3/29/03	32	20		In Love Wit Chu ....S:❶[1] / A:33		So So Def 52308
				DA BRAT Featuring Cherish		
8/2/03	87	7		Miss P. S:49		Reprise 16579
				CHERISH Featuring Da Brat		
				DA FLOCK ★		
12/6/03+	15S	6		Free		South Flock 001
				DA FLOCK Featuring BG		
				DAMIZZA ★		
				Born Damion Young in Brooklyn, New York. Male rap producer/remixer.		
12/20/03+	57	15		What Would You Do A:57		album cut
				DAMIZZA PRESENTS: Shade Sheist, Nate Dogg & Mariah Carey		
				DEAN, Kiley ★		
5/3/03	54	10		Make Me A Song......................................S:48 / A:53		Beatclub 000460
				DEBRECA ★		
4/26/03	42	12		21 Questions (Again)................................A:40		Mass Appeal 001 (T)
				DEF SQUAD — see MURRAY, Keith		

DEBUT DATE	PEAK POS	WKS CHR	G L D	ARTIST / Title	Sales/Air	Label & Number
				DE LA SOUL		
8/9/03	43^S	6		Shoomp		AOI 4125 **(T)**
				DE LA SOUL Feat Sean Paul		
				DILATED PEOPLES		
2/1/03	59^S	2		Live On Stage		ABB 1039 **(T)**
11/1/03	49^S	2		Marathon		ABB 1045 **(T)**
				DIPLOMATS, The		
3/29/03	94	1		Built This City	S:42	Roc-A-Fella 077007 **(T)**
				DIPLOMATS feat. Cam'ron, Jimmy Jones and Juelz Santana		
				samples "We Built This City" by Starship		
4/5/03	64	11		Dipset Anthem	S:24 / A:66	Roc-A-Fella 077995 **(T)**
				DIPLOMATS feat. Cam'ron and Juelz Santana		
				samples "One In A Million" by Sam Dees		
				DIVERSE ★		
				Born Kenneth Jenkins in 1975 in Chicago, Illinois. Male rapper.		
10/11/03	70^S	1		Explosive		Chocolate Ind. 037 **(T)**
				DIVERSE Featuring RJD2 and Lyrics Born		
				DJ KAYSLAY ★		
				Born Keith Grayson in Harlem, New York. Male DJ/rapper.		
3/15/03	53	14		Too Much For Me	A:53	album cut
				DJ KAYSLAY Featuring Nas, Foxy Brown, Baby and Amerie		
				from the album The Streetsweeper: Vol. 1 on Columbia 87048		
				DJ QUIK		
2/15/03	66	8		John Doe	A:64	album cut
				SHADE SHEIST Featuring DJ Quik, Hi-C, AMG & Swift		
				from the album Informal Introduction on Baby Ree 112957		
8/2/03	74	5		Let Me Know	A:73	album cut
				HI-C Featuring DJ Quik		
				DMX		
1/25/03	32	20		X Gon' Give It To Ya	S:13 / A:33	Def Jam 063776 **(T)**
				from the movie Cradle 2 The Grave starring Jet Li and DMX		
7/19/03	24	16		Where The Hood At	S:20 / A:24	Def Jam 001048 **(T)**
				contains an interpolation of "Young, Gifted And Black" by Big Daddy Kane		
10/25/03	57	20		Get It On The Floor	S:28 / A:60	Def Jam 001440 **(T)**
				DMX featuring Swizz Beatz		
				D.O.C., The		
3/1/03	53^S	3		The ?hit		Silverback 2114
				MC Ren, Ice Cube, Snoop Dogg and 6 Two (guest vocals)		
				DR. DRE		
1/11/03	63	15		Symphony In X Major	S:62 / A:62	Loud 79838 **(T)**
				XZIBIT Featuring Dr. Dre		
9/6/03	69	10		Girl I'm A Bad Boy	A:68	album cut
				FAT JOE & P. DIDDY Featuring Dre		
				DOUBLE DOZE ★		
12/6/03	96	1		Make Room	S:8	Realistic South 16074
				DOWNING, Will		
11/8/03+	58	20		A Million Ways	A:57	album cut
				from the album Emotions on GRP 000529		
				DRAG-ON		
9/20/03	80	10		Put Your Drinks Down	S:39	Ruff Ryders 38873 **(T)**
12/27/03	94	5		Bang Bang Boom		Ruff Ryders 47654 **(T)**
				samples "Nappy Head" by War		
				DRU HILL		
2/1/03	37^S	1		No Doubt (Work It)		Def Soul 063769 **(T)**
4/5/03	27	20		I Love You	A:26 / S:30	Def Soul 000785
				DSGB ★		
				Rap group from Atlanta: Rod "Lil Pete" Jackson, Tavares "Pinhead" Bridges, Steve "Blackoutt" Watkins and Rob "Klone" Klonel. DSGB: Down South Georgia Boyz.		
11/15/03	55^S	1		DSGB		Universal 001317 **(T)**
				DUARTE, Ryan ★		
12/27/03+	40^S	10↑		You		Marque 001814
				DUDENEM ★		
				Male rap duo from Chicago, Illinois: D-Skonie and B-Crazy.		
3/29/03	33^S	2		Life As We Know It		All Hearing 7103
				DUKES, Skent ★		
9/27/03	13^S	5		Grind Right		Wise Owl 94752
				SKENT DUKES featuring Sly Fam		

DEBUT DATE	PEAK POS	WKS CHR	G L D	ARTIST Title	Sales/Air	Label & Number
				DUPRI, Jermaine		
8/30/03	11	27		Wat Da Hook Gon Be	S:7 / A:11	Fo' Reel 001451 (T)
				MURPHY LEE Featuring Jermaine Dupri		
11/29/03+	34	16		Pop That Booty	S:14 / A:36	T.U.G. 67501 (T)
				MARQUES HOUSTON (Featuring Jermaine "JD" Dupri)		
				DWELE ★		
6/28/03	42	26		Find A Way	A:41 / S:43	Virgin 38865 (T)
				DYNASTY ★		
9/20/03	68^S	1		4X4		Matic 03 (T)
				EAMON ★		
12/13/03+	37	17↑		F**k It (I Don't Want You Back)	S:❶^9 / A:56	Jive 56647
				EARTHQUAKE INSTITUTE, The ★		
5/3/03	99	3		Super B-Boy Pimpin'	S:5	Richter Scale 60502
				EARTH, WIND & FIRE		
6/21/03	77	8		All In The Way	A:72	album cut
				from the album *The Promise* on Kalimba 973002		
				E-40 — see FEDERATION		
				ELEPHANT MAN ★		
5/24/03	29	26		Pon De River, Pon De Bank	A:30 / S:54	VP 6404 (T)
10/11/03	50^S	4		Let Me See U Bounce		Tommy Boy 2424 (T)
				BIZ MARKIE feat. Elephant Man		
11/29/03	15^S	1		Get Low Remix		BME 2394 (T)
				LIL JON & THE EAST SIDE BOYZ Featuring Elephant Man, Busta Rhymes & Ying Yang Twins		
				ELLIOTT, Missy "Misdemeanor"		
2/22/03	26	20		P***ycat	A:25	Goldmind 67340 (T)
				Tweet (additional vocals); B-side of her 2002 hit "Work It"		
4/26/03	86	7		Back In The Day	S:42	Goldmind 67387 (T)
				MISSY ELLIOTT (Featuring Jay-Z)		
				samples "I Don't Know What This World Is Coming To" by The Soul Children		
6/21/03	70^S	3		Ugly		Elektra 67394 (T)
				BLAQUE Featuring Missy Elliott		
7/12/03	49	14		Cop That Sh#!	S:15 / A:51	Blackground 001609 (T)
				TIMBALAND & MAGOO featuring Missy Elliott		
9/27/03	34	17		Party To Damascus	S:10 / A:34	J Records 54960 (T)
				WYCLEF JEAN (feat. Missy Elliott)		
10/11/03	17	20		Pass That Dutch	S:3 / A:16	EastWest 67506 (T)
				MISSY ELLIOTT		
				samples "Magic Mountain" by War and "Potholes In My Lawn" by De La Soul		
10/11/03	48^S	3		Honk Your Horn		Universal 019351
				DANI STEVENSON Featuring Missy Elliott		
11/29/03	22^S	4		Thugman		Elektra 67495 (T)
				TWEET featuring Missy Elliott		
				EMINEM		
2/1/03	44	20		Superman	A:43	album cut
				Dina Rae (female vocal)		
2/15/03	56	20		Patiently Waiting	A:56	album cut
				50 CENT Featuring Eminem		
5/10/03	33	15		Hail Mary	A:32	AP 105 (T)
				EMINEM, 50 CENT & BUSTA RHYMES		
8/9/03	66	13		My Name	A:62	album cut
				XZIBIT Featuring Eminem & Nate Dogg		
				from Xzibit's album *Man vs Machine* on Loud 85925		
				E.S.G. & SLIM THUG ★		
				Male rap duo: Cedric "E.S.G." Hill and Stayve "Slim Thug" Thomas. E.S.G.: Everyday Street Gangsta.		
1/25/03	80	12		Getchya Hands Up	A:75	album cut
				from the various artists album *Screwmania* on S-E-S Entertainment 2013		
				EVANS, Faith — see SCARFACE		
				EVE — see BLIGE, Mary J.		
				FABOLOUS		
2/8/03	69	4		Damn	A:69	album cut
				from the album *Street Dreams* on Desert Storm 62791		
2/15/03	2^3	28		Can't Let You Go	A:2 / S:19	Desert Storm 67428 (T)
				FABOLOUS featuring Mike Shorey & Lil' Mo		
3/8/03	13	23		4 Ever	A:12 / S:19	Elektra 67379 (T)
				LIL' MO (Featuring Fabolous)		

R&B SINGLES

DEBUT DATE	PEAK POS	WKS CHR	GLD	ARTIST Title	Sales/Air	Label & Number
				FABOLOUS — Cont'd		
5/24/03	6	26		Into You	A:6 / S:15	Desert Storm 67452 (T)
				FABOLOUS Featuring Ashanti or Tamia the version with Tamia is the 12" single above (samples "Fancy Dancer" by the Commodores); the version with Ashanti is from his album *Street Dreams* on Desert Storm 62791 (no sample)		
11/8/03	93	3		Make U Mine	S:18	Desert Storm 67493 (T)
				FABOLOUS Featuring Mike Shorey		
12/13/03+	29	14		Badaboom	A:29 / S:40	Epic 76716 (T)
				B2K featuring Fabolous from the movie *You Got Served* starring B2K		
				FAKTS ONE ★		
				Born in Chicago, Illinois. Male rapper.		
6/7/03	60ˢ	1		Show Starter		Coup d'Etat 10 (T)
				FANNYPACK ★		
7/12/03	75ˢ	1		Cameltoe	[N]	Tommy Boy 2402
				FAT JOE		
2/22/03	65	9		Who's That	A:62	album cut
				R. KELLY Featuring Fat Joe from Kelly's album *Chocolate Factory* on Jive 41812		
6/7/03	61	14		I Want You	A:61	Virgin 47305 (T)
				THALIA featuring Fat Joe samples "A Little Bit Of Love" by Brenda Russell		
9/6/03	69	10		Girl I'm A Bad Boy	A:68	album cut
				FAT JOE & P. DIDDY Feat. Dre from the movie *Bad Boys II* starring Will Smith and Martin Lawrence (soundtrack on Bad Boy 000716)		
				FEDERATION ★		
12/6/03+	88	15↑		Hyphy		Montbello 53673
				FEDERATION Featuring E-40		
				FIELD MOB		
5/17/03	77	7		All I Know	S:65	MCA 113950 (T)
				FIELD MOB Featuring Cee-Lo & Jazze Pha		
				50 CENT		
1/4/03	45ˢ	2		Rotten Apple		Full Clip 4001 (T)
2/15/03	56	20		Patiently Waiting	A:56	album cut
				50 CENT Featuring Eminem		
2/22/03	34	30		If I Can't	A:33	album cut
				above 2 from the album *Get Rich Or Die Tryin'* on Shady 493544		
3/8/03	❶⁷	28		21 Questions	S:❶¹ / A:❶⁸	Shady 080739 (T)
				50 CENT Feat. Nate Dogg samples "It's Only Love Doing Its Thing" by Barry White		
4/5/03	2³	26		Magic Stick	A:❶¹	album cut
				LIL' KIM (feat. 50 Cent) samples "The Thrill Is Gone" by B.B. King; from Lil' Kim's album *La Bella Mafia* on Queen Bee 83572		
4/12/03	2²	33		P.I.M.P.	A:2 / S:7	Shady 000888 (T)
5/3/03	26	24		What Up Gangsta	A:25	album cut
				from the album *Get Rich Or Die Tryin'* on Shady 493544		
5/10/03	33	15		Hail Mary	A:32	AP 105 (T)
				EMINEM, 50 CENT & BUSTA RHYMES		
				504 BOYZ		
2/15/03	66ˢ	1		Get Back		New No Limit 060096 (T)
				FLIPMODE SQUAD — see BUSTA RHYMES		
				FLOETRY		
2/8/03	8	30		Say Yes	A:8	album cut
8/23/03	31	20		Getting Late	A:30	album cut
				above 2 from the album *Floetic* on DreamWorks 450313		
				FOXX, Jamie — see TWISTA		
				FOXXX, Freddie		
5/31/03	56ˢ	2		Tha Konexion		Rapster 14 (T)
				FRANKIE J ★		
5/17/03	80	16		Don't Wanna Try	S:❶¹	Columbia 79872
8/23/03	54	20		Suga Suga	S:5 / A:50	Universal 001055
				BABY BASH Feat. Frankie J		
				FRANKLIN, Aretha		
7/19/03	53	15		The Only Thing Missin'	A:53	album cut
10/18/03	46	20		Wonderful	A:45	album cut
				above 2 from the album *So Damn Happy* on Arista 50174		
				FRANK-N-DANK ★		
				Male rap duo from Detroit, Michigan.		
12/27/03	59ˢ	1		48 Hours		ABB 155 (T)

DEBUT DATE	PEAK POS	WKS CHR	G L D	ARTIST Title	Sales/Air	Label & Number
				FREEWAY		
3/15/03	64	10		Alright	A:65	album cut
				FREEWAY Feat. Allen Anthony		
				from the album *Philadelphia Freeway* on Roc-A-Fella 586920		
5/10/03	40	20		Flipside	S:18 / A:41	Roc-A-Fella 000428 (T)
				FREEWAY feat. Peedi Crakk		
				FUNN CLUB ★		
				White female teen vocal group from Fort Lauderdale, Florida: Brittany, Danielle, Emmi and Kelsey.		
12/6/03+	17S	6		Whoomp! (There It Is)		album cut
				FUNN CLUB Featuring Tag Team		
				GANG STARR		
4/19/03	99	2		Nice Girl, Wrong Place	S:23	Virgin 38859 (T)
				GANG STARR feat. / Boy Big		
				samples "Kung Fu" by Curtis Mayfield		
10/11/03	27S	7		The Ownerz		Virgin 38874 (T)
				GHOSTFACE — see RONSON, Mark		
				GINUWINE		
1/25/03	16	20		Hell Yeah	A:14 / S:17	Epic 76881
				GINUWINE (feat. Baby)		
				written and produced by R. Kelly		
5/10/03	3	27		In Those Jeans	A:❶	album cut
				from the album *The Senior* on Epic 86960		
10/4/03	28	20		Love You More	A:28 / S:35	Epic 76890 (T)
				GOAPELE ★		
				Born Goapele Mohlabane on 7/11/77 in Oakland, California (African father/American mother). Female singer/songwriter. Name pronounced: gwa-pa-lay.		
5/31/03	83	20		Closer		Skyblaze 008 (T)
				GRAE, Jean		
3/8/03	67S	2		No Doubt		Third Earth 13 (T)
11/29/03	57S	1		Hater's Anthem		Babygrande 0013 (T)
				GRAFIC INTERNATIONAL ★		
6/14/03	96	2		Respect My Pimpin'	S:8	Graft 650000
				GREEN, Al — see SERMON, Eric		
				GREEN, Vivian		
6/14/03	52	13		Fanatic	A:51	album cut
10/18/03	75	9		What Is Love?	A:72	album cut
				above 2 from the album *A Love Story* on Columbia 86357		
				G-UNIT ★		
10/4/03	7	20		Stunt 101	S:4 / A:7	G-Unit 001601 (T)
12/6/03+	10↑	18↑		Wanna Get To Know You	A:10	album cut
				G-UNIT featuring Joe		
				samples "Come Live With Me Angel" by Marvin Gaye		
12/27/03	77	13		Smile	A:74	album cut
				above 2 from the album *Beg For Mercy* on G-Unit 001593		
				G-WIZ ★		
3/1/03	98	4		Just Like You	S:9	Compound 691007
				GWYNN, Nee-Nee ★		
2/22/03	89	10		No Means No	S:3	Base Hit 83022
				NEE-NEE GWYNN Featuring: Baby Diva		
				Tony Gwynn (backing vocals)		
				HAHZ THE RIPPA ★		
1/25/03	88	9		Everybody's Gotta Live	S:2	Body Head 6035
				samples "Everybody's Gotta Live" by Love		
				HALL, Ellis		
10/25/03	98	1		Gotta Get The Money	S:5	Crossover 70027
				HAMILTON, Anthony		
8/16/03	60	20		Comin' From Where I'm From	S:49 / A:59	So So Def 54118 (T)
				H.A.W.K. ★		
				Male rapper.		
5/31/03	73	12		You Already Know	A:71	album cut
				H.A.W.K. Featuring Big T		
				from the album *Game Face* on Ghetto Dreams 0001		
				HEADLEY, Heather		
3/8/03	15	37		I Wish I Wasn't..	A:15	album cut
				from the album *This Is Who I Am* on RCA 69376		

DEBUT DATE	PEAK POS	WKS CHR	G L D	ARTIST Title — Sales/Air	Label & Number
				HI-C ★	
				Born in 1972 in Louisiana; raised in California. Male rapper.	
8/2/03	74	5		Let Me Know A:73	album cut
				HI-C feat. DJ Quik	
				from the album *Hi-Life Hustle* on Hustle 42036	
				HIEROGLYPHICS	
8/23/03	75ˢ	1		Powers That Be	Hiero Imp. 230019 (T)
				HIGH & MIGHTY, The	
10/4/03	66ˢ	1		Take It Off!	Eastern Conf. 07 (T)
				HITMAN SAMMY SAM ★	
4/5/03	41	16		Step Daddy ....S:7 / A:43	Universal 000676
				samples "Double Dutch Bus" by Frankie Smith; a children's chorus sings "Itsy Bitsy Spider"	
				HOUSTON, Marques ★	
1/25/03	24	17		That Girl A:24	album cut
8/2/03	12	31		Clubbin A:12	album cut
				MARQUES HOUSTON Featuring Joe Budden & Pied Piper	
				written and produced by R. Kelly; above 2 from the album *MH* on T.U.G. 000046	
11/29/03+	34	16		Pop That Booty ....S:14 / A:36	T.U.G. 67501 (T)
				MARQUES HOUSTON (Featuring Jermaine "JD" Dupri)	
				HOUSTON, Whitney	
5/10/03	80	14	●	Try It On My Own S:59	Arista 51156 (D)
				IMMORTAL TECHNIQUE ★	
12/13/03	63ˢ	2		Industrial Revolution	Viper 01 (T)
				INNER CIRCLE — see CHECKER, Chubby	
				ISLEY BROTHERS, The	
2/15/03	14	27		What Would You Do? A:11	album cut
				THE ISLEY BROTHERS Featuring RONALD ISLEY AKA MR. BIGGS	
8/9/03	35	20		Busted...A:32	album cut
				THE ISLEY BROTHERS Featuring RONALD ISLEY AKA MR. BIGGS and JS	
				above 2 written and produced by R. Kelly; above 2 from the album *Body Kiss* on DreamWorks 450409	
				JACKI-O ★	
				Born Angela Kohn in Miami, Florida. Female rapper.	
8/23/03	61	12		Nookie (real good) A:61	Poe Boy 01
				JACKI-O Featuring Rodney	
				JACKSON, Michael	
10/25/03	40	19		One More Chance ....S:❶³ / A:43	Epic 76802 (M)
				written and co-produced by R. Kelly	
				JADAKISS	
8/16/03	65	12		Mighty D-Block (2 Guns Up) A:63	album cut
				SHEEK LOUCH Featuring Jadakiss, Styles & J-Hood	
				from the album *Walk Witt Me* on D-Block 001042	
9/6/03	98	2		Let's Get It...S:7	RapRock/Pyramid 10422
				SMOOT featuring Jadakiss & Swizz Beatz	
11/29/03	86	14		You'll Never Find (A Better Woman) S:38	TVT 2452 (T)
				TEEDRA MOSES Featuring Jadakiss	
				JAGGED EDGE	
8/16/03	2¹	34↑		Walked Outta Heaven ....S:❶¹² / A:2	So So Def 76974
11/1/03+	17	20		My Baby ....A:17 / S:53	Columbia 76779 (T)
				BOW WOW Featuring Jagged Edge	
				JAHEIM	
2/22/03	5	35		Put That Woman First A:5	album cut
				samples "I Forgot To Be Your Lover" by William Bell	
9/20/03	51	20		Backtight A:49	album cut
				samples "Somebody Told Me" by Teddy Pendergrass	
12/27/03+	64	15↑		Diamond In Da Ruff A:63	album cut
				above 3 from the album *Still Ghetto* on Divine Mill 48214	
				JAI, Jasmine ★	
				Born Jade Evonne Alston on 1/29/82 in Philadelphia, Pennsylvania. Singer/songwriter/producer.	
2/15/03	52ˢ	2		Be Easy	Jasmine Jai 6492
				JAKKI DA MOTAMOUTH ★	
7/5/03	67ˢ	1		I'm Trying	NCS 7003 (T)

DEBUT DATE	PEAK POS	WKS CHR	G L D	ARTIST Title	Sales/Air	Label & Number
				JA RULE		
4/26/03	68^S	1		Murder Reigns		Murder Inc. 015833 (T)
				contains an interpolation of "Africa" by Toto		
9/20/03	67	5		The Crown	A:65	album cut
				from the album *Blood In My Eye* on Murder Inc. 001577		
10/11/03	17	20		Clap Back	S:3 / A:17	Murder Inc. 001584 (T)
				JAVIER ★		
6/14/03	42	20		Crazy	A:44 / S:47	Capitol 52413
				JAY-EL ★		
5/31/03	18^S	18		Be About Yours		Powersource 91012 (M)
				JAYLIB ★		
				Collaboration of rappers/producers James "Jay Dilla" Yancey (from Detroit, Michigan) and Otis "Madlib" Jackson (from Oxnard, California).		
8/9/03	75^S	1		The Official		Stones Throw 2061 (T)
11/8/03	47^S	2		Champion Sound		Stones Throw 2062 (T)
				JAY-Z		
1/25/03	❶¹	23		Excuse Me Miss	A:❶¹ / S:4	Roc-A-Fella 063717 (T)
4/5/03	53	16		Stop	S:4 / A:54	Roc-A-Fella 000398 (T)
4/12/03	21	20		Beware Of The Boys (Mundian To Bach Ke)	S:❶¹ / A:21	Sequence 8012 (M)
				PAN'JABI MC Featuring Jay-Z Indian vocals by Labh Janjua; samples the theme from TV's *Knight Rider*		
4/12/03	37	23		La-La-La (Excuse Me Again)	A:34	album cut
				from the movie *Bad Boys II* starring Will Smith and Martin Lawrence (soundtrack on Bad Boy 000716)		
4/26/03	86	7		Back In The Day	S:42	Goldmind 67387 (T)
				MISSY ELLIOTT (Featuring Jay-Z) samples "I Don't Know What This World Is Coming To" by The Soul Children		
5/17/03	❶⁶	33		Frontin'	A:❶⁵ / S:2	Star Trak 58647
				PHARRELL Featuring Jay-Z		
5/24/03	❶³	25		Crazy In Love	A:❶⁴ / S:4	Columbia 79949 (D)
				BEYONCÉ (Featuring Jay-Z) samples "Are You My Woman (Tell Me So)" by The Chi-Lites		
11/8/03	6	20		Change Clothes	S:2 / A:6	Roc-A-Fella 001651 (T)
				Danne Doty (additional vocals)		
11/8/03	48	11		What More Can I Say	A:48	album cut
				from the album *The Black Album* on Roc-A-Fella 001528		
12/13/03+	3↑	17↑		Dirt Off Your Shoulder	S:4 / A:4	Roc-A-Fella 001936 (T)
				JEAN, Wyclef		
8/23/03	73	7		Industry	S:48 / A:69	album cut
				from the album *The Preacher's Son* on Yclef 55425		
9/27/03	34	17		Party To Damascus	S:10 / A:34	J Records 54960 (T)
				WYCLEF JEAN (feat. Missy Elliott)		
				JEDI MIND TRICKS ★		
3/15/03	43^S	3		Animal Rap		Babygrande 0102 (M)
				JEDI MIND TRICKS feat Kool G Rap		
				JHENÉ ★		
				Born in Los Angeles, California. Female singer. Cousin of Dreux "Lil Fizz" Frederic of B2K.		
10/25/03	91	5		No L.O.V.E.		T.U.G. 76934 (T)
				JIN ★		
				Born Jin Auyeung in 1982 in China; raised in Miami, Florida. Male rapper.		
12/20/03	74	10		Learn Chinese	S:29	Ruff Ryders 38885 (T)
				samples "Blind Man Can See It" by James Brown		
				J-KWON ★		
				Born in 1986 in St. Louis, Missouri. Male rapper.		
12/13/03+	2¹↑	17↑		Tipsy	S:2 / A:2	So So Def 58460 (T)
				J-LIVE		
2/1/03	66^S	1		Like This Anna		Coup d'Etat 0005 (T)
				JOE		
4/26/03	71	11		That Girl	A:71	album cut
				JOE Featuring Mr. Cheeks #1 hit for Stevie Wonder in 1982; from the various artists album *Conception: An Interpretation Of Stevie Wonder's Songs* on Motown 067314		
9/27/03	15	28↑		More & More	A:15	album cut
				written and produced by R. Kelly; from the album *And Then...* on Jive 53707		
12/6/03+	10↑	18↑		Wanna Get To Know You	A:10	album cut
				G-UNIT featuring Joe samples "Come Live With Me Angel" by Marvin Gaye		
				JOHNSON, Syleena		
4/19/03	75	4		Guess What (Guess Again) Remix	S:❶²	Jive 40099
				SYLEENA JOHNSON featuring R. Kelly remix of Johnson's original version titled "Guess What" (hit #29 in 2002)		
7/12/03	68	13		Faithful To You	A:67	album cut
				from the album *Chapter 2: The Voice* on Jive 41815		

R&B SINGLES

DEBUT DATE	PEAK POS	WKS CHR	G L D	ARTIST Title	Sales/Air	Label & Number
3/15/03	19^S	14		**JOLLY.GREEN** ★ .Yall Don't Know..		Zoe Pound 5601
2/15/03	39^S	8		**JONELL** So Whassup .... JONELL feat. Redman		Def Soul 063781 (T)
4/26/03	88	8		**JONES, Roy Jr.** Who Run This... ROY JONES, JR. Featuring Pastor Troy, Lil John And The Eastside Boyz	S:2	Body Head 274771
11/1/03	71	7		**JORDAN, Montell** Supa Star	A:70	Enterprise 5705 (T)
11/29/03	45^S	5		**J.R.** ★ Born James Hogan in Columbus, Georgia. Male rapper. My J's		Strong Arm 627
5/17/03	54	20		**JS** ★ Ice Cream .... from the album *Ice Cream* on DreamWorks 450332	A:54	album cut
8/9/03	35	20		Busted .... THE ISLEY BROTHERS Featuring RONALD ISLEY AKA MR. BIGGS and JS from the album *Body Kiss* on DreamWorks 450409	A:32	album cut
11/1/03+	61	18		Love Angel .... from the album *Ice Cream* on DreamWorks 450332; above 3 written and produced by R. Kelly	A:60	album cut
10/4/03	75^S	1		**JURASSIC 5** Freedom		Up Above 3037 (T)
10/11/03	73^S	2		**JUST-ICE** History...		Memnoch 008 (T)
12/13/03+	18	17↑		**JUVENILE** In My Life.. JUVENILE Featuring Mannie Fresh	S:16 / A:18	Cash Money 001827 (T)
6/14/03	56^S	2		**J-ZONE** 5 Star Hooptie..		Old Maid 32504 (T)
6/7/03+	58^S	3		**KANE, Big Daddy** Any Type Of Way		Mahogany 001 (T)
5/24/03	96	1		**KARDINAL OFFISHALL** Belly Dancer .... KARDINAL OFFISHALL Featuring Pharrell Williams	S:36	MCA 113949 (T)
11/22/03+	76	15		Back For More .... GLENN LEWIS Featuring Kardinal Offishall	S:71 / A:75	Red Star 76852 (T)
5/3/03	41	20		**KELIS** How You Want That.. LOON Fetauring Kelis samples "Saturday Night" by Schooly D	S:13 / A:40	Bad Boy 000430 (T)
9/6/03+	4	29		Milkshake	A:4 / S:6	Star Trak 58648 (D)
2/22/03	65	9		**KELLY, R.** Who's That... R. KELLY Featuring Fat Joe from the album *Choclate Factory* on Jive 41812	A:62	album cut
3/15/03	9	21		Snake R. KELLY featuring Cam'ron and Big Tigger	S:❶^1 / A:10	Jive 40108 (T)
4/5/03	29	31		I'll Never Leave .... from the album *Chocolate Factory* on Jive 41812	A:24	album cut
4/12/03	84	5		Soldier's Heart	S:21	Jive 40029
4/19/03	75	4		Guess What (Guess Again) Remix .... SYLEENA JOHNSON featuring R. Kelly remix of Johnson's original version titled "Guess What" (hit #29 in 2002)	S:❶^2	Jive 40099
1/26/03	16^S	17		Rich Man .... RUSSELL Feat. R. Kelly written and produced by R. Kelly		R Records 91008
6/28/03	71	17		Forever... from the album *Chocolate Factory* on Jive 41812	A:68	album cut
7/12/03	6	26		Thoia Thoing	S:5 / A:6	Jive 54283 (T)
9/13/03	65	6		Pick Up The Phone .... TYRESE and LUDACRIS feat. R. Kelly from the movie *2 Fast 2 Furious* starring Paul Walker and Tyrese (soundtrack on Def Jam South 000426)	A:63	album cut
10/11/03+	21	23		Gigolo .... NICK CANNON featuring R. Kelly	S:14 / A:22	Nick/Jive 56646 (T)
10/18/03+	6	25↑		Hotel CASSIDY feat. R. Kelly samples "Rapper's Delight" by Sugarhill Gang	S:3 / A:6	J Records 56053 (T)

DEBUT DATE	PEAK POS	WKS CHR	G L D	ARTIST Title	Sales/Air	Label & Number
				KELLY, R. — Cont'd		
10/25/03	49	20		Touched A Dream	A:45	album cut
				from the album *The R. In R&B Collection Volume One* on Jive 55077		
11/8/03+	38	19		Gangsta Girl	S:7 / A:41	Cash Money 001355 (T)
				BIG TYMERS featuring R. Kelly		
				written and produced by R. Kelly		
				KEM ★		
4/19/03	25	45		Love Calls	A:24	album cut
				from the album *Kemistry* on Motown 067516		
				KENNY G		
1/25/03	98	1		Auld Lang Syne (Freedom Mix)	S:5	[I-S]	Arista 15215
				contains audioclips from dozens of historical events		
				KEYS, Alicia		
11/1/03	**❶**⁹	23↑		You Don't Know My Name	A:**❶**⁹	J Records 56599 (T)
				samples "Let Me Prove My Love To You" by The Main Ingredient		
				KHADAFI, Tragedy ★		
				Born Percy Chapman on 8/13/71 in Queens, New York. Male rapper.		
11/22/03	70ˢ	1		Hood		25 To Life 1012 (T)
				KILLER MIKE		
1/4/03	8	35		Never Scared	S:5 / A:8	Break-Em-Off 50870 (T)
				BONE CRUSHER Featuring Killer Mike & T.I.		
				first released as a promotional CD maxi-single in very limited quantities with no bar-code on the actual product (label assigned it a number of 777); the 12" above is the widely available release		
2/8/03	42	17		A.D.I.D.A.S.	A:39	album cut
				KILLER MIKE Featuring Big Boi		
				A.D.I.D.A.S.: All Day I Dream About Sex; from the album *Monster* on Columbia 86862		
7/5/03	88	7		Dream Eyes	S:26	1972 Ent. 40094
				AX Featuring Killer Mike		
				KINDRED THE FAMILY SOUL ★		
				Husband-and wife vocal duo from Philadelphia, Pennsylvania: Fatin Dantzler and Aja Graydon.		
4/26/03	53	20		Far Away	A:52	album cut
				from the album *Surrender To Love* on Hidden Beach 86491		
				KNOC-TURN'AL		
5/24/03	61	20		Lights Out	A:58	album cut
				MACK 10 Featuring Westside Connection & Knoc-Turn'Al		
				from Mack 10's album *Ghetto, Gutter & Gangsta* on Hoo-Bangin' 970028		
12/20/03	78	16↑		The Way I Am	S:53	Desert Storm 67508 (T)
				KNOC-TURN'AL featuring Snoop Dogg		
				KOOL G RAP — see JEDI MIND TRICKS		
				KRONDON ★		
8/30/03	70ˢ	2		Feels Good		Strong Arm 001 (T)
				KWELI, Talib		
3/15/03	29	20		Get By	A:29 / S:31	Rawkus 113938 (T)
				LACKS ★		
				Born in Detroit, Michigan. Male rapper.		
8/30/03	74ˢ	1		The Idiology		Earth Angel 21001 (T)
				LAMAR, Nathaniel ★		
8/23/03	91	7		Soul Shake	S:3	Jenstar 1387
				LAST EMPEROR, The ★		
				Born in Philadelphia, Pennsylvania. Male rapper.		
12/20/03	61ˢ	1		Secret Wars Pt. 2		Highrise 12 (T)
				LATIF ★		
6/7/03	97	2		I Don't Wanna Hurt You	S:30	Motown 000439
				samples "Time Will Reveal" by DeBarge		
				LDS ★		
				Born David Eason in 1981 in Long Island, New York. Male rapper. LDS: Lyrically Destined to Shine.		
6/21/03	72ˢ	1		Drop It		Inner Circle 17162
				LEE, Murphy ★		
6/21/03	3	23		Shake Ya Tailfeather	A:3	album cut
				NELLY/P. DIDDY/MURPHY LEE		
				from the movie *Bad Boys II* starring Will Smith and Martin Lawrence (soundtrack on Bad Boy 000716)		
8/30/03	11	27		Wat Da Hook Gon Be	S:7 / A:11	Fo' Reel 001451 (T)
				MURPHY LEE Featuring Jermaine Dupri		
				LEVERT, Gerald		
2/15/03	57	19		Closure	A:55	album cut
				from the album *The G Spot* on Elektra 62795		
9/20/03	30	25		U Got That Love (Call It A Night)	A:30	album cut
				from the album *Stroke Of Genius* on Elektra 62903		

R&B SINGLES

DEBUT DATE	PEAK POS	WKS CHR	G L D	ARTIST / Title	Sales/Air	Label & Number
				LEWIS, Glenn		
11/22/03+	76	15		Back For More .... GLENN LEWIS Featuring Kardinal Offishall	S:71 / A:75	Red Star 76852 (T)
				LEXX ★		
2/15/03	90	6		How I Feel .... LEXX featuring Lil' Flip	S:5	Takeover 600001
				LIL BOW WOW		
6/21/03	12	20		Let's Get Down.......... BOW WOW (Feat. Baby)	S:2 / A:12	Columbia 79928
11/1/03+	17	20		My Baby .... BOW WOW Featuring Jagged Edge	A:17 / S:53	Columbia 76779 (T)
				LIL' FLIP		
2/15/03	90	6		How I Feel .... LEXX featuring Lil' Flip	S:5	Takeover 600001
3/22/03	15	31		Like A Pimp .... DAVID BANNER feat. Lil' Flip — samples "Take It Off" by UGK	A:15 / S:18	SRC 000402 (T)
4/19/03	98	2		Represent .... PAPA REU Featuring Lil' Flip, Lil' Keke & Hawk		Reu Musik 1001 (T)
5/31/03	62	19		Ridin Spinners .... THREE 6 MAFIA Featuring Lil' Flip — from the album *Da Unbreakables* on Hypnotize Minds 89030	A:62 / S:72	album cut
10/4/03	98	2		What Cha Gone Do.......... PLAYBOY SHANE Featuring Lil' Flip	S:7	Ball Hawg 60652
				LIL JON & THE EAST SIDE BOYZ		
4/12/03	2²	52↑		Get Low .... LIL JON & THE EAST SIDE BOYZ Featuring Ying Yang Twins	A:2 / S:6	BME 2377 (T)
4/26/03	88	8		Who Run This .... ROY JONES, JR. Featuring Pastor Troy, Lil John And The Eastside Boyz	S:2	Body Head 274771
6/28/03	2³	41↑		Damn! .... YOUNGBLOODZ Featuring Lil' Jon	A:2 / S:8	So So Def 52215 (T)
8/9/03	56	20		Shake That Monkey.......... TOO $HORT feat. Lil Jon & The Eastside Boyz	S:41 / A:56	$hort 55065 (T)
10/4/03+	9	27↑		Salt Shaker .... YING YANG TWINS Feat. LIL JON & THE EAST SIDE BOYZ	S:5 / A:9	Collipark 2485 (T)
11/22/03	48	20		Quick To Back Down.......... BRAVEHEARTS featuring Nas and Lil Jon	S:15 / A:51	Ill Will 76793 (T)
11/29/03	15ˢ	1		Get Low Remix .... LIL JON & THE EAST SIDE BOYZ Feat. Elephant Man, Busta Rhymes & Ying Yang Twins	[R]	BME 2394 (T)
12/27/03	81	6		Come Get Some .... TLC Featuring Lil' Jon & Sean Paul of YoungBloodZ	S:36	Arista 57820 (T)
				LIL' KEKE — see PAPA REU		
				LIL' KIM		
2/1/03	8	24		The Jump Off .... LIL' KIM (featuring Mr. Cheeks) — samples "Jeeps, Lex Coups, Bimaz & Benz" by Lost Boyz	S:3 / A:9	Queen Bee 88036 (T)
4/5/03	2³	26		Magic Stick .... LIL' KIM (feat. 50 Cent) — samples "The Thrill Is Gone" by B.B. King; from the album *La Bella Mafia* on Queen Bee 83572	A:❶	album cut
5/31/03	60	20		Thug Luv .... LIL' KIM (feat. Twista)	S:28 / A:60	Queen Bee 88246
				LIL' MO		
2/15/03	2³	28		Can't Let You Go .... FABOLOUS featuring Mike Shorey & Lil' Mo	A:2 / S:19	Desert Storm 67428 (T)
3/8/03	13	23		4 Ever.......... LIL' MO (Featuring Fabolous)	A:12 / S:19	Elektra 67379 (T)
5/10/03	50	11		21 Answers.......... LIL' MO Featuring Free	A:51	TKK 1533
				LIL SCRAPPY ★		
9/20/03+	73	20		Head Bussa	S:9 / A:75	BME 16506
				LIL WAYNE		
11/22/03	97	2		Get Something	S:55	Cash Money 001222 (T)
				LIL' ZANE		
7/26/03	87	11		Tonite, I'm Yours.......... ZANE featuring Tank	S:22	Priority 52480
				LITTLE BROTHER		
7/26/03	62ˢ	2		Way You Do It		ABB 1042 (T)
				LL COOL J		
5/17/03	73	11		Amazin'.......... LL COOL J Introducing Kandice Love	S:61 / A:73	Def Jam 000310 (T)
12/20/03+	56	14		She Is .... CARL THOMAS Featuring LL Cool J — from the album *Let's Talk About It* on Bad Boy 118802	A:55	album cut

DEBUT DATE	PEAK POS	WKS CHR	G L D	ARTIST Title	Sales/Air	Label & Number
				LOON ★		
5/3/03	41	20		How You Want That...S:13 / A:40		Bad Boy 000430 (T)
				LOON Featuring Kelis samples "Saturday Night" by Schooly D		
5/10/03	74	4		Just Friends S:57		Elektra 67390 (T)
				LSG Featuring Loon		
10/4/03	28	20		Down For Me A:27		album cut
				LOON Feat. Mario Winans from the album *Loon* on Bad Boy 000892		
				LOPEZ, Jennifer		
7/26/03	19ˢ	15		I'm Glad		Epic 79868
				samples "P.S.K. What Does It Mean?" by Schooly D		
				LSG		
5/10/03	74	4		Just Friends S:57		Elektra 67390 (T)
				LSG Featuring Loon		
				LUDACRIS		
5/10/03	20	20		Act A Fool ....S:8 / A:21		Def Jam S. 000539 (T)
				from the movie *2 Fast 2 Furious* starring Paul Walker and Tyrese		
8/16/03	❶⁵	32		Stand Up ....A:❶⁵ / S:6		Def Jam S. 001183 (T)
				LUDACRIS featuring Shawnna		
9/6/03	2¹	24		Holidae In ....A:2 / S:6		Disturb. Tha P. 52816 (T)
				CHINGY featuring Ludacris & Snoop Dogg		
9/13/03	65	6		Pick Up The Phone A:63		album cut
				TYRESE and LUDACRIS feat. R. Kelly from the movie *2 Fast 2 Furious* starring Paul Walker and Tyrese (soundtrack on Def Jam South 000426)		
9/27/03	29	18		Hot & Wet ....S:12 / A:31		Bad Boy 001150 (T)
				112 Featuring Ludacris		
11/29/03+	2¹	19↑		Splash Waterfalls ....A:2 / S:3		Disturb. Tha P. 001757 (T)
				LUMIDEE ★		
5/3/03	9	22		Never Leave You - Uh Oooh, Uh Oooh! ....A:9 / S:10		Universal 000652 (T)
				MACK 10		
5/24/03	61	20		Lights Out..A:58		album cut
				MACK 10 Featuring Westside Connection & Knoc-Turn'Al from the album *Ghetto, Gutter & Gangsta* on Hoo-Bangin' 970028		
				MADLIB ★ Born Otis Jackson in Oxnard, California. Male rapper/producer. One-half of Jaylib duo.		
6/14/03	43ˢ	2		Please Set Me At Ease		Astralwerks 77987 (T)
				MAD VILLAIN ★		
12/27/03+	63ˢ	3		Money Folder..		Stone Throw 2064 (T)
				MARIO		
2/1/03	61	15		C'mon..A:61		album cut
				from the album *Mario* on J Records 20026		
				MASTER P		
12/6/03+	40	18↑		Them Jeans A:40		Koch 5724 (T)
				McKNIGHT, Brian		
3/15/03	35	20		Shoulda, Woulda, Coulda A:35		album cut
				from the album *U Turn* on Motown 067315		
				MEDAPHOAR ★ Born in Los Angeles, California. Male rapper.		
11/15/03+	59ˢ	1		What U In It For?		Stone Throw 2076 (T)
				MEMPHIS BLEEK		
10/25/03	50ˢ	1		Need Me In Your Life		Roc-A-Fella 129711 (T)
				MERSILIS ★ Born James Allen on 3/28/75 in Wynnewood, Oklahoma. Male rapper. Former running back for the NFL's Chicago Bears.		
12/27/03	64ˢ	1		Nazty Girrrl		Mersilis 2015
				METHOD MAN — see BLIGE, Mary J.		
				MILLZ, Jae ★ Born in Harlem, New York. Male rapper.		
11/29/03	89	9		No, No, No S:28		Wanna Blow 42654 (T)
				MR. CHEEKS		
2/1/03	8	24		The Jump Off ....S:3 / A:9		Queen Bee 88036 (T)
				LIL' KIM (featuring Mr. Cheeks)		
2/22/03	52	20		Crush On You ....S:15 / A:52		Universal 000448 (T)
				MR. CHEEKS featuring Mario Winans		

DEBUT DATE	PEAK POS	WKS CHR	G L D	ARTIST Title	Sales/Air	Label & Number
				MR. CHEEKS — Cont'd		
4/26/03	**71**	11		That Girl A:71		album cut
				JOE Featuring Mr. Cheeks		
				#1 hit for Stevie Wonder in 1982; from the various artists album *Conception: An Interpretation Of Stevie Wonder's Songs* on Motown 067314		
7/5/03	**66**S	2		Hands High		Universal 000786 (T)
				MR. LIF		
3/8/03	**52**S	2		Live From The Plantation		Definitive Jux 45 (T)
				MOBB DEEP		
4/26/03	**81**	7		Double Shots..S:42		Landspeed 3019 (T)
				MOBB DEEP Featuring Big Noyd		
				MONICA		
4/5/03	**❶**5	31		So Gone A:❶3 / S:15		J Records 21260 (T)
				samples "You Are Number One" by The Whispers		
9/6/03	**24**	21		Knock Knock ....A:25 / S:26		J Records 57593 (D)
				samples "It's A Terrible Thing To Waste Your Love" by The Masqueraders; above 2 co-written and produced by Missy Elliott		
				M.O.P.		
3/29/03	**38**S	4		Stompdash*toutu (Vendetta)...............................S		Def Jam 000160 (T)
				CNN Featuring M.O.P.		
				samples "You've Got The Papers (I've Got The Man)" by Ann Peebles; from the movie *Cradle 2 The Grave* starring Jet Li and DMX		
7/12/03	**34**S	3		Call The Ambulance		J Records 53716 (T)
				BUSTA RHYMES (feat. Rah Digga & M.O.P.)		
				MOSES, Teedra ★		
11/29/03	**86**	14		You'll Never Find (A Better Woman) S:38		TVT 2452 (T)
				TEEDRA MOSES Featuring Jadakiss		
				MOSLEY, Lou		
4/19/03	**89**	12		If You Let Me..S:3		Jenstar 1383
				Vanessa Holmes (backing vocals); first recorded by the Four Tops in 1972		
				MOSS-SCOTT, Brandy		
3/15/03	**88**	9		Starting With Me..S:5		Heavenly Tunes 2005
				MS. JADE — see SLUM VILLAGE		
				MURRAY, Keith		
2/15/03	**50**	17		Yeah Yeah U Know It................................S:11 / A:51		Def Jam 000787
				KEITH MURRAY feat. Def Squad		
6/7/03	**63**	11		Candi Bar ....S:9 / A:68		Def Jam 000563 (T)
				Patti Austin (female vocal); samples "Havana Candi" by Patti Austin		
				MURS ★		
6/21/03	**73**S	1		Risky Business		Definitive Jux 53 (T)
				MUSIQ		
10/18/03	**18**	20		forthenight ....A:18 / S:21		Def Soul 001649 (T)
				MYA		
6/21/03	**17**	20		My Love Is Like...WO.............................S:3 / A:19		A&M 000768
				co-written and produced by Missy Elliott		
11/8/03	**35**	18		Fallen...S:10 / A:35		A&M 001681
				samples "Saudade Vem Corrondo" by Stan Getz & Luiz Bonfa		
				MYSTIKAL — see VIOLATOR		
				NAPPY ROOTS		
8/16/03	**53**	10		Roun' The Globe...S:38 / A:51		Atlantic 88228 (T)
				NAS		
1/4/03	**7**	26		I Can A:6 / S:11		Columbia 79941
				backing vocals by a children's chorus; melody is Beethoven's "Fur Elise"		
3/15/03	**53**	14		Too Much For Me...A:30		album cut
				DJ KAYSLAY Featuring Nas, Foxy Brown, Baby and Amerie		
				from the album *The Streetsweeper: Vol. 1* on Columbia 87048		
6/14/03	**76**	4		Get Down...S:45 / A:75		album cut
				from the album *God's Son* on Columbia 86930		
7/19/03	**72**	5		Nas' Angels...The Flyest..A:70		album cut
				NAS Feat. Pharrell		
				from the movie *Charlie's Angels: Full Throttle* starring Cameron Diaz (soundtrack on Columbia 90132)		
11/22/03	**48**	20		Quick To Back Down.............................S:15 / A:51		Ill Will 76793 (T)
				BRAVEHEARTS featuring Nas and Lil Jon		
				NATE DOGG		
3/8/03	**❶**7	28		21 Questions S:❶1 / A:❶8		Shady 080739 (T)
				50 CENT Feat. Nate Dogg		
				samples "It's Only Love Doing Its Thing" by Barry White		

DEBUT DATE	PEAK POS	WKS CHR	G L D	ARTIST / Title	Sales/Air	Label & Number
				NATE DOGG — Cont'd		
8/2/03	80	9		Ooh Wee	S:61	album cut
				MARK RONSON (featuring Ghostface & Nate Dogg)		
				from Ronson's album *Here Comes The Fuzz* on Elektra 62839		
8/9/03	66	13		My Name	A:62	album cut
				XZIBIT Featuring Eminem & Nate Dogg		
				from Xzibit's album *Man vs Machine* on Loud 85925		
10/18/03+	22	23		Gangsta Nation	S:7 / A:22	Hoo-Bangin' 53289 (T)
				WESTSIDE CONNECTION Featuring Nate Dogg		
11/22/03+	39	19		The Set Up	S:8 / A:39	Shady 002038 (T)
				OBIE TRICE Featuring Nas & Lil Jon		
12/20/03+	57	15		What Would You Do	A:57	album cut
				DAMIZZA PRESENTS: Shade Sheist, Nate Dogg & Mariah Carey		
				NELLY		
6/21/03	3	23		Shake Ya Tailfeather	A:3	album cut
				NELLY/P. DIDDY/MURPHY LEE		
				from the movie *Bad Boys II* starring Will Smith and Martin Lawrence (soundtrack on Bad Boy 000716)		
10/25/03	51	14		Iz U	S:34 / A:52	album cut
				from the album *Da Derrty Versions - The Reinvention* on Fo' Reel 001665		
				NORFUL, Smokie ★		
8/23/03	45	20		I Need You Now..	S:25 / A:45 [L]	EMI Gospel 77947
				NOTORIOUS B.I.G., The — see 2PAC		
				OL DIRTY BASTARD — see SIGEL, Beanie		
				112		
7/26/03	24	13		Na Na Na	S:4 / A:30	Bad Boy 000940
				112 featuring Super Cat		
9/27/03	29	18		Hot & Wet	S:12 / A:31	Bad Boy 001150 (T)
				112 Featuring Ludacris		
				OSBORNE, Jeffrey		
7/12/03	75	9		Rest Of Our Lives	A:72	album cut
				from the album *Music Is Life* on Jay Oz 8452		
				OUTERSPACE ★		
				Male rap duo from Philadelphia, Pennsylvania: Crypt Warchild and Planetary.		
3/22/03	45^S	1		151		Babygrande 0103 (T)
				OUTKAST		
2/8/03	42	17		A.D.I.D.A.S.	A:39	album cut
				KILLER MIKE Featuring Big Boi		
				A.D.I.D.A.S.: All Day I Dream About Sex; from Killer Mike's album *Monster* on Columbia 86862		
8/2/03	93	3		GhettoMusick	S:18	Arista 54249 (T)
				samples "Love, Want And Need You" by Patti LaBelle		
9/13/03+	2³	30↑	▲	The Way You Move /	A:2 / S:3	
				OUTKAST Featuring Sleepy Brown		
11/15/03+	9	21↑		Hey Ya!	A:9	Arista 54962 (D)
				PABLO, Petey		
1/18/03	98	3		Club Banger	S:65	Jive 40072 (T)
12/20/03+	17↑	16↑		Freek-A-Leek..	S:10 / A:16	Jive 58745 (T)
				PAN'JABI MC		
4/12/03	21	20		Beware Of The Boys (Mundian To Bach Ke).............	S:❶¹ / A:21	Sequence 8012 (M)
				PAN'JABI MC Featuring Jay-Z		
				Indian vocals by Labh Janjua; samples the theme from TV's *Knight Rider*		
				PAPA REU		
4/19/03	98	2		Represent		Reu Musik 1001 (T)
				PAPA REU Featuring Lil' Flip, Lil' Keke & Hawk		
				PASTOR TROY		
2/8/03	44^S	1		You Can't Pimp Me..		Madd Society 019635 (T)
4/26/03	88	8		Who Run This	S:2	Body Head 274771
				ROY JONES, JR. Featuring Pastor Troy, Lil John And The Eastside Boyz		
				PAUL, Sean		
2/15/03	❶¹	34		Get Busy	A:2 / S:6	VP/Atlantic 88020 (T)
5/31/03	9	20		Like Glue	A:9 / S:19	VP/Atlantic 88145 (T)
7/5/03	❶⁵	33		Baby Boy	A:❶⁵ / S:30	Columbia 76867 (T)
				BEYONCÉ feat. Sean Paul		
				Sean Paul is featured on the CD promo single (does NOT appear on the commercial 12" single)		
8/9/03	43^S	6		Shoomp		AOI 4125 (T)
				DE LA SOUL Feat Sean Paul		
11/15/03+	13↑	21↑		I'm Still In Love With You..	S:7 / A:13	VP/Atlantic 88253
				SEAN PAUL Featuring Sasha		

DEBUT DATE	PEAK POS	WKS CHR	G L D	ARTIST / Title	Sales/Air	Label & Number
				PEEDI CRAKK ★		
5/10/03	33ˢ	9		One For Peedi Crakk...		Roc-A-Fella 000396 (T)
8/16/03	95	2		When You Hear That...................................	S:35	Roc-A-Fella 000978 (T)
				BEANIE SIGEL feat. Peedi Crakk and Dirt McGirt		
				PHAROAHE MONCH		
6/28/03	48ˢ	4		Agent Orange		Rawkus 000760 (T)
				PHARRELL ★		
1/25/03	3	30		Beautiful	A:3 / S:7	Priority 77887 (T)
				SNOOP DOGG featuring Pharrell, Uncle Charlie Wilson		
4/5/03	86	3		Come Close Remix (Closer)...........................	S:15	MCA 000575
				COMMON Feat. Erykah Badu, Pharrell From The Neptunes, and Q-Tip		
				remix of Common's #21 hit for 2002		
5/17/03	❶⁶	33		Frontin'	A:❶⁵ / S:2	Star Trak 58647
				PHARRELL Featuring Jay-Z		
5/24/03	96	1		Belly Dancer..	S:36	MCA 113949 (T)
				KARDINAL OFFISHALL Featuring Pharrell Williams		
7/5/03	23	20		Light Your A** On Fire................................	S:5 / A:23	Star Trak 54245 (T)
				BUSTA RHYMES Featuring Pharrell		
7/19/03	72	5		Nas' Angels...The Flyest.............................	A:70	album cut
				NAS Feat. Pharrell		
				from the movie *Charlie's Angels: Full Throttle* starring Cameron Diaz (soundtrack on Columbia 90132)		
				PITCH BLACK ★		
				Male rap group from Brooklyn, New York: DG, Devious, Fast, GOD and Zakee.		
12/27/03	27ˢ	10		It's All Real...		Universal 001067 (T)
				PLANET ASIA ★		
				Born Jason Green in 1976 in Fresno, California. Male rapper.		
3/15/03	53ˢ	3		Golden Age		Threshold 3231 (T)
				PLANET ASIA Featuring KutMasta Kurt		
				PLAYBOY SHANE ★		
10/4/03	98	2		What Cha Gone Do....................................	S:7	Ball Hawg 60652
				PLAYBOY SHANE Featuring Lil Flip		
				POP SHOP ★		
				Born Lawrence Lucas in Charlotte, North Carolina. Male rapper.		
11/8/03	9ˢ	20↑		Look Ya		Gogetta 1069
				POWELL, Jesse		
10/4/03	99	1		By The Way...	S:9	D3/Riviera 9922
				POWW BROS., The ★		
				Vocal duo from Detroit, Michigan: brothers John and Shawn Powe (former members of UNV).		
1/18/03	97	1		Faithful To..	S:5	Powwer Moves 90457
				PRICE, Kelly		
3/8/03	58	19		He Proposed..	A:57	album cut
				from the album *Priceless* on Def Soul 586777		
				PROJECT 2B, The ★		
				Male rap duo from Florence, South Carolina: Danny Cayetano and Rockiem Joiner.		
7/5/03	17ˢ	17		Uh Oh		NyCe 1014
				PUFF DADDY		
3/29/03	54	9		Hooked..	A:54	album cut
				MARY J. BLIGE Featuring P. Diddy		
6/21/03	3	23		Shake Ya Tailfeather	A:3	album cut
				NELLY/P. DIDDY/MURPHY LEE		
				from the movie *Bad Boys II* starring Will Smith and Martin Lawrence (soundtrack on Bad Boy 000716)		
7/26/03	35	20		Summertime...	S:15 / A:34	Columbia 76915 (T)
				BEYONCÉ featuring P. Diddy		
				from the movie *The Fighting Temptations* starring Beyoncé and Cuba Gooding Jr.		
9/6/03	69	10		Girl I'm A Bad Boy.....................................	A:68	album cut
				FAT JOE & P. DIDDY Feat. Dre		
				from the movie *Bad Boys II* starring Will Smith and Martin Lawrence (soundtrack on Bad Boy 000716)		
				Q-TIP — see COMMON		
				RAEKWON		
6/14/03	56ˢ	4		Smith Bros		Ice Water 2999 (T)
				RAH DIGGA		
7/12/03	34ˢ	3		Call The Ambulance...................................		J Records 53716 (T)
				BUSTA RHYMES (feat. Rah Digga & M.O.P.)		
8/16/03	65	20		Party & Bullsh*t 2003	S:31 / A:60	Flipmode 55499 (T)
				RAHZEL		
5/31/03	73ˢ	1		Guess		Echelon 001 (T)

DEBUT DATE	PEAK POS	WKS CHR	GLD	ARTIST / Title	Sales/Air	Label & Number
				RAMSEY, Tarralyn ★		
12/27/03+	95	3		Up Against All Odds	S:32	Casablanca 001813
				RASHAD ★		
				Born Rashad Thomas in Ohio. Male singer.		
5/10/03	27^S	5		Sweet Misery		Fo' Reel 000260
				RAYNE, Tha'		
8/2/03	76	14		Didn't You Know	S:21	Arista 56688
				REDMAN — see JONELL		
				REVENUE ★		
2/8/03	92	10		Up In Da Club 2Nite	S:3	Stack A Grip 10002
				RJD2		
3/8/03	42^S	3		The Horror		Definitive Jux 46 (**T**)
10/11/03	70^S	1		Explosive		Chocolate Ind. 037 (**T**)
				DIVERSE Featuring RJD2 and Lyrics Born		
				ROCK, Pete, & C.L. Smooth		
4/26/03	49^S	3		Shine On Me!		St. Nick 0001 (**T**)
				ROEZ BOYZ ★		
4/26/03	97	4		63/64	S:7	Green Teeth 0452
				RONSON, Mark ★		
				Born in 1978 in London, England; raised in New York. White DJ/producer/remixer.		
8/2/03	80	9		Ooh Wee	S:61	album cut
				MARK RONSON (featuring Ghostface & Nate Dogg)		
				from the album *Here Comes The Fuzz* on Elektra 62839		
				ROSCOE		
5/17/03	95	2		Head To Toe		Priority 77911 (**T**)
				ROSCOE featuring Sleepy Brown		
7/5/03	73	12		Smooth Sailin'	A:71	Priority 52731
				samples "Brazilian Rhyme (Interlude)" by Earth, Wind & Fire		
				ROWLAND, Kelly		
2/22/03	72	7		Can't Nobody	S:68 / A:75	Music World 79839 (**T**)
				ROYCE DA 5'9"		
1/4/03	46^S	6		Mr. Baller		Game 2017 (**T**)
				ROYCE DA 5'9" Featuring Clipse		
				RUSSELL ★		
4/26/03	16^S	17		Rich Man		R Records 91008
				RUSSELL Feat. R. Kelly		
				written and produced by R. Kelly		
				SADAT X		
3/29/03	54^S	1		Plan X		Fat Beats 004 (**T**)
				SANTANA, Juelz ★		
				Born LaRon James in 1984 in Manhattan, New York. Male rapper. Member of The Diplomats.		
3/29/03	94	1		Built This City	S:42	Roc-A-Fella 077007 (**T**)
				DIPLOMATS feat. Cam'ron, Jimmy Jones and Juelz Santana		
				samples "We Built This City" by Starship		
4/5/03	64	11		Dipset Anthem	S:24 / A:66	Roc-A-Fella 077995 (**T**)
				DIPLOMATS feat. Cam'ron and Juelz Santana		
				samples "One In A Million" by Sam Dees		
8/2/03	70	10		Dipset (Santana's Town)	S:35 / A:74	Roc-A-Fella 000807 (**T**)
				JUELZ SANTANA Feat. Cam'ron		
				samples "Anvil Chorus" by The Chicago Symphony and Chorus		
				SARAI ★		
3/15/03	90	2		Pack Ya Bags	S:6	Epic 79841
				SASHA ★		
				Born in Kingston, Jamaica; raised in New York. Female dancehall reggae singer.		
8/30/03	79	8		Dat Sexy Body		VP 6366 (**T**)
11/15/03+	13↑	21↑		I'm Still In Love With You	S:7 / A:13	VP/Atlantic 88253
				SEAN PAUL Featuring Sasha		
				S.A. SMASH ★		
				Male rap duo from Columbus, Ohio: Camutao and Metro.		
6/7/03	64^S	1		Gangsta		Definitive Jux 52 (**T**)
11/29/03	69^S	1		Illy		Definitive Jux 69 (**T**)
				SCARFACE		
5/24/03	60^S	2		Someday		Def Jam S. 000399 (**T**)
				SCARFACE Featuring Faith Evans		

R&B SINGLES

DEBUT DATE	PEAK POS	WKS CHR	G L D	ARTIST / Title	Sales/Air	Label & Number
				SEDUCTION		
7/19/03	94	4		All Night Long	S:6	Jenstar 1384
				SEDUCTION with Saddler		
				SERMON, Erick		
2/1/03	80	9		Love Iz	S:47	J Records 21256 (T)
				ERICK SERMON Featuring Al Green		
				samples "Love & Happiness" by Al Green and "Here We Go" by Run-D.M.C.		
				702		
1/4/03	98	2		Star	S:7	Motown 019583
				702 Featuring Clipse		
2/15/03	31^S	4		Blah Blah Blah Blah		Motown 019716 (T)
3/22/03	49	20		I Still Love You	A:48	album cut
				from the album Star on Motown 066130		
				SHADE SHEIST		
2/15/03	66	8		John Doe	A:64	album cut
				SHADE SHEIST Featuring DJ Quik, Hi-C, AMG & Swift		
				from the album Informal Introduction on Baby Ree 112957		
12/20/03+	57	15		What Would You Do	A:57	album cut
				DAMIZZA PRESENTS: Shade Sheist, Nate Dogg & Mariah Carey		
				SHEEK LOUCH ★		
				Born Sean Jacobs in Yonkers, New York. Male rapper. Member of The Lox.		
7/12/03	92	3		OK	S:40	Universal 000774 (T)
8/16/03	65	12		Mighty D-Block (2 Guns Up)	A:63	album cut
				SHEEK LOUCH Featuring Jadakiss, Styles & J-Hood		
				from the album Walk Witt Me on D-Block 001042		
				SHOTGUN THE REPRESENTER ★		
6/21/03	10^S	15		Chow Chow Chow		Black 5 0005
				SIGEL, Beanie		
8/16/03	95	2		When You Hear That	S:35	Roc-A-Fella 000978 (T)
				BEANIE SIGEL feat. Peedi Crakk and Dirt McGirt		
				SKILLZ		
6/28/03	92	4		Off The Wall	S:53	Rawkus 000761 (T)
				SLUM VILLAGE		
1/11/03	93	3		Disco		Barak 51639 (T)
				SLUM VILLAGE Featuring Ms. Jade & Rajeshwari		
				SMOKE BULGA ★		
				Born in Boston, Massachusetts. Male rapper.		
6/21/03	60^S	2		Smoke Did It		Epic 79854 (T)
				SMOOT ★		
9/6/03	98	2		Let's Get It	S:7	RapRock/Pyramid 10422
				SMOOT featuring Jadakiss & Swizz Beatz		
				SNOOP DOGG		
1/25/03	3	30		Beautiful	A:3 / S:7	Priority 77887 (T)
				SNOOP DOGG featuring Pharrell, Uncle Charlie Wilson		
9/6/03	2^1	24		Holidae In	A:2 / S:6	Disturb. Tha P. 52816 (T)
				CHINGY featuring Ludacris & Snoop Dogg		
10/25/03	68	9		It Blows My Mind	A:65	album cut
				from the various artists album The Neptunes Present...Clones on Star Trak 51295		
12/20/03	78	16↑		The Way I Am	S:53	Desert Storm 67508 (T)
				KNOC-TURN'AL featuring Snoop Dogg		
				SOLANGE ★		
1/4/03	73	9		Feelin' You	S:3	Music World 79831 (M)
				SOUL POSITION ★		
10/4/03	74^S	2		Jerry Springer Episode		Fat Beats 2506 (T)
				SPARXXX, Bubba		
6/21/03	98	2		Jimmy Mathis	S:9	Beatclub 000746
				samples "Stone Fox Chase" by Area Code 615		
				STAGGA LEE ★		
3/15/03	68	16		Roll Wit M.V.P. (We Be Like! The La La Song)	S:19 / A:69	Artist Direct 01128
				samples "Lovin' You" by Minnie Riperton		
				STEVENSON, Dani ★		
10/11/03	48^S	3		Honk Your Horn		Universal 019351
				DANI STEVENSON Featuring Missy Elliott		
				STRICK! ★		
12/6/03	56^S	1		Born Wit It		Mac Mil 002 (T)

DEBUT DATE	PEAK POS	WKS CHR	G L D	ARTIST / Title	Sales/Air	Label & Number
				STUDDARD, Ruben		
6/21/03	2¹	20		Superstar	S:❶⁸ / A:33	J Records 51786
				#2 Pop hit for the Carpenters in 1971		
12/20/03+	2²	16↑		Sorry 2004	A:❶¹	album cut
				from the album *Soulful* on J Records 54639		
				STYLES		
8/16/03	65	12		Mighty D-Block (2 Guns Up) A:63		album cut
				SHEEK LOUCH Featuring Jadakiss, Styles & J-Hood		
				from the album *Walk Witt Me* on D-Block 001042		
				SUPER CAT — see 112		
				SWIZZ BEATZ		
9/6/03	98	2		Let's Get It S:7		RapRock/Pyramid 10422
				SMOOT featuring Jadakiss & Swizz Beatz		
10/25/03	57	20		Get It On The Floor ....S:28 / A:60		Def Jam 001440 (T)
				DMX featuring Swizz Beatz		
				TAG TEAM — see FUNN CLUB		
				TAMIA		
5/24/03	6	26		Into You	A:6 / S:15	Desert Storm 67452 (T)
				FABOLOUS Featuring Ashanti or Tamia		
				the version with Ashanti is from his album *Street Dreams* on Desert Storm 62791; the version with Tamia is available as a promo single only		
5/31/03	31	26		Officially Missing You ....S:9 / A:32		Elektra 67436 (M)
				TANK — see LIL' ZANE		
				THALIA ★		
6/7/03	61	14		I Want You A:61		Virgin 47305 (T)
				THALIA featuring Fat Joe		
				samples "A Little Bit Of Love" by Brenda Russell		
				THICKE ★		
3/15/03	34ˢ	9		When I Get You Alone		Nu America 497783
				THOMAS, Carl		
12/20/03+	56	14		She Is A:55		album cut
				CARL THOMAS Featuring LL Cool J		
				from the album *Let's Talk About It* on Bad Boy 118802		
				THREE 6 MAFIA		
5/31/03	62	19		Ridin Spinners ....A:62 / S:72		album cut
				THREE 6 MAFIA Featuring Lil' Flip		
				from the album *Da Unbreakables* on Hypnotize Minds 89030		
				T.I.		
1/4/03	8	35		Never Scared	S:5 / A:8	Break-Em-Off 50870 (T)
				BONE CRUSHER Featuring Killer Mike & T.I.		
				first released as a promotional CD maxi-single in very limited quantities with no bar-code on the actual product (label assigned it a number of 777); the 12" above is the widely available release		
5/24/03	27	25		24's ....A:28 / S:39		Atlantic 88124 (T)
10/25/03	55	20		Be Easy A:54		album cut
				from the album *Trap Muzik* on Grand Hustle 83650		
11/22/03+	15↑	20↑		Rubber Band Man.......................................S:14 / A:14		Atlantic 88322 (T)
				TIMBALAND AND MAGOO		
7/12/03	49	14		Cop That Sh#! ....S:15 / A:51		Blackground 001609 (T)
				TIMBALAND & MAGOO featuring Missy Elliott		
11/22/03+	52	20		I'll Be Around ....S:15 / A:52		Arista 59811 (T)
				CEE-LO Featuring Timbaland		
11/29/03	73	9		Indian Flute..A:70		album cut
				TIMBALAND & MAGOO Featuring Sebastian & Raje Shwari		
				from the album *Under Construction Part II* on Blackground 001185		
				TIMBERLAKE, Justin		
4/12/03	45	16		Rock Your Body...A:43		album cut
8/30/03	75	12		Still On My Brain A:75		album cut
				above 2 from the album *Justified* on Jive 41823		
				TLC		
5/10/03	40ˢ	5	●	Hands Up		Arista 51157 (D)
12/27/03	81	6		Come Get Some S:36		Arista 57820 (T)
				TLC Featuring Lil' Jon & Sean Paul of YoungBloodZ		
				TOO $HORT		
8/9/03	56	20		Shake That Monkey..................................S:41 / A:56		$hort 55065 (T)
				TOO $HORT feat Lil Jon & The Eastside Boyz		
				TRIBE CALLED QUEST, A — see VIOLATOR		

DEBUT DATE	PEAK POS	WKS CHR	G L D	ARTIST Title	Sales/Air	Label & Number
				TRICE, Obie		
8/30/03	**33**	13		Got Some Teeth..	S:13 / A:32	Shady 001116 (**T**)
				co-written and produced by Eminem		
11/22/03+	**39**	19		The Set Up..	S:8 / A:39	Shady 002038 (**T**)
				OBIE TRICE Featuring Nate Dogg		
				TRICK DADDY — see 2PAC		
				TRILLVILLE ★		
10/11/03+	**28**	26↑		Neva Eva...	S:4 / A:30	BME 16505
				TRIPLE THREAT ★		
				Male rap production trio from San Francisco, California: Apollo, Shortkut and Vinroc.		
3/15/03	**61**^S	2		Hit Em Off...		Fat Beats 2503 (**T**)
				TRIPLE THREAT Featuring Zion I		
				TWEET		
11/29/03	**22**^S	4		Thugman..		Elektra 67495 (**T**)
				TWEET featuring Missy Elliott		
				TWISTA		
5/31/03	**60**	20		Thug Luv...	S:28 / A:60	Queen Bee 88246
				LIL' KIM (feat. Twista)		
11/15/03+	**❶**²	21↑		Slow Jamz	A:❶² / S:5	Atlantic 88288 (**T**)
				TWISTA Featuring Kanye West & Jamie Foxx		
				samples "A House Is Not A Home" by Luther Vandross		
				213 ★		
8/23/03	**39**	19		Fly...	A:36	album cut
				2PAC		
2/22/03	**31**	23		Still Ballin...	A:31	album cut
				2PAC Featuring Trick Daddy		
				from the album *Better Dayz* on Amaru 497070		
10/11/03	**11**	21		Runnin (Dying To Live).......................................	S:3 / A:11	Amaru 001670 (**T**)
				TUPAC Featuring The Notorious B.I.G.		
				new mix (produced by Eminem) of their #62 hit in 1997		
				TYRESE		
5/17/03	**18**	23		Signs Of Love Makin'...	A:17	J Records 52518 (**D**)
9/13/03	**65**	6		Pick Up The Phone...	A:63	album cut
				TYRESE AND LUDACRIS feat. R. Kelly		
				from the movie *2 Fast 2 Furious* starring Paul Walker and Tyrese (soundtrack on Def Jam South 000426)		
				UNION TURNPIKE ★		
2/8/03	**47**^S	4		Oh!..		Epic 79827
				samples "The Stroke" by Billy Squier and "Jam Master Jay" by Run-D.M.C.; featured in the Fox-TV series *Fastlane*		
				URBAN MONARCHY ★		
11/29/03	**74**^S	1		411-69*69		Benchmark 001 (**T**)
				VAKILL ★		
				Born in Chicago, Illinois. Male rapper.		
3/22/03	**67**^S	1		End Of Days...		Moleman 013 (**T**)
				VALENTINE, Sunny ★		
				Born in Tyler, Texas. Male rapper.		
11/15/03	**23**^S	14		Leave It All Behind...		Camp David 5203
				SUNNY VALENTINE (featuring Sleepy Brown)		
				VANDROSS, Luther		
5/17/03	**28**	30		Dance With My Father..	A:27 / S:46	J Records 57595 (**D**)
				written by Vandross and Richard Marx; backing vocalists include Cissy Houston		
6/28/03	**67**^S	1		Smooth Love		Epic 32123
12/6/03+	**33**↑	18↑		Think About You...	A:33	album cut
				from the album *Dance With Me Father* on J Records 51885		
				VIOLATOR		
11/8/03	**89**	5		I C U (Doin' It)...	S:20	Violator 57358 (**T**)
				VIOLATOR FEATURING A TRIBE CALLED QUEST AND ERYKAH BADU		
				samples "High On Sunshine" by the Commodores and "Wild Thang" by 2 Much		
11/29/03+	**92**	8		Keep Doin' It..	S:36	Violator 57615 (**T**)
				VIOLATOR Featuring Mystikal, Dirtbag & Busta Rhymes		
				WC AND THE MAAD CIRCLE		
3/1/03	**97**	2		Flirt		Def Jam 163797 (**T**)
				WC Featuring Case		

DEBUT DATE	PEAK POS	WKS CHR	G L D	ARTIST Title	Sales/Air	Label & Number
				WEST, Kanye		
10/18/03+	8	25↑		Through The Wire	A:8 / S:10	Roc-A-Fella 001441 (T)
				samples "Through The Fire" by Chaka Khan		
11/15/03+	❶²	21↑		Slow Jamz	A:❶² / S:5	Atlantic 88288 (T)
				TWISTA Featuring Kanye West & Jamie Foxx		
				samples "A House Is Not A Home" by Luther Vandross		
				WESTSIDE CONNECTION		
5/24/03	61	20		Lights Out	A:58	album cut
				MACK 10 Featuring Westside Connection & Knoc-Turn'Al		
				from Mack 10's album *Ghetto, Gutter & Gangsta* on Hoo-Bangin' 970028		
10/18/03+	22	23		Gangsta Nation	S:7 / A:22	Hoo-Bangin' 53289 (T)
				WESTSIDE CONNECTION Featuring Nate Dogg		
				WILDCHILD		
4/19/03	33ˢ	2		Code Red		Stone Throw 2060 (T)
				WILSON, Charlie — see SNOOP DOGG		
				WINANS, Mario		
2/22/03	52	20		Crush On You	S:15 / A:52	Universal 000448 (T)
				MR. CHEEKS Featuring Mario Winans		
10/4/03	28	20		Down For Me	A:27	album cut
				LOON Feat. Mario Winans		
				from the album *Loon* on Bad Boy 000892		
				WONDER, Wayne		
10/18/03	85	9		Anything Goes	S:23	album cut
				CNN (CAPONE-N-N.O.R.E.), WAYNE WONDER and LEXXUS		
				from the various artists album *Red Star Sounds Presents Def Jamaica* on Def Jam 001195		
				XZIBIT		
1/11/03	63	15		Symphony In X Major	S:62 / A:62	Loud 79838 (T)
				XZIBIT Featuring Dr. Dre		
3/29/03	73	2		Choke Me, Spank Me (Pull My Hair)	A:73	album cut
8/9/03	66	13		My Name	A:62	album cut
				XZIBIT Featuring Eminem & Nate Dogg		
				above 2 from the album *Man vs Machine* on Loud 85925		
				YING YANG TWINS		
4/12/03	2²	52↑		Get Low	A:2 / S:6	BME 2377 (T)
				LIL JON & THE EAST SIDE BOYZ Featuring Ying Yang Twins		
7/5/03	43	20		Naggin	A:43 / S:44	Collipark 2481 (T)
10/4/03+	9	27↑		Salt Shaker	S:5 / A:9	Collipark 2485 (T)
				YING YANG TWINS Feat. LIL JON & THE EAST SIDE BOYZ		
11/29/03	15ˢ	1		Get Low Remix	[R]	BME 2394 (T)
				LIL JON & THE EAST SIDE BOYZ Feat. Elephant Man, Busta Rhymes & Ying Yang Twins		
				YOUNGBLOODZ		
6/28/03	2³	41↑		Damn!	A:2 / S:8	So So Def 52215 (T)
				YOUNGBLOODZ Featuring Lil' Jon		
11/15/03	94	4		Lean Low	S:34	So So Def 54629 (T)
				YOUNGBLOODZ Featuring Backbone		
12/27/03	81	6		Come Get Some	S:36	Arista 57820 (T)
				TLC Featuring Lil' Jon & Sean Paul of YoungBloodZ		
				YOUNG GUNZ ★		
5/31/03	10	29		Can't Stop, Won't Stop	A:9	album cut
				samples "Overweight Lovers In The House" by Heavy D and "Super Rappin'" by Grandmaster Flash; from the various artists album *The Chain Gang Vol. II* on Roc-A-Fella 000971		
				ZION ★		
6/7/03	92	5		Blowin' Me Up (Callin' Me)	S:5	Zion 6055

1. 50 CENT
990

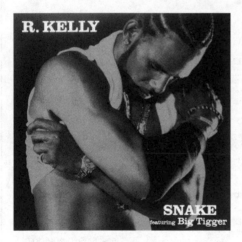

2. R. KELLY
730

3. JAY-Z
482

4.	410	BEYONCÉ ★		13.	264	AALIYAH
5.	352	LUDACRIS		14.	262	ASHANTI
6.	350	BUSTA RHYMES		15.	260	LIL' KIM
7.	302	P. DIDDY		16.	251	JAHEIM
8.	302	SEAN PAUL		17.	248	GINUWINE
9.	300 +	LIL JON & THE EAST SIDE BOYZ		18.	247	CHINGY ★
10.	292	MISSY ELLIOTT		19.	246	B2K
11.	279	FABOLOUS		20.	234	MONICA
12.	276	MARY J. BLIGE				

+ Subject to change since a title that peaked in 2003 by this artist is still charted as of the 4/3/04 cut-off date.

TOP 40 R&B/HIP-HOP SINGLES

PEAK DATE	CH	40	10	PK	RANK	RECORD TITLE	PEAK POSITION	ARTIST
						1		
2/15	32	28	16	9	1.	In Da Club		50 Cent
12/20	23 +	22 +	15	9	2.	You Don't Know My Name		Alicia Keys
5/3	28	23	14	7	3.	21 Questions		50 Cent Feat. Nate Dogg
8/16	33	27	13	6	4.	Frontin'		Pharrell Featuring Jay-Z
6/21	31	29	16	5	5.	So Gone		Monica
11/1	32	27	14	5	6.	Stand Up		Ludacris featuring Shawnna
9/27	33	25	12	5	7.	Baby Boy		Beyoncé feat. Sean Paul
1/25	37	32	16	3	8.	Miss You		Aaliyah
7/26	25	25	13	3	9.	Crazy In Love		Beyoncé (Featuring Jay-Z)
12/6	60 +	39 +	15	2	10.	Step In The Name Of Love		R. Kelly
4/26	34	31	13	1	11.	Get Busy		Sean Paul
4/19	23	19	12	1	12.	Excuse Me Miss		Jay-Z
						2		
2/1	36	34	18	5	13.	Ignition		R. Kelly
10/4	41 +	35 +	19	3	14.	Damn!		Youngbloodz Featuring Lil' Jon
5/17	28	24	12	3	15.	Can't Let You Go		Fabolous featuring Mike Shorey & Lil' Mo
6/14	26	22	12	3	16.	Magic Stick		Lil' Kim Featuring 50 Cent
9/6	52 +	43	19	2	17.	Get Low		Lil Jon & The East Side Boyz Featuring Ying Yang Twins
8/23	33	28	12	2	18.	P.I.M.P.		50 Cent
1/18	20	17	9	2	19.	Bump, Bump, Bump		B2K & P. Diddy
8/9	43	33	17	1	20.	Right Thurr		Chingy
12/27	34 +	31 +	16	1	21.	Walked Outta Heaven		Jagged Edge
5/24	29	23	13	1	22.	I Know What You Want		Busta Rhymes And Mariah Carey (feat. The Flipmode Squad)
11/8	29	22	8	1	23.	Rain On Me		Ashanti
11/15	24	20	8	1	24.	Holidae In		Chingy featuring Ludacris & Snoop Dogg
6/28	20	13	1	1	25.	Superstar		Ruben Studdard
						3		
4/12	30	23	12	3	26.	Beautiful		Snoop Dogg featuring Pharrell & Uncle Charlie Wilson
7/26	27	24	10	3	27.	In Those Jeans		Ginuwine
3/15	38	30	15	2	28.	How You Gonna Act Like That		Tyrese
9/20	23	22	7	1	29.	Shake Ya Tailfeather		Nelly/P. Diddy/Murphy Lee
						4		
2/8	31	25	7	2	30.	Wanksta		50 Cent
2/22	21	18	7	2	31.	All I Have		Jennifer Lopez Featuring LL Cool J
7/5	20	17	7	1	32.	Rock Wit U (Awww Baby)		Ashanti
						5		
12/27	35 +	29 +	14	5	33.	Read Your Mind		Avant
2/22	20	17	8	3	34.	Gossip Folks		Missy Elliott (Featuring Ludacris)
2/8	20	17	7	2	35.	Mesmerize		Ja Rule feat. Ashanti
5/24	35	30	8	1	36.	Put That Woman First		Jaheim
						6		
8/23	26	22	9	5	37.	Into You		Fabolous Featuring Tamia Or Ashanti
10/4	26	24	9	3	38.	Thoia Thoing		R. Kelly
1/11	28	19	7	3	39.	I Should Be...		Dru Hill
12/20	20	16	8	1	40.	Change Clothes		Jay-Z

#1 R&B/HIP-HOP SINGLES & TRACKS

	Date Hit #1	Wks @ #1	Title	Artist
1.	1/4	4	Love Of My Life (An Ode To Hip Hop) ..... *Erykah Badu Featuring Common* (includes 1 week at #1 in 2002)	
2.	1/25	3	Miss You .... *Aaliyah*	
3.	2/15	9	In Da Club .... *50 Cent*	
4.	4/19	1	Excuse Me Miss .... *Jay-Z*	
5.	4/26	1	Get Busy .... *Sean Paul*	
6.	5/3	7	21 Questions .... *50 Cent Feat. Nate Dogg*	
7.	6/21	5	So Gone .... *Monica*	
8.	7/26	3	Crazy In Love .... *Beyoncé (Featuring Jay-Z)*	
9.	8/16	6	Frontin' .... *Pharrell Featuring Jay-Z*	
10.	9/27	5	Baby Boy .... *Beyoncé (Featuring Sean Paul)*	
11.	11/1	5	Stand Up .... *Ludacris featuring Shawnna*	
12.	12/6	2	Step In The Name Of Love .... *R. Kelly*	
13.	12/20	9	You Don't Know My Name .... *Alicia Keys* (includes 7 weeks at #1 in 2004)	

#1 R&B/HIP-HOP AIRPLAY

	Date Hit #1	Wks @ #1	Title	Artist
1.	1/4	4	Love Of My Life (An Ode To Hip Hop) ...... *Erykah Badu Featuring Common* (includes 1 week at #1 in 2002)	
2.	1/25	3	Miss You .... *Aaliyah*	
3.	2/15	9	In Da Club .... *50 Cent*	
4.	4/19	1	Excuse Me Miss .... *Jay-Z*	
5.	4/26	8	21 Questions .... *50 Cent Feat. Nate Dogg*	
6.	6/21	1	Magic Stick .... *Lil' Kim Featuring 50 Cent*	
7.	6/28	3	So Gone .... *Monica*	
8.	7/19	4	Crazy In Love .... *Beyoncé (Featuring Jay-Z)*	
9.	8/16	1	In Those Jeans .... *Ginuwine*	
10.	8/23	5	Frontin' .... *Pharrell Featuring Jay-Z*	
11.	9/27	5	Baby Boy .... *Beyoncé (Featuring Sean Paul)*	
12.	11/1	5	Stand Up .... *Ludacris featuring Shawnna*	
13.	12/6	2	Step In The Name Of Love .... *H. Kelly*	
14.	12/20	9	You Don't Know My Name .... *Alicia Keys* (includes 7 weeks at #1 in 2004)	

#1 R&B/HIP-HOP SINGLES SALES

	Date Hit #1	Wks @ #1	Title	Artist
1.	1/4	17	**Ignition** .... *R. Kelly* (includes 9 weeks at #1 in 2002)	
2.	3/1	1	**Through The Rain** .... *Mariah Carey*	
3.	3/8	4	**Cry Me A River** .... *Justin Timberlake*	
4.	4/5	2	**Emotional Rollercoaster** .... *Vivian Green*	
5.	4/19	2	**Guess What (Guess Again) Remix** .... *Syleena Johnson featuring R. Kelly*	
6.	5/3	1	**All Life Long** .... *Mo Thugs*	
7.	5/10	1	**Beware Of The Boys (Mundian To Bach Ke)** ...*Panjabi MC Featuring Jay-Z*	
8.	5/17	2	**Miss You** .... *Aaliyah*	
9.	5/31	1	**21 Questions** .... *50 Cent Feat. Nate Dogg*	
10.	6/7	1	**In Love Wit Chu** .... *Da Brat Featuring Cherish*	
11.	6/14	1	**Don't Wanna Try** .... *Frankie J.*	
12.	6/21	1	**Snake/I'll Never Leave** .... *R. Kelly featuring Cam'ron and Big Tigger*	
13.	6/28	8	**Superstar/Flying Without Wings** .... *Ruben Studdard*	
14.	8/23	2	**Love @ 1st Sight** .... *Mary J. Blige featuring Method Man*	
15.	9/6	12↕	**Walked Outta Heaven** .... *Jagged Edge*	
16.	11/22	2↕	**Read Your Mind** .... *Avant*	
17.	12/13	3	**One More Chance** .... *Michael Jackson*	

#1 HOT RAP TRACKS

	Date Hit #1	Wks @ #1	Title	Artist
1.	1/4	12	**Work It** .... *Missy "Misdemeanor" Elliott* (includes 9 weeks at #1 in 2002)	
2.	1/25	2	**Air Force Ones** .... *Nelly Featuring Kyjuan, Ali & Murphy Lee*	
3.	2/8	12	**In Da Club** .... *50 Cent*	
4.	5/3	7	**21 Questions** .... *50 Cent Feat. Nate Dogg*	
5.	6/21	5	**Magic Stick** .... *Lil' Kim Featuring 50 Cent*	
6.	7/26	4	**Right Thurr** .... *Chingy*	
7.	8/23	2	**P.I.M.P.** .... *50 Cent*	
8.	9/6	3↕	**Get Low** .... *Lil Jon & The East Side Boyz Featuring Ying Yang Twins*	
9.	9/20	3	**Shake Ya Tailfeather** .... *Nelly/P. Diddy/Murphy Lee*	
10.	10/18	1	**Damn!** .... *Youngbloodz Featuring Lil' Jon*	
11.	10/25	8	**Stand Up** .... *Ludacris featuring Shawnna*	
12.	12/20	5	**The Way You Move** .... *OutKast Featuring Sleepy Brown* (includes 3 weeks at #1 in 2004)	

ADULT CONTEMPORARY

This section lists, by artist, every single and album track that debuted in 2003 on *Billboard's* weekly **Adult Contemporary** chart (a top 30 listing).

DEBUT DATE	PEAK POS	WKS CHR	G L D	ARTIST / Title	Label & Number
12/6/03+	**16**	18↑		**AGUILERA, Christina** The Voice Within .... from the album *Stripped* on RCA 68037	album cut
7/5/03	**13**	24	▲	**AIKEN, Clay** ★ This Is The Night /	
6/28/03	**29**	2		Bridge Over Troubled Water .... #1 Adult hit for Simon & Garfunkel in 1970	RCA 51785
10/25/03+	**8**	24↑		Invisible from the album *Measure Of A Man* on RCA 54638	album cut
12/13/03+	**9**	5		The First Noel [X]	album cut
12/13/03+	**16**	5		Silver Bells .... [X] **CLAY AIKEN & KIMBERLEY LOCKE** above 2 from the various artists album *American Idol: The Great Holiday Classics* on RCA 55424	album cut
				ASHTON, Susan — see BRICKMAN, Jim	
				BAND, Alex — see SANTANA	
				BEDINGFIELD, Daniel ★ Born in 1980 in New Zealand; raised in England. Pop singer/songwriter.	
4/19/03	**3**	34		If You're Not The One	Island 000267
9/27/03	**17**	14		**BOLTON, Michael** When I Fall In Love .... #6 Adult hit for Celine Dion & Clive Griffin in 1993 (originally a #20 Pop hit for Doris Day in 1952); from the album *Vintage* on PMG 73973	album cut
8/16/03+	**15**	25		**BRICKMAN, Jim** Peace (Where The Heart Is)......................... **JIM BRICKMAN Featuring Collin Raye and Susan Ashton**	album cut
12/6/03+	**❶**[1]	6		Sending You A Little Christmas [X] **JIM BRICKMAN with Kristy Starling** above 2 from the album *Peace* on Windham Hill 52896	album cut
8/9/03	**29**	1		**BUBLÉ, Michael** ★ Born on 9/9/75 in Burnaby, British Columbia, Canada. Traditional pop singer. Kissing A Fool.. #1 Adult hit for George Michael in 1988	album cut
9/20/03	**22**	9		How Can You Mend A Broken Heart .... #4 Adult hit for the Bee Gees in 1971; above 2 from the album *Michael Bublé* on 143 Records 48376	album cut
12/13/03	**6**	5		The Christmas Song [X] from the album *Let It Snow!* on 143 Records 48599	album cut
8/2/03	**25**	12		**CARLSON, Katrina** ★ Born in Paradise Valley, Arizona. Female singer/songwriter. I Know You By Heart.................................. **KATRINA CARLSON with Benny Mardones** from the album *Untucked* on Kataphonic 54619	album cut
				CARLTON, Vanessa — see COUNTING CROWS	
8/23/03	**27**	5		**CHAPMAN, Steven Curtis** ★ Born on 11/21/62 in Paducah, Kentucky. Contemporary Christian singer/songwriter. How Do I Love Her .... from the album *All About Love* on Sparrow 41762	album cut
				CHER — see STEWART, Rod	
8/30/03	**28**	3		**CLARKSON, Kelly** Miss Independent.. co-written by Christina Aguilera; from the album *Thankful* on RCA 68159	album cut
12/13/03+	**17**	5		My Grown Up Christmas List........................... [X] from the various artists album *American Idol: The Great Holiday Classics* on RCA 55424	album cut
3/15/03	**16**	13		**COLLINS, Phil** Come With Me (Lullaby) .... from the album *Testify* on Atlantic 83563	album cut
9/27/03+	**5**	28↑		Look Through My Eyes from the animated movie *Brother Bear* (soundtrack on Walt Disney 860127)	album cut
5/17/03	**5**	47↑		**COUNTING CROWS** Big Yellow Taxi **COUNTING CROWS Featuring Vanessa Carlton** #33 Adult hit for Joni Mitchell in 1970; from the album *Hard Candy* on Geffen 493356	album cut

ADULT CONTEMPORARY

DEBUT DATE	PEAK POS	WKS CHR	G L D	ARTIST / Title	Label & Number
				CROW, Sheryl	
2/22/03	17	26	●	Picture	Universal South 172274
				KID ROCK Featuring ALLISON MOORER or SHERYL CROW	
				commercial single features Moorer; the vast majority of radio stations played the original album version featuring Crow	
10/18/03+	2² ↑	25 ↑		The First Cut Is The Deepest	album cut
				written by Cat Stevens; #43 Adult hit for Rod Stewart in 1977; from the album *The Very Best Of Sheryl Crow* on A&M 152102	
				DIDO	
9/6/03+	4 ↑	30 ↑		White Flag	Arista 58336 (D)
				DION, Celine	
2/1/03	7	26		I Drove All Night	Epic 79931
				#43 Adult hit for Cyndi Lauper in 1989	
5/3/03	2¹⁴	34		Have You Ever Been In Love	album cut
10/18/03	17	18		Stand By Your Side	album cut
				above 2 from the album *One Heart* on Epic 87185	
				EAGLES	
6/7/03	5	26		Hole In The World	ERC II 3322 (D)
				includes a bonus audio CD of the song	
				EARTH, WIND & FIRE	
7/26/03	25	3		All In The Way	album cut
				from the album *The Promise* on Kalimba 973002	
				ESTEFAN, Gloria	
8/16/03	23	11		Wrapped	album cut
				from the album *Unwrapped* on Epic 86790	
				FLEETWOOD MAC	
3/29/03	10	16		Peacekeeper	album cut
7/12/03	17	13		Say You Will	album cut
				above 2 from the album *Say You Will* on Reprise 48394	
				FRANKIE J ★	
6/14/03	23	11		Don't Wanna Try...	Columbia 79872
				GARFUNKEL, Art	
2/22/03	30	2		Bounce..	album cut
				ART GARFUNKEL with Maia Sharp & Buddy Mondlock	
				from the album *Everything Waits To Be Noticed* on Manhattan 40990	
				GLOVER, Dana ★	
				Born in Rocky Mount, North Carolina. Female singer/songwriter.	
2/8/03	17	15		Thinking Over...	album cut
				from the album *Testimony* on DreamWorks 50299	
				GRANT, Amy	
8/9/03	23	10		Simple Things	album cut
				from the album *Simple Things* on A&M 000612	
				GRANT, Natalie ★	
				Born on 12/21/78 in Seattle, Washington. Christian singer/songwriter.	
3/22/03	25	14		No Sign Of It	album cut
				from the album *Deeper Life* on Curb 78761	
				GRAY, Dobie — see UNCLE KRACKER	
				GRAY, Tamyra ★	
				Born on 7/26/79 in Takoma Park, Maryland; raised in Norcross, Georgia. Black singer. Finalist on the second season of TV's *American Idol*.	
12/20/03	25	3		Have Yourself A Merry Little Christmas .... [X]	album cut
				RUBEN STUDDARD & TAMYRA GRAY	
				from the album *American Idol: The Great Holiday Classics* on RCA 55424	
				GROBAN, Josh	
2/8/03	10	22		You're Still You	album cut
				from the album *Josh Groban* on 143 Records 48154	
11/1/03+	❶⁴ ↑	23 ↑		You Raise Me Up	album cut
				from the album *Closer* on 143 Records 48450	
				HALL, Daryl	
8/2/03	21	13		Cab Driver...	album cut
				from the album *Can't Stop Dreaming* on Rhythm & Groove 12109	

DEBUT DATE	PEAK POS	WKS CHR	G L D	ARTIST Title	Label & Number
				HALL, Daryl, & John Oates	
5/31/03	16	14		Man On A Mission	album cut
11/1/03+	21	15		Getaway Car	album cut
				above 2 from the album *Do It For Love* on U-Watch 80100	
				HAMM, Regie ★	
				Born in Cleveland, Tennessee. Male singer/songwriter/pianist.	
1/18/03	16	19		Babies	album cut
				from the album *American Dreams* on Refugee 170362	
				HARRISON, George	
2/15/03	27	4		Stuck Inside A Cloud	album cut
				from the album *Brainwashed* on Dark Horse 41969	
				HILL, Faith	
4/26/03	7	26		One	album cut
				from the album *Cry* on Warner 48001	
				HOOTIE & THE BLOWFISH	
3/8/03	25	9		Innocence	album cut
				from the album *Hootie & The Blowfish* on Atlantic 83564	
				HOUSTON, Whitney	
3/1/03	10	22	●	Try It On My Own	Arista 51156 (D)
12/27/03+	20	3		One Wish (For Christmas) .... [X]	album cut
				from the album *One Wish: The Holiday Album* on Arista 50996	
				KID ROCK ★	
				Born Robert Ritchie on 1/17/71 in Romeo, Michigan. White hip-hop/rock singer.	
2/22/03	17	26	●	Picture	Universal South 172274
				KID ROCK Featuring ALLISON MOORER or SHERYL CROW	
				commercial single features Moorer; the vast majority of radio stations played the original album version featuring Crow	
				KROEGER, Chad — see SANTANA	
				LAVIGNE, Avril	
2/8/03	18	26	▲	I'm With You	Arista 51024 (D)
				LOCKE, Kimberley ★	
				Born on 1/1/78 in Portland, Tennessee. Black female singer. Finalist on the second season of TV's *American Idol*.	
12/13/03+	16	5		Silver Bells .... [X]	album cut
				CLAY AIKEN & KIMBERLEY LOCKE	
				from the various artists album *American Idol: The Great Holiday Classics* on RCA 55424	
				LOGGINS, Kenny	
8/16/03	22	16		With This Ring...	album cut
				written by Loggins and Richard Marx; from the album *It's About Time* on All The Best! 1	
				MARDONES, Benny — see CARLSON, Katrina	
				MATCHBOX TWENTY	
5/24/03	❶²	46↑		Unwell	album cut
				from the album *More Than You Think You Are* on Atlantic 83612	
				MATHIS, Johnny	
1/4/03	29	1		Frosty The Snowman .... [X]	album cut
				from the album *The Christmas Album* on Columbia 86814	
				MAYER, John	
12/6/03+	27	6		Bigger Than My Body	album cut
				from the album *Heavier Things* on Aware 86185	
				McDONALD, Michael	
6/21/03	20	14		I Heard It Through The Grapevine	album cut
				#1 Pop hit for Marvin Gaye in 1968	
11/8/03+	9↑	22↑		Ain't No Mountain High Enough	album cut
				#6 Adult hit for Diana Ross in 1970; above 2 from the album *Motown* on Motown 000651	
				McGRAW, Tim	
11/1/03+	13	20		Tiny Dancer	album cut
				#35 Adult hit for Elton John in 1972; from the album *Tim McGraw and The Dancehall Doctors* on Curb 78746	
				McLACHLAN, Sarah	
10/11/03+	12	26↑		Fallen..	Arista 60143

DEBUT DATE	PEAK POS	WKS CHR	G L D	ARTIST Title	Label & Number
				MERCYME	
5/24/03	5	30		I Can Only Imagine	INO/Curb 73150
				MIDLER, Bette	
12/20/03	15	4		White Christmas .... [X]	album cut
				co-produced by Barry Manilow; from the album *Bette Midler Sings The Rosemary Clooney Songbook* on Columbia 90350	
				MOORER, Allison see KID ROCK	
				NO DOUBT	
3/1/03	27	2		Underneath It All	Interscope 497768
				NO DOUBT featuring Lady Saw	
				RAITT, Bonnie	
3/22/03	27	5		Time Of Our Lives	album cut
				from the album *Silver Lining* on Capitol 31816	
				RAYE, Collin — see BRICKMAN, Jim	
				RIMES, LeAnn	
7/12/03	16	17		We Can	album cut
12/13/03+	14	5		O Holy Night .... [X]	album cut
				Sheila E. (drums); above 2 from the album *Greatest Hits* on Curb 78829	
				RONEY, Burke ★	
				Born in Santa Monica, California. Singer/songwriter/guitarist.	
11/29/03	22	9		Let It All Come Down	album cut
				from the album *Let It All Come Down* on R World 570011	
				SANTANA	
11/22/03+	16	20↑		Why Don't You & I	album cut
				SANTANA Featuring Alex Band or Chad Kroeger	
				the Chad Kroeger (of Nickelback) version is from Santana's album *Shaman* on Arista 14737; the Alex Band (of The Calling) vesion is available as a promo single only (Arista 53233)	
				SEAL	
9/20/03	20	20		Waiting For You	Warner 16574
				SIMPLY RED	
8/9/03	5	32		Sunrise	album cut
				samples "I Can't Go For That (No Can Do)" by Daryl Hall & John Oates; from the album *Home* on simplyred.com 0001	
				SIXPENCE NONE THE RICHER	
3/8/03	12	22		Don't Dream It's Over..	Squint/Curb 886260
				#9 Adult hit for Crowded House in 1987	
				STARLING, Kristy — see BRICKMAN, Jim	
				STEWART, Rod	
5/10/03	27	6		They Can't Take That Away From Me...................	album cut
				#1 Pop hit for Fred Astaire in 1937; from the album *It Had To Be You...The Great American Songbook* on J Records 20039	
11/8/03+	17	16		Bewitched, Bothered & Bewildered.....................	album cut
				ROD STEWART & CHER	
				#3 Pop hit for Bill Snyder in 1950; from the album *As Time Goes By...The Great American Songbook Vol. II* on J Records 55710	
				STUDDARD, Ruben ★	
6/21/03	27	8	●	Flying Without Wings	J Records 51786
12/20/03	25	3		Have Yourself A Merry Little Christmas .... [X]	album cut
				RUBEN STUDDARD & TAMYRA GRAY	
				from the various artists album *American Idol: The Great Holiday Classics* on RCA 55424	
				TAYLOR, James	
3/15/03	25	11		September Grass	album cut
				from the album *October Road* on Columbia 63584	
				3 DOORS DOWN ★	
				Rock group from Escatawpa, Mississippi: Brad Arnold (vocals), Matt Roberts (guitar), Todd Harrell (bass) and Chris Henderson (drums).	
12/27/03+	15	13↑		Here Without You	album cut
				from the album *Away From The Sun* on Republic 066165	
				TRAIN	
7/19/03+	❶³	38↑		Calling All Angels	album cut
				from the album *My Private Nation* on Columbia 86593	

DEBUT DATE	PEAK POS	WKS CHR	G L D	ARTIST Title	Label & Number
				TWAIN, Shania	
5/10/03	❶⁶	48↑		Forever And For Always	album cut
				from the album *Up!* on Mercury 170314	
				UNCLE KRACKER	
1/18/03	26	8		In A Little While	album cut
3/22/03	❶²⁸	55↑		Drift Away	album cut
				UNCLE KRACKER Featuring Dobie Gray	
				new version of Gray's #12 Adult hit in 1973 (including new vocals by Gray); above 2 from Uncle Kracker's album *No Stranger To Shame* on Lava 83542	
				VANDROSS, Luther	
6/21/03	4	27		Dance With My Father	J Records 57595 (D)
				written by Vandross and Richard Marx; backing vocalists include Cissy Houston	

1. UNCLE KRACKER
478+

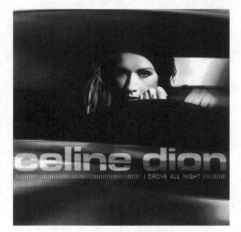

2. CELINE DION
405

3. SHANIA TWAIN
198+

4.	191	SANTANA	13.	136	NORAH JONES
5.	186	DIXIE CHICKS	14.	128	ROD STEWART
6.	182	CHRISTINA AGUILERA	15.	127+	DOBIE GRAY
7.	165	MICHAEL BUBLÉ ★	16.	126	CLAY AIKEN ★
8.	157	AVRIL LAVIGNE	17.	118	JAMES TAYLOR
9.	156+	MATCHBOX TWENTY	18.	117+	COUNTING CROWS
10.	153	DARYL HALL & JOHN OATES	19.	102	SIMPLY RED
11.	144	DANIEL BEDINGFIELD ★	20.	101	RUBEN STUDDARD ★
12.	139	FLEETWOOD MAC			

+ Subject to change since a title that peaked in 2003 by this artist is still charted as of the 4/3/04 cut-off date.

PEAK DATE	WEEKS				RANK	RECORD TITLE	PEAK POSITION	ARTIST
	CH	20	10	PK				
						1		
6/7	55 +	51 +	47 +	27	1.	Drift Away		Uncle Kracker Featuring Dobie Gray
2/15	26	21	16	7	2.	Landslide		Dixie Chicks
11/15	48 +	46 +	37 +	6	3.	Forever And For Always		Shania Twain
4/19	42	39	24	5	4.	Beautiful...		Christina Aguilera
4/5	61	60	51	4	5.	The Game Of Love		Santana featuring Michelle Branch
12/20	46 +	42 +	35 +	2	6.	Unwell...		Matchbox Twenty
						2		
6/21	34	33	30	14	7.	Have You Ever Been In Love		Celine Dion
						3		
6/14	34	32	24	11	8.	If You're Not The One		Daniel Bedingfield
						4		
4/26	66	57	20	5	9.	Don't Know Why...		Norah Jones
9/20	27	26	18	2	10.	Dance With My Father		Luther Vandross
1/4	26	22	4	1	11.	You............................		Jim Brickman Featuring Jane Krakowski
						5		
11/15	32	29	14	6	12.	Sunrise		Simply Red
11/1	47 +	44 +	31	4	13.	Big Yellow Taxi...		Counting Crows Featuring Vanessa Carlton
8/23	26	25	14	3	14.	Hole In The World		Eagles
11/8	30	23	11	1	15.	I Can Only Imagine.................................		Mercyme
						6		
12/20	5	5	1	1	16.	The Christmas Song		Michael Bublé
						7		
3/22	29	26	17	3	17.	Forever For You		Daryl Hall & John Oates
7/5	26	24	8	3	18.	One		Faith Hill
4/12	26	17	8	3	19.	I Drove All Night		Celine Dion
1/4	5	5	1	1	20.	It Wouldn't Be Christmas (Without You).........		John Tesh
						10		
5/10	16	14	3	3	21.	Peacekeeper		Fleetwood Mac
5/3	22	17	1	1	22.	Try It On My Own		Whitney Houston
4/12	22	13	1	1	23.	You're Still You		Josh Groban
						11		
1/4	4	2		1	24.	Santa Claus Is Coming To Town		Steve Tyrell
						12		
5/3	22	11		1	25.	Don't Dream It's Over		Sixpence None The Richer
						13		
2/8	22	12		4	26.	These Foolish Things		Rod Stewart
1/18	26	19		2	27.	Complicated...		Avril Lavigne
8/23	24	15		1	28.	This Is The Night...		Clay Aiken
1/4	3	2		1	29.	The Gift...		Aselin Debison
						14		
1/18	25	17		1	30.	When You Lie Next To Me		Kellie Coffey

#1 ADULT CONTEMPORARY

	Date Hit #1	Wks @ #1	Title	Artist
1.	1/4	2	**O Holy Night** .... *Josh Groban*	
			(includes 1 week at #1 in 2002)	
2.	1/11	11 ↕	**Cry** .... *Faith Hill*	
			(includes 6 weeks at #1 in 2002)	
3.	2/15	7	**Landslide** .... *Dixie Chicks*	
4.	4/5	4 ↕	**The Game Of Love** .... *Santana featuring Michelle Branch*	
5.	4/19	5	**Beautiful**... *Christina Aguilera*	
6.	6/7	28 ↕	**Drift Away** .... *Uncle Kracker (Featuring Dobie Gray)*	
			(includes 3 weeks at #1 in 2004)	
7.	11/15	6 ↕	**Forever And For Always**................................*Shania Twain*	
			(includes 3 weeks at #1 in 2004)	
8.	12/20	2	**Unwell** .... *Matchbox Twenty*	

#1 ADULT TOP 40 TRACKS

	Date Hit #1	Wks @ #1	Title	Artist
1.	1/4	13	**The Game Of Love** .... *Santana featuring Michelle Branch*	
			(includes 6 weeks at #1 in 2002)	
2.	2/22	10	**I'm With You** .... *Avril Lavigne*	
3.	5/3	18	**Unwell** .... *Matchbox Twenty*	
4.	9/6	5	**Calling All Angels**... *Train*	
5.	10/11	9	**Why Don't You & I** .... *Santana Featuring Alex Band or Chad Kroeger*	
6.	12/13	13	**Here Without You** .... *3 Doors Down*	
			(includes 10 weeks at #1 in 2004)	

DANCE CLUB PLAY

This brand new section lists, by artist, every title that debuted in 2003 on *Billboard's* weekly **Hot Dance Club Play** chart (a top 50 listing). It provides updated information to our recently released, first of its kind, *Hot Dance/Disco 1974-2003* book, which contains chart research through July 5, 2003.

DEBUT DATE	PEAK POS	WKS CHR	G L D	ARTIST Title	Label & Number
				AGEHA ★	
8/30/03	3	16		A Better World	Gate 1169
				AGEHA Featuring Jocelyn Brown & Loleatta Holloway	
				AGUILERA, Christina	
3/1/03	**0**¹	15		Beautiful	RCA 51195
				ALCAZAR	
1/25/03	30	11		Don't You Want Me	E-magine 013
				AMOS, Tori	
6/21/03	6	14		Don't Make Me Come To Vegas	Epic 79888
				AMUKA ★	
8/9/03	7	14		Appreciate Me	Star 69 1262
				AMUKA Featuring Sheila Brody	
				ANANDA PROJECT, The	
7/19/03	15	15		Can You Find The Heart	Integrooves 187
				THE ANANDA PROJECT Featuring Nicola Hitchcock	
				ANASTACIA	
3/29/03	**0**¹	14		Love Is A Crime	Daylight (promo)
				ANDERSON, Sunshine — see GROOVE ARMADA	
				ARENA, Tina — see ROC PROJECT	
				ASHANTI ★	
				Born Ashanti Douglas on 10/13/80 in Glen Cove, Long Island, New York. Female hip-hop singer/songwriter.	
10/11/03	6	15		Rock Wit U (Awww Baby)	Murder Inc. (promo)
				ATB	
6/21/03	26	9		I Don't Wanna Stop	Radikal 99180
9/6/03	10	13		Long Way Home	Radikal 99193
				ATLAS, Natacha -- see GHOSTLAND	
				AUBREY	
5/3/03	24	10		Willing & Able............................	Dee Vee (promo)
10/25/03	10	15		I'm Waiting	Vish (promo)
				AUBREY VS JOHNNY VICIOUS	
				AVIANCE, Kevin	
12/20/03+	**0**¹	16↑		Give It Up	Robbins 72099
				BAELING, Becky ★	
				Born in 1978 in Rochester, Michigan. White female singer.	
1/25/03	3	16		If You Love Me	Universal (promo)
5/10/03	**0**¹	13		Getaway	Universal (promo)
				BAJOFONDOTANGOCLUB ★	
				Studio group assembled in Argentina by producers Emilio Kauderer and Didi Gutman.	
10/18/03	28	10		Los Tangueros .... [F]	Surco (promo)
				BAKER, Arthur	
12/20/03+	22	13		1000 Years	Tommy Boy Silver 2430
				ARTHUR BAKER Featuring Astrid Williamson	
				BASEMENT JAXX	
11/15/03+	3	15		Lucky Star	XL 38878
				BASEMENT JAXX Featuring Dizzee Rascal	
				BEAT HUSTLERZ ★	
				Electronic production duo: Ellis Miah and Jody Den Broeder.	
10/18/03	15	14		Just About Had Enough	Star 69 1268
				BEAT HUSTLERZ Featuring Thea Austin	
				BEDINGFIELD, Daniel	
4/12/03	4	15		If You're Not The One	Island 000243
				BEYONCÉ	
8/2/03	**0**¹	14		Crazy In Love	Columbia 79947
10/25/03	2²	13		Baby Boy	Columbia 76867
				BIG BANG THEORY ★	
11/15/03	17	14		Do U Got Funk?................................	Uncommon Trax 002
				BLUE MAN GROUP ★	
				Experimental musical theatre trio: Matt Goldman, Phil Stanton and Chris Wink. Perform with various inventive percussion instruments while dressed in blue-painted skin, skullcaps and black clothing.	
10/18/03	7	14		I Feel Love	Blue Man Group (promo)
				BLUE MAN GROUP Featuring Venus Hum	
				#3 Dance hit for Donna Summer in 1977	

DEBUT DATE	PEAK POS	WKS CHR	G L D	ARTIST Title	Label & Number
				BOOMKAT	
9/6/03	❶¹	14		What U Do 2 Me	DreamWorks (promo)
				BOWIE, David	
2/8/03	42	6		Everyone Says Hi	Columbia (promo)
				BRANCH, Michelle ★	
				Born on 7/2/83 in Sedona, Arizona. Adult Alternative pop-rock singer/songwriter/guitarist.	
12/13/03+	3	14		Breathe	Maverick 42689
				BRIGHTMAN, Sarah	
7/19/03	❶¹	14		Harem (Cancao do Mar)	Angel 53240
				adapted from the song "Cancao do Mar" first recorded by female Portugese singer Dulce Pontes in 1996	
				BROWN, Jocelyn — see AGEHA	
				BT	
5/24/03	5	15		Somnambulist	Nettwerk 33190
				a Somnambulist is a sleep walker; song also known as "Simply Being Loved"	
				CALDERONE, Victor	
3/8/03	46	6		The Drive..	Statrax 34001
10/18/03	39	9		Deep Dark Jungle.................................	Statrax 34003
				CAREY, Mariah	
9/20/03	5	14		Bringin' On The Heartbreak	Monarc (promo)
				#61 Pop hit for Def Leppard in 1984	
				CEEVOX — see HOUSEKEEPERZ	
				CHER	
2/22/03	❶¹	13		When The Money's Gone	Warner 42496
				CLARE QUILTY ★	
				Adult-alternative group from Charlottesville, Virginia: Jenn Rhubright (vocals), Michael Rodi (guitar), Chris Ruotolo (bass) and Jimmy Amburgey (drums).	
7/12/03	33	8		Tremble	Dcide 001
				COLDPLAY ★	
				Rock group from Edinburgh, Scotland: Chris Martin (vocals), Jon Buckland (guitar), Guy Berryman (bass) and Will Champion (drums). Martin married actress Gwyneth Paltrow on 12/5/2003.	
6/7/03	31	9		Clocks	Capitol (promo)
				COLOURFUL KARMA ★	
6/14/03	7	18		For The Music	DotDotDot 014
				COLOURFUL KARMA Featuring Terra Deva	
				CONJURE ONE	
9/13/03	3	13		Center Of The Sun	Nettwerk 33203
				COOLER KIDS	
7/19/03	4	15		Morning Star	DreamWorks (promo)
				COOPER, Deborah	
5/31/03	4	14		Real Love	Emerge 30070
				CORSTEN, Ferry	
12/27/03+	24	13		Rock Your Body, Rock	Moonshine 88492
				COX, Chris	
2/15/03	❶¹	14		I Believe	The Right Stuff 77875
				CHRIS COX VS. HAPPY CLAPPERS	
				COX, Deborah	
5/31/03	❶¹	12		Play Your Part	J Records (promo)
				CRUZ, Celia ★	
				Born on 10/21/24 in Havana, Cuba. Died of brain cancer on 7/16/2003 (age 78). Known as "The Queen of Salsa Music."	
12/13/03+	35	9		Rio Y Llora.................................... [F]	Sony Discos (promo)
				CRUZ, DJ Mike	
7/12/03	24	9		Medicine	Nervous 20485
				DJ MIKE CRUZ PRESENTS CHYNA RO & SANDY B	
				CYN ★	
1/18/03	18	12		Fantasy Reality....................................	Star 69 12511
				DAMIAN ★	
12/27/03+	32	10		Oneness....................................	Naimad 001
				DAMIAN Featuring Sasha Lazard	

DEBUT DATE	PEAK POS	WKS CHR	G L D	ARTIST Title	Label & Number
7/26/03	21	12		**DEAD OR ALIVE** You Spin Me Round (Like A Record)............ [R] remix of their #4 Dance hit in 1985	Legacy (promo)
2/22/03	37	8		**DE-JAVU** ★ I Can't Stop	Neutone 003
6/14/03	9	14		**DELERIUM** After All DELERIUM Featuring Jael	Nettwerk 33194
				DeLORY, Donna — see QUAYLE, Mac	
11/15/03+	❶¹	17		**DIDO** Stoned	Arista 56070
2/15/03	2²	15		**DION, Celine** I Drove All Night #6 Pop hit for Cyndi Lauper in 1989	Epic (promo)
7/12/03	3	14		**DORIA, Andrea** ★ Bucci Bag	Star 69 1263
7/19/03	38	6		**DOUGAN, Rob** ★ Born in Sydney, Australia. Electronic musician/producer. Furious Angels	Reprise (promo)
5/24/03	31	10		**DRU HILL** ★ Male R&B vocal trio from Baltimore, Maryland: Mark "Sisqo" Andrews, Tamir "Nokio" Ruffin and Larry "Jazz" Anthony. Group named after Druid Hill Park in Baltimore. I Love You	Def Soul 000305
4/5/03	42	7		**DRUNKENMUNKY** ★ E...	Ultra 1153
				DUTCH -- see SCUMFROG	
8/9/03	40	6		**EDER, Linda** I Am What I Am.................................. from the Broadway show La Cage Aux Folles; #3 Dance hit for Gloria Gaynor in 1983	Atlantic 88183
3/22/03	❶¹	12		**ELLIOTT, Missy "Misdemeanor"** Gossip Folks MISSY "MISDEMEANOR" ELLIOTT (Featuring Ludacris) samples "Double Dutch Bus" by Frankie Smith	The Gold Mind 67387
11/8/03	22	12		**EMMANUEL** Guajira .... [F]	Universal Latino (promo)
2/15/03	17	13		**ENRIQUEZ, Jocelyn** No Way No How	Jem (promo)
2/1/03	18	12		**FISCHERSPOONER** Electro-pop duo from New York: Warren Fischer and Casey Spooner. Emerge..	Capitol 77886
5/3/03	21	11		The 15th	Capitol (promo)
7/19/03	37	6		**FRANKIE J** ★ Don't Wanna Try................................	Columbia (promo)
9/27/03	7	13		**FRANKLIN, Aretha** The Only Thing Missin'	Arista 56474
1/25/03	❶¹	14		**FRIBURN & URIK** Dance To The Rhythm	Tommy Boy 2392
4/26/03	13	13		Elefants	Star 69 12571
1/18/03	❶¹	15		**FUNKY GREEN DOGS** Rise Up	Star 69 1255
6/7/03	❶¹	13		Alright	Tommy Boy 2405
11/1/03	❶¹	15		Believe MURK (above 2)	Tommy Boy 2431
6/14/03	3	14		**GAHAN, Dave** ★ Dirty Sticky Floors	Mute 42620
8/30/03	5	12		I Need You	Mute 42643
8/16/03	34	9		**GARDEWEG** ★ All I Want..	Radikal 99170

DANCE CLUB PLAY

DEBUT DATE	PEAK POS	WKS CHR	G L D	ARTIST Title	Label & Number
				GEORGIE PORGIE	
8/23/03	❶¹	15		I Love I Love	Vinyl Soul 124
				GHOSTLAND ★	
				Electronic trio from London, England: Justin Adams (guitar), Caroline Dale (cello) and John Reynolds (producer).	
3/29/03	20	14		Guide Me God..	Tommy Boy 2396
				GHOSTLAND Featuring Sinéad O'Connor & Natacha Atlas	
				GIOVANNA ★	
12/6/03	39	8		You Got Me	Act 2 002
				GREEN, Vivian ★	
				Born in 1979 in Philadelphia, Pennsylvania. R&B singer/songwriter.	
1/11/03	❶¹	15		Emotional Rollercoaster	Columbia (promo)
7/26/03	7	13		Fanatic	Columbia 79904
				GRIFFIN, Mary	
3/8/03	6	14		Without You	Curb 77101
				GROOVE ARMADA	
5/24/03	5	13		Easy	Jive Electro 40056
				GROOVE ARMADA Featuring Sunshine Anderson	
				GUETTA, David ★	
				Born in France. White DJ/producer.	
12/27/03+	15	14		Just A Little More Love	Astralwerks 47592
				GUSGUS	
4/19/03	43	8		David	Moonshine (promo)
				HALL, Daryl, & John Oates	
10/18/03	40	4		Intuition.................	U-Watch 1022
				HAPPY CLAPPERS	
2/15/03	❶¹	14		I Believe	The Right Stuff 77875
				CHRIS COX VS. HAPPY CLAPPERS	
				HARRIS, Barry	
3/15/03	31	8		S'cream	Nervous 20529
				HAYDN, Lili ★	
				Born in Toronto, Ontario, Canada. Eclectic violinist/songwriter.	
9/27/03	16	12		Anything	Private Music (promo)
				HEADLEY, Heather	
7/5/03	5	14		I Wish I Wasn't	RCA (promo)
				HELLER, Pete	
4/19/03	36	10		Big Room Drama....................	JBO (import)
				PETE HELLER & TEDD PATTERSON PRESENT THE LOOK & FEEL	
				HILL, Saffron ★	
10/11/03	7	16		My Love Is Always	Uncommon Trax 003
				HOLLOWAY, Loleatta	
5/3/03	5	12		Relight My Fire	Sony Discos (import)
				MARTIN Featuring Loleatta Holloway	
8/30/03	3	16		A Better World	Gate 1169
				AGEHA Featuring Jocelyn Brown & Loleatta Holloway	
				HOUSEKEEPERZ ★	
9/6/03	26	10		Wurkin'....................	Harlequin 51251
				HOUSEKEEPERZ Featuring Ceevox	
				HOUSTON, Whitney	
2/22/03	❶¹	14		Try It On My Own	Arista 50538
5/10/03	❶¹	13		Love That Man	Arista 52396
				IGLESIAS, Enrique	
11/22/03+	4	14		Addicted	Interscope (promo)
				IIO	
2/15/03	41	10		At The End	Made (import)

DEBUT DATE	PEAK POS	WKS CHR	G L D	ARTIST Title	Label & Number
				INDIA	
4/5/03	2²	14		Seduce Me Now	Sony Discos 8655
				INDUSTRY	
11/22/03+	7	14		Release Me	Star 69 1270
				IN-GRID ★	
9/20/03	6	16		You Promised Me	ZYX 5218
				JAEL — see DELERIUM	
				JEWEL	
5/31/03	❶¹	14		Intuition	Atlantic 88122
10/18/03	❶¹	13		Stand	Atlantic 88233
				JOHN, Elton	
1/11/03	5	13		Your Song [R]	Rocket (promo)
				new version of Elton's #8 Pop hit from 1971	
11/1/03+	❶¹	15		Are You Ready For Love	Southern Fried 1177
				new mix of a recording from Elton's 1979 album *The Thom Bell Sessions*	
				JUNG ★	
				Electronic trio from New York: Lisa "Hope" Molina (vocals), Norty Cotto and Yianni Papadopoulous.	
5/10/03	14	14		You Mean The World To Me	Cutting 458
				JUNG Featuring Hope	
				JUNIOR SENIOR ★	
				White trip-hop duo from Jutland, Denmark: Jesper "Junior" Mortensen and Jeppe "Senior" Laursen.	
8/30/03	45	6		Move Your Feet	Crunchy Frog 88149
				KELIS	
10/25/03	❶¹	18		Milkshake	Star Trak (promo)
				KENNA ★	
				Born in Ethiopia; raised in Virginia Beach, Virginia. Male alternative-funk singer/musician.	
9/6/03	19	11		Freetime	Columbia 79860
				KINGS OF TOMORROW	
1/18/03	26	11		I Want You (For Myself)	Yoshitoshi 093
				KIRA ★	
				Born Natasja DeWitte on 3/5/77 in Belgium. Female singer.	
5/3/03	34	8		I'll Be Your Angel	Nu Life 98845
				K-KLASS ★	
				Electronic group from Wrexham, Wales: Andy Williams, Carl Thomas, Paul Roberts and Russ Morgan.	
6/28/03	9	14		Talk 2 Me	Tommy Boy 2407
				K-KLASS Featuring Kinane	
				KRISTA ★	
6/21/03	24	10		Let Me Be Your Angel	Henry Street 584
				KRISTINE W	
10/11/03	❶¹	16		Fly Again	Tommy Boy 2422
				LA BOUCHE	
2/8/03	9	13		In Your Life	Logic 98814
				LATIN PROJECT, The ★	
				Studio project assembled by musicians/producers Jez Colin and Matt Cooper	
9/13/03	❶¹	14		Lei Lo Lai	Electric Monkey 1008
				LAUPER, Cyndi	
12/6/03+	10	15		Walk On By	Daylight (promo)
				#6 Pop hit for Dionne Warwick in 1964	
				LAWRENCE, Seth ★	
9/20/03	9	13		Future Funk	Tommy Boy 2413
				LAZARD, Sasha	
1/25/03	43	5		Battle Of Erishkigal	Omtown (promo)
12/27/03+	32	10		Oneness	Naimad 001
				DAMIAN Featuring Sasha Lazard	
				LEE-CABRERA ★	
9/13/03	42	7		Shake It	Creedence (import)

DEBUT DATE	PEAK POS	WKS CHR	G L D	ARTIST / Title	Label & Number
				LENNOX, Annie	
7/5/03	❶²	14		Pavement Cracks	J Records 55884
11/22/03+	❶¹	16		Wonderful	J Records (promo)
11/22/03+	❶¹	15		A Thousand Beautiful Things	J Records (promo)
				LIMERICK, Alison	
3/1/03	16	14		Where Love Lives .... [R]	Logic 98844
				new mix of her #3 Dance hit in 1991	
				LOPEZ, Jennifer	
5/17/03	4	14		I'm Glad	Epic 79952
				LUDACRIS — see ELLIOTT, Missy "Misdemeanor"	
				MADE BY MONKEYS ★	
				Electronic trio formed in Montreal, Quebec, Canada: female vocalist Maria Matto (from Miami, Florida) and producers Andrew Kapur and Saad Malick.	
5/24/03	28	10		I Try	Star 69 1265
				MADONNA	
4/26/03	❶¹	12		American Life	Maverick 42614
7/12/03	❶¹	12		Hollywood	Maverick 42638
11/8/03	4	14		Nobody Knows Me	Maverick 42682
11/22/03	❶²	13		Me Against The Music	Jive 57757
				BRITNEY SPEARS Featuring Madonna	
12/20/03+	❶¹	15		Nothing Fails	Maverick 42682
				MANTRONIX	
7/26/03	3	14		77 Strings (How Did You Know)	Uncommon Trax 001
				KURTIS MANTRONIK Presents Chamonix	
				MARASCIA ★	
3/8/03	4	15		Shake It	Tommy Boy 2394
				MARTIN, Billie Ray	
2/22/03	3	15		Honey	Nervous 20528
				MARTIN, Ricky	
5/3/03	5	12		Relight My Fire	Sony Discos (import)
				MARTIN Featuring Loleatta Holloway	
				#1 Dance hit for Dan Hartman in 1980	
10/4/03	13	12		Jaleo .... [F]	Sony Discos (promo)
				title is Spanish for "Commotion"	
				McLACHLAN, Sarah	
12/6/03+	3	16		Fallen	Arista (promo)
				MIA	
1/25/03	46	1		Dream Girl Part 2	MiaDreamworld 003
				samples "Won't Get Fooled Again" by The Who	
6/21/03	3	13		Addicted	MiaDreamworld 004
11/29/03	25	10		Forever	MiaDreamworld 005
				MINOGUE, Kylie	
12/20/03+	❶¹	16↑		Slow	Capitol 53362
				MITCHELL, Vernessa	
4/19/03	37	8		Serious	JVM 014
				MONICA	
6/7/03	❶¹	13		So Gone	J Records 21260
12/13/03+	13	16		Get It Off	J Records (promo)
				MOORE, Rose ★	
				Born in New Mexico. Native American singer/songwriter. Also known as Cherokee Rose.	
3/8/03	36	6		Why/E Si Do Maya E Si	Omtown (promo)
				written by Moore in response to the 9/11 terrorist attacks	
				MOTORCYCLE ★	
12/13/03+	41	17↑		As The Rush Comes	Ultra 1192
				MUSIQ	
2/8/03	31	10		dontchange.......................................	Def Soul 063790
				NATÉ, Ultra	
6/28/03	8	14		Brass In Pocket	Blufire 002
				#28 Dance hit for The Pretenders in 1980	

DEBUT DATE	PEAK POS	WKS CHR	G L D	ARTIST Title	Label & Number
				NESBY, Ann	
8/30/03	6	12		Shelter	It's Time Child 002
				OAKENFOLD	
11/8/03	41	7		Hypnotised	Perfecto 42661
				O'CONNOR, Sinéad — see GHOSTLAND	
				ONO, Yoko	
3/15/03	❶¹	14		Walking On Thin Ice [R]	Mindtrain 82669
				ONO	
				remix of her #13 Dance hit from 1981	
				ORANGE FACTORY, The ★	
8/2/03	19	12		White Horse	Tommy Boy 2408
				#1 Dance hit for Laid Back in 1984	
				ORBIT, William — see P!NK	
				PALMER, Holly ★	
				Born in Santa Monica, California; raised in Seattle, Washington. Adult-alternative singer/songwriter.	
10/4/03	3	14		Just So You Know	Warner 42644
				PARADISE ★	
2/8/03	37	7		Rising Sun	5050 (import)
				PAUSINI, Laura	
4/12/03	❶¹	15		If That's Love	Atlantic (promo)
				PERPETUOUS DREAMER	
4/12/03	7	14		Dust.Wav	Radikal 99159
				PET SHOP BOYS	
3/29/03	15	12		Sexy Northerner	Sanctuary (promo)
				P!NK	
8/16/03	8	12		Feel Good Time	Columbia (promo)
				P!NK Featuring William Orbit	
				samples "Fresh Garbage" by Spirit; from the movie *Charlie's Angeles: Full Throttle* starring Cameron Diaz, Drew Barrymore and Lucy Liu	
				PRAXIS	
7/5/03	42	6		Turn Me Out .... [R]	2-Xist 001
				PRAXIS Featuring Kathy Brown	
				new mix of their #1 Dance hit from 1997	
				PURETONE	
5/3/03	4	13		Stuck In A Groove	MTA 27781
				PURPLE KITTY ★	
6/7/03	17	11		Bang On	Nervous 20524
				PURPLE KITTY Featuring Latanza Waters	
				QUAYLE, Mac ★	
				Born in Virginia; later based in New York. Prolific DJ/producer/remixer.	
12/6/03+	8	14		The Hurting	Dee Vee 001
				MAC QUAYLE Featuring Donna Delory	
				RAUHOFER, Peter	
4/5/03	5	15		I Am Ready	Star 69 1252
				SIZE QUEEN	
11/1/03	32	11		This Is My House	Star 69 1269
				RIMES, LeAnn	
3/1/03	10	13		Tic Toc	Curb (promo)
8/16/03	19	12		We Can	Curb (promo)
				RIVERA, Robbie	
1/25/03	❶¹	14		The Hum Melody	Juicy (import)
				ROCKIK ★	
6/14/03	31	8		Memories	Tommy Boy 2406
				ROC PROJECT, The ★	
				Dance studio production of Ray "Roc" Checo.	
5/3/03	4	15		Never (Past Tense)	Tommy Boy 2401
				THE ROC PROJECT Feat. Tina Arena	

DEBUT DATE	PEAK POS	WKS CHR	G L D	ARTIST / Title	Label & Number
				ROLLING STONES, The	
11/15/03	34	9		Sympathy For The Devil	Abkco 719666
				new mixes of their original 1968 recording	
				RUBIN-VEGA, Daphne ★	
				Born on 11/18/68 in Panama City, Panama. Singer/actress/dancer. Starred in Broadway's *Rent*.	
10/25/03	42	6		Rocket Man	Emerge 16178
				#6 Pop hit for Elton John in 1972	
				SANDY B — see DJ MIKE CRUZ	
				SAPPHIRECUT ★	
				Born Megan Taylor in Pittsburgh, Pennsylvania. White singer/songwriter/keyboardist.	
2/1/03	9	13		Free Your Mind	Twisted 77856
				SCUMFROG, The ★	
				Born Jesse Houk in 1971 in Amsterdam, the Netherlands. Prolific electronic musician/producer/remixer. Also recorded as Dutch.	
6/14/03	4	13		Music Revolution	Effin 1001
7/26/03	❶¹	15		My Time	Effin 1002
				DUTCH Featuring Crystal Waters	
				SEAL	
8/23/03	❶²	14		Get It Together	Warner 42645
11/1/03	❶¹	15		Waiting For You	Warner 42656
				SEIKO	
3/8/03	15	13		Just For Tonight...	Flora 60094
				SHALIM	
				Born in Puerto Rico. Male singer.	
8/16/03	46	2		Se Me Olvido Tu Nombre .... [F]	Crescent Moon (promo)
				title is Spanish for "I Forgot Your Name"	
				SHEIK, Duncan	
3/1/03	❶¹	14		On A High	Atlantic (promo)
				SIMONE, Nina ★	
				Born Eunice Waymon on 2/21/33 in Tryon, South Carolina. Died of cancer on 4/21/2003 (age 70). Jazz-styled singer.	
8/9/03	10	14		Sinnerman	Verve 000910
				SIMPLY RED	
7/19/03	❶¹	14		Sunrise	simplyred.com (promo)
				samples "I Can't Go For That (No Can Do)" by Daryl Hall & John Oates	
12/20/03+	❶¹	15		Fake	simplyred.com (promo)
				SINCLAIR, Bob ★	
				Born in Paris, France. Male DJ/producer.	
12/27/03+	23	12		Kiss My Eyes	Star 69 1273
				SMASH MOUTH	
8/23/03	11	13		You Are My Number One...	Interscope (promo)
				SOLID SESSIONS ★	
				Electronic production duo from the Netherlands: Cyril Helwig and Thymen Holleman.	
3/8/03	23	13		Janeiro	Radikal 99163
				SPEARS, Britney	
11/22/03	❶²	13		Me Against The Music	Jive 57757
				BRITNEY SPEARS Featuring Madonna	
				STAKEY, Renée ★	
3/29/03	10	15		Rainy Day	Robbins 72084
				STANSFIELD, Lisa	
5/17/03	34	9		All Around The World... [R]	BMG Heritage (promo)
				remix of her #1 Dance hit from 1990	
				STING	
9/6/03	❶¹	14		Send Your Love	A&M (promo)
				STONE, Angie	
3/29/03	18	12		Bottles & Cans	J Records (promo)

DEBUT DATE	PEAK POS	WKS CHR	G L D	ARTIST Title	Label & Number
				SUMMER, Donna	
11/8/03+	5	15		You're So Beautiful	Mercury (promo)
				SUPERCHUMBO	
10/4/03	❶¹	16		This Beat Is	Twisted 50020
				SUPREME BEINGS OF LEISURE	
2/1/03	5	14		Ghetto	Palm 7085
				SUZY K ★	
				Born in Manhattan, New York. White singer.	
1/11/03	45	2		Circle	Vellum 54579
				TALLMAN, Dawn	
2/1/03	13	13		Let It Go	Nervous 20523
4/12/03	11	14		Heavenly Light	Slaag 002
				TAMIA	
7/26/03	4	14		Officially Missing You	Elektra 47436
				t.A.T.u.	
4/26/03	❶¹	16		Not Gonna Get Us	Interscope (promo)
				THALIA	
8/9/03	27	10		I Want You	EMI Latin 47305
				THALIA Featuring Fat Joe	
11/15/03+	12	13		Baby, I'm In Love	EMI Latin 38872
				30 DIRTY JUNKIES ★	
4/12/03	6	13		People Are People	Topaz (import)
				TIGA ★	
				Born in Montreal, Quebec, Canada. Male electronic producer/musician.	
9/20/03	22	11		Hot In Herre	!K7 (promo)
				#1 Pop hit for Nelly in 2002	
				TIMBERLAKE, Justin	
2/1/03	2¹	14		Cry Me A River	Jive 40073
4/19/03	❶¹	14		Rock Your Body	Jive (promo)
				TINA ANN	
6/7/03	10	13		I Do	Heart 82002
				TURNER, Laura ★	
				Born in Houston, Texas; raised in Jackson Hole, Wyoming. Classical-styled singer.	
8/23/03	14	14		Soul Deep	Curb (promo)
				TURNER, Marisa ★	
				Born in Detroit, Michigan. Black female singer.	
1/11/03	6	16		What I Want	Jellybean 2648
				UNDERWORLD	
2/1/03	6	16		Dinosaur Adventure 3D	JBO 27778
12/27/03+	9	13		Born Slippy Nuxx	JBO 27802
				VAN DYK, Paul ★	
				Born on 12/16/71 in Eisenhuttenstadt, East Germany. Techno-dance DJ/producer.	
5/10/03	6	13		Nothing But You [I]	Mute 9204
				PAUL VAN DYK Feat. Hemstock & Jennings	
11/1/03	36	10		Time Of Our Lives	Mute 9225
				PAUL VAN DYK Featuring Vega 4	
				VELOCITY CODE ★	
11/29/03	32	9		Beautiful Outside	Mean Red (promo)
				VENUS HUM ★	
				Trip-hop trio from Nashville, Tennessee: Annette Strean (vocals), Kip Kubin and Tony Miracle (instruments).	
3/29/03	6	14		Montana	MCA (promo)
9/6/03	6	14		Soul Sloshing	Geffen (promo)
10/18/03	7	14		I Feel Love	Blue Man Group (promo)
				BLUE MAN GROUP Featuring Venus Hum	
				VICIOUS, Johnny	
10/25/03	10	15		I'm Waiting	Vish (promo)
				AUBREY VS JOHNNY VICIOUS	
				WATERS, Crystal — see DUTCH	

DANCE CLUB PLAY

DEBUT DATE	PEAK POS	WKS CHR	G L D	ARTIST / Title	Label & Number
				WATLEY, Jody	
7/5/03	19	12		Whenever	Peace Bisquit 106
				WEEKEND PLAYERS ★	
				Electronic duo from England: Rachel Foster (vocals) and Andy Cato (producer). Cato is also a member of Groove Armada.	
3/22/03	❶¹	15		I'll Be There	ffrr (promo)
8/9/03	❶¹	15		Into The Sun	Multiply (promo)
				WHORIZON ★	
8/23/03	35	8		I'm Feelin' High	Cutting 458
				WOODWARD, Lucy ★	
8/2/03	3	15		Blindsided	Atlantic 88172

130

1. **FUNKY GREEN DOGS**
459

2. **MADONNA**
345

3. **JUSTIN TIMBERLAKE**
331

4.	239	SEAL	13.	198	MARIAH CAREY
5.	232	KRISTINE W	14.	198	THE SCUMFROG ★
6.	231	BOOMKAT	15.	189	CONJURE ONE
7.	230	WEEKEND PLAYERS ★	16.	188	VIVIAN GREEN ★
8.	229	LAURA PAUSINI	17.	184	MIA
9.	227	WHITNEY HOUSTON	18.	182	FRIBURN & URIK
10.	227	JEWEL	19.	179	DAVE GAHAN ★
11.	222	BEYONCÉ	20.	176	YOKO ONO
12.	212	BECKY BAELING ★			

TOP 30 DANCE CLUB PLAY

PEAK DATE	WEEKS				RANK	RECORD TITLE	PEAK POSITION	ARTIST
	CH	20	10	PK				
							1	
9/27	14	10	7	2	1.	Get It Together		Seal
8/9	14	8	6	2	2.	Pavement Cracks		Annie Lennox
12/27	13	8	6	2	3.	Me Against The Music		Britney Spears Featuring Madonna
10/11	15	10	8	1	4.	Into The Sun		Weekend Players
2/15	17	11	7	1	5.	Head		Thunderpuss & Barnes
1/25	16	11	7	1	6.	Some Lovin'		Murk vs Kristine W
2/1	14	11	7	1	7.	Surrender		Laura Pausini
12/20	15	9	7	1	8.	Believe		Murk
12/13	15	9	7	1	9.	Waiting For You		Seal
9/20	15	8	7	1	10.	My Time		Dutch Featuring Crystal Waters
10/18	14	8	7	1	11.	Send Your Love		Sting
7/19	13	8	7	1	12.	So Gone		Monica
3/1	17	11	6	1	13.	The Wreckoning		Boomkat
11/29	16	11	6	1	14.	Fly Again		Kristine W
7/5	16	10	6	1	15.	Not Gonna Get Us		t.A.T.u.
6/14	15	10	6	1	16.	If That's Love		Laura Pausini
10/25	15	10	6	1	17.	I Love I Love		Georgie Porgie
5/10	14	10	6	1	18.	Walking On Thin Ice		Ono
8/2	13	10	6	1	19.	Alright		Murk
3/8	15	9	6	1	20.	Rise Up		Funky Green Dogs
5/17	15	9	6	1	21.	I'll Be There		Weekend Players
6/7	14	9	6	1	22.	Rock Your Body		Justin Timberlake
3/15	14	9	6	1	23.	The Hum Melody		Robbie Rivera
5/24	14	9	6	1	24.	Love Is A Crime		Anastacia
4/12	14	9	6	1	25.	Try It On My Own		Whitney Houston
7/26	14	9	6	1	26.	Intuition		Jewel
1/18	13	9	6	1	27.	Like I Love You		Justin Timberlake
2/8	14	8	6	1	28.	Through The Rain		Mariah Carey
11/8	14	8	6	1	29.	What U Do 2 Me		Boomkat
8/30	14	8	6	1	30.	Sunrise		Simply Red

#1 HOT DANCE CLUB PLAY *

	Date Hit #1	Wks. @ #1	Title	Artist
1.	1/4	3	Dark Beat (Addicted 2 Drums)................ Oscar G & Ralph Falcon (includes 1 week at #1 in 2002)	
2.	1/18	1	Like I Love You .... Justin Timberlake	
3.	1/25	1	Some Lovin' .... Murk vs Kristine W	
4.	2/1	1	Surrender .... Laura Pausini	
5.	2/8	1	Through The Rain .... Mariah Carey	
6.	2/15	1	Head .... Thunderpuss & Barnes	
7.	2/22	1	Emotional Rollercoaster........................... Vivian Green	
8.	3/1	1	The Wreckoning .... Boomkat	
9.	3/8	1	Rise Up..Funky Green Dogs	
10.	3/15	1	The Hum Melody.. Robbie Rivera	
11.	3/22	1	Dance To The Rhythm .... Friburn & Urik	
12.	3/29	1	I Believe .... Chris Cox Vs. Happy Clappers	
13.	4/5	1	When The Money's Gone.. Cher	
14.	4/12	1	Try It On My Own................................. Whitney Houston	
15.	4/19	1	Beautiful ....Christina Aguilera	
16.	4/26	1	On A High .... Duncan Sheik	
17.	5/3	1	Gossip Folks ....Missy "Misdemeanor" Elliott Featuring Ludacris	
18.	5/10	1	Walking On Thin Ice .... Ono	
19.	5/17	1	I'll Be There... Weekend Players	
20.	5/24	1	Love Is A Crime ....Anastacia	
21.	5/31	1	American Life ....Madonna	
22.	6/7	1	Rock Your Body .... Justin Timberlake	
23.	6/14	1	If That's Love .... Laura Pausini	
24.	6/21	1	Love That Man .... Whitney Houston	
25.	6/28	1	Getaway .... Becky Baeling	
26.	7/5	1	Not Gonna Get Us .... t.A.T.u.	
27.	7/12	1	Play Your Part .... Deborah Cox	
28.	7/19	1	So Gone .... Monica	
29.	7/26	1	Intuition .... Jewel	
30.	8/2	1	Alright .... Murk	
31.	8/9	2	Pavement Cracks .... Annie Lennox	
32.	8/23	1	Hollywood ....Madonna	
33.	8/30	1	Sunrise.. Simply Red	
34.	9/6	1	Harem .... Sarah Brightman	
35.	9/13	1	Crazy In Love .... Beyoncé	
36.	9/20	1	My Time ....Dutch Featuring Crystal Waters	
37.	9/27	2	Get It Together ....Seal	
38.	10/11	1	Into The Sun .... Weekend Players	
39.	10/18	1	Send Your Love .... Sting	
40.	10/25	1	I Love I Love ....Georgie Porgie	
41.	11/1	1	Lei Lo Lai .... The Latin Project	
42.	11/8	1	What U Do 2 Me .... Boomkat	
43.	11/15	1	This Beat Is .... Superchumbo	
44.	11/22	1	Stand.. Jewel	
45.	11/29	1	Fly Again .... Kristine W	
46.	12/6	1	Milkshake .... Kelis	
47.	12/13	1	Waiting For You ....Seal	
48.	12/20	1	Believe .... Murk	
49.	12/27	2	Me Against The Music .... Britney Spears Featuring Madonna (includes 1 week at #1 in 2004)	

* Chart renamed on 10/25/03 (previously known as "Club Play").

#1 HOT DANCE SINGLES SALES *

	Date Hit #1	Wks. @ #1	Title	Artist
1.	1/4	16	**Die Another Day** .... *Madonna* (includes 8 weeks at #1 in 2002)	
2.	3/1	1	**Through The Rain** .... *Mariah Carey*	
3.	3/8	5	**Cry Me A River** .... *Justin Timberlake*	
4.	4/12	10↕	**If You're Not The One** .... *Daniel Bedingfield*	
5.	5/17	1	**American Life** .... *Madonna*	
6.	6/28	5↕	**Stuck** .... *Stacie Orrico*	
7.	7/26	7↕	**Hollywood** .... *Madonna*	
8.	9/6	1	**Officially Missing You** .... *Tamia*	
9.	9/27	12↕	**Rubberneckin'** .... *Elvis Presley*	
10.	10/4	1	**Sympathy For The Devil** .... *The Rolling Stones*	
11.	12/27	1	**Nothing Fails/Nobody Knows Me** .... *Madonna*	

* Chart renamed on 3/1/03 to "Dance Singles Sales" and renamed again to current name on 10/25/03 (previously known as "Maxi-Singles Sales").

#1 HOT DANCE RADIO AIRPLAY *

	Date Hit #1	Wks. @ #1	Title	Artist
1.	10/25	3	**Just The Way You Are** .... *Milky*	
2.	11/15	1	**Baby Boy** .... *Beyoncé*	
3.	11/22	11↕	**Something Happened On The Way To Heaven** .... *Deborah Cox* (includes 5 weeks at #1 in 2004)	

* Chart first published in *Billboard* on 10/25/03.

MAINSTREAM ROCK TRACKS

This section lists, by artist, every album track that debuted in 2003 on *Billboard's* **Mainstream Rock Tracks** chart — a weekly compilation of the 40 most-played album tracks on the nation's mainstream rock radio stations.

As of August 2, 2003 Billboard reduced the size of the chart published in the magazine to a Top 20, and on October 25, 2003 the chart was discontinued in the magazine. However, the full weekly Top 40 chart continues to be available on Billboard's Web site.

The album title as well as the album label and number are listed to the immediate right of the rock track.

DEBUT DATE	PEAK POS	WKS CHR	ARTIST / Rock Track	Album Title	Album Label & Number
			ADEMA		
7/19/03	25	11	Unstable	*Unstable*	Arista 53914
			AFI ★		
3/15/03	33	10	Girl's Not Grey	*Sing The Sorrow*	Nitro 450380
8/2/03	31	10	The Leaving Song Pt. II	*Sing The Sorrow*	Nitro 450380
			ALIEN ANT FARM		
8/9/03	38	1	These Days	*truANT*	El Tonal 000568
			ALLMAN BROTHERS BAND, The		
4/12/03	37	7	Firing Line	*Hittin' The Note*	Peach 84599
			ATARIS, The ★		
8/30/03	36	5	The Boys Of Summer	*So Long, Astoria*	Columbia 86184
			#1 Mainstream Rock hit for Don Henley in 1984		
			AUDIOSLAVE		
2/1/03	❶^{12}	39	Like A Stone	*Audioslave*	Interscope 86968
6/14/03	2^1	38	Show Me How To Live	*Audioslave*	Interscope 86968
10/4/03+	2^2	27↑	I Am The Highway	*Audioslave*	Interscope 86968
			BLACK LABEL SOCIETY ★		
			Hard-rock duo from Jersey City, New Jersey: Zakk Wylde (vocals, guitar, bass) and Craig Nunenmacher (drums). Wylde was lead guitarist for Ozzy Osbourne and his own group, Pride & Glory.		
4/12/03	12	26	Stillborn — ZAKK WYLDE'S BLACK LABEL SOCIETY	*The Blessed Hellride*	Spitfire 15091
			BLANK THEORY, The ★		
			Rock group from Chicago, Illinois: brothers Nathan (vocals, guitar) and Matthew (bass) Leone, Michael Foderaro (guitar), Shawn Currie (keyboards) and James Knight (drums).		
1/25/03	36	5	Middle Of Nowhere	*Beyond The Calm Of The Corridor*	Scratchie 39021
			BLINDSIDE		
2/22/03	31	9	Sleepwalking	*Silence*	Elektra 62765
			BON JOVI		
3/1/03	39	1	Bounce	*Bounce*	Island 063055
			BREAKING BENJAMIN		
3/8/03	24	14	Skin	*Saturate*	Hollywood 62356
			CAVE IN ★		
			Rock group from Boston, Massachusetts: Stephen Brodsky (vocals, guitar), Adam McGrath (guitar), Caleb Scofield (bass) and John-Robert Conners (drums).		
6/7/03	37	1	Anchor	*Antenna*	RCA 68131
			CHEVELLE		
2/8/03	❶^4	35	Send The Pain Below	*Wonder What's Next*	Epic 86157
9/20/03+	17	23	Closure	*Wonder What's Next*	Epic 86157
			COLD		
3/15/03	4	28	Stupid Girl	*Year Of The Spider*	Flip 000006
9/6/03	17	16	Suffocate	*Year Of The Spider*	Flip 000006
			DARKNESS, The ★		
			Rock group from England: brothers Justin (vocals) and Dan (guitar) Hawkins, Frankie Poullain (bass) and Ed Graham (drums).		
12/27/03+	23	15↑	I Believe In A Thing Called Love	*Permission To Land*	Atlantic 60817
			DEFAULT		
11/1/03	25	15	(Taking My) Life Away	*Elocation*	TVT 6000
			DEFTONES		
5/10/03	16	14	Minerva	*Deftones*	Maverick 48350
			DIE TRYING ★		
			Rock group from Sacramento, California: Jassen Jenson (vocals), Jack Sinamian (guitar), Steve Avery (bass) and Matt Conley (drums).		
6/7/03	35	8	Oxygen's Gone	*Die Trying*	Island 000099
			DISTURBED		
6/21/03	4	27	Liberate	*Believe*	Reprise 48320
			DONNAS, The ★		
1/4/03	31	10	Take It Off	*Spend The Night*	Atlantic 83567

MAINSTREAM ROCK TRACKS

DEBUT DATE	PEAK POS	WKS CHR	ARTIST / Rock Track	Album Title	Album Label & Number
			DOUBLEDRIVE		
4/5/03	22	19	Imprint	*Blue In The Face*	Roadrunner 618441
			ELEMENT EIGHTY ★		
			Hard-rock group from Tyler, Texas: Dave Galloway (vocals), Matt Woods (guitar), Roon (bass) and Ryan Carroll (drums).		
11/29/03	36	9	Broken Promises	*Element Eighty*	Republic 128402
			EVANESCENCE ★		
3/15/03	11	26	Bring Me To Life	*Fallen*	Wind-Up 13063
			Paul McCoy (of rock group 12 Stones; guest vocal); featured in the movie *Daredevil* starring Ben Affleck		
8/2/03	26	15	Going Under	*Fallen*	Wind-Up 13063
			FINCH ★		
			Rock group from Los Angeles, California: Nate Barcalow (vocals), Randy Strohmeyer and Alex Linares (guitars), Derek Doherty (bass) and Alex Pappas (drums).		
3/1/03	35	10	What It Is To Burn	*What It Is To Burn*	Drive-Thru 860991
			FINGER ELEVEN		
10/4/03	38	8	One Thing	*Finger Eleven*	Wind-Up 13058
			FINGERTIGHT ★		
			Rock group from San Francisco, California: Scott Rose (vocals), Sergio Renoso (guitar), Jesse Del Rio (bass) and Kirk Shelton (drums).		
9/13/03	34	6	Guilt (Hold Down)	*In The Name Of Progress*	Columbia 86377
			FOO FIGHTERS		
2/1/03	5	26	Times Like These	*One By One*	Roswell 68008
7/26/03	23	10	Low	*One By One*	Roswell 68008
			40 BELOW SUMMER ★		
			Hard-rock group from New Jersey: Max Illidge (vocals), Joe D'Amico (guitar), Jordan Plingos (guitar), Hector Graziani (bass) and Carlos Aguilar (drums).		
12/27/03+	39	3	Self Medicate	*The Mourning After*	Razor & Tie 82898
			FUEL		
1/4/03	22	11	Won't Back Down	*Daredevil (soundtrack)*	Wind-Up 13079
8/9/03	9	26	Falls On Me	*Natural Selection*	Epic 86392
			GODSMACK		
2/15/03	❶[2]	29	Straight Out Of Line	*Faceless*	Republic 067854
7/5/03	7	26	Serenity	*Faceless*	Republic 067854
11/29/03+	3	19↑	Re-Align	*Faceless*	Republic 067854
			(HED)PLANET EARTH		
2/15/03	21	15	Blackout	*Blackout*	Volcano 41817
8/16/03	40	1	Other Side	*Blackout*	Volcano 41817
			HOOBASTANK		
10/25/03+	16	19	Out Of Control	*The Reason*	Island 001488
			HOTWIRE ★		
			Hard-rock group from Newbury Park, California: Russ Martin (vocals, guitar), Gabe Garcia (guitar), Chris Strauser (bass) and Brian Borg (drums).		
9/13/03	40	1	Not Today	*The Routine*	RCA 50669
			ILL NIÑO		
8/30/03	26	16	How Can I Live	*Freddy vs. Jason (soundtrack)*	Roadrunner 618347
			JANE'S ADDICTION		
6/14/03	4	19	Just Because	*Strays*	Capitol 90186
10/18/03	35	5	True Nature	*Strays*	Capitol 90186
			JET ★		
9/27/03+	7	28↑	Are You Gonna Be My Girl	*Get Born*	Elektra 62892

DEBUT DATE	PEAK POS	WKS CHR	ARTIST / Rock Track	Album Title	Album Label & Number
			KID ROCK		
11/8/03	33	12	Feel Like Makin Love	*Kid Rock*	Top Dog 83865
			#10 Pop hit for Bad Company in 1975		
			KORN		
7/12/03	12	19	Did My Time	*Take A Look In The Mirror*	Immortal 90335
			featured in the movie *Lara Croft Tomb Raider: The Cradle Of Life* starring Angelina Jolie		
10/18/03	11	19	Right Now	*Take A Look In The Mirror*	Immortal 90335
			LEISUREWORLD ★		
			Rock group from Toronto, Ontario, Canada: Cade Lakeshore (vocals), Patricia Melia (guitar), Patrick Worthington (bass) and Brent Empress (drums).		
3/1/03	37	2	I'm Dead	*Double Wide Double High*	Artist Direct 1122
			LIMP BIZKIT		
8/23/03	16	10	Eat You Alive	*Results May Vary*	Flip 001235
10/25/03+	11	24↑	Behind Blue Eyes	*Results May Vary*	Flip 001235
			#34 Pop hit for The Who in 1971		
			LINKIN PARK		
3/15/03	❶[1]	26	Somewhere I Belong	*Meteora*	Warner 48186
6/21/03	2[2]	28	Faint	*Meteora*	Warner 48186
10/11/03+	❶[3]	26↑	Numb	*Meteora*	Warner 48186
			LIVE		
5/10/03	33	7	Heaven	*Birds Of Pray*	Radioactive 000374
			LOSTPROPHETS ★		
			Rock group formed in Wales: Ian Watkins (vocals), Mike Lewis and Lee Gaze (guitars), Stuart Richardson (bass) and Mike Chiplin (drums).		
12/27/03+	14↑	15↑	Last Train Home	*Start Something*	Columbia 86554
			LYNYRD SKYNYRD		
4/26/03	27	16	Red White & Blue	*Vicious Cycle*	Sanctuary 84607
			MANMADE GOD ★		
			Rock group from San Francisco, California: Pann (vocals), Craig Locicero (guitar), James Walker (bass) and Steve Jacobs (drums).		
6/21/03	36	8	Safe Passage	*Manmade God*	American 014102
			MANSON, Marilyn		
5/3/03	18	13	mOBSCENE	*The Golden Age Of Grotesque*	Nothing 000370
			MEMENTO ★		
			Rock group from Australia: Justin Cotta (vocals), Jason "Space" Smith (guitar), Leighton "Lats" Kearns (bass) and Steve Clark (drums).		
5/24/03	28	10	Nothing Sacred	*Beginnings*	Columbia 86631
11/15/03	35	6	Saviour	*Beginnings*	Columbia 86631
			METALLICA		
6/14/03	2[2]	11	St. Anger	*St. Anger*	Elektra 62853
8/9/03	21	10	Frantic	*St. Anger*	Elektra 62853
12/20/03+	28	11	The Unnamed Feeling	*St. Anger*	Elektra 62853
			MOTOGRATER ★		
			Hard-rock group from Texas: Ghost (vocals), Nuke (guitar), Smur (bass) and Crispy (drums).		
8/16/03	29	12	Down	*Motograter*	Elektra 62837
			MUDVAYNE		
5/31/03	16	26	World So Cold	*The End Of All Things To Come*	Epic 86487
			NICKELBACK		
8/16/03	2[8]	26	Someday	*The Long Road*	Roadrunner 618400
11/15/03+	❶[11]↑	21↑	Figured You Out	*The Long Road*	Roadrunner 618400
			OFFSPRING, The		
11/15/03+	6	21↑	Hit That	*Splinter*	Columbia 89026
			OLEANDER		
2/15/03	25	10	Hands Off The Wheel	*Joyride*	Sanctuary 84593

MAINSTREAM ROCK TRACKS

DEBUT DATE	PEAK POS	WKS CHR	ARTIST / Rock Track	Album Title	Album Label & Number
			OUTSPOKEN ★		
			Rock group from Louisville, Kentucky: David Frazier (vocals), Kevin McCreery (guitar), Shaun Kennedy (guitar), Frank Green (bass) and Donnie Highland (drums).		
1/25/03	22	10	Farther	*Bitter Shovel* ....Lava 83589	
			PERFECT CIRCLE, A		
8/16/03	❶²	26	Weak And Powerless	*Thirteenth Step*.................Virgin 80918	
12/20/03+	3↑	16↑	The Outsider	*Thirteenth Step*.................Virgin 80918	
			PILLAR ★		
			Christian hard-rock group from Hays, Kansas: Rob Beckley (vocals), Noah Hanson (guitar), Michael "Kalel" Wittig (bass) and Brad Noone (drums).		
6/28/03	37	6	Fireproof	*Fireproof*....................Flicker 2617	
			P.O.D.		
5/3/03	20	9	Sleeping Awake	*The Matrix Reloaded (soundtrack)*..........Warner Sunset 48411	
10/11/03	12	18	Will You	*Payable On Death*................Atlantic 83676	
			POWERMAN 5000		
4/5/03	10	25	Free	*Transform* ....DreamWorks 450433	
9/6/03	27	9	Action	*Transform* ....DreamWorks 450433	
			PRESENCE ★		
			Rock group from Tallahassee, Florida: Jay Slim (vocals), Dave Fulmer (guitar), D.J. Stange (bass) and Nick Wells (drums).		
4/26/03	31	7	Tonz Of Fun	*Rise*.....................Curb 78766	
			PROJECT 86 ★		
			Christian rock group from Anaheim, California: Andrew Schwab (vocals), Randy Torres (guitar), Steven Dail (bass) and Alex Albert (drums).		
3/8/03	35	5	Hollow Again	*Truthless Heros*.............Atlantic 83568	
			PUDDLE OF MUDD		
10/25/03	❶³	24↑	Away From Me	*Life On Display* ....Flawless 001080	
			QUEENS OF THE STONE AGE		
5/3/03	24	11	Go With The Flow	*Songs For The Deaf* ....Interscope 493425	
			QUEENSRŸCHE		
8/2/03	38	1	Open	*Tribe* ....Sanctuary 84578	
			RA		
5/24/03	30	8	Rectifier..	*From One* ....Republic 066093	
			RED HOT CHILI PEPPERS		
1/4/03	15	26	Can't Stop	*By The Way* ....Warner 48140	
11/22/03	22	13	Fortune Faded	*Greatest Hits* ....Warner 48545	
			REVIS ★		
			Rock group from Carbondale, Illinois: Justin Holman (vocals), Robert Davis (guitar), Nathaniel Cox (guitars), Bob Thiemann (bass) and David Piribauer (drums).		
3/8/03	8	26	Caught In The Rain	*Places For Breathing* ....Epic 86514	
10/11/03	29	10	Seven...	*Places For Breathing* ....Epic 86514	
			SALIVA		
3/15/03	11	17	Rest In Pieces..	*Back Into Your System* ....Island 063153	
7/19/03	29	8	Raise Up	*Back Into Your System* ....Island 063153	
			SEETHER		
3/22/03	13	26	Driven Under..	*Disclaimer* ....Wind-Up 13068	
9/13/03	8	26	Gasoline	*Disclaimer* ....Wind-Up 13068	
			SEVENDUST		
9/6/03	10	26	Enemy	*Seasons*.......................TVT 5990	
			SHINEDOWN ★		
			Rock group from Jacksonville, Florida: Brent Smith (vocals), Jasin Todd (guitar), Brad Stewart (bass) and Barry Kerch (drums).		
4/19/03	5	29	Fly From The Inside	*Leave A Whisper* ....Atlantic 83566	
11/1/03+	7↑	23↑	45	*Leave A Whisper* ....Atlantic 83566	
			SKRAPE		
12/6/03	34	10	Stand Up (Summer Song)............................	*Up The Dose*................................RCA 54528	

140

DEBUT DATE	PEAK POS	WKS CHR	ARTIST / Rock Track	Album Title	Album Label & Number
			SLOTH ★		
			Rock group from Los Angeles, California: Rich Love (vocals), Kristo Panos (guitar), Andy Kovatch (bass) and Adam Figura (drums).		
8/16/03	25	13	Someday	*Dead Generation*	Hollywood 162374
			SMILE EMPTY SOUL ★		
5/10/03	8	27	Bottom Of A Bottle	*Smile Empty Soul*	Throback 83639
11/22/03+	26	16	Nowhere Kids	*Smile Empty Soul*	Throback 83639
			SOCIALBURN		
5/31/03	23	11	Everyone	*Where You Are*	Elektra 62790
			SPARTA ★		
			Rock group from El Paso, Texas: Jim Ward (vocals, guitar), Paul Hinojos (guitar), Matt Miller (bass) and Tony Hajjar (drums). Ward, Hinojos and Hajjar are also members of At The Drive-In.		
1/4/03	35	3	Air	*Wiretap Scars*	DreamWorks 450366
			STAIND		
4/19/03	2^1	17	Price To Play	*14 Shades Of Grey*	Flip 62882
6/28/03	❶^{14}	41↑	So Far Away	*14 Shades Of Grey*	Flip 62882
11/22/03+	10	20↑	How About You	*14 Shades Of Grey*	Flip 62882
			STATIC-X		
9/27/03	22	16	The Only	*Shadow Zone*	Warner 48427
			STEREOMUD		
1/25/03	29	11	Breathing	*Every Given Moment*	Columbia 86488
			STONE SOUR		
2/22/03	18	11	Inhale	*Stone Sour*	Roadrunner 618425
			STONE TEMPLE PILOTS		
11/1/03	5	16	All In The Suit That You Wear	*Thank You*	Atlantic 83586
			STYX		
3/1/03	37	2	Waiting For Our Time	*Cyclorama*	Sanctuary 86337
			SYSTEMATIC		
4/26/03	39	3	Leaving Only Scars	*Pleasure To Burn*	Elektra 62845
			TAPROOT		
3/29/03	23	12	Mine	*Welcome*	Atlantic 83561
			THEORY OF A DEADMAN		
2/1/03	13	19	Make Up Your Mind	*Theory Of A Deadman*	Roadrunner 618421
			THREE DAYS GRACE ★		
8/2/03	4	35↑	(I Hate) Everything About You	*Three Days Grace*	Jive 53479
			3 DOORS DOWN		
4/5/03	8	22	The Road I'm On	*Away From The Sun*	Republic 066165
8/16/03	14	26	Here Without You	*Away From The Sun*	Republic 066165
			THRICE ★		
			Punk-rock group from Anaheim, California: Dustin Kensrue (vocals, guitar), brothers Ed (bass) and Riley (drums) Breckenridge and Teppi Teranishi (guitar).		
9/20/03	36	4	All That's Left	*The Artist In The Ambulance*	Island 000295
			TRAIN		
6/14/03	40	1	Calling All Angels	*My Private Nation*	Columbia 86593
			TRAPT		
7/12/03	❶^1	36	Still Frame	*Trapt*	Warner 48296
			TYPE O NEGATIVE		
7/5/03	40	1	I Don't Wanna Be Me	*Life Is Killing Me*	Roadrunner 618438
			UNLOCO ★		
			Hard-rock group from Austin, Texas: Joey Duenas (vocals), Marc Serrano (guitar), Victor Escareno (bass) and Peter Navarrette (drums).		
3/22/03	25	13	Failure	*Becoming I*	Maverick 48352
			VELVET REVOLVER ★		
			All-star rock group: Scott Weiland (vocals; Stone Temple Pilots) and Dave Kushner (guitar), with former Guns N' Roses members Slash (guitar), Duff McKagen (bass) and Matt Sorum (drums).		
7/5/03	17	11	Set Me Free	*Hulk (soundtrack)*	Decca 63302

DEBUT DATE	PEAK POS	WKS CHR	ARTIST Rock Track	Album Title	Album Label & Number
			V SHAPE MIND ★		
			Hard-rock group from Decatur, Illinois: Brad Hursh (vocals, guitar), Jeff McElyea (guitar), Vic Zientara (bass) and Scott Parjani (drums).		
11/8/03	**40**	2	Monsters .... *Cul-De-Sac* ....Republic 101002		
			WHITE STRIPES, The ★		
7/12/03	**12**	26	Seven Nation Army .... *Elephant*............................Third Man 27148		
			ZOMBIE, Rob		
11/15/03	**39**	2	Two-Lane Blacktop .... *Past, Present & Future*.........Geffen 001041		

1. **STAIND**
378+

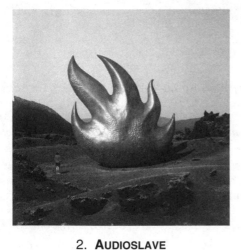

2. **AUDIOSLAVE**
377

3. **SEETHER**
307

4.	305	**SALIVA**		13.	161	**METALLICA**
5.	291	**TRAPT**		14.	155	**TAPROOT**
6.	291	**CHEVELLE**		15.	154	**QUEENS OF THE STONE AGE**
7.	249	**LINKIN PARK**		16.	151	**FOO FIGHTERS**
8.	225	**GODSMACK**		17.	151	**NICKELBACK**
9.	187	**DISTURBED**		18.	148	**KORN**
10.	164	**COLD**		19.	144 +	**PUDDLE OF MUDD**
11.	163	**3 DOORS DOWN**		20.	142	**FUEL**
12.	162	**MUDVAYNE**			142	**SOCIALBURN**

+ Subject to change since a title that peaked in 2003 by this artist is still charted as of the 4/3/04 cut-off date.

PEAK DATE	WEEKS				RANK	RECORD TITLE	PEAK POSITION	ARTIST
	CH	20	10	PK				
							1	
8/16	41 +	39 +	31	14	1.	So Far Away		Staind
4/19	39	37	28	12	2.	Like A Stone		Audioslave
7/12	35	30	22	4	3.	Send The Pain Below		Chevelle
12/13	24 +	21	18	3	4.	Away From Me		Puddle Of Mudd
3/29	29	29	23	2	5.	Straight Out Of Line		Godsmack
11/22	26	25	20	2	6.	Weak And Powerless		A Perfect Circle
7/26	55	42	30	1	7.	Headstrong		Trapt
4/12	26	25	20	1	8.	Somewhere I Belong		Linkin Park
12/6	36	29	19	1	9.	Still Frame		Trapt
							2	
1/4	35	34	21	12	10.	Always		Saliva
9/13	26	20	14	8	11.	Someday		Nickelback
8/23	28	26	17	2	12.	Faint		Linkin Park
6/14	11	9	8	2	13.	St. Anger		Metallica
9/6	38	35	19	1	14.	Show Me How To Live		Audioslave
6/7	17	12	11	1	15.	Price To Play		Staind
							3	
2/15	48	40	19	5	16.	Fine Again		Seether
2/1	43	36	19	2	17.	The Red		Chevelle
							4	
12/20	35 +	21 +	18 +	8	18.	(I Hate) Everything About You		Three Days Grace
11/1	27	23	15	2	19.	Liberate		Disturbed
7/19	28	21	13	2	20.	Stupid Girl		Cold
8/9	19	12	8	1	21.	Just Because		Jane's Addiction
							5	
9/6	29	19	11	4	22.	Fly From The Inside		Shinedown
4/12	26	17	10	2	23.	Times Like These		Foo Fighters
11/22	16	11	7	2	24.	All In The Suit That You Wear		Stone Temple Pilots
2/15	28	23	8	1	25.	Poem		Taproot
3/8	28	23	8	1	26.	No One Knows		Queens Of The Stone Age
							6	
4/12	30	28	17	3	27.	Remember		Disturbed
							7	
10/11	26	22	12	3	28.	Serenity		Godsmack
2/1	26	12	5	1	29.	Weathered		Creed
							8	
7/19	26	21	10	3	30.	Caught In The Rain		Revis

#1 MAINSTREAM ROCK TRACKS

	Date Hit #1	Wks @ #1	Title	Artist
1.	1/4	17	**When I'm Gone** ....*3 Doors Down* (includes 5 weeks at #1 in 2002)	
2.	3/29	2	**Straight Out Of Line**..*Godsmack*	
3.	4/12	1	**Somewhere I Belong**...*Linkin Park*	
4.	4/19	12	**Like A Stone**...*Audioslave*	
5.	7/12	4↕	**Send The Pain Below** ....*Chevelle*	
6.	7/26	1	**Headstrong** ....*Trapt*	
7.	8/16	14	**So Far Away** ....*Staind*	
8.	11/22	2	**Weak And Powerless**...................................*A Perfect Circle*	
9.	12/6	1	**Still Frame**..*Trapt*	
10.	12/13	3	**Away From Me** ....*Puddle Of Mudd*	

MODERN ROCK TRACKS

This section lists, by artist, every album track that debuted in 2003 on *Billboard's* **Modern Rock Tracks** chart — a weekly compilation of the 40 most-played album tracks on modern rock radio stations.

The album title as well as the album label and number are listed to the immediate right of the rock track.

DEBUT DATE	PEAK POS	WKS CHR	ARTIST / Rock Track	Album Title	Album Label & Number
			ADEMA		
8/16/03	37	4	Unstable	*Unstable*	Arista 53914
			AFI ★		
2/15/03	7	23	Girl's Not Grey	*Sing The Sorrow*	Nitro 450380
7/5/03	16	18	The Leaving Song Pt. II	*Sing The Sorrow*	Nitro 450380
12/6/03+	8↑	18↑	Silver And Cold	*Sing The Sorrow*	Nitro 450380
			ALIEN ANT FARM		
7/26/03	29	7	These Days	*truANT*	El Tonal 000568
			ALKALINE TRIO ★		
			Punk-rock trio from Chicago, Illinois: Matt Skiba (vocals, guitar), Daniel Andriano (bass) and Derek Grant (drums).		
7/5/03	38	1	We've Had Enough	*Good Mourning*	Vagrant 381
			ALL-AMERICAN REJECTS, The		
5/24/03	29	8	The Last Song	*The All-American Rejects*	Doghouse 450407
			AMERICAN HI-FI		
2/1/03	33	7	The Art Of Losing	*The Art Of Losing*	Island 063657
			ATARIS, The ★		
3/1/03	11	15	In This Diary	*So Long, Astoria*	Columbia 86184
6/14/03	2¹	22	The Boys Of Summer	*So Long, Astoria*	Columbia 86184
			#1 Mainstream Rock hit for Don Henley in 1984		
11/1/03	27	7	The Saddest Song	*So Long, Astoria*	Columbia 86184
			AUDIOSLAVE		
2/1/03	❶²	33	Like A Stone	*Audioslave*	Interscope 86968
6/28/03	4	26	Show Me How To Live	*Audioslave*	Interscope 86968
10/18/03+	3	25↑	I Am The Highway	*Audioslave*	Interscope 86968
			BECK		
3/15/03	36	2	Lost Cause	*Sea Change*	DGC 493393
			BILLY TALENT ★		
			Punk-rock group from Streetsville, Ontario, Canada: Ben Kowalewicz (vocals), Ian D'Sa (guitar), Jon Gallant (bass) and Aaron Solowoniuk (drums).		
8/16/03	24	11	Try Honesty	*Billy Talent*	Atlantic 83614
			BLINK-182		
10/18/03	2³	25↑	Feeling This	*Blink-182*	Geffen 001334
			BLUR		
3/29/03	22	9	Crazy Beat	*Think Tank*	Food 84242
			BRAND NEW ★		
			Punk-rock group from Merrick, New York: Jesse Lacey (vocals), Vincent Accardi (guitar), Garrett Tierney (bass) and Brian Lane (drums).		
9/6/03	37	6	The Quiet Things That No One Ever Knows	*Deja Entendu*	Triple Crown 82896
			BREAKING BENJAMIN		
4/12/03	37	4	Skin	*Saturate*	Hollywood 62356
			BURNING BRIDES ★		
			Hard-rock trio from Philadelphia, Pennsylvania: Dimitri Coats (vocals, guitar), Melanie Campbell (bass) and Mike Ambs (drums).		
3/1/03	31	6	Arctic Snow	*Fall Of The Plastic Empire*	File 13 35
			CASH, Johnny ★		
			Born J.R. Cash on 2/26/32 in Kingsland, Arkansas; raised in Dyess, Arkansas. Died of diabetes on 9/12/2003 (age 71). Legendary country singer/songwriter/guitarist. Inducted into the Rock and Roll Hall of Fame in 1992. Won Grammy's Lifetime Achievement Award in 1999.		
3/15/03	33	2	Hurt	*American IV: The Man Comes Around*	American 063339
			#8 Modern Rock hit for Nine Inch Nails in 1995		
			CAVE IN ★		
5/10/03	34	4	Anchor	*Antenna*	RCA 68131
			CHEVELLE		
2/15/03	❶¹	36	Send The Pain Below	*Wonder What's Next*	Epic 86157
10/11/03+	11	22	Closure	*Wonder What's Next*	Epic 86157
			COLD		
3/29/03	6	26	Stupid Girl	*Year Of The Spider*	Flip 000006
9/20/03	21	12	Suffocate	*Year Of The Spider*	Flip 000006

DEBUT DATE	PEAK POS	WKS CHR	ARTIST / Rock Track	Album Title	Album Label & Number
			COLDPLAY		
4/26/03	18	12	The Scientist	*A Rush Of Blood To The Head*	Capitol 40504
11/8/03	24	12	Moses [L]	*Coldplay Live 2003*	Capitol 99014
			CRYSTAL METHOD, The		
12/20/03+	26	11	Born Too Slow	*Legion Of Boom*	V2 27176
			DARKNESS, The ★		
12/13/03+	9	17↑	I Believe In A Thing Called Love	*Permission To Land*	Atlantic 60817
			DASHBOARD CONFESSIONAL		
7/26/03	8	21	Hands Down	*A Mark, A Mission, A Brand, A Scar*	Vagrant 0385
			DEFTONES		
5/3/03	9	15	Minerva	*Deftones*	Maverick 48350
			D4, The ★		
			Punk-rock group from Auckland, New Zealand: Jimmy Christmas (vocals, guitar), Dion (vocals, guitar), Vaughan (bass) and Beaver (drums).		
4/5/03	39	1	Get Loose	*6twenty*	Flying Nun 162388
			DIE TRYING ★		
6/21/03	29	6	Oxygen's Gone	*Die Trying*	Island 000099
			DISTILLERS, The ★		
			Punk-rock group from Australia: Brody Dalle (vocals, guitar), Tony Bradley (vocals, guitar), Ryan Sinn (bass) and Andy Granelli (drums).		
11/22/03	28	10	Drain The Blood	*Coral Fang*	Hellcat 48586
			DISTURBED		
1/4/03	22	25	Remember	*Believe*	Reprise 48320
7/12/03	22	21	Liberate	*Believe*	Reprise 48320
			EVANESCENCE ★		
1/25/03	❶²	26	Bring Me To Life	*Fallen*	Wind-Up 13063
			Paul McCoy (of rock group 12 Stones; guest vocal); featured in the movie *Daredevil* starring Ben Affleck		
6/28/03	5	25	Going Under	*Fallen*	Wind-Up 13063
			EVERCLEAR		
2/1/03	30	6	Volvo Driving Soccer Mom	*Slow Motion Daydream*	Capitol 38270
			EVE 6		
6/14/03	9	17	Think Twice	*It's All In Your Head*	RCA 52346
			FINCH ★		
2/22/03	15	16	What It Is To Burn	*What It Is To Burn*	Drive-Thru 860991
			FINGER ELEVEN ★		
			Rock group from Toronto, Ontario, Canada: brothers Scott (vocals) and Sean (bass) Anderson, Rick Jackett and James Black (guitars) and Rob Gommerman (drums).		
11/29/03+	5	19↑	One Thing	*Finger Eleven*	Wind-Up 13058
			FOO FIGHTERS		
1/25/03	5	28	Times Like These	*One By One*	Roswell 68008
7/19/03	15	11	Low	*One By One*	Roswell 68008
11/29/03+	15	19↑	Darling Nikki	*(single only)*	Roswell 56370
			first recorded by Prince in 1984; only available as an Australian import single		
			FOUNTAINS OF WAYNE		
9/13/03	31	7	Stacy's Mom	*Welcome Interstate Managers*	S-Curve 90875
			FUEL		
2/8/03	37	3	Won't Back Down	*Daredevil (soundtrack)*	Wind-Up 13079
8/9/03	11	17	Falls On Me	*Natural Selection*	Epic 86392
			GODSMACK		
2/15/03	9	25	Straight Out Of Line	*Faceless*	Republic 067854
7/19/03	10	25	Serenity	*Faceless*	Republic 067854
12/27/03+	28	15↑	Re-Align	*Faceless*	Republic 067854

DEBUT DATE	PEAK POS	WKS CHR	ARTIST / Rock Track	Album Title	Album Label & Number
			GOOD CHARLOTTE		
2/1/03	**10**	18	The Anthem	The Young And The Hopeless	Daylight 86486
6/7/03	**28**	6	The Young And The Hopeless	The Young And The Hopeless	Daylight 86486
			(HED)PLANET EARTH		
3/22/03	**32**	8	Blackout	Blackout	Volcano 41817
			HOOBASTANK		
11/1/03	**9**	17	Out Of Control	The Reason	Island 001488
			HOT ACTION COP ★		
			Hard-rock/hip-hop group formed in Nashville, Tennessee: Rob Werthner (vocals), Tim Flaherty (guitar), Luis Espaillat (bass) and Kory Knipp (drums).		
4/12/03	**38**	1	Fever For The Flava	Hot Action Cop	Lava 83554
			HOT HOT HEAT ★		
			Rock group from Victoria, British Columbia, Canada: Steve Bays (vocals, keyboards), Dante DeCaro (guitar), Dustin Hawthorne (bass) and Paul Hawley (drums).		
5/10/03	**19**	19	Bandages	Make Up The Breakdown	Sub Pop 70599
10/18/03	**33**	5	Talk To Me, Dance With Me	Make Up The Breakdown	Sub Pop 70599
			JANE'S ADDICTION		
6/14/03	**❶**[1]	19	Just Because	Strays	Capitol 90186
10/18/03	**30**	5	True Nature	Strays	Capitol 90186
			JET ★		
9/13/03+	**3**	30↑	Are You Gonna Be My Girl	Get Born	Elektra 62892
			JOHNSON, Jack		
4/12/03	**31**	10	The Horizon Has Been Defeated	On And On	Moonshine Conspiracy 075012
			KORN		
7/12/03	**17**	14	Did My Time	Take A Look In The Mirror	Immortal 90335
			featured in the movie *Lara Croft Tomb Raider: The Cradle Of Life* starring Angelina Jolie		
10/25/03	**13**	16	Right Now	Take A Look In The Mirror	Immortal 90335
			LESS THAN JAKE		
8/9/03	**36**	5	The Science Of Selling Yourself Short	Anthem	Sire 48459
			LIMP BIZKIT		
8/23/03	**20**	8	Eat You Alive	Results May Vary	Flip 001235
12/20/03+	**18**	16↑	Behind Blue Eyes	Results May Vary	Flip 001235
			#34 Pop hit for The Who in 1971		
			LINKIN PARK		
3/15/03	**❶**[5]	26	Somewhere I Belong	Meteora	Warner 48186
5/17/03	**❶**[6]	37	Faint	Meteora	Warner 48186
10/4/03	**❶**[12]	27↑	Numb	Meteora	Warner 48186
			LIVE		
5/3/03	**33**	6	Heaven	Birds Of Pray	Radioactive 000374
			LOSTPROPHETS		
12/27/03+	**3**↑	15↑	Last Train Home	Start Something	Columbia 86554
			LYNCH, Liam ★		
			Born on 9/5/70 in Ohio. Singer/songwriter/guitarist. Co-creator of the short-lived MTV sock-puppet comedy series *The Sifl & Olly Show*.		
3/29/03	**34**	6	United States Of Whatever	Fake Songs	S-Curve 83743
			MANSON, Marilyn		
5/3/03	**26**	10	mOBSCENE	The Golden Age Of Grotesque	Nothing 000370
			MAROON5 ★		
1/18/03	**31**	9	Harder To Breathe	Songs About Jane	Octone 50001
			MATTHEWS, Dave, Band		
9/13/03	**35**	5	Gravedigger	Some Devil	RCA 55167

151

MODERN ROCK TRACKS

DEBUT DATE	PEAK POS	WKS CHR	ARTIST Rock Track	Album Title	Album Label & Number
			MATTHEWS, Dave, Band		
9/13/03	35	5	Gravedigger	*Some Devil*	RCA 55167
			METALLICA		
6/14/03	17	8	St. Anger	*St. Anger*	Elektra 62853
			NICKELBACK		
8/16/03	4	26	Someday	*The Long Road*	Roadrunner 618400
12/6/03+	4	18↑	Figured You Out	*The Long Road*	Roadrunner 618400
			OFFSPRING, The		
11/15/03+	❶[1]	21↑	Hit That	*Splinter*	Columbia 89026
			OUTKAST ★		
			Male hip-hop duo from Atlanta, Georgia: Andre "Dre" Benjamin and Antoine "Big Boi" Patton.		
10/18/03	16	18	Hey Ya!	*Speakerboxxx/The Love Below*	Arista 50133
			PACIFIER ★		
			Rock group from New Zealand: Jon Toogood (vocals, guitar), Phil Knight (guitar), Karl Kippenberger (bass) and Tom Larkin (drums).		
2/15/03	37	5	Bullitproof	*Pacifier*	Arista 14794
			PEARL JAM		
1/4/03	29	6	Save You	*Riot Act*	Epic 86825
			PERFECT CIRCLE, A		
8/16/03	❶[2]	26	Weak And Powerless	*Thirteenth Step*	Virgin 80918
12/13/03+	10↑	17↑	The Outsider	*Thirteenth Step*	Virgin 80918
			P.O.D.		
5/3/03	14	9	Sleeping Awake	*The Matrix Reloaded (soundtrack)*	Warner Sunset 48411
10/11/03	12	16	Will You	*Payable On Death*	Atlantic 83676
			POP, Iggy		
12/6/03	35	8	Little Know It All	*Skull Ring*	Virgin 80774
			POWERMAN 5000		
5/31/03	38	2	Free	*Transform*	DreamWorks 450433
			PUDDLE OF MUDD		
10/25/03	5	20	Away From Me	*Life On Display*	Flawless 001080
			QUEENS OF THE STONE AGE		
4/12/03	7	25	Go With The Flow	*Songs For The Deaf*	Interscope 493425
			RADIOHEAD		
5/10/03	14	15	There There	*Hail To The Thief*	Capitol 84543
9/13/03	32	5	Go To Sleep	*Hail To The Thief*	Capitol 84543
			RANCID		
8/2/03	13	11	Fall Back Down	*Indestructible*	Hellcat 48529
			RED HOT CHILI PEPPERS		
5/31/03	13	14	Dosed	*By The Way*	Warner 48140
11/22/03	8	15	Fortune Faded	*Greatest Hits*	Warner 48545
			REVIS ★		
3/22/03	20	16	Caught In The Rain	*Places For Breathing*	Epic 86514
			SALIVA		
3/22/03	20	14	Rest In Pieces	*Back Into Your System*	Island 063153
			SEETHER		
3/22/03	13	22	Driven Under	*Disclaimer*	Wind-Up 13068
10/4/03	37	5	Gasoline	*Disclaimer*	Wind-Up 13068
			SEVENDUST		
9/20/03	30	11	Enemy	*Seasons*	TVT 5990

DEBUT DATE	PEAK POS	WKS CHR	ARTIST Rock Track	Album Title	Album Label & Number
			SHINEDOWN ★		
6/21/03	34	5	Fly From The Inside	*Leave A Whisper*	Atlantic 83566
			SMILE EMPTY SOUL ★		
5/10/03	7	26	Bottom Of A Bottle	*Smile Empty Soul*	Throback 83639
12/6/03+	27	11	Nowhere Kids	*Smile Empty Soul*	Throback 83639
			SOCIALBURN		
6/7/03	27	10	Everyone	*Where You Are*	Elektra 62790
			SOMETHING CORPORATE		
11/8/03	37	5	Space	*North*	Drive-Thru 001190
			STAIND		
4/19/03	6	17	Price To Play	*14 Shades Of Grey*	Flip 62882
6/28/03	❶7	30	So Far Away	*14 Shades Of Grey*	Flip 62882
11/29/03+	10	16	How About You	*14 Shades Of Grey*	Flip 62882
			STONE TEMPLE PILOTS		
11/8/03	19	8	All In The Suit That You Wear	*Thank You*	Atlantic 83586
			STORY OF THE YEAR ★		
			Rock group from St. Louis, Missouri: Dan Marsala (vocals), Ryan Phillips (guitar), Philip Sneed (guitar), Adam Russell (bass) and Josh Wills (drums).		
11/1/03+	12	23↑	Until The Day I Die	*Page Avenue*	Maverick 48438
			STROKES, The		
9/27/03	15	18	12:51	*Room On Fire*	RCA 55497
			SUM 41		
3/15/03	13	15	The Hell Song	*Does This Look Infected?*	Island 063491
			SWITCHFOOT ★		
8/9/03+	5	33	Meant To Live	*The Beautiful Letdown*	Red Ink 71083
			TAPROOT		
4/5/03	26	10	Mine	*Welcome*	Atlantic 83561
			THEORY OF A DEADMAN ★		
			Rock group from Vancouver, British Columbia, Canada: Tyler Connolly (vocals, guitar), David Brenner (guitar), Dean Back (bass) and Tim Hart (drums).		
3/22/03	38	2	Make Up Your Mind	*Theory Of A Deadman*	Roadrunner 618421
			THIRD EYE BLIND		
4/19/03	35	5	Blinded (When I See You)	*Out Of The Vein*	Elektra 62888
			THREE DAYS GRACE ★		
7/19/03	2²	38↑	(I Hate) Everything About You	*Three Days Grace*	Jive 53479
			3 DOORS DOWN		
4/12/03	24	13	The Road I'm On	*Away From The Sun*	Republic 066165
8/30/03	22	22	Here Without You	*Away From The Sun*	Republic 066165
			311		
7/12/03	3	19	Creatures (For A While)	*Evolver*	Volcano 53714
11/22/03	39	2	Beyond The Gray Sky	*Evolver*	Volcano 53714
			THRICE ★		
7/26/03	24	11	All That's Left	*The Artist In The Ambulance*	Island 000295
			THURSDAY ★		
			Hard-rock group from New Brunswick, New Jersey: Geoff Rickly (vocals), Steve Pedulla (guitar), Tom Keeley (guitar), Tim Payne (bass) and Tucker Rule (drums).		
10/18/03	30	7	Signals Over The Air	*War All The Time*	Victory 000293
			TRAPT		
7/19/03	3	30	Still Frame	*Trapt*	Warner 48296
			UNWRITTEN LAW		
1/4/03	16	12	Rest Of My Life	*Music In High Places*	Lava 83632
			USED, The		
2/15/03	13	14	Buried Myself Alive	*The Used*	Reprise 48287
6/14/03	23	11	Blue And Yellow	*The Used*	Reprise 48287
			VELVET REVOLVER ★		
7/12/03	32	4	Set Me Free	*Hulk (soundtrack)*	Decca 63302

DEBUT DATE	PEAK POS	WKS CHR	ARTIST Rock Track	Album Title	Album Label & Number
			VENDETTA RED ★		
			Hard-rock group from Seattle, Washington: Zach Davidson (vocals, guitar), Justin Cronk (guitar), Erik Chapman (keyboards), Michael Vermillion (bass) and Joseph Lee Childres (drums).		
5/24/03	16	15	Shatterday..	*Between The Never And The Now*.................................Epic 86415	
			WHITE STRIPES, The		
3/8/03	❶³	38	Seven Nation Army	*Elephant*...........................Third Man 27148	
8/9/03	8	23	The Hardest Button To Button	*Elephant*...........................Third Man 27148	
			YELLOWCARD ★		
			Punk-rock group from Jacksonville, Florida: Ryan Key (vocals, guitar), Sean Mackin (violin, vocals), Benjamin Harper (guitar), Alex Lewis (bass) and Longineu Parsons (drums).		
9/6/03	25	12	Way Away	*Ocean Avenue* ....Capitol 39844	
			YORN, Pete		
5/17/03	32	5	Come Back Home...	*Day I Forgot* ....Columbia 86922	

1. **LINKIN PARK**
590+

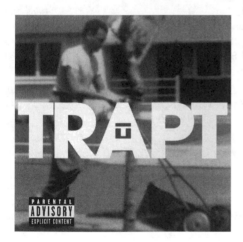

2. **TRAPT**
295

3. **RED HOT CHILI PEPPERS**
291

4.	267	**STAIND**		13.	191	**SALIVA**
5.	251	**QUEENS OF THE STONE AGE**		14.	170	**GODSMACK**
6.	250	**3 DOORS DOWN**		15.	169	**JANE'S ADDICTION**
7.	241	**WHITE STRIPES**		16.	164	**FOO FIGHTERS**
8.	239	**AUDIOSLAVE**		17.	156	**SUM 41**
9.	234	**ATARIS** ★		18.	151	**AFI** ★
10.	231	**EVANESCENCE** ★		19.	143	**COLD**
11.	220	**SEETHER**		20.	141	**311**
12.	205	**COLDPLAY**			141	**TAPROOT**

+ Subject to change since a title that peaked in 2003 by this artist is still charted as of the 4/3/04 cut-off date.

TOP 30 MODERN ROCK TRACKS

PEAK DATE	WEEKS				RANK	RECORD TITLE	PEAK POSITION	ARTIST
	CH	20	10	PK				
					1			
11/22	27 +	24 +	21	12	1.	**Numb**		Linkin Park
9/20	30	28	23	7	2.	**So Far Away**		Staind
8/9	37	32	21	6	3.	**Faint**		Linkin Park
5/31	45	34	25	5	4.	**Headstrong**		Trapt
4/12	26	22	17	5	5.	**Somewhere I Belong**		Linkin Park
2/8	36	33	20	4	6.	**No One Knows**	Queens Of The Stone Age	
7/12	38	36	26	3	7.	**Seven Nation Army**	The White Stripes	
3/8	27	25	17	3	8.	**Can't Stop**	Red Hot Chili Peppers	
5/17	33	32	23	2	9.	**Like A Stone**	Audioslave	
3/29	26	22	17	2	10.	**Bring Me To Life**	Evanescence	
11/1	26	19	14	2	11.	**Weak And Powerless**	A Perfect Circle	
7/5	36	31	21	1	12.	**Send The Pain Below**	Chevelle	
2/1	27	26	19	1	13.	**Always**	Saliva	
8/2	19	13	10	1	14.	**Just Because**	Jane's Addiction	
					2			
11/29	25 +	17	14	3	15.	**Feeling This**	Blink-182	
2/15	30	29	15	2	16.	**When I'm Gone**	3 Doors Down	
12/20	38 +	28 +	21	2	17.	**(I Hate) Everything About You**	Three Days Grace	
8/16	22	16	12	1	18.	**The Boys Of Summer**	Ataris	
					3			
11/8	30	20	13	1	19.	**Still Frame**	Trapt	
9/13	19	12	9	1	20.	**Creatures (For A While)**	311	
					4			
10/4	26	15	11	5	21.	**Someday**	Nickelback	
9/20	26	22	13	2	22.	**Show Me How To Live**	Audioslave	
					5			
3/8	28	26	20	4	23.	**Times Like These**	Foo Fighters	
10/11	25	18	8	3	24.	**Going Under**	Evanescence	
12/13	20	14	12	1	25.	**Away From Me**	Puddle Of Mudd	
					6			
1/25	38	30	14	5	26.	**Fine Again**	Seether	
5/24	17	11	9	3	27.	**Price To Play**	Staind	
7/5	26	18	10	1	28.	**Stupid Girl**	Cold	
					7			
4/12	23	13	8	4	29.	**Girl's Not Grey**	AFI	
9/6	26	20	9	3	30.	**Bottom Of A Bottle**	Smile Empty Soul	

	Date Hit #1	Wks @ #1	Title	Artist
1.	1/4	10	**All My Life** ....*Foo Fighters*	
			(includes 6 weeks at #1 in 2002)	
2.	2/1	1	**Always**..*Saliva*	
3.	2/8	4	**No One Knows** ....*Queens Of The Stone Age*	
4.	3/8	3	**Can't Stop** ....*Red Hot Chili Peppers*	
5.	3/29	2	**Bring Me To Life** ....*Evanescence*	
6.	4/12	5	**Somewhere I Belong**.....................................*Linkin Park*	
7.	5/17	2	**Like A Stone**..*Audioslave*	
8.	5/31	5	**Headstrong** ....*Trapt*	
9.	7/5	1	**Send The Pain Below**.......................................*Chevelle*	
10.	7/12	3	**Seven Nation Army**..*White Stripes*	
11.	8/2	1	**Just Because** ....*Jane's Addiction*	
12.	8/9	6	**Faint** ....*Linkin Park*	
13.	9/20	7↕	**So Far Away** ....*Staind*	
14.	11/1	2	**Weak And Powerless**.......................................*A Perfect Circle*	
15.	11/22	12	**Numb** ....*Linkin Park*	
			(includes 6 weeks at #1 in 2004)	

2002 SINGLES UPDATES

The following titles were listed in the *2002 Music Yearbook* and were still charted when that book went to press in 2003. This list completes the weeks charted (WKS CHR) and peak position (PK POS) data for those singles.

HOT 100 *

	WKS CHR
Kelly, R. .... *Ignition*	42
3 Doors Down...*When I'm Gone*	45

*These two titles were still on the chart in the *2002 Music Yearbook* and were still on the chart when the *Top Pop Singles 1955-2002* book was published. All other titles in the *2002 Music Yearbook* were updated in the *Top Pop Singles 1955-2002* book and therefore not shown here.

COUNTRY SINGLES

	WKS CHR	PK POS
Allan, Gary.. *Man To Man*	31	
Andrews, Jessica .... *There's More To Me Than You*	26	17
Cagle, Chris.. *What A Beautiful Day*	32	4
Carter, Deana... *There's No Limit*	26	14
Clark, Terri.. *I Just Wanna Be Mad*	34	
Cochran, Tammy..*Love Won't Let Me*	20	31
Diamond Rio.. *I Believe*	34	1[2]
Dixie Chicks... *Travelin' Soldier*	25	
Hill, Faith .... *When The Lights Go Down*	20	
Jackson, Alan .... *That'd Be Alright*	24	2[1]
Keith, Toby, with Willie Nelson................................. *Beer For My Horses*	39	1[6]
Kid Rock Featuring Allison Moorer or Sheryl Crow..................................... *Picture*	33	21
McBride, Martina ....*Concrete Angel*	26	5
McGraw, Tim .... *Tiny Dancer*	15	
McGraw, Tim .... *She's My Kind Of Rain*	22	2[3]
Montgomery Gentry.. *Speed*	33	5
Morgan, Craig... *Almost Home*	37	6
Nichols, Joe.. *Brokenheartsville*	32	
Shelton, Blake .... *The Baby*	24	
Tippin, Aaron, Featuring Thea Tippin.................. *Love Like There's No Tomorrow*	19	35
Travis, Randy ....*Three Wooden Crosses*	34	1[1]
Twain, Shania.. *Up!*	20	
Urban, Keith .... *Somebody Like You*	41	
Urban, Keith .... *Raining On Sunday*	30	3
Wills, Mark ....*19 Somethin'*	34	

R&B/HIP-HOP SINGLES

Artist	Title	WKS CHR	PK POS
Aaliyah	I Care 4 U	44	
Aaliyah	Miss You	37	-
Baby (AKA The Birdman) Featuring Clipse	What Happened To That Boy	20	
Badu, Erykah, Featuring Common	Love Of My Life (An Ode To Hip Hop)	40	
BLACKstreet	Deep	20	
B2K Featuring P. Diddy	Bump, Bump, Bump	20	
Busta Rhymes (feat. Spliff Star)	Make It Clap	24	
Choppa Featuring Master P	Choppa Style	22	49
Clipse featuring Faith Evans	Ma, I Don't Love Her	20	
Common Featuring Mary J. Blige	Come Close To Me	20	
Da En Tourage	Bunny Hop	20	
Dru Hill	I Should Be...	28	
Elliott, Missy	Work It	29	
Elliott, Missy, (Featuring Ludacris)	Gossip Folks	20	
Eminem	8 Mile	18	
Fat Joe Featuring Tony Sunshine & Armageddon	All I Need	20	35
Field Mob	Sick Of Being Lonely	34	
50 Cent	Wanksta	31	
50 Cent	In Da Club	32	1^9
50 Cent Featuring The Notorious B.I.G.	Realest Niggaz	22	30
Green, Vivian	Emotional Rollercoaster	36	13
Jaheim Featuring Tha Rayne	Fabulous	36	
Ja Rule feat. Ashanti	Mesmerize	20	
Johnson, Syleena	Guess What	28	29
K-Ci & JoJo	This Very Moment	20	
Kelly, R.	Ignition	36	2^5
Lil Jon & The East Side Boyz	I Don't Give A @#&%	20	50
Lopez, Jennifer, Featuring LL Cool J	All I Have	21	
Martinez, Angie, Featuring Kelis	Take You Home	17	
Musiq	dontchange	42	
Nelly	Pimp Juice	23	27
Nelly Featuring Kyjuan, Ali and Murphy Lee	Air Force Ones	28	
Nivea	Laundromat	20	
Notorious B.I.G., The	Big Poppa/Warning	88	
Perez, Amanda	Angel	20	
Racket City	Throw Up	43	
Smilez & Southstar	Tell Me (What's Goin' On)	20	
Timberlake, Justin	Cry Me A River	20	
2Pac	Thugz Mansion	22	
Tyrese	How You Gonna Act Like That	38	
Wonder, Stevie	No Letting Go	37	14

ADULT CONTEMPORARY

Artist	Title	WKS CHR	PK POS
Aguilera, Christina	Beautiful	42	1^5
Carlton, Vanessa	A Thousand Miles	74	
Clarkson, Kelly	A Moment Like This	28	
Collins, Phil	Can't Stop Loving You	60	
Crow, Sheryl	Soak Up The Sun	60	
Dixie Chicks	Landslide	26	
Five For Fighting	Superman (It's Not Easy)	87	
Hall, Daryl, & John Oates	Forever For You	29	7
Hill, Faith	Cry	47	
Iglesias, Enrique	Hero	88	
Jones, Norah	Don't Know Why	66	4
Mayer, John	Your Body Is A Wonderland	26	17
Santana featuring Michelle Branch	The Game Of Love	61	1^4
Stewart, Rod	These Foolish Things	22	
Twain, Shania	I'm Gonna Getcha Good!	26	

MAINSTREAM ROCK TRACKS

		WKS CHR	PK POS
Audioslave	Cochise	26	
Chevelle	The Red	43	
Creed	Weathered	26	
Disturbed	Prayer	36	
Disturbed	Remember	30	6
Foo Fighters	All My Life	32	
Mudvayne	Not Falling	31	
Nirvana	You Know You're Right	26	
Queens Of The Stone Age	No One Knows	28	
RA	Do You Call My Name	26	
Saliva	Always	35	
Seether	Fine Again	48	
Socialburn	Down	26	
Taproot	Poem	28	
3 Doors Down	When I'm Gone	40	
Trapt	Headstrong	55	1[1]

MODERN ROCK TRACKS

		WKS CHR	PK POS
All-American Rejects, The	Swing, Swing	23	8
Chevelle	The Red	39	
Coldplay	Clocks	26	
Donnas, The	Take It Off	15	
Foo Fighters	All My Life	35	
Mudvayne	Not Falling	18	28
Nirvana	You Know You're Right	26	
Queens Of The Stone Age	No One Knows	36	
Red Hot Chili Peppers	Can't Stop	27	
Saliva	Always	27	
Seether	Fine Again	38	
Socialburn	Down	21	
Sum 41	Still Waiting	26	
Taproot	Poem	26	
3 Doors Down	When I'm Gone	30	
Trapt	Headstrong	45	1[5]
Zwan	Honestly	18	

#1 SINGLES
ON VARIOUS OTHER BILLBOARD CHARTS

Hot Latin Tracks

Eurochart — Singles

Hits Of The United Kingdom — Singles

EXPLANATION OF COLUMNAR HEADINGS

DATE HIT #1: Date title first peaked at the #1 position in <u>2003</u>

WKS @ #1: Total weeks title held the #1 position

LABEL: Original label

$\updownarrow$: Indicates title hit #1, dropped down, and then returned to the #1 spot

A note below some titles indicates the title also held the #1 position in years other than 2003.

#1 HOT LATIN TRACKS

	Date Hit #1	Wks. @ #1	Title	Artist...Label
1.	1/4	8	**El Problema** .... *Ricardo Arjona*...Sony Discos
			(includes 4 weeks at #1 in 2002)	
2.	2/1	2	**Asi Es La Vida** .... *Olga Tañón*...Warner Latina
3.	2/15	3 ↕	**Seduceme** .... *India*...Sony Discos
4.	2/22	1	**Quizas** .... *Enrique Iglesias*...Universal Latino
5.	3/1	1	**Que Me Quedes Tu** .... *Shakira*...Sony Discos
6.	3/22	3	**Una Vez Mas** .... *Conjunto Primavera*...Fonovisa
7.	4/12	11 ↕	**Tal Vez** .... *Ricky Martin*...Sony Discos
8.	5/31	1	**Para Que La Vida** .... *Enrique Iglesias*...Universal Latino
9.	7/5	1	**Mana** .... *Mariposa Traicionera*...Warner Latina
10.	7/12	1	**Tu Amor O Tu Desprecio** .... *Marco Antonio Solis*...Fonovisa
11.	7/19	5 ↕	**Fotografia** .... *Juanes Featuring Nelly Furtado*...Surco
12.	8/2	1	**Casi** .... *Soraya*...EMI Latin
13.	8/9	1	**Jaleo** .... *Ricky Martin*...Sony Discos
14.	9/6	1	**Un Siglo Sin Ti** .... *Chayanne*...Sony Discos
15.	9/13	4 ↕	**Antes** .... *Obie Bermudez*...EMI Latin
16.	10/4	4 ↕	**Hoy** .... *Gloria Estefan*...Sony Discos
17.	10/25	2 ↕	**Te Necesito** .... *Luis Miguel*...Warner Latina
18.	11/22	8 ↕	**Mientes Tan Bien** .... *Sin Bandera*...Sony Discos
			(includes 2 weeks at #1 in 2004)	

#1 EUROCHART — SINGLES

	Date Hit #1	Wks. @ #1	Title	Artist...Label
1.	1/4	17	**The Ketchup Song** .... *Las Ketchup*...Columbia
			(includes 15 weeks at #1 in 2002)	
2.	1/18	8 ↕	**Lose Yourself** .... *Eminem*...Interscope
3.	2/15	5	**All The Things She Said** .... *t.A.T.u.* ...Interscope
4.	4/19	8	**In Da Club** .... *50 Cent*...Interscope
5.	6/14	1	**I Know What You Want**
			...*Busta Rhymes And Mariah Carey (feat. The Flipmode Squad)*...J Records
6.	6/21	6 ↕	**Bring Me To Life** .... *Evanescence*...Wind-Up
7.	7/26	4	**Crazy In Love** .... *Beyoncé (Featuring Jay-Z)*...Columbia
8.	8/30	2	**Never Leave You - Uh Oooh, Uh Oooh!** .... *Lumidee*...MCA
9.	9/13	1	**Breathe** .... *Blu Cantrell Featuring Sean Paul*...Arista
10.	9/20	3	**White Flag** .... *Dido*...Cheeky
11.	10/11	7	**Where Is The Love?** .... *Black Eyed Peas*...A&M
12.	11/29	3	**Me Against The Music** .... *Britney Spears Featuring Madonna*...Jive
13.	12/20	13	**Shut Up** .... *Black Eyed Peas*...Interscope
			(includes 11 weeks at #1 in 2004)	

#1 HITS OF THE UNITED KINGDOM — SINGLES

	Date Hit #1	Wks. @ #1	Title	Artist...Label
1.	1/4	4	**Sound Of The Underground**	*Girls Aloud*...Polydor
2.	2/1	2	**Stop Living The Lie**...	*David Sneddon*...Mercury
3.	2/15	4	**All The Things She Said**...	*t.A.T.u.* ...Interscope
4.	3/15	2	**Beautiful**	*Christina Aguilera*...RCA
5.	3/29	2	**Spirit In The Sky**...................................	*Gareth Gates & The Kumars*...RCA
6.	4/12	4	**Make Luv** ....*Room 5 Featuring Oliver Cheatham*...Positiva
7.	5/10	1	**You Said No**..*Busted*...Universal
8.	5/17	1	**Loneliness** ....*Tomcraft*...Data
9.	5/24	4	**Ignition**.. *R. Kelly*...Jive
10.	6/21	4	**Bring Me To Life**.. *Evanescence*...Epic
11.	7/19	3	**Crazy In Love** .... *Beyoncé (Featuring Jay-Z)*...Columbia
12.	8/9	1	**Never Gonna Leave Your Side** ....*Daniel Bedingfield*...Polydor
13.	8/16	4	**Breathe** .... *Blu Cantrell Featuring Sean Paul*...Arista
14.	9/13	1	**Are You Ready For Love**.................................... *Elton John*...Southern Fried
15.	9/20	6	**Where Is The Love?**...*Black Eyed Peas*...A&M
16.	11/1	1	**Hole In The Head**... *Sugababes*...Island
17.	11/8	2	**Be Faithful** .... *Fatman Scoop Featuring Crooklyn Clan*...Def Jam
18.	11/22	1	**Slow** ....*Kylie Minogue*...Parlophone
19.	11/29	1	**Crashed The Wedding**..*Busted*...Universal
20.	12/6	1	**Mandy** .... *Westlife*...BMG
21.	12/13	2	**Leave Right Now**... *Will Young*...BMG
22.	12/27	1	**Changes**....................................... *Ozzy & Kelly Osborne*...Sanctuary

SINGLES SONG TITLE SECTION

This section is an all-inclusive, alphabetically-arranged listing of every song title to appear in the *The Singles* sections.

Each song is listed once, with the chart data listed below it. The chart data consists of the highest position reached and the chart symbol. For a song that hit more than one chart, the chart on which it peaked the highest appears first, and so on. If a composition has more than one charted version, its title is listed once with the artists listed below in descending order of peak position. If a song has the same title, but is not by the same composer, the title is listed again.

CHART SYMBOLS

HT - Hot 100		**RS** - R&B Sales	
HS - Hot 100 Sales		**AC** - Adult Contemporary	
BU - Bubbling Under Hot 100		**DN** - Dance Club Play	
CW - Country Singles		**RK** - Mainstream Rock Tracks	
RB - R&B Singles		**MD** - Modern Rock Tracks	

↑: Indicates the highest position is subject to change since the title was climbing the chart as of the 4/3/04 cut-off date.

A

A.D.I.D.A.S. *Killer Mike*
42-RB 60-HT

AKshon (Yeah!) *Killer Mike*
74-HS

Abracadabra *Apani B*
55-RS

Act A Fool *Ludacris*
20-RB 32-HT

Action *Powerman 5000*
27-RK

Addicted *Mia*
3-DN

Addicted *Enrique Iglesias*
4-DN 101-BU

Addicted *Simple Plan*
45-HT

After All *Delerium*
9-DN 57-HS

After All *Brett James*
39-CW

Again *Fantasy*
37-HS

Agent Orange *Pharoahe Monch*
48-RS

Ain't No Mountain High Enough
Michael McDonald
9↑-AC

Air *Sparta*
35-RK

All Around The World
Lisa Stansfield
34-DN

All Around The World (Punk Debutante) *Cooler Kids*
45-HS

All I Know *Field Mob*
77-RB

All I Need *Fat Joe*
86-HT

All I Want *Gardeweg*
34-DN

All I Want For Christmas Is A Real Good Tan *Kenny Chesney*
30-CW

All In The Suit That You Wear
Stone Temple Pilots
5-RK 19-MD 118-BU

All In The Way *Earth, Wind & Fire*
25-AC 77-RB

All Life Long *Mo Thugs*
10-HS 83-RB

All Night Long *Seduction w/Saddler*
29-HS 94-RB

All That's Left *Thrice*
24-MD 36-RK

All The Things She Said *t.A.T.u.*
20-HT

Allways *Kev Brown*
72-RS

Almost Home *Craig Morgan*
59-HT

Alone *Lasgo*
83-HT

Alright *Murk*
1-DN

Alright *Allen Anthony*
42-RS

Alright *Freeway*
64-RB

Amame *Alexandre Pires*
114-BU

Amazin' *LL Cool J*
73-RB

Amazing *Josh Kelley*
79-HT

American Life *Madonna*
1-DN 37-HT

American Soldier *Toby Keith*
1-CW 28-HT

Anchor *Cave In*
34-MD 37-RK

And The Crowd Goes Wild
Mark Wills
29-CW

Angel *Amanda Perez*
20-HT

Angel *Renee McCrary*
57-CW

Animal Rap *Jedi Mind Tricks*
43-RS 58-HS

Another Postcard
Barenaked Ladies
82-HT

Antes *Obie Bermudez*
120-BU

Anthem, The *Good Charlotte*
10-MD 43-HT

Any Type Of Way *Big Daddy Kane*
58-RS

Anything *Lili Haydn*
16-DN

Anything Goes
CNN, Wayne Wonder & Lexxus
85-RB

Appreciate Me *Amuka*
7-DN

Arctic Snow *Burning Brides*
31-MD

Are You Gonna Be My Girl *Jet*
3-MD 7-RK 32↑-HT

Are You Happy Now?
Michelle Branch
16-HT

Are You Ready For Love
Elton John
1-DN

Art Is Hard *Art Is Hard*
18-HS

Art Of Losing *American Hi-Fi*
33-MD

As The Rush Comes *Motorcycle*
41-DN

Asi Es La Vida *Olga Tañón*
121-BU

At The End *iio*
41-DN

Auld Lang Syne (Freedom Mix)
Kenny G
50-RD

Away From Me *Puddle Of Mudd*
1-RK 5-MD 72-HT

B

B R Right *Trina*
83-HT

Babies *Regie Hamm*
16-AC

Baby Boy *Beyoncé*
1-HT 1-RB 2-DN

Baby, I'm In Love *Thalia*
12-DN 51-HS

Baby You Can Do It *Baby*
73-RS

Back For More *Glenn Lewis*
76-RB

Back In The Day *Missy Elliott*
62-HS 86-RB

Back In The Day (Puff)
Erykah Badu
62-RB

Back Of Your Hand *Dwight Yoakam*
52-CW

Back To Memphis *Billy Ray Cyrus*
60-CW

Backseat Of A Greyhound Bus
Sara Evans
16-CW 103-BU

Backtight *Jaheim*
51-RB

Bad Boy This Bad Boy That
Bad Boy's Da Band
15-RB 50-HT

Badaboom *B2K*
29-RB 59-HT

Bandages *Hot Hot Heat*
19-MD

Bang Bang Boom *Drag-On*
94-RB

Bang On *Purple Kitty*
17-DN

Battle Is The Lord's
Yolanda Adams
75-RB

Battle Of Erishkigal *Sasha Lazard*
43-DN

Be About Yours *Jay-El*
18-RS 56-HS

Be Easy *Jasmine Jai*
52-RS

Be Easy *T.I.*
55-RB

Beautiful *Christina Aguilera*
1-DN

Beautiful *Snoop Dogg*
3-RB 6-HT

Beautiful Goodbye *Jennifer Hanson*
76-HT

Beautiful Outside *Velocity Code*
32-DN

Beautiful You *Carly Hennessey*
45-HS

Beer For My Horses
Toby Keith w/Willie Nelson
22-HT

Behind Blue Eyes *Limp Bizkit*
11-RK 18-MD

Believe *Murk*
1-DN

Belly Dancer *Kardinal Offishall*
68-HS 96-RB

Better World *AgeHa*
3-DN

Beware Of The Boys (Mundian To Bach Ke) *Pan'jabi MC*
21-RB 33-HT

Bewitched, Bothered & Bewildered
Rod Stewart & Cher
17-AC

Beyond The Gray Sky *311*
39-MD

Big Room Drama
*Pete Heller & Tedd Patterson
Present The Look & Feel*
36-DN

Big Star *Kenny Chesney*
2-CW 28-HT

Big Yellow Taxi *Counting Crows*
5-AC 42-HT

Bigger Than My Body *John Mayer*
27-AC 33-HT

Blackout *(HED)Planet Earth*
21-RK 32-MD

Blah Blah Blah Blah *702*
31-RS

Blinded (When I See You)
Third Eye Blind
35-MD 116-BU

Blindsided *Lucy Woodward*
3-DN

Blowin' Me Up (Callin' Me) *Zion*
23-HS 92-RB

Blowin' Me Up (With Her Love)
JC Chasez
15-RS 35-HT

Blue And Yellow *Used*
23-MD

Blues Beach *Steely Dan*
17-HS

Born Slippy Nuxx *Underworld*
9-DN

Born Too Slow *Crystal Method*
26-MD

Born Wit It *Strick!*
56-RS

Bottles & Cans *Angie Stone*
18-DN

Bottom Of A Bottle
Smile Empty Soul
7-MD 8-RK 107-BU

Bounce *Art Garfunkel*
30-AC

Bounce *Bon Jovi*
39-RK

Boy (I Need You) *Mariah Carey*
68-RB

Boy Like You *Trick Pony*
47-CW

Boys Of Summer *Ataris*
2-MD 20-HT 36-RK

Brass In Pocket *Ultra Naté*
8-DN

Break The Record *Warren Brothers*
54-CW

Break You Off *Roots*
99-HT

Breathe *Michelle Branch*
3-DN 36-HT

Breathe *Blu Cantrell*
70-HT

Breathing *Stereomud*
29-RK

Bridge Over Troubled Water
Clay Aiken
29-AC

Bright Lights *Matchbox Twenty*
23-HT

Bring Me To Life *Evanescence*
1-MD 5-HT 11-RK

Bringin' On The Heartbreak
Mariah Carey
5-DN

Broken Promises *Element Eighty*
36-RK

Brokenheartsville *Joe Nichols*
27-HT

Bucci Bag *Andrea Doria*
3-DN

Built This City *Diplomats*
94-RB

Bullitproof *Pacifier*
37-MD

Buried Myself Alive *Used*
13-MD

Busted *Isley Brothers*
35-RB 112-BU

By The Way *Jesse Powell*
51-HS 99-RB

C

Cab Driver *Daryl Hall*
21-AC

Cadillac On 22's *David Banner*
83-RB

Call The Ambulance *Busta Rhymes*
34-RS

Calling All Angels *Train*
1-AC 19-HT 40-RK

Calling All Girls *ATL*
11-HS 48-RB

Cameltoe *Fannypack*
63-HS 75-RS

Can You Find The Heart
Ananda Project
15-DN

**Can You Hear Me When I Talk To
You?** *Ashley Gearing*
27-HS 36-CW

Can't Hold Us Down
Christina Aguilera
12-HT

Can't Let You Go *Fabolous*
2-RB 4-HT

Can't Nobody *Kelly Rowland*
72-RB 97-HT

Can't Stop *Red Hot Chili Peppers*
15-RK 57-HT

Can't Stop Loving You *Phil Collins*
76-HT

Can't Stop, Won't Stop
Young Gunz
10-RB 14-HT

Candi Bar *Keith Murray*
47-HS 63-RB

Carry On *Alana Davis*
30-HS

Carry The Flag *Dean Justin*
4-CS 29-HS

Casi *Soraya*
125-BU

Caught In The Rain *Revis*
8-RK 20-MD

Celebrity *Brad Paisley*
3-CW 31-HT

Center Of The Sun *Conjure One*
3-DN

Champion Sound *Jaylib*
47-RS

Change Clothes *Jay-Z*
6-RB 10-HT

Chicks Dig It *Chris Cagle*
5-CW 53-HT

Choke Me, Spank Me (Pull My Hair)
Xzibit
73-RB

Choppa Style *Choppa*
94-HT

Chow Chow Chow
Shotgun The Representer
10-RS 36-HS

Christmas Song *Michael Bublé*
6-AC

Chrome *Trace Adkins*
74-HT

Circle *Suzy K*
45-DN

Clap Back *Ja Rule*
17-RB 44-HT

Clocks *Coldplay*
29-HT 31-DN

Closer *Goapele*
83-RB

Closure *Chevelle*
11-MD 17-RK 120-BU

Closure *Gerald Levert*
57-RB

Club Banger *Petey Pablo*
98-RB

Clubbin *Marques Houston*
12-RB 39-HT

Coat Of Many Colors
Shania Twain w/Alison Krauss
57-CW

Code Red *Wildchild*
33-RS

Come Back Home *Pete Yorn*
32-MD

Come Close Remix (Closer)
Common
22-HS 86-RB

Come Get Some *TLC*
81-RB

C'mon *Mario*
61-RB

Come Over *Aaliyah*
9-RB 32-HT

Come With Me (Lullaby) *Phil Collins*
16-AC

Comin' From Where I'm From
Anthony Hamilton
60-RB

Concrete Angel *Martina McBride*
47-HT

Cool To Be A Fool *Joe Nichols*
18-CW

Cop That Sh#! *Timbaland & Magoo*
49-RB 95-HT

Country Ain't Country *Travis Tritt*
26-CW

Country Girl *DF Dub*
120-BU

Country Thang
John Michael Montgomery
45-CW

Cowboys Like Us *George Strait*
2-CW 38-HT

Crazy *Javier*
42-RB 95-HT

Crazy Beat *Blur*
22-MD

Crazy In Love *Beyoncé*
1-HT 1-RB 1-DN

Creatures (For A While) *311*
3-MD 118-BU

Feeling This *Blink-182*
2-MD 102-BU
Feels Good *Krondon*
70-RS
Feliz Navidad *Clay Walker*
49-CW
Fever For The Flava *Hot Action Cop*
38-MD
Few Questions *Clay Walker*
9-CW 55-HT
15th, The *Fischerspooner*
21-DN
Fighter *Christina Aguilera*
20-HT
Figured You Out *Nickelback*
1-RK 4-MD
Find A Way *Dwele*
42-RB 93-HT
Fire It Up *Copywrite*
56-RS
Fire (Yes, Yes Y'all) *Joe Budden*
48-RB 51-HS
Fireproof *Pillar*
37-RK
Firing Line *Allman Brothers Band*
37-RK
First Cut Is The Deepest
Sheryl Crow
2↑-AC 14↑-HT 35-CW
First Noel *Clay Aiken*
9-AC
5 Star Hooptie *J-Zone*
56-RS
Flipside *Freeway*
40-RB 95-HT
Flirt *WC*
97-RB
Fly *213*
39-RB 102-BU
Fly Again *Kristine W*
1-DN 60-HS
Fly From The Inside *Shinedown*
5-RK 34-MD
Flying Without Wings
Ruben Studdard
2-HT 27-AC
Focus *Joe Budden*
58-HS
For The Music *Colourful Karma*
7-DN
forthenight *Musiq*
18-RB 53-HT
4 Ever *Lil' Mo*
13-RB 37-HT
Forever *Mia*
25-DN
Forever *R. Kelly*
71-RB
Forever And For Always
Shania Twain
1-AC 4-CW 20-HT
Forrest County Line *4 Runner*
59-CW
Fortune Faded
Red Hot Chili Peppers
8-MD 22-RK 112-BU
48 Hours *Frank-N-Dank*
59-RS
45 *Shinedown*
7↑-RK
Fotografía *Juanes w/Nelly Furtado*
116-BU

4X4 *Dynasty*
68-RS
411-69*69 *Urban Monarchy*
74-RS
Four-Wheel Drive
John Michael Montgomery
52-CW
Frantic *Metallica*
21-RK
Free *Powerman 5000*
10-RK 38-MD
Free *Da Flock*
15-RS
Free Your Mind *Sapphirecut*
9-DN
Freedom *Jurassic 5*
75-RS
Freek-A-Leek *Petey Pablo*
17↑-RB
Freetime *Kenna*
19-DN
Fridaynititus *Brad Tyler*
57-CW
Frontin' *Pharrell*
1-RB 5-HT
Frosty The Snowman
Johnny Mathis
29-AC
Fk It (I Don't Want You Back)**
Eamon
16-HT 37-RB
Furious Angels *Rob Dougan*
38-DN
Future Funk *Seth Lawrence*
9-DN

G

Gangsta *S.A. Smash*
64-RS
Gangsta Girl *Big Tymers*
38-RB 85-HT
Gangsta Nation
Westside Connection
22-RB 33-HT
Gasoline *Seether*
8-RK 37-MD
Get Back *504 Boyz*
66-RS
Get Busy *Sean Paul*
1-HT 1-RB
Get By *Talib Kweli*
29-RB 77-HT
Get Down *Nas*
76-RB
Get It Off *Monica*
13-DN
Get It On The Floor *DMX*
57-RB 73-HS
Get It Together *Seal*
1-DN 40-HS
Get Loose *D4*
39-MD
Get Low
Lil Jon & The East Side Boyz
2-HT 2-RB
Lil Jon & The East Side Boyz
[Remix]
15-RS 56-HS
Get Something *Lil Wayne*
97-RB

Getaway *Becky Baeling*
1-DN
Getaway Car
Daryl Hall & John Oates
21-AC
Getchya Hands Up
E.S.G. & Slim Thug
80-RB
Getting Late *Floetry*
31-RB 114-BU
Ghetto *Supreme Beings Of Leisure*
5-DN
GhettoMusick *OutKast*
61-HS 93-RB
Gigolo *Nick Cannon*
21-RB 24-HT
Girl All The Bad Guys Want
Bowling For Soup
64-HT
Girl I'm A Bad Boy
Fat Joe & P. Diddy
69-RB 122-BU
Girl's Not Grey *AFI*
7-MD 33-RK 114-BU
Girlfriend *B2K*
19-RB 30-HT
Girls And Boys *Good Charlotte*
48-HT
Give It Up *Kevin Aviance*
1-DN
Go To Sleep *Radiohead*
8-HS 32-MD
Go With The Flow
Queens Of The Stone Age
7-MD 24-RK 116-BU
God Bless The U.S.A.
American Idol Finalists
4-HT
God Is A DJ *P!nk*
103-BU
God's Work *Murs*
64-HS
Godspeed (Sweet Dreams)
Dixie Chicks
48-CW
Going Under *Evanescence*
5-MD 26-RK 104-BU
Golden Age *Planet Asia*
53-RS
Good Little Girls *Blue County*
16↑-CW
Good Time *Jessica Andrews*
49-CW
Gossip Folks
Missy "Misdemeanor" Elliott
1-DN
Got Some Teeth *Obie Trice*
33-RB 54-HT
Gotta Get The Money *Ellis Hall*
32-HS 98-RB
Gravedigger *Dave Matthews Band*
35-MD
Grey Street *Dave Matthews Band*
119-BU
Grind Right *Skent Dukes*
13-RS 34-HS
Guajira *Emmanuel*
22-DN
Guess *Rahzel*
73-RS

Guess What
Syleena Johnson
104-BU
Syleena Johnson [Remix]
8-HS 75-RB
Guide Me God Ghostland
20-DN 67-HS
Guilt (Hold Down) Fingertight
34-RK
Guy Like Me Pat Green
31↑-CW

H

Hail Mary Eminem, 50 Cent &
Busta Rhymes
33-RB 111-BU
Half A Heart Tattoo
Jennifer Hanson
40-CW
Half A Man Anthony Smith
40-CW
Handprints On The Wall
Kenny Rogers
40-CW
Hands Down
Dashboard Confessional
8-MD
Hands High Mr. Cheeks
66-RS
Hands Off The Wheel Oleander
25-RK
Hands Up TLC
18-HS 40-RS
Harder To Breathe Maroon5
18-HT 31-MD
Hardest Button To Button
White Stripes
8-MD
Harem (Cancao do Mar)
Sarah Brightman
1-DN 27-HS
Hater's Anthem Jean Grae
57-RS
Have You Ever Been In Love
Celine Dion
2-AC 104-BU
Have You Forgotten? Darryl Worley
1-CW 22-HT
Have Yourself A Merry Little
Christmas
Ruben Studdard & Tamyra Gray
25-AC
He Proposed Kelly Price
58-RB
Head Bussa Lil Scrappy
18-HS 73-RB
Head On Collision
New Found Glory
34-HS
Head To Toe Roscoe
95-RB
Headstrong Trapt
16-HT
Hearts On Fire Big Advice
32-HS 99-RB
Heaven Live
33-MD 33-RK 59-HT
Heaven Help Me Wynonna
37-CW

Heavenly Light Dawn Tallman
11-DN
Heavy Liftin' Blake Shelton
32-CW
Hell Is A Flame Big C
28-HS 96-RB
Hell Song Sum 41
13-MD
Hell Yeah Montgomery Gentry
4-CW 45-HT
Hell Yeah Ginuwine
16-RB 17-HT
Help Pour Out The Rain (Lacey's
Song) Buddy Jewell
3-CW 29-HT
Here Without You 3 Doors Down
5-HT 14-RK 15-AC 22-MD
Here's Your Sign Christmas
Bill Engvall
1-CS 8-HS
Hey Love, No Fair Leland Martin
59-CW
Hey Mr. President Warren Brothers
28-CW
Hey Ya! OutKast
1-HT 9-RB 16-MD
Hey You! Shorty What's Yo Name?
Collardgreens
42-RS
Hidden Agenda Craig David
119-BU
History Just-Ice
73-RS
Hit Em Off Triple Threat
61-RS
Hit That Offspring
1-MD 6-RK 64-HT
Hold You Close Clear
25-RS 38-HS
Hole In The World Eagles
5-AC 69-HT
Holidae In Chingy
2-RB 3-HT
Hollow Again Project 86
35-RK
Hollywood Madonna
1-DN 4-HS
Honesty (Write Me A List)
Rodney Atkins
4-CW 57-HT
Honey Billie Ray Martin
3-DN
Honk Your Horn Dani Stevenson
24-HS 48-RS
Hood Tragedy Khadafi
70-RS
Hood Money Capone-N-Noreaga
53-RS
Hooked Mary J. Blige
54-RB
Horizon Has Been Defeated
Jack Johnson
31-MD
Horror, The RJD2
42-RS 55-HS
Hot & Wet 112
29-RB 70-HT
Hot Damn Clipse
56-HS 58-RB
Hot In Herre Tiga
22-DN
Hot Mama Trace Adkins
5-CW

Hotel Cassidy
4-HT 6-RB
Hottest Of The Hot B.G.
74-RB
How About You Staind
10-MD 10-RK
How Can I Live Ill Niño
26-RK
How Can You Mend A Broken
Heart Michael Bublé
22-AC
How Do I Love Her
Steven Curtis Chapman
27-AC
How I Feel Lexx
13-HS 90-RB
How You Gonna Act Like That
Tyrese
7-HT
How You Want That Loon
41-RB 88-HT
Hum Melody Robbie Rivera
1-DN
Hurt Johnny Cash
10-HS 33-MD 56-CW
Hurting, The Mac Quayle
8-DN
Hyphy Federation
88-RB
Hypnotised Oakenfold
41-DN
Hypocrite Akrobatik
48-RS

I

I Am Ready Size Queen
5-DN
I Am The Highway Audioslave
2-RK 3-MD
I Am What I Am Linda Eder
40-DN 70-HS
I Believe
Chris Cox Vs. Happy Clappers
1-DN
I Believe Diamond Rio
31-HT
I Believe In A Thing Called Love
Darkness
9-MD 23-RK
I C U (Doin' It) Violator
43-HS 89-RB
I Can Nas
7-RB 12-HT
I Can Only Imagine
Mercyme
5-AC 52-CW 71-HT
Jeff Carson
50-CW
I Can't Be Your Friend Rushlow
16-CW 106-BU
I Can't Sleep Clay Walker
25↑-CW
I Can't Stop De-Javu
37-DN
I Can't Stop Al Green
67-HS
I Can't Take You Anywhere
Scotty Emerick w/Toby Keith
24-CW 91-HT

I Do *Tina Ann*
10-DN

I Don't Wanna Be Me
Type O Negative
40-RK

I Don't Wanna Hurt You *Latif*
46-HS 97-RB

I Don't Wanna Stop *ATB*
26-DN

I Drove All Night *Celine Dion*
2-DN 7-AC 45-HT

I Feel Love *Blue Man Group*
7-DN

I Got'cha Ma *Caddillac Tah*
88-RB

(I Hate) Everything About You
Three Days Grace
2-MD 4-RK 55-HT

I Heard It Through The Grapevine
Michael McDonald
20-AC

I Know What You Want
Busta Rhymes & Mariah Carey
2-RB 3-HT

I Know You By Heart *Katrina*
Carlson w/Benny Mardones
25-AC

I Like *AJ*
32-HS 91-RB

I Love I Love *Georgie Porgie*
1-DN

I Love This Bar *Toby Keith*
1-CW 26-HT

I Love You *Dru Hill*
27-RB 77-HT

I Love You *Dru Hill*
31-DN

I Love You This Much
Jimmy Wayne
6-CW

I Melt *Rascal Flatts*
2-CW 34-HT

I Need A Man *Foxy Brown*
52-HS 62-RB

I Need A Vacation
Rebecca Lynn Howard
49-CW

I Need You *Dave Gahan*
5-DN 61-HS

I Need You Now *Smokie Norful*
45-RB 96-HT

I Raq And Roll *Clint Black*
42-CW

I Still Love You *702*
49-RB

I Think You're Beautiful *Amy Dalley*
43-CW

I Try *Made By Monkeys*
28-DN

I Wanna Do It All *Terri Clark*
3-CW 38-HT

I Want My Island Girl
Darrell Labrado
22-HS

I Want My Money Back
Sammy Kershaw
33-CW

I Want You *Thalia*
22-HT 27-DN 61-RB

I Want You (For Myself)
Kings Of Tomorrow
26-DN

I Will Hold My Ground
Darryl Worley
57-CW

I Wish *Jo Dee Messina*
15-CW

I Wish I Wasn't *Heather Headley*
5-DN 15-RB 55-HT

I Wish You'd Stay *Brad Paisley*
57-HT

I'd Do Anything *Simple Plan*
51-HT

I'll Be Around *Sawyer Brown*
48-CW

I'll Be Around *Cee-Lo*
52-RB

I'll Be Home For Christmas
Kenny Chesney
60-CW

I'll Be There *Weekend Players*
1-DN

I'll Be Your Angel *Kira*
34-DN

I'll Never Leave *R. Kelly*
29-RB 103-BU

I'm Dead *Leisureworld*
37-RK

I'm Feelin' High *Whorizon*
35-DN

I'm Glad *Jennifer Lopez*
4-DN 19-RS 32-HT

I'm Gonna Take That Mountain
Reba McEntire
14-CW 103-BU

I'm Good *Blaque*
95-RB

I'm In Love With A Married Woman
Mark Chesnutt
48-CW

I'm In Love With You *Billy Dean*
52-CW

I'm Just A Girl *Deana Carter*
35-CW

I'm Missing You *Kenny Rogers*
49-CW

I'm One Of You *Hank Williams, Jr.*
39-CW

I'm Still In Love With You
Sean Paul
13↑-RB

I'm Trying *Jakki Da Motamouth*
67-RS

I'm Waiting
Aubrey vs Johnny Vicious
10-DN

I'm With You *Avril Lavigne*
18-AC

I'm Your Man *Steve Wariner*
58-CW

I've Never Been Anywhere
Sammy Kershaw
58-CW

Ice Cream *JS*
54-RB 124-BU

Idiology, The *Lacks*
74-RS

If I Can't *50 Cent*
34-RB 76-HT

If That's Love *Laura Pausini*
1-DN

If There Ain't There Ought'a Be
Marty Stuart
41-CW

If You Let Me *Lou Mosley*
15-HS 89-RB

If You Love Me *Becky Baeling*
3-DN

If You're Not The One
Daniel Bedingfield
3-AC 4-DN 15-HT

Illy *S.A. Smash*
69-RS

Immaculate *Survivalist*
23-HS

Imprint *Doubledrive*
22-RK

In A Little While *Uncle Kracker*
26-AC

In Da Club
50 Cent
1-HT
Beyoncé
67-RB

In Love Wit Chu *Da Brat*
32-RB 44-HT

In My Daughter's Eyes
Martina McBride
4-CW

In My Dreams *Rick Trevino*
41-CW

In My Life *Juvenile*
18-RB

In This Diary *Ataris*
11-MD

In Those Jeans *Ginuwine*
3-RB 8-HT

In Your Life *La Bouche*
9-DN 49-HS

In Your Love *Rhett Akins*
57-CW

Incomplete *C-Ianae*
10-HS 90-RB

Indian Flute *Timbaland & Magoo*
73-RB

Industrial Revolution
Immortal Technique
63-RS

Industry *Wyclef Jean*
73-RB

Inhale *Stone Sour*
18-RK

Innocence *Hootie & The Blowfish*
25-AC

Into The Sun *Weekend Players*
1-DN

Into You *Fabolous*
4-HT 6-RB

Intuition *Jewel*
1-DN 20-HT

Intuition *Daryl Hall & John Oates*
40-DN

Invisible *Clay Aiken*
8-AC 37-HT

It Blows My Mind *Snoop Dogg*
68-RB

It Can All Be Gone
Jamie Lee Thurston
59-CW

It Doesn't Mean I Don't Love You
McHayes
41-CW

It's All Real *Pitch Black*
27-RS

It's Five O'Clock Somewhere
Alan Jackson & Jimmy Buffett
1-CW 17-HT

It's Goin' Down *Baby D*
88-RB
It's My Life *No Doubt*
10-HT
Iz U *Nelly*
51-RB   103-BU

J

Jah is My Rock *Caribbean Pulse*
13-HS   87-RB
Jaleo *Ricky Martin*
13-DN   122-BU
Janeiro *Solid Sessions*
23-DN
Jerry Springer Episode
Soul Position
74-RS
Jimmy Mathis *Bubba Sparxxx*
10-HS   98-RB
Jingle Bells
Kenny Chesney
49-CW
Alan Jackson
58-CW
John Doe *Shade Sheist*
66-RB
Jump Off *Lil' Kim*
8-RB   17-HT
Just A Dog *Big Moe*
69-RB
Just A Little More Love
David Guetta
15-DN
Just About Had Enough
Beat Hustlerz
15-DN
Just Because *Jane's Addiction*
1-MD   4-RK   72-HT
Just For Tonight *Seiko*
15-DN
Just Friends *LSG*
74-RB
Just Like You *G-Wiz*
27-HS   98-RB
Just So You Know *Holly Palmer*
3-DN

K

Keep Doin' It *Violator*
92-RB
Kiss My Eyes *Bob Sinclair*
23-DN
Kissing A Fool *Michael Bublé*
29-AC
Knock Knock *Monica*
24-RB   75-HT
Konexion, Tha *Freddie Foxxx*
56-RS

L

La-La-La (Excuse Me Again) *Jay-Z*
37-HS   112-BU
Ladies *Sarai*
101-BU

Last Song *All-American Rejects*
29-MD
Last Train Home *Lostprophets*
3↑-MD   14↑-RK
Late Great Golden State
Dwight Yoakam
52-CW
Laundromat *Nivea*
58-HT
Lean Low *Youngbloodz*
94-RB
Learn Chinese *Jin*
74-RB
Leave It All Behind *Sunny Valentine*
23-RS
Leaving Only Scars *Systematic*
39-RK
Leaving Song I *AFI*
16-MD   31-RK
Lei Lo Lai *Latin Project*
1-DN
Let It All Come Down *Burke Roney*
22-AC
Let It Go *Dawn Tallman*
13-DN
Let Me Be Your Angel *Krista*
24-DN
Let Me Know *Hi-C*
74-RB
Let Me See U Bounce *Biz Markie*
50-RS
Let's Get Down *Bow Wow*
12-RB   14-HT
Let's Get It *Smoot*
43-HS   98-RB
Let's Get Up *Craig-G*
65-RS
Letter (Almost Home) *Clint Daniels*
56-CW
Liberate *Disturbed*
4-RK   22-MD   121-BU
Life As We Know It *Dudenem*
33-RS
Life Goes By *Special Goodness*
19-HS
Light Your A** On Fire
Busta Rhymes
23-RB   58-HT
Lights Out *Mack 10*
61-RB
Lights Out *Lisa Marie Presley*
114-BU
Like A Pimp *David Banner*
15-RB   48-HT
Like A Stone *Audioslave*
1-RK   1-MD   31-HT
Like Glue *Sean Paul*
9-RB   13-HT
Like This Anna *J-Live*
66-RS
Limbo Rock *Chubby C & OD*
9-RS   29-HS
Little Drummer Boy ..see: Peace
On Earth
Little Know It All *Iggy Pop*
35-MD
Little Moments *Brad Paisley*
2-CW   35-HT
Live From The Plantation *Mr. Lif*
52-RS   72-HS
Live On Stage *Dilated Peoples*
59-RS

Lonesome, On'ry And Mean
Travis Tritt
50-CW
Long Black Train *Josh Turner*
13-CW   72-HT
Long Way Home *ATB*
10-DN
Look Through My Eyes *Phil Collins*
5-AC
Look Ya *Pop Shop*
9-RS
Los Tangueros *Bajofondotangoclub*
28-DN
Losing Grip *Avril Lavigne*
64-HT
Lost Cause *Beck*
36-MD
Love American *Give Up The Ghost*
72-HS
Love Angel *JS*
61-RB
Love @ 1st Sight *Mary J. Blige*
10-RB   22-HT
Love Calls *Kem*
25-RB   106-BU
Love Changes Everything
Aaron Lines
39-CW
Love Is A Crime *Anastacia*
1-DN
Love Iz *Erick Sermon*
73-HS   80-RB
Love Song *Jeff Bates*
8-CW   59-HT
Love That Man *Whitney Houston*
1-DN
Love You More *Ginuwine*
28-RB   78-HT
Love You Out Loud *Rascal Flatts*
3-CW   30-HT
Love's Got An Attitude (It Is What It
Is) *Amy Dalley*
27-CW
Lovin' All Night *Patty Loveless*
18-CW   81-HT
Low *Foo Fighters*
10-HS   15-MD   23-RK
Low *Kelly Clarkson*
58-HT
Lucky One *Alison Krauss*
46-CW
Lucky Star *Basement Jaxx*
3-DN

M

Ma, I Don't Love Her *Clipse*
86-HT
Magic Stick *Lil' Kim*
2-HT   2-RB
Make Me A Song *Kiley Dean*
54-RB   99-HT
Make Me Smile (Come Up And See
Me) *Erasure*
40-HS
Make Room *Double Doze*
30-HS   96-RB
Make U Mine *Fabolous*
93-RB

Make Up Your Mind
  Theory Of A Deadman
  13-RK 38-MD
Man On A Mission
  Daryl Hall & John Oates
  16-AC
Man To Man *Gary Allan*
  25-HT
Marathon *Dilated Peoples*
  49-RS
Mariposa Traicionera *Maná*
  120-BU
Martie, Emily & Natalie
  Cledus T. Judd
  55-CW
Me Against The Music
  Britney Spears
  1-DN 35-HT
Me And Giuliani Down By The
  School Yard *!!! (Chk Chk Chk)*
  33-HS
Me Cansé De Ti *Obie Bermudez*
  118-BU
Me, Myself And I *Beyoncé*
  2-RB 4-HT
Meant To Live *Switchfoot*
  5-MD
Medicine *DJ Mike Cruz Presents*
  Chyna Ro & Sandy B
  24-DN
Memories *Rockik*
  31-DN
Middle Age Crazy *T. Graham Brown*
  58-CW
Middle Of Nowhere *Blank Theory*
  36-RK
Midnight Creep
  Alchemist Presents...
  59-RS
Mientes Tan Bien *Sin Bandera*
  114-BU
Mighty D-Block (2 Guns Up)
  Sheek Louch
  65-RB
Milkshake *Kelis*
  1-DN 3-HT 4-RB
Million Ways *Will Downing*
  58-RB
Mine *Taproot*
  23-RK 26-MD
Minerva *Deftones*
  9-MD 16-RK 120-BU
Miss Independent *Kelly Clarkson*
  9-HT 28-AC
Miss P. *Cherish*
  87-RB
Misunderstood *Bon Jovi*
  106-BU
mOBSCENE *Marilyn Manson*
  5-HS 18-RK 26-MD
Money Folder *Mad Villain*
  63-RS
Monsters *V Shape Mind*
  40-RK
Montana *Venus Hum*
  6-DN
More & More *Joe*
  15-RB 48-HT
Morning Star *Cooler Kids*
  4-DN
Moses *Coldplay*
  24-MD

Move Your Feet *Junior Senior*
  45-DN
Mr. Baller *Royce Da 5'9"*
  46-RS
Murder Reigns *Ja Rule*
  68-RS
Music Revolution *Scumfrog*
  4-DN
My Baby *Bow Wow*
  17-RB 42-HT
My Beautiful America
  Charlie Daniels Band
  58-CW
My Front Porch Looking In
  Lonestar
  1-CW 23-HT
My Grown Up Christmas List
  Kelly Clarkson
  17-AC
My J's *J.R.*
  45-RS
My Last Name *Dierks Bentley*
  18↑-CW
My Love Is Always *Saffron Hill*
  7-DN
My Love Is Like...WO *Mya*
  13-HT 17-RB
My Name *Xzibit*
  66-RB
My Time *Dutch*
  1-DN

N

Na Na Na *112*
  24-RB 75-HT
Naggin *Ying Yang Twins*
  43-RB 87-HT
Nas' Angels...The Flyest *Nas*
  72-RB
Nazty Girrrl *Mersilis*
  64-RS
Need Me In Your Life
  Memphis Bleek
  50-RS
Neva Eva *Trillville*
  28-RB 77-HT
Never Leave You - Uh Oooh, Uh
  Oooh! *Lumidee*
  3-HT 9-RB
Never (Past Tense) *Roc Project*
  97-HT 4-DN
Never Scared *Bone Crusher*
  8-RB 26-HT
New York Christmas *Rob Thomas*
  22-HS
Next Big Thing *Vince Gill*
  105-BU
Nice Girl, Wrong Place *Gang Starr*
  31-HS 99-RB
99.9% Sure (I've Never Been Here
  Before) *Brian McComas*
  10-CW 57-HT
Nitefall *Kev Brown*
  71-RS
No Doubt *Jean Grae*
  67-RS
No Doubt (Work It) *Dru Hill*
  37-RS
No Letting Go *Wayne Wonder*
  11-HT

No L.O.V.E. *Jhené*
  91-RB
No Means No *Nee-Nee Gwynn*
  16-HS 89-RB
No, No, No *Jae Millz*
  89-RB
No One's Gonna Change You
  Reina
  96-HT
No Regrets Yet *Sonya Isaacs*
  36-CW
No Shoes, No Shirt, No Problems
  Kenny Chesney
  2-CW 28-HT
No Sign Of It *Natalie Grant*
  25-AC
No Way No How *Jocelyn Enriquez*
  17-DN
Nobody Knows Me *Madonna*
  4-DN
Nookie (real good) *Jacki-O*
  61-RB
Not Falling *Mudvayne*
  17-HS
Not Gonna Get Us *t.A.T.u.*
  1-DN
Not Today *Mary J. Blige*
  21-RB 41-HT
Not Today *Hotwire*
  40-RK
Nothing At All *Santana*
  37-HS
Nothing But You *Paul Van Dyk*
  6-DN 37-HS
Nothing Fails *Madonna*
  1-HS 1-DN
Nothing Sacred *Memento*
  28-RK
Nowhere Kids *Smile Empty Soul*
  26-RK 27-MD
Numb *Linkin Park*
  1-RK 1-MD 11-HT

O

O Holy Night
  LeAnn Rimes
  14-AC
  Josh Groban
  109-BU
OK *Sheek Louch*
  92-RB
Off The Wall *Skillz*
  92-RB
Official, The *Jaylib*
  75-RS
Officially Missing You *Tamia*
  4-DN 31-RB 83-HT
Oh! *Union Turnpike*
  47-RS 63-HS
Oh L'Amour *Erasure*
  68-HS
Oíche Chiún (Silent Night) *Enya*
  16-HS
Old Weakness (Coming On Strong)
  Tanya Tucker
  49-CW
On A High *Duncan Sheik*
  1-DN
On Your Way Home *Patty Loveless*
  29-CW

One *Faith Hill*
7-AC   124-BU
151 *Outerspace*
45-RS
One For Peedi Crakk *Peedi Crakk*
33-RS
One Last Time *Dusty Drake*
26-CW
One Mississippi *Jill King*
60-CW
One More Chance *Michael Jackson*
40-RB   83-HT
One Of Those Days *Brad Martin*
50-CW
One Step Closer *American Juniors*
6-HS
One Thing *Finger Eleven*
5-MD   38-RK
One Wish (For Christmas)
Whitney Houston
20-AC
Oneness *Damian*
32-DN
Only, The *Static-X*
22-RK
Only God (Could Stop Me Loving You) *Emerson Drive*
23-CW   124-BU
Only Thing Missin' *Aretha Franklin*
7-DN   53-RB
Ooh! *Mary J. Blige*
14-RB   29-HT
Ooh Wee *Mark Ronson*
80-RB
Open *Queensrÿche*
38-RK
Other Side *(HED)Planet Earth*
40-RK
Out Of Control *Hoobastank*
9-MD   16-RK
Outsider, The *Perfect Circle*
3↑-RK   10↑-MD
Ownerz, The *Gang Starr*
27-RS   61-HS
Oxygen's Gone *Die Trying*
29-MD   35-RK

P

Pack Ya Bags *Sarai*
18-HS   90-RB
Paint Me A Birmingham
Tracy Lawrence
15↑-CW
Paper Angels *Jimmy Wayne*
40-CW
Para Qué La Vida *Enrique Iglesias*
102-BU
Party & Bullsh*t 2003 *Rah Digga*
65-RB
Party To Damascus *Wyclef Jean*
34-RB   65-HT
Pass That Dutch *Missy Elliott*
17-RB   27-HT
Patiently Waiting *50 Cent*
56-RB
Pavement Cracks *Annie Lennox*
1-DN   17-HS
Peace On Earth/Little Drummer Boy *David Bowie & Bing Crosby*
66-HS

Peace (Where The Heart Is)
Jim Brickman
15-AC
Peacekeeper *Fleetwood Mac*
10-AC   80-HT
People Are People *30 Dirty Junkies*
6-DN
Perfect *Sara Evans*
2↑-CW
Perfect *Simple Plan*
24-HT
Pick Up The Phone
Tyrese & Ludacris
65-RB
Picture *Kid Rock*
17-AC
P.I.M.P. *50 Cent*
2-RB   3-HT
Pimp Juice *Nelly*
58-HT
Plan X *Sadat X*
54-RS
Play Your Part *Deborah Cox*
1-DN
Playboys Of The Southwestern World *Blake Shelton*
24-CW
Please Set Me At Ease *Madlib*
43-RS
Poet Has Come *Blaq Poet*
46-RS
Pon De River, Pon De Bank
Elephant Man
29-RB   86-HT
Pop That Booty *Marques Houston*
34-RB   76-HT
Powerless (Say What You Want)
Nelly Furtado
109-BU
Powers That Be *Hieroglyphics*
75-RS
Pray For The Fish *Randy Travis*
48-CW
Pretty Baby *Vanessa Carlton*
101-BU
Price To Play *Staind*
2-RK   6-MD   66-HT
Pump It Up *Joe Budden*
16-RB   38-HT
P*ycat** *Missy "Misdemeanor" Elliott*
26-RB   77-HT
Put That Woman First *Jaheim*
5-RB   20-HT
Put Your Drinks Down *Drag-On*
80-RB

Q

Quick To Back Down *Bravehearts*
48-RB
Quiet Things That No One Ever Knows *Brand New*
37-MD
Quizás *Enrique Iglesias*
121-BU

R

Rain On Me *Ashanti*
2-RB   7-HT
Rainbow Man *Jeff Bates*
47-CW
Raining On Sunday *Keith Urban*
38-HT
Rainy Day *Renée Stakey*
10-DN   72-HS
Raise Up *Saliva*
29-RK
Re-Align *Godsmack*
3-RK   28-MD
Read Your Mind *Avant*
5-RB   13-HT
Real Emotions *Los Lonely Boys*
71-HS
Real Good Man *Tim McGraw*
1-CW   27-HT
Real Love *Deborah Cooper*
4-DN
Real Thing *George Strait*
60-CW
Realest N*ggas *50 Cent*
106-BU
Reckoning (Don't Tread On Me)
Iced Earth
13-HS
Rectifier *RA*
30-RK
Red Dirt Road *Brooks & Dunn*
1-CW   25-HT
Red White & Blue *Lynyrd Skynyrd*
27-RK
Redneck 12 Days Of Christmas
Jeff Foxworthy
1-CS   8-HS
Release Me *Industry*
7-DN
Relight My Fire *Ricky Martin*
5-DN
Remedy (I Won't Worry)
Jason Mraz
15-HT
Remember *Disturbed*
22-MD   110-BU
Remember When *Alan Jackson*
1-CW   29-HT
Represent *Papa Reu*
98-RB
Respect Me *Gyrlz Society*
54-HS
Respect My Pimpin'
Grafic International
25-HS   96-RB
Rest In Pieces *Saliva*
11-RK   20-MD   93-HT
Rest Of My Life *Unwritten Law*
16-MD
Rest Of Our Lives *Jeffrey Osborne*
75-RB
Rich Man *Russell*
16-RS   41-HS
Ridin Spinners *Three 6 Mafia*
62-RB
Rie Y Llora *Celia Cruz*
35-DN
Right Now *Korn*
11-RK   13-MD   119-BU
Right Thurr *Chingy*
2-HT   2-RB

Rise Up *Funky Green Dogs*
1-DN

Rising Sun *Paradise*
37-DN

Risky Business *Murs*
73-RS

Road I'm On *3 Doors Down*
8-RK   24-MD

Roc Ya Body "Mic Check 1, 2"
M.V.P. (Most Valuable Playas)
82-HT

Rock-A-Bye Heart *Steve Holy*
37-CW

Rock Wit U (Awww Baby) *Ashanti*
2-HT   4-RB   6-DN

Rock You Baby *Toby Keith*
13-CW   66-HT

Rock Your Body *Justin Timberlake*
1-DN   5-HT   45-RB

Rock Your Body, Rock
Ferry Corsten
24-DN

Rocket Man *Daphne Rubin-Vega*
42-DN

Rockin' Little Christmas
Brooks & Dunn
57-CW

**Roll Wit M.V.P. (We Be Like! The La
La Song)** *Stagga Lee*
68-RB   91-HT

Room With A View *Brother Ali*
58-RS

Rotten Apple *50 Cent*
45-RS

Roun' The Globe *Nappy Roots*
53-RB   96-HT

Round Round *Sugababes*
34-HS

Rubber Band Man *T.I.*
15↑-RB

Rubberneckin' *Elvis Presley*
94-HT

Run, Run, Run *Ryan Tyler*
36-CW

Runnin (Dying To Live) *Tupac*
11-RB   19-HT

Running *No Doubt*
62-HT

S

Saddest Song *Ataris*
27-MD

Safe Passage *Manmade God*
36-RK

Salt Shaker *Ying Yang Twins*
9-HT   9-RB

Same Man *Rachel Loy*
47-HS

San Francisco *Slr Ivan*
48-HS

Save You *Pearl Jam*
4-HS   29-MD

Saviour *Memento*
35-RK

Say How I Feel *Rhian Benson*
45-HS   66-RB

Say Yes *Floetry*
8-RB   24-HT

Say You Will *Fleetwood Mac*
17-AC

Scary Old World *Radney Foster*
52-CW

Science Of Selling Yourself Short
Less Than Jake
36-MD

Scientist, The *Coldplay*
18-MD

S'cream *Barry Harris*
31-DN

Se Me Olvido Tu Nombre *Shalim*
46-DN

Secret Wars *Last Emperor*
61-RS

Seduce Me Now *India*
2-DN   123-BU

Self Medicate *40 Below Summer*
39-RK

Sell A Lot Of Beer *Warren Brothers*
51-CW

Send The Pain Below *Chevelle*
1-RK   1-MD   65-HT

Send Your Love *Sting*
1-DN

Sending You A Little Christmas
Jim Brickman w/Kristy Starling
1-AC

Señorita *Justin Timberlake*
27-HT

September Grass *James Taylor*
25-AC

Serenity *Godsmack*
7-RK   10-MD   113-BU

Serious *Vernessa Mitchell*
37-DN

Set Me Free *Velvet Revolver*
17-RK   32-MD

Set Up *Obie Trice*
39-RB

Seven *Revis*
29-RK

Seven Nation Army *White Stripes*
1-MD   12-RK   76-HT

77 Strings (How Did You Know)
*Kurtis Mantronik Presents
Chamonix*
3-DN

Sexy Northerner *Pet Shop Boys*
15-DN

Shake It *Marascia*
4-DN

Shake It *Lee-Cabrera*
42-DN

Shake That Monkey *Too $hort*
56-RB   84-HT

Shake Ya Tailfeather
Nelly/P. Diddy/Murphy Lee
1-HT   3-RB

Shape Of Things To Come...
My Ruin
60-HS

Shatterday *Vendetta Red*
16-MD

She Is *Susan Ashton*
56-CW

She Is *Carl Thomas*
56-RB

**She Only Smokes When She
Drinks** *Joe Nichols*
17-CW   72-HT

She's My Kind Of Rain
Tim McGraw
27-HT

She's Not Just A Pretty Face
Shania Twain
9-CW   56-HT

Shelter *Ann Nesby*
6-DN

Shine On Me!
Pete Rock & C.L. Smooth
49-RS   64-HS

?hit, The *D.O.C.*
48-HS   53-RS

Shoomp *De La Soul*
43-RS

Shoulda, Woulda, Coulda
Brian McKnight
35-RB   106-BU

Show Me How To Live *Audioslave*
2-RK   4-MD   67-HT

Show Starter *Fakts One*
60-RS

Signals Over The Air *Thursday*
30-MD

Signs Of Love Makin' *Tyrese*
18-RB   57-HT

Silver And Cold *AFI*
8↑-MD

Silver Bells
Clay Aiken & Kimberley Locke
16-AC

Simple Life *Carolyn Dawn Johnson*
17↑-CW

Simple Things *Amy Grant*
23-AC

Sing For The Moment *Eminem*
14-HT

Sinnerman *Nina Simone*
10-DN

63/64 *Roez Boyz*
33-HS   97-RB

Skin *Breaking Benjamin*
24-RK   37-MD

Sleeping Awake *P.O.D.*
14-MD   20-RK

Sleepwalking *Blindside*
31-RK

Slow *Kylie Minogue*
1-DN

Slow Jamz *Twista*
1-HT   1-RB

Smaller Pieces *Dusty Drake*
50-CW

Smile *G-Unit*
77-RB

Smith Bros *Raekwon*
56-RS

Smoke Did It *Smoke Bulga*
60-RS

Smooth Love *Luther Vandross*
67-RS

Smooth Sailin' *Roscoe*
73-RB

Snake *R. Kelly*
9-RB   16-HT

Snowfall On The Sand
Steve Wariner
52-CW

So Far Away *Staind*
1-RK   1-MD   24-HT

So Gone *Monica*
1-RB   1-DN   10-HT

So Says I *Shins*
14-HS

So Whassup *Jonell*
39-RS   49-HS

So Yesterday *Hilary Duff*
42-HT

Soldier's Heart *R. Kelly*
80-HT   84-RB

Solsbury Hill *Erasure*
10-HS

Some Lovin' *Murk vs Kristine W*
39-HS

Someday *Nickelback*
2-RK   4-MD   7-HT

Someday *Sloth*
25-RK

Someday *Vince Gill*
31-CW

Someday *Scarface*
60-RS

Somewhere I Belong *Linkin Park*
1-MD   1-RK   32-HT

Somnambulist *BT*
5-DN   98-HT

Songs About Rain *Gary Allan*
14↑-CW

Sorry 2004 *Ruben Studdard*
2-RB

Sorta Fairytale *Tori Amos*
9-HS

Soul Deep *Laura Turner*
14-DN

Soul Shake *Nathaniel Lamar*
31-HS   91-RB

Soul Sloshing *Venus Hum*
6-DN

Southern Boy *Charlie Daniels Band w/Travis Tritt*
51-CW

Space *Something Corporate*
37-MD

Speed *Montgomery Gentry*
47-HT

Spend My Time *Clint Black*
16-CW

Splash Waterfalls *Ludacris*
2-RB

St. Anger *Metallica*
2-RK   17-MD   107-BU

Stacy's Mom *Fountains Of Wayne*
21-HT   31-MD

Stand *Jewel*
1-DN   16-HS

Stand By Your Side *Celine Dion*
17-AC

Stand Up *Ludacris*
1-HT   1-RB

Stand Up In It *Theodis Ealey*
5-HS

Stand Up (Summer Song) *Skrape*
34-RK

Star *702*
98-RB

Stardust *Martin L. Gore*
55-HS

Starting With Me
Brandy Moss-Scott
16-HS   88-RB

Stay Gone *Jimmy Wayne*
3-CW   32-HT

Stay Real *Black Moon*
64-RS

Step Daddy *Hitman Sammy Sam*
41-RB   90-HT

Step In The Name Of Love *R. Kelly*
9-HT

Step Into My Office, Baby
Belle & Sebastian
64-HS

Still Ballin *2Pac*
31-RB   69-HT

Still Frame *Trapt*
1-RK   3-MD   69-HT

Still On My Brain *Justin Timberlake*
75-RB

Stillborn *Black Label Society*
12-RK

Stompdash*toutu (Vendetta)
Capone-N-Noreaga
38-RS   55-HS

Stoned *Dido*
1-DN

Stop *Jay-Z*
18-HS   53-RB

Straight Out Of Line *Godsmack*
1-RK   9-MD   73-HT

Streets Of Heaven *Sherrié Austin*
18-CW   113-BU

Strictly Business *Brad Wolf*
58-CW

Stuck *Stacie Orrico*
52-HT

Stuck In A Groove *Puretone*
4-DN

Stuck Inside A Cloud
George Harrison
27-AC

Stunt 101 *G-Unit*
7-RB   13-HT

Stupid Girl *Cold*
4-RK   6-MD   87-HT

Such Great Heights *Postal Service*
21-HS

Suddenly *LeAnn Rimes*
43-CW

Sueña *Intocable*
118-BU

Suffocate *Cold*
17-RK   21-MD

Suga Suga *Baby Bash*
7-HT   54-RB

Summertime *Beyoncé*
35-RB   58-HS   108-BU

Sunrise *Simply Red*
1-DN   5-AC   122-BU

Supa Star *Montell Jordan*
71-RB

Super B-Boy Pimpin'
Earthquake Institute
22-HS   99-RB

Superman *Eminem*
15-HT   44-RB

Superstar *Ruben Studdard*
2-RB   112-BU

Sweet Misery *Rashad*
27-RS

Sweet Southern Comfort
Buddy Jewell
3↑-CW

Sweetest Sin *Jessica Simpson*
6-HS

Swing, Swing *All-American Rejects*
60-HT

Sympathy *Goo Goo Dolls*
115-BU

Sympathy For The Devil
Rolling Stones
34-DN   97-HT

Symphony In X Major *Xzibit*
63-RB

T

Take It Off *Donnas*
31-RK

Take It Off! *High & Mighty*
66-RS

Take Me Away *Fefe Dobson*
87-HT

Take You Home *Angie Martinez*
85-HT

(Taking My) Life Away *Default*
25-RK

Tal Vez *Ricky Martin*
74-HT

Talk 2 Me *K-Klass*
9-DN

Talk To Me, Dance With Me
Hot Hot Heat
33-MD

Te Necesito *Luis Miguel*
119-BU

Tear It Up *Andrew W.K.*
26-HS

Tell Me Something Bad About Tulsa *George Strait*
11-CW   69-HT

Tell Me (What's Goin' On)
Smilez & Southstar
28-HT

Tennessee River Run *Darryl Worley*
31-CW

Texas Plates *Kellie Coffey*
24-CW

That Girl *Marques Houston*
24-RB   63-HT

That Girl *Joe*
71-RB

That Was Us *Chad Brock*
58-CW

That'd Be Alright *Alan Jackson*
29-HT

That's A Woman *Mark Wills*
40-CW

Them Jeans *Master P*
40-RB

Then They Do *Trace Adkins*
9-CW   52-HT

There Goes My Life *Kenny Chesney*
1-CW   29-HT

There Is No War *Donovan Chapman*
58-CW

There There *Radiohead*
14-MD

There's A Winner In You
Tiffany Evans
18-HS

(there's gotta be) More To Life
Stacie Orrico
30-HT

There's More To Me Than You
Jessica Andrews
108-BU

There's No Limit *Deana Carter*
102-BU

These Days *Alien Ant Farm*
29-MD   38-RK

They Can't Take That Away From Me *Rod Stewart*
27-AC

Think About You *Luther Vandross*
33↑-RB

Think Twice *Eve 6*
9-MD

Thinking Over *Dana Glover*
17-AC

This Beat Is *Superchumbo*
1-DN

This Far Gone *Jennifer Hanson*
42-CW

This Is God *Phil Vassar*
17-CW   109-BU

This Is How We Do *Big Tymers*
53-RB   97-HT

This Is My House *Peter Rauhofer*
32-DN

This Is The Night *Clay Aiken*
1-HT   13-AC

This Love *LeAnn Rimes*
37-CW

This One's For The Girls
Martina McBride
3-CW   39-HT

Thoia Thoing *R. Kelly*
6-RB   13-HT

Thousand Beautiful Things
Annie Lennox
1-DN

1000 Years *Arthur Baker*
22-DN

Three Mississippi *Terri Clark*
30-CW

Three Wooden Crosses
Randy Travis
31-HT

Through The Rain *Mariah Carey*
69-RB

Through The Wire *Kanye West*
8-RB   15-HT

Thug Luv *Lil' Kim*
48-HS   60-RB

Thugman *Tweet*
22-RS

Tic Toc *LeAnn Rimes*
10-DN

Time Of Our Lives *Bonnie Raitt*
27-AC

Time Of Our Lives *Paul Van Dyk*
36-DN   63-HS

Times Like These *Foo Fighters*
5-RK   5-MD   65-HT

Tiny Dancer *Tim McGraw*
13-AC

Tipsy *J-Kwon*
2↑-RB

Toast To Men *Willa Ford*
45-HS

Tonite, I'm Yours *Zane*
44-HS   87-RB

Tonz Of Fun *Presence*
31-RK

Too Much For Me *DJ Kayslay*
53-RB

Too Much Month (At The End Of The Money) *Marty Stuart*
54-CW

Touched A Dream *R. Kelly*
49-RB

Tough Little Boys *Gary Allan*
1-CW   32-HT

Train *Goldfrapp*
64-HS

Travelin' Soldier *Dixie Chicks*
25-HT

Tremble *Clare Quilty*
33-DN

Trouble *P!nk*
68-HT

Trouble With Love Is *Kelly Clarkson*
101-BU

Troy (The Phoenix From The Flame) *Sinéad O'Connor*
53-HS

True Nature *Jane's Addiction*
30-MD   35-RK

Truth About Men *Tracy Byrd*
13-CW   77-HT

Try Honesty *Billy Talent*
24-MD

Try It On My Own *Whitney Houston*
1-DN   10-AC   80-RB   84-HT

Tu Amor O Tu Desprecio
Marco Antonio Solís
121-BU

Turn Me On *Norah Jones*
2-HS

Turn Me Out *Praxis*
42-DN

12:51 *Strokes*
15-MD

24's *T.I.*
27-RB   78-HT

21 Answers *Lil' Mo*
50-RB

21 Questions *50 Cent*
1-HT   1-RB

21 Questions (Again) *Debreca*
42-RB

Two-Lane Blacktop *Rob Zombie*
39-RK

U

U Got That Love (Call It A Night)
Gerald Levert
30-RB   103-BU

Ugly *Blaque*
70-RS

Uh Oh *Project 2B*
17-RS

Ultimate Love *Phil Vassar*
41-CW

Un Siglo Sin Ti *Chayanne*
120-BU

Una Vez Mas *Conjunto Primavera*
111-BU

Underneath It All *No Doubt*
27-AC

United States Of Whatever
Liam Lynch
34-MD

Unkissed *Holly Lamar*
59-CW

Unnamed Feeling *Metallica*
28-RK

Unstable *Adema*
25-RK   37-MD

Until The Day I Die
Story Of The Year
12-MD

Untitled #1 *Sigur Ros*
11-HS

Unusually Unusual *Lonestar*
66-HT

Unwell *Matchbox Twenty*
1-AC   5-HT

Up! *Shania Twain*
63-HT

Up Against All Odds
Tarralyn Ramsey
31-HS   95-RB

Up In Da Club 2Nite *Revenue*
12-HS   92-RB

V

Voice Within *Christina Aguilera*
16-AC   33-HT

Volvo Driving Soccer Mom
Everclear
30-MD

W

Waiting For Our Time *Styx*
37-RK

Waiting For You *Seal*
1-DN   20-AC   89-HT

Walk A Little Straighter
Billy Currington
8-CW   67-HT

Walk On By *Cyndi Lauper*
10-DN

Walked Outta Heaven *Jagged Edge*
2-RB   6-HT

Walking In Memphis *Lonestar*
8-CW   61-HT

Walking On A Cloud *Brand Nubian*
75-RS

Walking On Thin Ice *Ono*
1-DN   25-HS

Walter *Charlie Robison*
58-CW

Wanna Get To Know You *G-Unit*
10↑-RB

Was That My Life *Jo Dee Messina*
21-CW   114-BU

Wat Da Hook Gon Be *Murphy Lee*
11-RB   17-HT

Watch The Wind Blow By
Tim McGraw
1-CW   32-HT

Wave On Wave *Pat Green*
3-CW   39-HT

Way Away *Yellowcard*
25-MD

Way I Am *Knoc-Turn'Al*
78-RB

Way You Do It *Little Brother*
62-RS

Way You Move *OutKast*
1-HT   2-RB

We Can *LeAnn Rimes*
16-AC   19-DN

We Shook Hands (Man To Man)
Tebey
47-CW

We've Had Enough *Alkaline Trio*
38-MD

THE ALBUMS

Lists alphabetically, by artist, in three separate sections, all albums that debuted on *Billboard's Pop (The Billboard 200)*, *Country*, and *R&B/Hip-Hop* albums charts from January 4 through December 27.

All #1 titles are identified by a special #1 symbol (❶). All Top 10 albums are shaded and all titles and peak positions are shown in bold (dark) typeface.

EXPLANATION OF COLUMNAR HEADINGS

DEBUT DATE: Date album first charted

PEAK POS: Album's highest charted position (highlighted in bold type)

WKS CHR: Total weeks charted

GLD: ●   RIAA-certified gold album (500,000 units sold or 250,000 for EPs)

▲ RIAA-certified platinum album (one million units sold or 500,000 for EPs) A superscript number to the right of a platinum triangle indicates multi-platinum status (ex.: ▲^{2} indicates an album was certified double platinum)

LABEL & NUMBER: Original album label and number

Letter(s) in brackets indicates:

C - Comedy Recording	**L** - Live
E - Early Recording	**M** - Mini Album (E.P.)
F - Foreign Language	**S** - Movie Soundtrack
G - Greatest Hits	**TV** - Television Album
I - Instrumental Recording	**V** - Various Artists
K - Compilation	**X** - Christmas Recording

OTHER DATA AND SYMBOLS

1: A superior number after #1 and #2 albums indicates total weeks album held that position.

+: Indicates album peaked in 2004

[ ]: Number in brackets following label number indicates amount of discs in a multi-disc CD album

↑: Indicates the highest position and/or weeks charted data are subject to change since the album was still charted as of the 4/3/04 cut-off date

25^C: Superscript C following the peak position in the "PEAK" column indicates album only charted on the Catalog Albums chart and <u>not</u> on the Pop Albums chart.

15^X: Superscript X following the peak position in the "PEAK" column indicates album only charted on the Christmas Albums chart and <u>not</u> on the Pop Albums chart.

★: Artist's first appearance on chart

Biographical information is shown for nearly every new artist. If a new artist made both the Pop Albums section and one or more of the other albums sections, their biographical information appears in the Pop Albums section only.

TOP 20 ARTISTS

At the back of each album section is a listing, in rank order, of the *Top 20 Artists* of 2003. The ranking is compiled from those albums which appeared in the Top 10 only in 2003.

★ Indicates those top artists who debuted on that particular chart during 2003.

An inverse point system is used to calculate a point total for each artist based on the weekly Top 10 chart positions of their albums. For each week an album appears in the Top 10, points are awarded based on the album's chart position (#1 = 10 points, #2 = 9 points, #3 = 8 points, etc.). These weekly points are added together to create an overall point total for each artist. If an album appeared in the Top 10 in 2003 and also appeared in the Top 10 in other years, only the 2003 chart positions are calculated in.

Ties are broken in this order: most weeks at the #1 position, and then, most weeks in the Top 10.

TOP 30 ALBUMS

Following is the chronology used in ranking each year's hit albums:

1) The album's peak position

   All albums peaking at #1 are listed first, then albums that peaked at #2 are grouped together and shown secondly, then the #3s, etc. Ties among each highest position grouping are broken down in this order:

2) Total weeks album held its peak position

3) Total weeks charted in Top 10

4) Total weeks charted in Top 40

5) Total weeks charted

If there are still ties, a computerized inverse point system is used to calculate a point total for each hit based on its weekly chart positions. For each week an album appears on the charts, it is given points based on its chart position for that week. The maximum points awarded is based on the size of the chart. For example, for *The Billboard 200* chart the point scaling is as follows: #1 = 200 points, #2 = 199 points, etc. The maximum points a #1 hit receives on a top 75 chart is 75 points, and so on. These points are added together to create a raw point total for each album, which is used to break any remaining ties.

POP ALBUMS

This section lists, by artist, every album that debuted in 2003 on **The Billboard 200** weekly chart (a top 200 listing).

DEBUT DATE	PEAK POS	WKS CHR	G L D	ARTIST Title	Label & Number
				ABK ★	
				Born James Lowery on 6/26/75 in Detroit, Michigan. Native American hardcore rapper. Performs with white face paint. Affiliated with Insane Clown Posse. ABK: Any Body Killa.	
4/26/03	98	1		Hatchet Warrior	Psychopathic 4012
				ADAMS, Ryan	
11/22/03	33	4		Rock N Roll	Lost Highway 001376
11/22/03	78	1		Love Is Hell Pt. 1 .... [M]	Lost Highway 001548
12/27/03	171	1		Love Is Hell Pt. 2 .... [M]	Lost Highway 001549
				ADEMA	
9/6/03	43	4		Unstable	Arista 53914
				ADKINS, Trace	
7/26/03	9	24	●	Greatest Hits Collection, Volume I [G]	Capitol 81512
12/20/03	31	16↑	●	Comin' On Strong	Capitol 40517
				AESOP ROCK ★	
				Born Ian Bavitz in Manhattan, New York. Male rapper.	
10/11/03	112	1		Bazooka Tooth	Definitive Jux 68
				AFI	
3/29/03	5	45↑	●	Sing The Sorrow	Nitro 450380
				AGUILAR, Pepe ★	
				Born in Zacatecas, Mexico. Latin singer.	
4/12/03	118	4		Y Tenerte Otra Vez.. [F]	Univision 310119
				title is Spanish for "And Once Again Perhaps"	
				AIKEN, Clay ★	
				Born on 11/30/78 in Chapel Hill, North Carolina. White male vocalist. Finished in second place on the second season of TV's *American Idol* in 2003.	
11/1/03	❶²	23↑	▲²	Measure Of A Man	RCA 54638
				AIR SUPPLY	
6/21/03	186	1		Ultimate Air Supply .... [G]	Arista 52204
				ALABAMA	
2/22/03	15	11		In The Mood: Love Songs... [K]	RCA 67052 [2]
10/25/03	64	5		The American Farewell Tour .... [K]	RCA 54371
				ALIEN ANT FARM	
9/6/03	42	4		truANT...	El Tonal 000568
				ALKALINE TRIO	
5/31/03	20	12		Good Mourning	Vagrant 381
				ALL-AMERICAN REJECTS, The ★	
				Punk-rock group from Stillwater, Oklahoma: Tyson Ritter (vocals, bass), Mike Kennerty and Nick Wheeler (guitars), and Chris Gaylor (drums).	
2/22/03	25	41	●	The All-American Rejects..	Doghouse 450407
				ALLAN, Gary	
10/18/03	17	25↑	●	See If I Care	MCA Nashville 000111
				ALLMAN BROTHERS BAND, The	
4/5/03	37	7		Hittin' The Note...	Peach 84599
				AMERICAN HI-FI	
3/15/03	80	2		The Art Of Losing..	Island 063657
				AMOS, Tori	
12/6/03	40	9		A Tori Amos Collection: Tales Of A Librarian .... [G]	Atlantic 83658
				ANASTASIO, Trey	
5/17/03	102	1		Plasma .... [L]	Elektra 62867 [2]
				ANDREWS, Jessica	
5/3/03	34	8		Now	DreamWorks 450356
				ANDREW W.K.	
9/27/03	61	1		The Wolf..	Island 001051
				ANTHRAX	
5/24/03	122	1		We've Come For You All..	Sanctuary 84609
				ANTI-FLAG ★	
				Punk-rock group from Pittsburgh, Pennsylvania: Justin Sane (vocals, guitar), Chris Head (guitar), Chris #2 (bass) and Pat Thetic (drums).	
11/8/03	91	1		The Terror State	Fat Wreck Chords 643
				ASHANTI	
6/7/03	142	6		Ashanti: The 7 Series .... [K-M]	Murder Inc. 000494
				contains seven songs from her *Ashanti* album	
7/19/03	❶²	30	▲	Chapter II	Murder Inc. 000143
12/6/03	160	5		Ashanti's Christmas .... [X]	The Inc. 001612

DEBUT DATE	PEAK POS	WKS CHR	G L D	ARTIST Title	Label & Number
				ATARIS, The ★	
				Punk-rock group from Los Angeles, California: Kris Roe (vocals, guitar), John Collura (guitar), Mike Davenport (bass) and Chris Knapp (drums).	
3/22/03	24	36	●	So Long, Astoria	Columbia 86184
				ATMOSPHERE	
10/11/03	83	2		Seven's Travels	Rhymesayers 86690
				AUDIO ADRENALINE	
3/15/03	116	3		Worldwide	Forefront 40877
				AUSTIN, Sherrié	
8/30/03	144	1		Streets Of Heaven	Broken Bow 75872
				AVALON	
4/12/03	112	12		The Very Best Of Avalon: Testify To Love .... [G]	Sparrow 42949
				AVANT	
12/27/03	18	15↑	●	Private Room	Magic Johnson 001567
				BABY BASH ★	
				Born Ronald Bryant in Vallejo, California; raised in Houston, Texas. Latin male rapper.	
10/11/03	48	26↑	●	Tha Smokin' Nephew	Universal 001258
				BACHARACH, Burt — see ISLEY BROTHERS	
				BAD BOY'S DA BAND ★	
				Rap group assembled by P. Diddy for the reality TV series *Making The Band 2*: Dylan John, Sara Stokes, Lloyd "Ness" Mathis, Frederick Watson, Lynese "Babs" Wiley and Rodney "Young City" Hill.	
10/18/03	2¹	9	●	Too Hot For T.V.	Bad Boy 001118
				BADU, Erykah	
10/4/03	3	11	●	World Wide Underground	Motown 000739
				BANNER, David ★	
				Born in Mississippi. Male rapper.	
6/7/03	9	22		Mississippi: The Album	SRC 000312
				BANTON, Buju	
3/29/03	198	1		Friends For Life	VP 83634
				BARENAKED LADIES	
11/8/03	10	10		Everything To Everyone	Reprise 48209
				BARNARD, Shane, & Shane Everett ★	
				Christian singing/songwriting duo from Texas.	
4/12/03	149	1		Carry Away	Inpop 71264
				BASEMENT JAXX	
11/8/03	172	1		Kish Kash	XL 93878
				BATES, Jeff ★	
				Born on 9/19/63 in Bunker Hill, Mississippi. Country singer/songwriter/guitarist.	
6/7/03	117	3		Rainbow Man	RCA 67071
				BEACH BOYS, The	
6/28/03	16	41↑	●	The Very Best Of The Beach Boys: Sounds Of Summer .... [G]	Capitol 82710
				BEATLES, The	
12/6/03	5	14	▲	Let It Be...Naked [R]	Apple 95713
				re-issue of their #1 album from 1970 (minus the orchestral overdubs by Phil Spector)	
				BECK, Jeff	
8/23/03	122	1		Jeff .... [I]	Epic 86941
				BELLE AND SEBASTIAN	
10/25/03	84	2		Dear Catastrophe Waitress	Rough Trade 83216
				BELUSHI - AYKROYD ★	
				Duo of actors/singers/comedians. Jim Belushi was born on 6/15/54 in Chicago, Illinois. Dan Aykroyd was born on 7/1/52 in Ottawa, Ontario, Canada. Aykroyd and Jim's older brother John (died of a drug overdose on 3/5/82, age 33) were the original Blues Brothers.	
6/21/03	166	2		Have Love Will Travel	Have Love 480200
				BENATAR, Pat	
8/30/03	187	1		Go	Bel Chiasso 79743
				BENSON, George	
7/26/03	138	1		The Greatest Hits Of All .... [G]	Rhino 78284
				BENTLEY, Dierks ★	
				Born on 11/20/75 in Phoenix, Arizona. Country singer/songwriter/guitarist.	
9/6/03	26	31↑	●	Dierks Bentley	Capitol 39814

DEBUT DATE	PEAK POS	WKS CHR	G L D	ARTIST / Title	Label & Number
2/1/03	65	3		**BENZINO** Redemption	Surrender 62827
3/15/03	98	4		**BERING STRAIT** ★ Country group from Obninsk, Russia: Natasha Borzilova (vocals, guitar), Ilya Toshinsky (guitar), Lydia Salnikova (keyboards), Alexander "Sasha" Ostrovsky (dobro), Sergei "Spooky" Olkhovsky (bass) and Alexander Arzamastsev (drums). Bering Strait	Universal South 170218
7/12/03	❶¹	39↑	▲³	**BEYONCÉ** ★ Born Beyoncé Knowles on 9/4/81 in Houston, Texas. R&B singer/songwriter/actress. Member of Destiny's Child. Dangerously In Love	Columbia 86386
3/15/03	21	12		**B.G.** Livin' Legend	Koch 8465
7/26/03	195	1		**BIG BAD VOODOO DADDY** Save My Soul	Big Bad 79742
10/18/03	177	1		**BIG DADDY WEAVE** ★ Christian pop group from Nashville, Tennessee: brothers Mike Weaver (vocals, guitar) and Jay Weaver (bass), Jeremy Redmon (guitar), Joe Shirk (sax) and Jeff Jones (drums). Fields Of Grace	Fervent 30040
8/30/03	161	2		**BIG GIPP** ★ Born Cameron Gipp in Atlanta, Georgia. Male rapper. Member of Goodie Mob. Mutant Mindframe	Koch 8481
12/27/03	21	15↑	●	**BIG TYMERS** Big Money Heavyweight	Cash Money 000815
10/4/03	194	1		**BILLY TALENT** ★ Punk-rock group from Streetsville, Ontario, Canada: Ben Kowalewicz (vocals), Ian D'Sa (guitar), Jon Gallant (bass) and Aaron Solowoniuk (drums). Billy Talent	Atlantic 83614
7/12/03	26	39↑	▲	**BLACK EYED PEAS** Elephunk	A&M 000699
5/10/03	50	7		**BLACK LABEL SOCIETY** The Blessed Hellride	Spitfire 15091
9/20/03	47	4		**BLACK REBEL MOTORCYCLE CLUB** ★ Eclectic-rock trio from San Francsico, California: Peter Hayes (vocals, guitar), Robert Turner (bass) and Nick Jago (drums). Take Them On, On Your Own	Virgin 80095
3/29/03	14	5		**BLACKstreet** Level II	DreamWorks 450392
9/13/03	❶¹	25	▲	**BLIGE, Mary J.** Love & Life	Geffen 000956
12/20/03+	164	3		**BLIND BOYS OF ALABAMA, The** ★ Legendary gospel group from Talladega, Alabama: Bobby Butler, Jimmy Carter, Clarence Fountain, Ricke McKinnie, Tracie Pierce, George Scott and Joe Williams. Go Tell It On The Mountain [X]	Real World 90600
12/6/03	3	18↑	▲	**BLINK-182** Blink-182	Geffen 001336
5/10/03	60	6		**BLUE MAN GROUP** The Complex	Blue Man Group 83631
8/23/03	147	1		**BLUES TRAVELER** Truth Be Told	Sanctuary 84620
5/24/03	56	3		**BLUR** Think Tank	Parlophone 84242
9/20/03	76	5		**BOLTON, Michael** Vintage	PMG 73973
5/17/03	11	19		**BONE CRUSHER** ★ Born Wayne Hardnett on 8/23/71 in Atlanta, Georgia. Male rapper. AttenCHUN!	Break-Em-Off 50995
11/22/03	14	12		**BON JOVI** This Left Feels Right _contains new acoustic versions of several previous hits_	Island 001540
9/13/03	195	1		**BOO & GOTTI** ★ Male rap duo from Chicago, Illinois. Perfect Timing	Cash Money 000542

POP ALBUMS

DEBUT DATE	PEAK POS	WKS CHR	GLD	ARTIST / Title	Label & Number
				BOOMKAT ★	
				Pop duo from Tuscon, Arizona: brother-and sister Kellin and Taryn Manning. Taryn acted in such movies as *Crossroads* and *8 Mile*.	
4/26/03	88	2		Boomkatalog.One	DreamWorks 450386
				BOUNCING SOULS, The ★	
				Punk-rock group from New Jersey: Greg Attonito (vocals), Pete Steinkopf (guitar), Bryan Kienlen (bass) and Michael McDermott (drums).	
9/13/03	168	1		Anchors Aweigh..................................	Epitaph 86669
				BOWIE, David	
10/4/03	29	4		Reality	Iso 90576
				BOWLING FOR SOUP ★	
				Punk-rock group from Wichita Falls, Texas: Jaret Reddick (vocals, guitar), Chris Burney (guitar), Erik Chandler (bass) and Gary Wiseman (drums).	
3/15/03	129	15		Drunk Enough To Dance	Ffroe 41819
				BOYSETSFIRE	
4/19/03	141	1		Tomorrow Come Today...........................	Wind-Up 13071
				BRANCH, Michelle	
7/12/03	2[1]	33	▲	Hotel Paper	Maverick 48426
				BRAND NEW ★	
				Punk-rock group from Merrick, New York: Jesse Lacey (vocals), Vincent Accardi (guitar), Garrett Tierney (bass) and Brian Lane (drums).	
7/5/03	63	26		Deja Entendu	Triple Crown 82896
				BRAXTON, Toni	
11/22/03	119	2		Ultimate Toni Braxton .... [G]	Arista 51699
				BRICKELL, Edie	
11/1/03	188	1		Volcano	Universal 000963
				BRICKMAN, Jim	
11/15/03	87	8		Peace .... [X]	Windham Hill 52896
				BRIGHTMAN, Sarah	
6/28/03	29	16		Harem..	Angel 37180
				BRONCO ★	
				Latin group from Apodaca, Mexico: Ramiro Delgado, Aurelio Esparza, José Esparza, Javier Villarreal and José Villarreal.	
4/19/03	153	2		30 Inolvidables .... [F-G]	Fonovisa 350787
				title is Spanish for "30 Unforgettables"	
8/9/03	97	5		Siempre Arriba .... [F]	Fonovisa 350927
				title is Spanish for "Always Above"	
				BROOKLYN TABERNACLE CHOIR, The	
12/6/03	137	1		Live...This Is Your House .... [L]	Word-Curb 82502 [2]
				BROOKS & DUNN	
8/2/03	4	36↑	●	Red Dirt Road	Arista Nashville 67070
				BROTHA LYNCH HUNG	
6/28/03	132	2		Lynch By Inch: Suicide Note	Siccmade 70132 [2]
				BT	
8/23/03	138	1		Emotional Technology	Nettwerk 30344
				B2K	
7/19/03	192	1		B2K: The Remixes - Vol. 2 .... [K]	Epic 86885
				BUBLÉ, Michael ★	
				Born on 9/9/75 in Burnaby, British Columbia, Canada. Traditional pop singer.	
3/1/03	47	37↑	●	Michael Bublé	143 Records 48376
12/20/03	56	3		Let It Snow! .... [X-M]	143 Records 48599
				BUDDEN, Joe ★	
				Born in 1980 in Jersey City, New Jersey. Male rapper.	
6/28/03	8	16		Joe Budden	Def Jam 000505
				BUFFETT, Jimmy	
5/3/03	9	31↑	▲2	Meet Me In Margaritaville: The Ultimate Collection	Mailboat 067781 [2]
				BYRD, Tracy	
7/19/03	33	7		The Truth About Men	RCA 67073
				CAEDMON'S CALL	
2/22/03	66	4		Back Home	Essential 10694
				CAGLE, Chris	
4/19/03	15	36	●	Chris Cagle	Capitol 40516

DEBUT DATE	PEAK POS	WKS CHR	G L D	ARTIST / Title	Label & Number
				CAMPBELL, Glen	
2/15/03	89	1		All The Best .... [G]	Capitol 41816
				CANIBUS	
8/9/03	194	1		Rip The Jacker	Babygrande 5
				CANNON, Nick ★	
				Born on 10/17/80 in San Diego, California. R&B singer/actor. Regular on TV's *All That* (1998-2001). Starred in the movie *Drumline*.	
12/27/03	83	10		Nick Cannon	Nick 48500
				CANTRELL, Blu	
7/12/03	37	7		Bittersweet..	Arista 52728
				CAREY, Mariah	
11/1/03	26	5		The Remixes .... [K]	Columbia 87154 [2]
				CARRINGTON, Rodney	
3/1/03	82	7		Nut Sack .... [C]	Capitol 36579
				CARTER, Deana	
4/5/03	58	3		I'm Just A Girl	Arista Nashville 67054
				CARTER, Regina ★	
				Born in Detroit, Michigan. Black female classical violinist.	
5/31/03	189	1		Paganini: After A Dream....................... [I]	Verve 065554
				CASH, Johnny	
9/27/03	8[C]	10		Super Hits [G]	Columbia 66773
9/27/03	102	10		The Essential Johnny Cash .... [G]	Legacy 86290 [2]
				CASH, Rosanne	
4/12/03	130	3		Rules Of Travel................................	Capitol 37757
				CASSIDY, Eva	
8/30/03	112	5		American Tune	Blix Street 10079
				CASTING CROWNS ★	
				Christian pop group from Daytona Beach, Florida: Mark Hall (vocals), Hector Cervantes (guitar), Juan Devevo (guitar), Megan Garrett (keyboards), Melodee Devevo (violin), Chris Huffman (bass) and Andy Williams (drums).	
10/18/03+	80↑	13↑		Casting Crowns................................	Beat Street 10723
				CAT POWER ★	
				Born Chan (pronounced: Shawn) Marshall in 1974 in Florida. Female singer/songwriter/pianist.	
3/8/03	105	4		You Are Free................................	Matador 427
				CAVE, Nick, and The Bad Seeds	
3/1/03	182	1		Nocturama	Mute 86668
				CAVE IN ★	
				Rock group from Boston, Massachusetts: Stephen Brodsky (vocals, guitar), Adam McGrath (guitar), Caleb Scofield (bass) and John-Robert Conners (drums).	
4/5/03	169	1		Antenna................................	RCA 68131
				C-BO	
8/9/03	199	1		The Mobfather	West Coast Mafia 2010
				CHAPMAN, Steven Curtis	
2/15/03	12	12		All About Love................................	Sparrow 41762
				CHAYANNE	
9/13/03	87	5		Sincero................................ [F]	Sony Discos 70627
				CHEAP TRICK	
8/9/03	128	1		Special One	Cheap Trick Unlim. 36333
				CHEMICAL BROTHERS, The	
10/18/03	123	1		Singles 93 - 03 .... [G]	Freestyle Dust 92714 [2]
				CHER	
4/19/03	4	51↑	▲[2]	The Very Best Of Cher [G]	Warner 73852
9/13/03	40	6		Live: The Farewell Tour .... [L]	Warner 73953
9/13/03	83	5		The Very Best Of Cher: Special Edition.................... [G-L]	Warner 73956 [2]
				deluxe package of first two albums listed above	
				CHESNEY, Kenny	
10/25/03	42	12	●	All I Want For Christmas Is A Real Good Tan .... [X]	BNA 51808
				CHESNUTT, Cody ★	
				Born in Atlanta, Georgia. Male R&B singer/songwriter.	
4/5/03	128	1		The Headphone Masterpiece	Ready Set Go! 001 [2]
				CHICAGO	
12/6/03	102	4		Christmas: What's It Gonna Be, Santa? .... [X]	Rhino 73892

DEBUT DATE	PEAK POS	WKS CHR	G L D	ARTIST / Title	Label & Number
				CHIEFTAINS, The	
9/27/03	180	2		Further Down The Old Plank Road	Victor 52897
				CHIMAIRA ★	
				Hard-rock group from Cleveland, Ohio: Mark Hunter (vocals), Rob Arnold (guitar), Matt DeVries (guitar), Chris Spicuzza (electronics), Jim LaMarca (bass) and Andols Herrick (drums).	
5/31/03	117	1		The Impossibility Of Reason	Roadrunner 618397
				CHINGY ★	
				Born Howard Bailey on 3/9/80 in St. Louis, Missouri. Male rapper.	
8/2/03	2¹	36↑	▲²	Jackpot	Disturbing Tha P. 82976
				CHOPPA ★	
				Born Darwin Turner in New Orleans, Louisiana. Male rapper.	
3/22/03	54	8		Straight From The N.O.	New No Limit 075007
				CINCOTTI, Peter ★	
				Born on 7/11/83 in Manhattan, New York. Jazz singer/pianist.	
3/29/03	118	6		Peter Cincotti	Concord 2159
				CLARK, Terri	
2/1/03	27	8		Pain To Kill	Mercury 170325
				CLARK SHEARD, Karen	
11/22/03	188	1		The Heavens Are Telling	Elektra 62894
				CLARKSON, Kelly ★	
				Born on 4/24/82 in Burleson, Texas. Female pop singer. Winner of TV's first *American Idol* talent series.	
5/3/03	❶¹	47	▲²	Thankful	RCA 68159
				CLASH, The	
3/29/03	99	2		The Essential Clash	[G] Epic 89056 [2]
				COHEED AND CAMBRIA ★	
				Hard-rock group from Nyack, New York: Claudio Sanchez (vocals, guitar), Travis Stever (guitar), Mic Todd (bass) and Josh Eppard (drums).	
10/25/03	52	3		In Keeping Secrets Of Silent Earth: 3	Equal Vision 87
				COLD	
5/31/03	3	21		Year Of The Spider	Flip 000006
				COLDPLAY	
11/22/03	13	16	●	Coldplay Live 2003	[L] Capitol 99014
				COMO, Perry	
11/15/03	50ˣ	1		Christmas With Perry Como	[X] BMG 44553
				CONJUNTO PRIMAVERA	
4/19/03	159	3		Nuestra Historia	[F-G] Fonovisa 50786
				title is Spanish for "Our History"	
9/6/03	124	4		Decide Tú	[F] Fonovisa 350875
				title is Spanish for "You Decide"	
				CONNICK, Harry Jr.	
11/15/03	12	9	●	Harry For The Holidays	[X] Columbia 90550
				CONTROL ★	
9/6/03	196	1		La Historia	[F-G] EMI Latin 90878
				COODER, Ry	
2/15/03	52	8		Mambo Sinuendo	[F] Perro Verde 79691
				RY COODER MANUEL GALBÁN	
				COOPER, Alice	
10/18/03	184	1		The Eyes Of Alice Cooper	Eagle 20028
				CORAL, The ★	
				Pop-rock group from Holylake, Wirral, England: James Skelly (vocals, guitar), Lee Southall (guitar), Bill Ryder-Jones (trumpet), Nick Power (organ), Paul Duffy (bass) and Ian Skelly (drums).	
3/22/03	189	1		The Coral	Deltasonic 87192
				COSTELLO, Elvis	
10/11/03	57	3		North	Deutsche Gr. 000999
				COUNTING CROWS	
12/13/03	32	16	●	Films About Ghosts: The Best Of	[G] Geffen 001676
				CRADLE OF FILTH ★	
				Goth-rock group from England: Dani Davey (vocals), Paul Allender (guitar), Martin Powell (keyboards), Dave Pubis (bass) and Adrian Erlandsson (drums).	
4/12/03	140	1		Damnation And A Day	Red Ink 71423
				CRISTIAN	
10/18/03	167	1		Amar Es	[F] Ariola 55195
				title is Spanish for "Love Is"	

DEBUT DATE	PEAK POS	WKS CHR	G L D	ARTIST Title	Label & Number
				CROSS MOVEMENT, The ★	
				Christian hip-hop group from New Jersey: William Branch, Virgil Byrd, Brady Goodwin and John Wells.	
5/10/03	134	1		Holy Culture	BEC 82654
				CROW, Sheryl	
11/22/03+	2²	20↑	▲²	The Very Best Of Sheryl Crow	[G] A&M 001521
				CROWDER, David, Band ★	
				Born in Waco, Texas. Christian singer/songwriter.	
10/4/03	84	1		Illuminate	Sixsteps 90230
				CRUZ, Celia ★	
				Born on 10/21/24 in Havana, Cuba. Died of brain cancer pn 7/16/2003 (age 78). Known as "The Queen of Salsa Music."	
8/2/03	106	7		Hits Mix	[F] Sony Discos 87607
8/16/03	40	7		Regalo Del Alma	[F] Sony Discos 70620
				title is Spanish for "Gift Of The Soul"	
8/16/03	95	7		Éxitos Eternos	[F] Universal Latino 000756
				CULBERTSON, Brian ★	
				Born in Decatur, Illinois. Smooth jazz singer/pianist.	
7/12/03	197	1		Come On Up	Warner 48300
				CURRINGTON, Billy ★	
				Born on 11/19/73 in Savannah, Georgia; raised in Rincon, Georgia. Country singer/songwriter/pianist.	
10/18/03	107	2		Billy Currington	Mercury 000164
				CYRUS, Billy Ray	
11/15/03	131	1		The Other Side	Word-Curb 886274
				DA BRAT	
8/2/03	17	6		Limelite, Luv & Niteclubz	So So Def 51586
				DANDY WARHOLS, The	
9/6/03	118	2		Welcome To The Monkey House	Capitol 84368
				DASHBOARD CONFESSIONAL	
1/4/03	111	6		MTV Unplugged V 2.0	[L] Vagrant 0378
8/30/03	2¹	22	●	A Mark • A Mission • A Brand • A Scar	Vagrant 0385
				DAVIS, Sammy Jr. — see SINATRA, Frank	
				DAY, Howie ★	
				Born in Bangor, Maine. Adult Alternative singer/songwriter.	
5/17/03	135	1		The Madrigals	[M] Epic 89083
10/25/03	46	4		Stop All The World Now	Epic 86807
				DEAD PREZ	
11/8/03	144	1		Turn Off The Radio The Mixtape Vol. 2: Get Free Or Die Tryin'	Boss Up 9228
				DEATH CAB FOR CUTIE ★	
				Pop-rock group from Bellingham, Washington: Benjamin Gibbard (vocals, guitar), Chris Walla (keyboards), Nick Harmer (bass) and Jason McGerr (drums). Gibbard is also one-half of The Postal Service.	
10/25/03	97	2		Transatlanticism	Barsuk 32
				DEFAULT	
12/13/03	105	3		Elocation	TVT 6000
				DEFTONES	
6/7/03	2¹	13	●	Deftones	Maverick 48350
				DEGRAW, Gavin ★	
				Born in 1977 in Buffalo, New York. Adult Alternative singer/songwriter.	
8/9/03+	103	9		Chariot	J Records 20058
				DeVITO, Louie	
5/3/03	174	3		Dance Divas	Dee Vee 0005
7/5/03	132	5		Louie DeVito's Dance Factory Level 2	Dee Vee 0006
9/13/03	93	4		Ultra.Dance 04	Ultra 1175 [2]
				DF DUB ★	
				Born William Green in Detroit, Michigan. White rapper. Worked as DJ "Billy The Kid" on WILD-FM in Dallas, Texas.	
4/5/03	144	1		Country Girl	3Sixty 89089
				D4, The ★	
				Punk-rock group from Auckland, New Zealand: Jimmy Christmas (vocals, guitar), Dion (vocals, guitar), Vaughan (bass) and Beaver (drums).	
4/12/03	164	1		6twenty	Flying Nun 162388
				DIAMOND, Neil	
10/18/03	137	2		Stages: Performances 1970-2002	[L] Columbia 90540 [5]

DEBUT DATE	PEAK POS	WKS CHR	G L D	ARTIST Title	Label & Number
				DIDO	
10/18/03	4	25↑	▲	Life For Rent	Arista 50137
				DIFRANCO, Ani	
3/29/03	30	7		Evolve	Righteous Babe 030
				DIMMU BORGIR ★	
				Death-metal group from Norway: Shagrath (vocals), Galder (guitar), Silenoz (guitar), Mustis (keyboards), Vortex (bass) and Barker (drums).	
9/27/03	170	1		Death Cult Armageddon	Nuclear Blast 1047
				DION, Celine	
4/12/03	2[1]	32	▲2	One Heart	Epic 87185
				DIPLOMATS, The ★	
				Hip-hop group from Harlem, New York: Cam'ron Giles, Jimmy Jones, Ezekiel "Freaky Zeeky" Jiles and LeRon "Juelz Santana" James.	
4/12/03	8	18	●	Diplomatic Immunity	Roc-A-Fella 063211 [2]
				DIRTY	
3/15/03	63	4		Keep It Pimp & Gangsta	Universal 018415
10/25/03	160	1		Love Us Or Hate Us	Nfinity 42030
				DISTILLERS, The ★	
				Punk-rock group from Australia: Brody Dalle (vocals, guitar), Tony Bradley (vocals, guitar), Ryan Sinn (bass) and Andy Granelli (drums).	
11/1/03	97	1		Coral Fang	Hellcat 48586
				DIXIE CHICKS	
12/6/03	27	18↑	●	Top Of The World Tour Live [L]	Monument 90794 [2]
				DJ ENVY ★	
				Born in Queens, New York. Male DJ/remixer. One of the leading "mixtape" producers.	
3/1/03	57	4		The Desert Storm Mixtape: Blok Party Vol. 1	Desert Storm 86737
				DJ KAYSLAY ★	
				Born Keith Grayson in Harlem, New York. Male DJ/rapper.	
6/7/03	22	8		The Streetsweeper Vol. 1	Columbia 87048
				DMX	
10/4/03	❶[1]	24	▲	Grand Champ	Ruff Ryders 063369
				DOBSON, Fefe ★	
				Born in Toronto, Ontario, Canada. Black female rock singer/songwriter.	
12/27/03+	67	15↑		Fefe Dobson	Island 001244
				D.O.C., The	
3/15/03	184	1		Deuce	Silverback 2113
				DO OR DIE	
9/6/03+	115	3		Pimpin' Ain't Dead	J Prince 42029
				DOORS, The	
8/30/03	63	4		Legacy: The Absolute Best [G]	Elektra 73889 [2]
				DOWNING, Will	
11/1/03	92	6		Emotions	GRP 000529
				DREAM THEATER	
11/29/03	53	2		Train Of Thought	Elektra 62891
				DROPKICK MURPHYS	
6/28/03	83	6		Blackout	Hellcat 80446
				DUFF, Hilary	
9/13/03	❶[1]	30↑	▲3	Metamorphosis	Buena Vista 861006
				DWELE ★	
				Born Andwele Gardner in Detroit, Michigan. Male R&B singer/songwriter/producer.	
6/7/03	108	11		Subject	Virgin 80919
				EAGLES	
11/8/03	3	22↑	▲2	The Very Best Of [G]	Warner 73971 [2]
				EARLY NOVEMBER, The ★	
				Punk-rock group from Hammonton, New Jersey: Arthur "Ace" Enders (vocals, guitar), Joseph Marro (guitar), Sergio Anello (bass) and Jeff Kummer (drums).	
10/25/03	107	1		The Room's Too Cold	Drive-Thru 001480
				EARTH, WIND & FIRE	
6/7/03	89	4		The Promise	Kalimba 973002
10/11/03	22[C]	4		Greatest Hits [G]	Legacy 65779
				EDER, Linda	
3/8/03	115	4		Broadway My Way	Atlantic 83580

DEBUT DATE	PEAK POS	WKS CHR	G L D	ARTIST Title	Label & Number
				EELS	
6/21/03	145	1		Shootenanny!	DreamWorks 000039
				E-40	
9/27/03	16	5		Breakin News	Sick Wid' It 41857
				ELEPHANT MAN ★	
				Born O'Neil Bryant in Kingston, Jamaica. Dancehall reggae singer.	
12/20/03	74	2		Good 2 Go	VP 83681
				ELLIOTT, Missy	
12/13/03	13	17↑	▲	This Is Not A Test!	Gold Mind 62905
				ENIGMA	
10/18/03	94	5		Voyageur	Virgin 90447
				ERASURE	
2/15/03	138	1		Other People's Songs	Mute 9198
				ESTEFAN, Gloria	
10/11/03	39	5		Unwrapped	Epic 86790
				EVANESCENCE ★	
				Rock group from Little Rock, Arkansas: Amy Lee (vocals), Ben Moody (guitar), Josh LeCompt (bass) and Rocky Gray (drums). Won the 2003 Best New Artist Grammy Award.	
3/22/03	3	55↑	▲⁴	Fallen	Wind-Up 13063
				EVANS, Sara	
9/6/03	20	8		Restless	RCA 67074
				EVERCLEAR	
3/29/03	33	4		Slow Motion Daydream	Capitol 38270
				EVE 6	
8/9/03	27	9		It's All In Your Head	RCA 52346
				EXIES, The ★	
				Rock group from Los Angeles, California: Scott Stevens (vocals, guitar), David Walsh (guitar), Freddy Herrera (bass) and Dennis Wolfe (drums).	
1/25/03	115	4		Inertia	Melisma 13309
				FABOLOUS	
3/22/03	3	35	▲	Street Dreams	Desert Storm 62791
11/22/03	28	3		More Street Dreams Pt. 2: The Mixtape	Desert Storm 62924
				FELICIANO, José	
5/24/03	173	1		Señor Bolero 2 [F]	Universal Latino 000083
				FERNÁNDEZ, Alejandro	
11/8/03	196	1		En Vivo: Juntos Por Ultima Vez [F-L]	Sony Discos 91088 [2]
				VICENTE Y ALEJANDRO FERNANDEZ	
				FFH	
5/3/03	89	5		Ready To Fly	Essential 10705
				50 CENT ★	
				Born Curtis Jackson on 7/6/76 in Jamaica, Queens, New York. Male rapper/songwriter.	
1/11/03	28	10		Guess Who's Back?	Full Clip 2003
2/22/03	❶⁶	59↑	▲⁶	Get Rich Or Die Tryin'	Shady 493544
5/3/03	2¹	17		The New Breed	Shady 000108
				54TH PLATOON ★	
				Male rap group from New Orleans, Louisiana: Jackie "Big Nut" Washington, Jochan "JS" Scott, Thomas "Nu Black" Valentine and Tevin "TL" Lashley.	
5/24/03	128	2		All Or N.O.thin	Fubu 9001
				FINGER ELEVEN ★	
				Rock group from Toronto, Ontario, Canada: brothers Scott (vocals) and Sean (bass) Anderson, Rick Jackett and James Black (guitars) and Rob Gommerman (drums).	
7/5/03+	114↑	10↑		Finger Eleven	Wind-Up 13058
				FIRE THEFT, The ★	
				Rock trio from Seattle, Washington: Jeremy Enigk (vocals, guitar), Nate Mendel (bass) and William Goldsmith (drums). Mendel and Goldsmith were members of Foo Fighters; Goldsmith was also with Sunny Day Real Estate.	
10/11/03	198	1		The Fire Theft	Rykodisc 10642
				FLAMING LIPS, The	
5/10/03	93	2		Fight Test [M]	Warner 48433
				FLECK, Bela, & The Flecktones	
8/30/03	196	1		Little Worlds	Columbia 86353 [3]

POP ALBUMS

DEBUT DATE	PEAK POS	WKS CHR	G L D	ARTIST / Title	Label & Number
				FLEETWOOD MAC	
5/3/03	3	23	●	Say You Will	Reprise 48394
				FLOETRY	
12/6/03	74	3		Floacism "Live" .... [L]	DreamWorks 001438
				FONSI, Luis	
11/15/03	138	1		Abrazar La Vida .... [F]	Universal Latino 001403
				title is Spanish for "Embrace The Life"	
				FOUNTAINS OF WAYNE ★	
				Pop-rock group from New York: Chris Collingwood (vocals, guitar), Jody Porter (guitar), Adam Schlesinger (bass) and Brian Young (drums).	
6/28/03	115	28		Welcome Interstate Managers	S-Curve 90875
				FOXWORTHY, Jeff	
9/20/03	76	5		The Best Of Jeff Foxworthy: Double Wide, Single Minded .... [C-K]	Warner 73903
				FRANKIE J ★	
				Born Francis Jay Bautista in Tijuana, Mexico; raised in San Diego, California. Latino singer/songwriter/producer.	
6/14/03	53	15		What's A Man To Do?	Columbia 90073
				FRANKLIN, Aretha	
10/4/03	33	11		So Damn Happy	Arista 50174
				FRAYSER BOY ★	
				Born Frayser Coleman in Memphis, Tennessee. Male rapper.	
9/13/03	178	1		Gone On That Bay	Hypnotize Minds 3606
				FREEWAY ★	
				Born Leslie Pridgen in Philadelphia, Pennsylvania. Male rapper.	
3/15/03	5	14		Philadelphia Freeway	Roc-A-Fella 586920
				FROM AUTUMN TO ASHES ★	
				Rock group from Long Island, New York: Benjamin Perri (vocals), Scott Gross (guitar), Brian Deneeve (guitar), Mike Pilato (bass) and Francis Mark (drums).	
9/27/03	73	2		The Fiction We Live	Vagrant 386
				FUEL	
10/11/03	15	14		Natural Selection	Epic 86392
				FURTADO, Nelly	
12/13/03	38	11	●	Folklore	DreamWorks 001007
				FURTHER SEEMS FOREVER ★	
				Rock group from Pompano Beach, Florida: Jason Gleason (vocals), Josh Colbert (guitar), Derick Cordoba (guitar), Chad Neptune (bass) and Steve Kleisath (drums).	
3/1/03	133	2		How To Start A Fire	Tooth & Nail 39418
				GABRIEL, Peter	
11/22/03	100	3		Hit .... [G]	Real World 001486 [2]
				GAHAN, Dave ★	
				Born on 5/9/62 in Epping, Essex, England. Lead singer of Depeche Mode.	
6/21/03	127	1		Paper Monsters	Mute 48471
				GAITHER, Bill & Gloria, & Their Homecoming Friends	
2/15/03	55	5		Heaven .... [L]	Spring House 42415
2/15/03	64	2		Going Home .... [L]	Spring House 42416
10/4/03	99	1		Red Rocks Homecoming .... [L]	Spring House 42418
10/4/03	121	1		Rocky Mountain Homecoming .... [L]	Spring House 42417
				GAITHER VOCAL BAND, The	
10/18/03	174	1		a cappella	Spring House 42516
				GANG STARR	
7/12/03	18	8		The Ownerz	Virgin 80247
				GILL, Vince	
3/1/03	14	9		Next Big Thing	MCA Nashville 170286
				GILMAN, Billy	
5/3/03	109	2		Music Through Heartsongs: Songs Based On The Poems Of Mattie J.T. Stepanek	Epic 86954
				GINUWINE	
4/26/03	6	27	●	The Senior	Epic 86960
				GODSMACK	
4/26/03	❶[1]	49↑	▲	Faceless	Republic 067854
				GOV'T MULE	
10/25/03	153	1		The Deepest End: Live In Concert .... [L]	ATO 21517 [2]

194

DEBUT DATE	PEAK POS	WKS CHR	G L D	ARTIST Title	Label & Number
				GRANDADDY ★	
				Rock group from Modesto, California: Jason Lytle (vocals), Jim Fairchild (guitar), Tim Dryden (keyboards), Kevin Garcia (bass) and Aaron Burtch (drums).	
6/28/03	84	3		Sumday	V2 27155
				GRANT, Amy	
9/6/03	23	6		Simple Things	A&M 000612
12/20/03	166	1		20th Century Masters: The Best Of Amy Grant -	
				The Christmas Collection .... [X]	A&M 000695
				GRATEFUL DEAD	
10/4/03	69	4		The Very Best Of Grateful Dead................................... [G]	Warner 73899
				GRAY, Macy	
8/2/03	44	6		The Trouble With Being Myself...................................	Epic 86535
				GREEN, Al	
2/15/03	91	3		The Love Song Collection .... [K]	Right Stuff 80327
12/6/03	53	12		I Can't Stop	Blue Note 93556
				GREEN, Pat	
8/2/03	10	24	●	Wave On Wave	Republic 000562
				GRIFFITH, Andy	
12/20/03	141	1		The Christmas Guest: Stories And Songs Of	
				Christmas .... [X]	Sparrow 51815
				GROBAN, Josh	
11/29/03+	❶¹	19↑	▲³	Closer	143 Records 48450
				GRUPO MONTEZ DE DURANGO ★	
				Latin group from Mexico: José Terrazas, his son José Terrazas Jr., Daniel Avila, Francisco López, Armando Ramirez, Alfredo Corral and Ismael Miljarez.	
10/18/03	88	6		De Durango A Chicago.. [F]	Disa 724088
				GUARINI, Justin ★	
				Born on 10/28/78 in Columbus, Georgia. Finalist on the second season of TV's *American Idol* talent series.	
6/28/03	20	5		Justin Guarini	RCA 68188
				GUIDED BY VOICES	
9/6/03	193	1		Earthquake Glue	Matador 574
				GUINEY, Bob ★	
				Born in 1971 in Riverview, Michigan. Star of the first season of the TV reality series *The Bachelor*.	
12/13/03	114	1		3 Sides	Wind-Up 13090
				G-UNIT ★	
				Male rap trio from Jamaica, Queens, New York: Curtis "50 Cent" Jackson, Christopher Lloyd "Banks" and David "Young Black" Brown.	
11/29/03	2¹	19↑	▲²	Beg For Mercy	G-Unit 001593
				GUSTER	
7/12/03	35	12		Keep It Together..	Palm 48306
				GUY, Buddy	
6/21/03	188	1		Blues Singer	Silvertone 41843
				HAGAR, Sammy	
6/7/03	152	1		Sammy And The Wabo's Live: Hallelujah.................... [L]	Sanctuary 84608
				HALL, Daryl, & John Oates	
3/1/03	77	7		Do It For Love..	U-Watch 80100
				HAMILTON, Anthony ★	
				Born in Charlotte, North Carolina. R&B singer/songwriter.	
10/11/03	33	25↑		Comin' Where I Come From	So So Def 52107
				HANSON, Jennifer ★	
				Born in Whittier, California; raised in La Habra, California. Country singer/songwriter.	
3/8/03	125	2		Jennifer Hanson	Capitol 35247
				HARGROVE, Roy ★	
				Born on 10/16/69 in Waco, Texas. Trumpet player.	
6/7/03	185	1		Hard Groove .... [I]	Verve 065192
				ROY HARGROVE PRESENTS THE RH FACTOR	
				HARPER, Ben	
3/29/03	19	23		Diamonds On The Inside..	Virgin 80640
				HARRIS, Emmylou	
10/11/03	58	7		Stumble Into Grace...	Nonesuch 79805
				HATEBREED	
11/15/03	30	3		The Rise Of Brutality	No Name 001442

DEBUT DATE	PEAK POS	WKS CHR	G L D	ARTIST Title	Label & Number
				(HED)PLANET EARTH	
4/5/03	33	6		Blackout..	Volcano 41817
				HENDRIX, Jimi	
10/4/03	191	1		Live At Berkeley .... [L]	Ex. Hendrix 001102
				THE JIMI HENDRIX EXPERIENCE	
				recorded on 5/3/70 at the Berkeley Communtity Theatre	
				HIATT, John	
5/24/03	73	4		Beneath This Gruff Exterior	New West 6045
				JOHN HIATT & THE GONERS	
				HIEROGLYPHICS ★	
				Rap group from Oakland, California: A Plus, Tajai, Del, Pep Love, Jay Biz, Opio, Phesto, Casual, Domino and Toure.	
10/25/03	155	1		Full Circle..	Hiero Imperium 230109
				HITMAN SAMMY SAM ★	
				Born Sammy King in Atlanta, Georgia. Male rapper.	
5/17/03	116	4		The Step Daddy	ColliPark 000380
				HOLLISTER, Dave	
11/29/03	42	2		Real Talk	DreamWorks 450500
				HOOBASTANK	
12/27/03+	25↑	15↑		The Reason	Island 001488
				HOOTIE & THE BLOWFISH	
3/22/03	46	6		Hootie & The Blowfish	Atlantic 83564
				HOT BOY$	
4/12/03	14	6		Let 'Em Burn..	Cash Money 860966
				HOT HOT HEAT ★	
				Rock group from Victoria, British Columbia, Canada: Steve Bays (vocals, keyboards), Dante DeCaro (guitar), Dustin Hawthorne (bass) and Paul Hawley (drums).	
7/26/03	146	9		Make Up The Breakdown	Sub Pop 70599
				HOUSTON, Marques ★	
				Born on 8/4/81 in Los Angeles, California. R&B singer. Member of Immature.	
11/8/03	18	9		MH	T.U.G. 62935
				HOUSTON, Whitney	
12/6/03	49	6		One Wish: The Holiday Album .... [X]	Arista 50996
				IGLESIAS, Enrique	
12/13/03	31	10		Seven	Interscope 001711
				ILL NIÑO ★	
				Rock group from New Jersey: Cristian Machado (vocals), Arhue Luster (guitar), Jardel Paisante (guitar), Danny Couto (percussion), Lazaro Pina (bass) and Dave Chavarri (drums).	
10/18/03	37	3		Confession	Roadrunner 618391
				INSPECTAH DECK	
6/28/03	137	1		The Movement...	Koch 8660
				INTOCABLE	
3/1/03	60	5		La Historia .... [F-G]	EMI Latin 80819 [2]
3/1/03	161	9		La Historia .... [F-G]	EMI Latin 80818
9/6/03	95	4		Nuestro Destino Estaba Escrito .... [F]	EMI Latin 90524
				title is Spanish for "Our Destiny Was Written"	
				IRISH TENORS, The	
12/27/03	112	1		We Three Kings .... [X]	Razor & Tie 82897
				IRON MAIDEN	
9/27/03	18	4		Dance Of Death	Columbia 89061
				ISLEY BROTHERS, The	
5/24/03	❶[1]	23	●	Body Kiss	DreamWorks 450409
11/29/03	73	2		Here I Am: Isley Meets Bacharach	DreamWorks 001005
				RONALD ISLEY / BURT BACHARACH	
				JACKSON, Alan	
8/30/03	❶[1]	32↑	▲[3]	Greatest Hits Volume II and Some Other Stuff [G]	Arista Nashville 53097 [2]
				JACKSON, Michael	
12/6/03	13	18↑	●	Number Ones.. [G]	Epic 88998
				JAGGED EDGE	
11/1/03	3	23↑	●	Hard	Columbia 87017

DEBUT DATE	PEAK POS	WKS CHR	G L D	ARTIST / Title	Label & Number
				JAKES, T.D.	
4/12/03	63	4		A Wing And A Prayer	Dexterity Sounds 20378
				BISHOP T.D. JAKES And The POTTER'S HOUSE MASS CHOIR	
				JAMES, Etta	
5/24/03	195	1		Let's Roll	Private Music 11646
				JANE'S ADDICTION	
8/9/03	4	10	●	Strays	Capitol 90186
				JARS OF CLAY	
2/22/03	64	9		Furthermore: From The Studio, From The Stage .... [L]	Essential 10689 [2]
11/22/03	103	5		Who We Are Instead	Essential 10709
				JA RULE	
11/22/03	6	10		Blood In My Eye	Murder Inc. 001577
				JAVIER ★	
				Born Javier Colon in 1978 in Hartford, Connecticut. R&B singer/songwriter/guitarist.	
8/23/03	91	5		Javier	Capitol 39843
				JAYHAWKS, The	
4/26/03	51	6		Rainy Day Music	American 000076
				JAY-Z	
4/26/03	17	13		Blueprint 2.1	Roc-A-Fella 000297
11/29/03	❶²	19↑	▲²	The Black Album	Roc-A-Fella 001528
				JEAN, Wyclef	
11/22/03	22	5		The Preacher's Son	Yclef 55425
				JET ★	
				Rock group from Melbourne, Australia: brothers Nick (guitar) and Chris (drums) Cester, Cameron Muncey (vocals, guitar) and Mark Wilson (bass).	
10/25/03+	36↑	24↑	●	Get Born	Elektra 62892
				JETHRO TULL	
11/15/03	35ˣ	1		The Jethro Tull Christmas Album .... [X]	Fuel 2000 061340
				JEWEL	
6/21/03	2¹	21	●	0304	Atlantic 83638
				JEWELL, Buddy ★	
				Born on 4/2/61 in Lepanto, Arkansas. Country singer/songwriter. Winner on the first season of TV's *Nashville Star* talent show in 2003.	
7/19/03	13	18↑	●	Buddy Jewell	Columbia 90131
				JOHNSON, Jack	
5/24/03	3	41↑	●	On And On	Moonshine Con. 075012
				JONES, George	
4/19/03	131	7		The Gospel Collection: George Jones Sings The Greatest Stories Ever Told	Bandit 67063 [2]
				JONES, Norah — see MALICK, Peter	
				JONES, Rickie Lee	
10/25/03	189	1		The Evening Of My Best Day	V2 27171
				JONES, Tom	
11/1/03	127	10		Reloaded: Greatest Hits .... [G]	Decca 001421
				JS ★	
				R&B vocal duo from Los Angeles, California: sisters Kim and Kandy Johnson. JS: Johnson Sisters.	
8/16/03	33	9		Ice Cream	DreamWorks 450332
				JUDD, Cledus T.	
5/17/03	130	1		A Six Pack Of Judd .... [M-N]	Monument 89223
				JULIANA THEORY, The ★	
				Rock group from Greensburg, Pennsylvania: Brett Detar (vocals), Josh Fiedler (guitar), Josh Kosker (guitar), Chad Alan (bass) and Neil Hebrank (drums).	
2/22/03	71	5		Love	Epic 86163
				JUMP5	
10/25/03	150	3		Accelerate	Sparrow 83553
				JUNIOR SENIOR ★	
				White trip-hop duo from Jutland, Denmark: Jesper "Junior" Mortensen and Jeppe "Senior" Laursen.	
8/23/03	94	4		D-D-Don't Don't Stop The Beat	Crunchy Frog 83663
				KEEN, Robert Earl	
10/25/03	172	1		Farm Fresh Onions	Audium 8191

DEBUT DATE	PEAK POS	WKS CHR	G L D	ARTIST / Title	Label & Number
				KEITH, Toby	
5/3/03	45	9		The Best Of Toby Keith: 20th Century Masters	
				The Millennium Collection .... [G]	Mercury 170351
11/15/03	40ˣ	2		Christmas To Christmas .... [X]	Mercury 527909
11/22/03	❶¹	20↑	▲³	Shock'n Y'all	DreamWorks 450435
				KELIS	
12/27/03	27	15↑	●	Tasty	Star Trak 52132
				KELLEY, Josh ★	
				Born in Augusta, Georgia. Pop singer/songwriter/guitarist.	
8/2/03	159	11		For The Ride Home	Hollywood 162377
				KELLY, R.	
3/8/03	❶¹	57↑	▲²	Chocolate Factory	Jive 41849
10/11/03	4	26↑	▲	The R. In R&B Collection Volume One [G]	Jive 55214
11/8/03	135	2	●	The R. In R&B: The Video Collection .... [G]	Jive 53709
				KEM ★	
				Born Kem Owens in Nashville, Tennessee; later based in Detroit, Michigan. Male R&B singer/songwriter.	
3/15/03	90	46↑		Kemistry	Motown 067516
				KENNY G	
6/28/03	42	10		Ultimate Kenny G .... [G-I]	Arista 50997
				KEYS, Alicia	
12/20/03	❶²	16↑	▲²	The Diary Of Alicia Keys	J Records 55712
				KID ROCK	
11/29/03	8	19↑	▲	Kid Rock	Top Dog 83685
				KIDZ BOP KIDS	
3/22/03	17	25	●	Kidz Bop 3	Razor & Tie 89060
8/30/03	14	27	●	Kidz Bop 4	Razor & Tie 89074
				KILLER MIKE ★	
				Born Michael Render in Atlanta, Georgia. Male rapper. Discovered by OutKast.	
3/29/03	10	10		Monster	Aquemini 86862
				KINDRED THE FAMILY SOUL ★	
				Husband-and-wife R&B vocal duo from Philadelphia, Pennsylvania: Fatin Dantzler and Aja Graydon.	
4/12/03	159	2		Surrender To Love	Hidden Beach 86491
				KING, B.B.	
6/28/03	165	2		Reflections	MCA 000532
				KING CRIMSON	
3/22/03	150	1		The Power To Believe	Sanctuary 84585
				KINGS OF LEON ★	
				Rock group from Nashville, Tennessee: brothers Caleb Followill (vocals, guitar), Jared Followill (bass) and Nathan Followill (drums), with their cousin Matthew Followill (guitar).	
9/6/03	113	5		Youth & Young Manhood	RCA 52394
				KISS	
8/9/03	18	4		Symphony: Alive IV .... [L]	Kiss 84624 [2]
				recorded on 2/28/03 with the Melbourne Symphony Orchestra	
8/23/03	132	1		The Best Of Kiss: 20th Century Masters - The	
				Millennium Collection .... [G]	Mercury 000827
				KORN	
12/6/03	9	18↑	▲	Take A Look In The Mirror	Immortal 90335
				KOZ, Dave	
10/25/03	129	3		Saxophonic .... [I]	Capitol 34226
				KREVIAZUK, Chantal ★	
				Born on 5/18/73 in Winnipeg, Manitoba, Canada. Female Adult Alternative singer/pianist.	
5/10/03	119	2		What If It All Means Something	Columbia 86482
				KRS-ONE	
7/12/03	186	1		Kristyles	Koch 8342
				KUMBIA KINGS	
3/15/03	86	9		4 .... [F]	EMI Latin 40514
				A.B. Qunitanilla III Presents KUMBIA KINGS	
11/8/03	109	6		La Historia .... [F-G]	EMI Latin 93488
				A.B. QUINTANILLA III & KUMBIA KINGS	
				LACHEY, Nick ★	
				Born on 11/9/73 in Harlan, Kentucky. White male singer. Member of 98°. Married Jessica Simpson on 10/26/2002 (they appeared as themselves in the 2003 MTV reality series *Newlyweds*).	
11/29/03	51	2		SoulO	Universal 000190

DEBUT DATE	PEAK POS	WKS CHR	G L D	ARTIST / Title	Label & Number
				LAGWAGON ★	
				Punk-rock group from Goleta, California: Joey Cape (vocals), Chris Flippin (guitar), Chris Rest (guitar), Jesse Buglione (bass) and Dave Raun (drums).	
4/26/03	172	1		Blaze	Fat Wreck Chords 642
				LANG, Jonny	
11/1/03	17	17		Long Time Coming	A&M 001145
				LANOIS, Daniel	
5/10/03	143	2		Shine	Anti 86661
				LATTIMORE, Kenny	
3/1/03	31	15		Things That Lovers Do	Arista 14751
				KENNY LATTIMORE & CHANTÉ MOORE	
				LAUPER, Cyndi	
12/6/03	38	14		At Last	Daylight 90760
				LeDOUX, Chris	
8/9/03	162	1		Horsepower	Capitol 81580
				LED ZEPPELIN	
6/14/03	❶¹	16	▲	How The West Was Won [K-L]	Atlantic 83587 [3]
				LEE, Murphy ★	
				Born Tohri Harper in St. Louis, Missouri. Male rapper. Member of St. Lunatics.	
10/11/03	8	26↑	●	Murphy's Law	Fo' Reel 001132
				LENNOX, Annie	
6/28/03	4	20	●	Bare	J Records 52350
				LES NUBIANS	
4/12/03	79	11		One Step Forward	Omtown 82569
				LESS THAN JAKE	
6/7/03	45	12		Anthem	Sire 48459
				LEVERT, Gerald	
11/15/03	6	12		Stroke Of Genius	Elektra 62903
				LIL BOW WOW	
9/6/03	3	25	●	Unleashed	Columbia 87103
				BOW WOW	
				LIL' FLIP	
4/19/03	167	2		Lil' Flip And Sucka Free Present 7-1-3 And The Undaground Legend: Remixed	Sucka Free 89228 [2]
				LIL JON & THE EAST SIDE BOYZ	
11/22/03	197	1		Certified Crunk	Ichiban 01037
12/13/03	37	17↑		Part II	BME 2378
				LIL' KIM	
3/22/03	5	29	▲	La Bella Mafia	Queen Bee 83572
				LILLIX ★	
				Female rock group from Cranbrook, British Columbia, Canada: sisters Tasha-Ray Ervin (vocals, guitar) and Lacey-Lee Ervin (keyboards), with Louise Burns (bass) and Kim Urhahn (drums).	
6/14/03	188	2		Falling Uphill	Maverick 48323
				LIL' MO	
5/17/03	17	10		Meet The Girl Next Door	Elektra 62835
				LIL' ROMEO	
1/4/03	33	11		Game Time	New No Limit 060055
				LIL WYTE ★	
				Born in Memphis, Tennessee. White male rapper.	
3/22/03	197	1		Doubt Me Now	Hypnotize Minds 3604
				LIL' ZANE	
9/6/03	191	1		The Big Zane Theory	Priority 50191
				ZANE	
				LIMP BIZKIT	
10/11/03	3	26↑	●	Results May Vary	Flip 001235
				LINE, Lorie ★	
				Born in Reno, Nevada. New Age/light classical pianist.	
1/18/03	18ˣ	1		Sharing The Season: Volume Four [X-I]	Time Line 21
				LORIE LINE & Her Pop Chamber Orchestra	
				LINES, Aaron ★	
				Born in 1978 in Fort McMurray, Alberta, Canada. Country singer/songwriter/guitarist.	
1/25/03	68	6		Living Out Loud	RCA 67057

DEBUT DATE	PEAK POS	WKS CHR	G L D	ARTIST Title	Label & Number
				LINKIN PARK	
4/12/03	❶²	52↑	▲⁴	Meteora	Warner 48186
12/6/03	23	18↑	●	Live In Texas .... [L]	Warner 48563
				LIVE	
6/7/03	28	19		Birds Of Pray	Radioactive 000374
				LONESTAR	
6/21/03	7	38	▲	From There To Here: Greatest Hits [G]	BNA 67076
				LOON ★	
				Born Chauncey Hawkins in Harlem, New York. Male rapper.	
11/8/03	6	6		Loon	Bad Boy 000892
				LOPEZ, Jennifer	
12/6/03	69	5		The Reel Me .... [K]	Epic 90767
				LOS BUKIS ★	
				Latin group from Mexico: Marco Antonio Solis, Joel Solis, Roberto Guadarrama, Pepe Guadarrama, Eusebio Cortez, El Chivo and Pedro Sanchez.	
1/25/03	169	4		30 Inolvidables .... [F]	Fonovisa 350691
4/19/03	127	7		20 Inolvidables .... [F]	Fonovisa 350832
				LOS BUKIS/LOS TEMERARIOS	
8/23/03	121	6		25 Joyas Musicales .... [F]	Fonovisa 350895
				LOS TEMERARIOS	
4/19/03	127	7		20 Inolvidables .... [F]	Fonovisa 350832
				LOS BUKIS/LOS TEMERARIOS	
12/13/03	179	2		Tributo Al Amor .... [F]	Fonovisa 351005
				LOS TIGRES DEL NORTE	
7/19/03	67	8		Herencia Musical: 20 Corridos Inolvidables .... [F]	Fonovisa 350871
				LOVELESS, Patty	
10/4/03	77	3		On Your Way Home	Epic 86620
				LOVETT, Lyle	
3/15/03	106	4		Smile: Songs From The Movies	Curb 113184
10/18/03	63	7		My Baby Don't Tolerate	Curb 001162
				LSG	
8/16/03	6	8		LSG2	Elektra 62851
				LUDACRIS	
10/25/03	❶¹	24↑	▲	Chicken*N*Beer	Disturb. Tha P. 000930
				LUMIDEE ★	
				Born Lumidee Cedeno in Harlem, New York (Puerto Rican parents). Female singer/rapper/songwriter.	
7/12/03	22	11		Almost Famous	Straight Face 000681
				LYNNE, Shelby	
10/4/03	160	1		Identity Crisis	Capitol 90508
				LYNYRD SKYNYRD	
6/7/03	30	11		Vicious Cycle	Sanctuary 84607
8/30/03	16	15	●	Thyrty - The 30th Anniversary Collection .... [G]	UTV 000284 [2]
				MA, Yo-Yo	
8/16/03	58	14		Obrigado Brazil .... [I]	Sony Classical 89935
				MACK 10	
8/9/03	105	1		Ghetto, Gutter & Gangsta	Hoo-Bangin' 970028
				MADONNA	
5/10/03	❶¹	14	▲	American Life	Maverick 48439
12/13/03	115	1		Remixed & Revisited .... [K]	Maverick 48624
				MAGIC	
4/5/03	147	2		White Eyes	New No Limit 860993
				MALICK, Peter ★	
				Born in Boston, Massachusetts. Blues guitarist.	
7/26/03	54	11		New York City	Koch 8678
				THE PETER MALICK GROUP Featuring Norah Jones	
				MALKMUS, Stephen	
4/5/03	97	2		Pig Lib	Matador 0572
				STEPHEN MALKMUS & THE JICKS	
				MANÁ	
12/6/03	181	1		Eclipse .... [F]	Warner Latina 61046

DEBUT DATE	PEAK POS	WKS CHR	G L D	ARTIST Title	Label & Number
				MANNHEIM STEAMROLLER	
2/8/03	41	6		Romantic Melodies .... [I]	American Gram. 214
6/7/03	78	8		American Spirit	American Gram. 1776
				MANNHEIM STEAMROLLER/C.W McCALL	
10/18/03	53	5		Halloween .... [I-N]	American Gram. 1031
				MANSON, Marilyn	
5/31/03	❶[1]	16		The Golden Age Of Grotesque	Nothing 000370
				MARLEY, Ziggy	
5/3/03	138	8		Dragonfly	Tuff Gong 11636
				MAROON5 ★	
				Alternative pop-rock group from Los Angeles, California: Adam Levine (vocals, guitar), James Valentine (guitar), Jesse Carmichael (keyboards), Mickey Madden (bass) and Ryan Dusick (drums).	
5/31/03+	7	45↑	▲	Songs About Jane	Octone 50001
				MARS VOLTA, The ★	
				Rock group from El Paso, Texas: Cedric Bixler (vocals), Omar Rodriguez (guitar), Jeremy Ward (keyboards) Jon Theodore (bass) and Ikey Owens (drums). Bixler and Rodriguez were members of At The Drive-In. Ward died of a drug overdose on 5/25/2003 (age 27).	
7/12/03	39	11		De-Loused In The Comatorium........................	Strummer 000593
				MARTIN, Dean — see SINATRA, Frank	
				MARTIN, Ricky	
6/7/03	12	9		Almas Del Silencio........................ [F]	Sony Discos 70439
				title is Spanish for "Souls Of Silence"	
				MASSIVE ATTACK	
3/1/03	69	7		100th Window........................	Virgin 81239
				MATCHBOX TWENTY	
11/29/03	43	2		EP .... [L-M]	Melisma 83701
				MATTHEWS, Dave, Band	
10/11/03	2[1]	22	▲	Some Devil	RCA 55167
				DAVE MATTHEWS	
12/6/03	14	13	▲	The Central Park Concert........................ [L]	Bama Rags 57501 [3]
				MAYER, John	
3/1/03	17	31	▲	Any Given Thursday .... [L]	Aware 87199 [2]
9/27/03	❶[1]	28↑	▲	Heavier Things	Aware 86185
				McBRIDE, Martina	
10/18/03	7	25↑	▲	Martina	RCA 54207
				McCALL, C.W. — see MANNHEIM STEAMROLLER	
				McCLURKIN, Donnie	
3/22/03	31	16		Donnie McClurkin...Again	Verity 43199
				McCOMAS, Brian ★	
				Born on 5/23/72 in Bethesda, Maryland; raised in Harrison, Arkansas. Country singer/songwriter.	
8/9/03	149	1		Brian McComas........................	Lyric Street 165025
				McDONALD, Michael	
7/12/03+	14	35↑	▲	Motown	Motown 000651
				McENTIRE, Reba	
12/6/03	25	12	●	Room To Breathe........................	MCA Nashville 000451
				REBA	
				McKNIGHT, Brian	
4/12/03	7	15	●	U Turn	Motown 067315
				McLACHLAN, Sarah	
11/22/03	2[1]	20↑	▲[2]	Afterglow	Arista 50150
				MEAT LOAF	
10/11/03	85	4		Couldn't Have Said It Better........................	Sanctuary 84653
				ME FIRST AND THE GIMME GIMMES ★	
				Punk-rock group from San Francisco, California: Spike (vocals), Jake Jackson (guitar), Joey Cape (guitar), Fat Mike (bass) and Dave (drums).	
7/19/03	131	2		Take A Break	Fat Wreck Chords 650
				MELLENCAMP, John	
6/21/03	31	7		Trouble No More	Columbia 90133
				MESSINA, Jo Dee	
6/7/03	14	20		Greatest Hits .... [G]	Curb 78790
				MEST ★	
				Punk-rock group from Chicago, Illinois: cousins Tony Lovato (vocals, guitar) and Matt Lovato (bass), Jeremiah Rangel (guitar) and Nick Gigel (drums).	
6/28/03	64	10		Mest........................	Maverick 48456

DEBUT DATE	PEAK POS	WKS CHR	G L D	ARTIST Title	Label & Number
				METALLICA	
6/21/03	❶¹	23	▲²	St. Anger	Elektra 62853
				METHENY, Pat	
6/14/03	167	1		One Quiet Night.. [I]	Warner 48473
				MIDLER, Bette	
10/18/03	14	22	●	Bette Midler Sings The Rosemary Clooney Songbook	Columbia 90350
				MIGUEL, Luis	
10/18/03	43	6		33 .... [F]	Warner Latina 60873
				MILLER, Steve, Band	
10/4/03	37	13		Young Hearts: Complete Greatest Hits .... [G]	Capitol 90509
				MINISTRY	
3/8/03	157	1		Animositisomina	Sanctuary 84568
				MISFITS	
8/16/03	133	1		Project 1950	Misfits 10643
				MR. CHEEKS	
4/5/03	75	4		Back Again!	Universal 067615
				MOBB DEEP	
5/10/03	21	9		Free Agents: The Murda Mix Tape................................	Landspeed 9222
				MOGWAI ★ Rock group from Glasgow, Scotland: Stuart Braithwaite (vocals, guitar), Dominic Aitchison (guitar), John Cummings (guitar), Brandan O'Hare (bass) and Martin Bulloch (drums).	
7/5/03	182	1		Happy Songs For Happy People..............................	Matador 567
				MONICA	
7/5/03	❶¹	24	●	After The Storm	J Records 20031
				MONKEES, The	
5/17/03	51	6		The Best Of The Monkees .... [G]	Rhino 73875
				MONTGOMERY, John Michael	
9/13/03	77	4		The Very Best Of John Michael Montgomery............. [G]	Warner 73918
				MOODY BLUES, The	
11/15/03	10ˣ	2		December [X]	Universal 001563
				MOORE, Chanté — see LATTIMORE, Kenny	
				MOORE, Mandy	
11/8/03	14	13		Coverage..	Epic 90127
				MORGAN, Craig ★ Born Craig Morgan Greer in Kingston Springs, Tennessee. Country singer/songwriter.	
5/3/03	124	15		I Love It	Broken Bow 75672
				MORRISON, Van	
11/8/03	32	10		What's Wrong With This Picture?	Blue Note 90167
				MORTON, Bishop Paul S. ★ Born in Canada; later based in New Orleans, Louisiana. Leader of the Greater St. Stephens Full Gospel Church.	
8/9/03	169	1		Let It Rain.. [L] BISHOP PAUL S. MORTON & THE FGBCF MASS CHOIR	Tehillah 5497
				MOVIELIFE, The ★ Punk-rock group from Long Island, New York: Vinnie Caruana (vocals), Brandon Reilly (guitar), Dan Navetta (guitar), Phil Navetta (bass) and Evan Baken (drums).	
3/15/03	164	1		Forty Hour Train Back To Penn	Drive-Thru 060092
				MRAZ, Jason ★ Born on 10/20/72 in Mechanicsville, Virginia. Singer/songwriter/guitarist.	
4/5/03	55	53↑	●	Waiting For My Rocket To Come	Elektra 62829
				MS. DYNAMITE ★ Born Niomi McLean-Daley in London, England. Female R&B singer.	
3/29/03	179	1		A Little Deeper...	Polydor 076043
				MULLINS, Rich	
5/24/03	179	1		Here In America.. [L]	Reunion 10052
				MURRAY, Keith	
8/2/03	40	4		He's Keith Murray..	Def Jam 000316
				MUSHROOMHEAD	
11/1/03	40	40		XIII	Filthy Hands 001036
				MUSIC, The ★ Rock group from Kippax, Leeds, England: Robert Harvey (vocals), Adam Nutter (guitar), Stuart Coleman (bass) and Phil Jordan (drums).	
3/15/03	128	2		The Music	Capitol 80328

DEBUT DATE	PEAK POS	WKS CHR	G L D	ARTIST Title	Label & Number
				MUSIQ	
12/27/03	13	15↑	●	soulstar	Def Soul 001616
				MXPX	
10/4/03	51	2		Before Everything & After	A&M 000941
				MYA	
8/9/03	3	18	●	Moodring	A&M 000734
				MY MORNING JACKET ★	
				Rock group from Louisville, Kentucky: Jim James (vocals), Johnny Quaid (guitar), Danny Cash (keyboards), Two-Tone Tommy (bass) and Patrick Hallahan (drums).	
9/27/03	121	3		It Still Moves	ATO 52979
				NAPPY ROOTS	
9/13/03	12	8		Wooden Leather	Atlantic 83646
				NAZARIO, Ednita	
12/6/03	116	1		Por Ti .... [F] EDNITA	Sony Discos 70618
				NDEGÉOCELLO, Me'Shell	
11/1/03	150	1		Comfort Woman	Maverick 48547
				NELLY	
12/13/03	12	17↑	▲	Da Derrty Versions - The Reinvention .... [K]	Fo' Reel 001665
				NELSON, Willie	
4/19/03	179	5		The Essential Willie Nelson .... [G]	Legacy 86740 [2]
7/12/03	42	8		Live And Kickin' .... [L] WILLIE NELSON & FRIENDS	Lost Highway 000453
				NEVILLE, Aaron	
2/15/03	191	1		Believe	Tell It 20381
				NEW PORNOGRAPHERS, The ★	
				Rock group from Vancouver, British Columbia, Canada: Neko Case (female vocals), Carl Newman (male vocals), Todd Fancey (guitar), Blaine Thurier (keyboards), John Collins (bass) and Kurt Dahle (drums).	
5/24/03	196	1		Electric Version	Matador 551
				NEWSBOYS	
4/26/03	33	17		Adoration: The Worship Album	Sparrow 41763
				NEWSONG	
9/27/03	172	1		More Life	Reunion 10054
				NEXT	
1/4/03	120	9		The Next Episode	J Records 20016
				NICKELBACK	
10/11/03	6	26↑	▲²	The Long Road	Roadrunner 618400
				NO DOUBT	
12/13/03	2¹	17↑	▲	The Singles 1992-2003 [G]	Interscope 001495
				NOFX	
4/12/03	187	1		Regaining Unconsciousness .... [M]	Fat Wreck Chords 656
5/24/03	44	6		The War On Errorism	Fat Wreck Chords 657
				NORFUL, Smokie ★	
				Born William Norful in Pine Bluff, Arkansas. Gospel singer/songwriter/organist.	
3/8/03	154	9		I Need You Now	EMI Gospel 20374
11/8/03	90	4		Smokie Norful: Limited Edition..	EMI Gospel 95086
				NOTHINGFACE ★	
				Hard-rock group from Washington DC: Matt Holt (vocals), Tom Maxwell (guitar), Bill Gaal (bass) and Chris Houck (drums).	
5/10/03	125	1		Skeletons	TVT 5980
				O.A.R.	
6/14/03	54	5		In Between Now And Then	Everfine 83643
				OFFSPRING, The	
12/27/03	30	15↑	●	Splinter..	Columbia 89026
				ONE TWELVE	
12/6/03	22	14		Hot & Wet...	Bad Boy 000927
				OPERA BABES ★	
				Classical female vocal duo from London, England: Karen England and Rebecca Knight.	
2/8/03	199	1		Beyond Imagination..	Sony Classical 87803

POP ALBUMS

DEBUT DATE	PEAK POS	WKS CHR	G L D	ARTIST Title	Label & Number
				OPETH ★	
				Hard-rock group from Sweden: Mikael Akerfeldt (vocals, guitar), Peter Lindgren (guitar), Martin Mendez (bass) and Martin Lopez (drums).	
5/10/03	192	1		Damnation	Koch 8652
				ORBISON, Roy	
2/8/03	48^C	1		16 Biggest Hits .... [G]	Monument 69738
				ORRICO, Stacie	
4/12/03	59	49	●	Stacie Orrico..................................	ForeFront 32589
				OSBOURNE, Ozzy	
3/1/03	81	6		The Essential Ozzy Osbourne....................... [G]	Legacy 86812 [2]
				OUR LADY PEACE	
7/19/03	112	1		Live .... [L]	Columbia 85855
				OUTKAST	
10/11/03	❶⁷	26↑	▲⁹	Speakerboxxx/The Love Below	Arista 50133 [2]
				PAISLEY, Brad	
8/9/03	8	35↑	●	Mud On The Tires	Arista Nashville 50605
				PANTERA	
10/11/03	38	5		The Best Of Pantera: Far Beyond The Great Southern Cowboys' Vulgar Hits.................. [G]	Elektra 73932
				PARTON, Dolly	
6/21/03	130	2		Ultimate Dolly Parton .... [G]	RCA 52008
11/29/03	167	1		For God And Country	Blue Eye 79756
				PASSION	
9/6/03	107	3		Sacred Revolution: The Songs From OneDay03	Sixsteps 84393
				PAVAROTTI, Luciano	
10/11/03	135	2		Ti Adoro .... [F]	Decca 001096
				PEARL JAM	
6/28/03	182	1		Tokyo, Japan: March 3rd 2003............ [L]	Epic 90336 [2]
8/2/03	169	1		State College Pennsylvania: May 3rd 2003 .... [L]	Epic 90500 [3]
11/29/03	15	11	●	Lost Dogs .... [K]	Epic 85738 [2]
				PENNYWISE	
9/27/03	54	2		From The Ashes	Epitaph 86664
				PEREZ, Amanda ★	
				Born in Fort Wayne, Indiana. R&B-dance singer/songwriter.	
3/15/03	73	15		Angel	Powerhouse 82131
				PERFECT CIRCLE, A	
10/4/03	2¹	27↑	●	Thirteenth Step	Virgin 80918
				PET SHOP BOYS	
2/22/03	188	1		Disco 3	Sanctuary 84595
				PHAIR, Liz	
7/12/03	27	18		Liz Phair	Capitol 22084
				PHILLIPS, CRAIG & DEAN	
2/15/03	142	4		Let Your Glory Fall	Sparrow 51979
				PILLAR	
6/28/03	185	1		Fireproof	Flicker 2617
				P!NK	
11/29/03	9	15	▲	Try This	Arista 52139
				PLANT, Robert	
11/22/03	134	1		Sixty Six To Timbuktu .... [K]	Atlantic 83626 [2]
				PLAY	
6/28/03	67	7		Replay	Columbia 87177
				P.O.D.	
11/22/03	9	13	●	Payable On Death	Atlantic 83676
				POINT OF GRACE	
4/26/03	136	7		24	Word/Curb 886251 [2]
				POISON	
8/23/03	141	1		Best Of Ballads & Blues........................... [K]	Capitol 91407

DEBUT DATE	PEAK POS	WKS CHR	G L D	ARTIST / Title	Label & Number
				POISON THE WELL ★	
				Hard-rock group from Florida: Jeff Moreira (vocals), Derek Miller (guitar), Ryan Primack (guitar), Geoff Vegas (bass) and Chris Hornbrook (drums).	
7/19/03	98	3		You Come Before You	Atlantic 83645
				POWERMAN 5000	
6/7/03	27	9		Transform	DreamWorks 450433
				PRESLEY, Elvis	
10/25/03	3	16	▲	Elvis: 2nd To None [K]	RCA 55895
12/20/03	175	2		Elvis: Christmas Peace [X-K]	RCA 52393 [2]
				PRESLEY, Lisa Marie ★	
				Born on 2/1/68 in Memphis, Tennessee. Pop-dance singer. Daughter of Priscilla and Elvis Presley. Married to Michael Jackson from 1994-96. Married actor Nicolas Cage on 8/10/2002 (since seperated).	
4/26/03	5	18		To Whom It May Concern	Capitol 96668
				PRICE, Kelly	
5/17/03	10	12		Priceless	Def Soul 586777
				PRIMUS	
10/25/03	44	2		Animals Should Not Try To Act Like People	Interscope 001323
				PRINCE PAUL	
5/24/03	200	1		Politics Of The Business	Razor & Tie 82888
				PUDDLE OF MUDD	
12/13/03	20	17↑	●	Life On Display	Geffen 001080
				QUEENSRŸCHE	
8/9/03	56	2		Tribe	Sanctuary 84578
				RA ★	
				Rock group from Brooklyn, New York: Sahaj Ticotin (vocals, guitar), Ben Carroll (guitar), Sean Corcoran (bass) and Skoota Warner (drums).	
1/25/03	154	3		From One	Republic 066093
				RADIOHEAD	
6/28/03	3	20	●	Hail To The Thief	Capitol 84543
				RAGE AGAINST THE MACHINE	
12/13/03	94	4		Live At The Grand Royal Olympic Auditorium [L]	Epic 85114
				RAITT, Bonnie	
10/18/03	47	5		The Best Of Bonnie Raitt 1989-2003 [G]	Capitol 90491
				RANCID	
9/6/03	15	7		Indestructible	Hellcat 48529
				RANDOLPH, Robert, & The Family Band ★	
				Born in Newark, New Jersey. Black pedal steel guitarist/vocalist. The Family Band: John Ginty (organ), Danyel Morgan (bass) and Marcus Randolph (drums).	
8/23/03	145	3		Unclassified	Dare 48472
				RAPTURE, The ★	
				Rock group from New York: Luke Jenner (vocals, guitar), Mattie Safer (vocals, bass), Gabriel Andruzzi (sax) and Vito Roccoforte (drums).	
11/8/03	121	1		Echoes	Strummer 001283
				RAVEONETTES, The ★	
				Male-female rock duo from Copenhagen, Denmark: Sune Rose Wagner (vocals, guitar) and Sharin Foo (vocals, bass).	
9/20/03	123	2		Chain Gang Of Love	Columbia 90353
				RED HOT CHILI PEPPERS	
12/6/03+	18	18↑	●	Greatest Hits [G]	Warner 48545
				RELIENT K	
3/29/03	38	15		Two Lefts Don't Make A Right...But Three Do	Gotee 2890
				R.E.M.	
11/15/03	8	13	●	In Time 1988-2003: The Best Of R.E.M. [G]	Warner 48381
11/15/03	16	4		In Time 1988-2003: The Best Of R.E.M. (Limited Edition) [G]	Warner 48550 [2]
				REVIS ★	
				Rock group from Carbondale, Illinois: Justin Holman (vocals), Robert Davis (guitar), Nathaniel Cox (guitars), Bob Thiemann (bass) and David Piribauer (drums).	
6/7/03	115	11		Places For Breathing	Epic 86514
				RICE, Chris	
3/22/03	161	2		Run The Earth, Watch The Sky	Rocketown 20001

DEBUT DATE	PEAK POS	WKS CHR	G L D	ARTIST Title	Label & Number
				RICE, Damien ★	
				Born in Celbridge, Kildare, Ireland. Adult-Alternative singer/songwriter.	
8/23/03	169	10		O	DRM 48507
				RICHARDSON, Calvin ★	
				Born in Monroe, North Carolina. R&B singer/songwriter.	
9/27/03	65	10		2:35 PM	Hollywood 162351
				RICHIE, Lionel	
2/22/03	19	28	●	The Definitive Collection .... [G]	Motown 068140
				RIMES, LeAnn	
12/6/03	24	18↑	●	Greatest Hits .... [G]	Curb 78829
				ROONEY ★	
				Pop-rock group from Los Angeles, California: Robert Carmine (vocals, guitar), Taylor Locke (guitar), Louie Stephens (keyboards), Matt Winter (bass) and Ned Brower (drums).	
6/7/03+	125	24↑		Rooney	Geffen 000242
				ROSCOE ★	
				Born in Philadelphia, Pennsylvania. Male rapper. Younger brother of rapper Kurupt (of Tha Dogg Pound).	
6/28/03	148	2		Young Roscoe Philaphornia	Priority 28291
				RUFIO ★	
				Punk-rock group from Los Angeles, California: Scott Sellers (vocals, guitar), Clark Domae (guitar), Jon Berry (bass) and Mike Jimenez (drums).	
7/5/03	168	1		MCMLXXXV..	Nitro 15853
				RUSH	
3/1/03	62	7		The Spirit Of Radio: Greatest Hits 1974-1987 .... [G]	Mercury 063335
11/8/03	33	2	●	Rush In Rio .... [L]	Anthem 83672 [3]
				RX BANDITS ★	
				Ska-punk group from Anaheim, California: Matthew Embree (vocals, guitar), Steve Choi (guitar), Steven Borth (sax), Chris Sheets (trombone), Joseph Troy (bass) and Christopher Tsagakis (drums).	
8/2/03	148	1		The Resignation	Drive-Thru 000835
				RZA	
10/25/03	49	4		Birth Of A Prince	Wu-Records 84652
				SAADIQ, Raphael	
11/1/03	182	1		All Hits At The House Of Blues........................ [L]	Pookie 1001 [2]
				SANBORN, David	
6/21/03	177	1		timeagain .... [I]	Verve 065578
				SANTANA, Juelz ★	
				Born LaRon James in 1984 in Manhattan, New York. Male rapper. Member of The Diplomats.	
9/6/03	8	8		From Me To U	Roc-A-Fella 000142
				SANZ, Alejandro	
9/20/03	128	3		No Es Lo Mismo...................................... [F]	Warner Latina 60516
				title is Spanish for "It's Not The Same"	
				SARAI ★	
				Born Sarai Howard in 1982 in Kingston, New York. White female rapper/songwriter.	
8/16/03	187	1		The Original	Sweat 85859
				SAVES THE DAY	
10/4/03	27	3		In Reverie..	Vagrant 001115
				SCAGGS, Boz	
5/24/03	167	1		But Beautiful..	Gray Cat 4000
				SCARFACE	
4/26/03	20	8		Balls And My Word	Rap-A-Lot 42024
				SCRUGGS, Earl	
8/9/03	179	4		The Three Pickers	Rounder 610526
				EARL SCRUGGS / DOC WATSON / RICKY SKAGGS	
				SEAL	
9/27/03	3	28↑	●	Seal IV	Warner 47947
				SEGER, Bob	
11/22/03	23	20↑	●	Greatest Hits 2 .... [G]	Capitol 52772
				SELENA	
7/12/03	117	1		Greatest Hits .... [G]	EMI Latin 90398
				SENSES FAIL ★	
				Hard-rock group from New Jersey: Buddy Nielsen (vocals), Dave Miller (guitar), Garret Zablocki (guitar), Mike Glita (bass) and Dan Trapp (drums).	
5/17/03	144	1		From The Depths Of Dreams .... [M]	Drive-Thru 000155

DEBUT DATE	PEAK POS	WKS CHR	G L D	ARTIST / Title	Label & Number
				SEVENDUST	
10/25/03	14	6		Seasons	TVT 5990
				702	
4/12/03	45	3		Star	Motown 066130
				SHEEK LOUCH ★	
				Born Sean Jacobs in Yonkers, New York. Male rapper. Member of The Lox.	
10/4/03	9	6		Walk Witt Me	D-Block 001042
				SHELTON, Blake	
2/22/03	8	12		The Dreamer	Warner 48237
				SHINEDOWN ★	
				Rock group from Jacksonville, Florida: Brent Smith (vocals), Jasin Todd (guitar), Brad Stewart (bass) and Barry Kerch (drums).	
8/2/03	159	1		Leave A Whisper	Atlantic 83566
				SHINS, The ★	
				Pop-rock group from Albuquerque, New Mexico: James Mercer (vocals, guitar), Marty Crandall (keyboards), Neal Langford (bass) and Jesse Sandoval (drums).	
11/8/03	86	5		Chutes Too Narrow	Sub Pop 625
				SILK	
10/11/03	178	1		Silktime	Silk 12147
				SIMON & GARFUNKEL	
3/15/03	24[C]	9	▲	The Best Of Simon & Garfunkel.................. [G]	Legacy 66022
11/1/03	27	11		The Essential Simon & Garfunkel.............. [G]	Legacy 90716 [2]
				SIMPSON, Jessica	
9/6/03+	2[1]↑	31↑	▲	In This Skin	Columbia 86560
				SINATRA, Frank	
3/1/03	44[C]	1		Gold .... [K]	Capitol 19705
11/1/03	38	8		Live And Swingin': The Ultimate Rat Pack Collection .... [K-L]	Reprise 73922
				FRANK SINATRA, DEAN MARTIN & SAMMY DAVIS JR.	
				SISTER HAZEL	
2/1/03	177	1		Chasing Daylight..	Sixthman 61015
				SKAGGS, Ricky — see SCRUGGS, Earl	
				SKILLET	
12/6/03	179	1		Collide	Ardent 72522
				SMASH MOUTH	
8/23/03	100	2		Get The Picture?	Interscope 000795
				SMILE EMPTY SOUL ★	
				Hard-rock trio from Los Angeles, California: Sean Danielsen (vocals, guitar), Ryan Martin (bass) and Derek Gledhill (drums).	
7/12/03	94	21		Smile Empty Soul..	Throback 83639
				SMITH, Michael W.	
10/25/03	38	9		The Second Decade: 1993-2003 .... [G]	Reunion 10080
				SOCIALBURN ★	
				Rock group from Blountstown, Florida: Neil Alday (vocals, guitar), Chris Cobb (guitar), Dusty Price (bass) and Brandon Bittner (drums).	
3/1/03	178	2		Where You Are	Elektra 62790
				SOLANGE ★	
				Born Solange Knowles on 6/24/86 in Houston, Texas. Female R&B singer. Sister of Beyoncé Knowles of Destiny's Child.	
2/8/03	49	5		Solo Star	Music World 86354
				SOLÍS, Marco Antonio	
5/31/03	59	5		Tu Amor O Tu Desprecio .... [F]	Fonovisa 350840
				title is Spanish for "Your Love Or Your Scorn"	
11/15/03	114	3		La Historia Continúa... .... [F-K]	Fonovisa 350950
				SOMETHING CORPORATE	
11/8/03	24	8		North	Drive-Thru 001190
				SPARXXX, Bubba	
10/4/03	10	10		Deliverance	Beat Club 001147
				SPEARS, Britney	
12/6/03	❶[1]	18↑	▲[2]	In The Zone	Jive 53748
				SPINESHANK	
9/27/03	89	2		Self-Destructive Pattern	Roadrunner 618454
				SPRINGSTEEN, Bruce	
11/29/03	14	13	▲	The Essential Bruce Springsteen .... [G]	Legacy 90773 [3]

DEBUT DATE	PEAK POS	WKS CHR	G L D	ARTIST / Title	Label & Number
				STAIND	
6/7/03	❶¹	41	▲	14 Shades Of Grey	Flip 62882
				STARR, Ringo	
4/12/03	113	2		Ringo Rama	Koch 8429
				STATIC-X	
10/25/03	20	6		Shadow Zone	Warner 48427
				STEELY DAN	
6/28/03	9	12		Everything Must Go	Reprise 48435
				STEREOMUD	
4/19/03	146	1		Every Given Moment	Columbia 86488
				STEWART, Rod	
9/13/03	66	5		Encore: The Very Best Of Rod Stewart Vol. 2 .... [G]	Warner 73911
11/8/03	2²	22↑	▲²	As Time Goes By...The Great American Songbook Vol. II	J Records 55710
				STICKY FINGAZ	
5/17/03	176	1		Decade	D3 9916
				STING	
10/18/03	3	25↑	▲	Sacred Love	A&M 001141
				STONE, Joss ★	
				Born Joscelyn Stoker on 4/11/87 in Dover, England. White female soul-styled singer.	
10/4/03+	56↑	19↑		The Soul Sessions .... [M]	S-Curve 42234
				STONE TEMPLE PILOTS	
11/29/03	26	11		Thank You .... [G]	Atlantic 83586
				STORY OF THE YEAR ★	
				Rock group from St. Louis, Missouri: Dan Marsala (vocals), Ryan Phillips (guitar), Philip Sneed (guitar), Adam Russell (bass) and Josh Wills (drums).	
10/4/03+	51↑	15↑		Page Avenue	Maverick 48438
				STRAIT, George	
3/1/03	7	22	●	For The Last Time: Live From The Astrodome [L]	MCA Nashville 170319
6/28/03	5	32↑	●	Honkytonkville	MCA Nashville 000114
				STREISAND, Barbra	
11/1/03	5	14	●	The Movie Album	Columbia 89018
				STRING CHEESE INCIDENT, The	
10/11/03	157	1		Untying The Not	SCI Fidelity 1015
				STROKES, The	
11/15/03	4	13	●	Room On Fire	RCA 55497
				STRUMMER, Joe, & The Mescaleros ★	
				Born John Mellor on 8/21/52 in Ankara, Turkey (British parents). Died of a heart attack on 12/22/2002 (age 50). Punk-rock singer/songwriter/guitarist. Leader of legendary punk band The Clash. The Mescaleros: Martin Slattery, Tymon Dogg, Simon Stanford and Scott Shields.	
11/8/03	160	1		Streetcore	Hellcat 80454
				STUDDARD, Ruben ★	
				Born on 7/14/78 in Birmingham, Alabama. Black male vocalist. Winner on the second season of TV's *American Idol* in 2003.	
12/27/03	❶¹	15↑	▲	Soulful	J Records 54639
				STYX	
3/8/03	127	1		Cyclorama..	Sanctuary 86337
				SUBLIME	
12/13/03	190	1		The Best Of Sublime: 20th Century Masters: The Millennium Collection.......................... [G]	Gasoline Alley 112921
				SUGAR RAY	
6/21/03	29	7		In The Pursuit Of Leisure	Atlantic 83616
				SUMMER, Donna	
10/18/03	111	4		The Journey: The Very Best Of Donna Summer .... [G]	Mercury 001009
				SUPERGRASS ★	
				Rock trio from Oxford, England: Gaz Coombes (vocals, guitar), Mick Quinn (bass) and Danny Goffey (drums).	
3/1/03	195	1		Life On Other Planets	Island 063685
				SUPERJOINT RITUAL	
8/9/03	55	4		A Lethal Dose Of American Hatred	Sanctuary 70022
				SUPERSTAR KIDZ ★	
				Studio group featuring vocalists Michele Fischer, Renee Sandstrom, Marco Marinangeli, Julie Griffin, Kelly Hansen, Michael Morabito, Chaka Blackmon and Randy Crenshaw.	
8/23/03	59	5		Superstar Kidz....................................	Walt Disney 860087

DEBUT DATE	PEAK POS	WKS CHR	G L D	ARTIST / Title	Label & Number
				SWEAT, Keith	
2/22/03	86	4		Keith Sweat Live .... [L]	Elektra 62855
				SWITCHFOOT ★	
				Christian rock group from San Diego, California: brothers Jonathan Foreman (vocals, guitar) and Tim Foreman (bass), with Jerome Fontamillas (keyboards) and Chad Butler (drums).	
3/15/03+	44↑	52↑	●	The Beautiful Letdown	Red Ink 71083
				TAKING BACK SUNDAY ★	
				Rock group from Amityville, Long Island, New York: Adam Lazzara (vocals), Ed Reyes (guitar), Mark O'Connell (keyboards), Shaun Cooper (bass) and John Nolan (drums).	
2/1/03	183	1		Tell All Your Friends	Victory 176
				t.A.T.u. ★	
				Female teen dance-rock duo from Moscow, Russia: Julia Volkova and Lena Katina.	
1/18/03	13	33	●	200 KM/H In The Wrong Lane................................	Interscope 064107
				TAYLOR, James	
4/26/03	11	39↑	●	The Best Of James Taylor .... [G]	Warner 73837
				TEMPTATIONS, The	
12/13/03+	18^X	2		The Best Of The Temptations: 20th Century Masters The Christmas Collection........................ [X]	Motown 000620
				THALIA	
7/26/03	11	9		Thalia..	EMI Latin 81023
				THICKE ★	
				Born Robin Thicke in Los Angeles, California. "Blue-eyed soul" singer/songwriter. Son of actress Gloria Loring and actor Alan Thicke.	
5/3/03	152	1		A Beautiful World...................................	Nu America 493375
				THIRD DAY	
3/22/03	18	31	●	Offerings II: All I Have To Give	Essential 10706
				THIRD EYE BLIND	
5/31/03	12	9		Out Of The Vein	Elektra 62888
				THOMPSON, Richard	
5/24/03	121	2		The Old Kit Bag	Cooking Vinyl 126
				THORNS, The ★	
				All-star adult-alternative trio: Matthew Sweet (vocals, bass), Shawn Mullins (vocals, guitar) and Pete Droge (vocals, drums).	
6/7/03	62	9		The Thorns	Aware 86958
				THREE DAYS GRACE ★	
				Hard-rock trio from Norwood, Ontario, Canada: Adam Gontier (vocals, guitar), Brad Walst (bass) and Neil Sanderson (drums).	
10/25/03+	72↑	24↑	●	Three Days Grace	Jive 53479
				3 DOORS DOWN	
11/29/03	21	19↑		Another 700 Miles .... [L-M]	Republic 001603
				311	
8/9/03	7	10		Evolver	Volcano 53714
				THREE 6 MAFIA	
7/12/03	4	14		Da Unbreakables	Hypnotize Minds 89030
				THRICE ★	
				Punk-rock group from Anaheim, California: Dustin Kensrue (vocals, guitar), brothers Ed (bass) and Riley (drums) Breckenridge and Teppi Teranishi (guitar).	
8/9/03	16	12		The Artist In The Ambulance	Island 000295
				THURSDAY	
10/4/03	7	9		War All The Time	Victory 000293
				T.I.	
9/6/03	4	29↑	●	Trap Muzik	Grand Hustle 83650
				TIMBALAND AND MAGOO	
12/6/03	50	3		Under Construction Part II	Blackground 001185
				TINSLEY, Boyd ★	
				Born on 5/16/64 in Charlottesville, West Virginia. Black adult-alternative singer/violinist. Member of the Dave Matthews Band.	
7/5/03	97	1		True Reflections	Bama Rags 52633
				TOMAHAWK	
				Hard-rock group formed San Francisco, Cliafornia: Mike Patton (vocals), Duane Denison (guitar), Kevin Rutmanis (bass) and John Stainer (drums). Patton was also leader of Faith No More and Mr. Bungle.	
5/24/03	137	2		Mit Gas	Ipecac 40

POP ALBUMS

DEBUT DATE	PEAK POS	WKS CHR	G L D	ARTIST Title	Label & Number
				TOO $HORT	
11/22/03	49	8		Married To The Game	$hort 53722
				TRAIN	
6/21/03	6	42↑	▲	My Private Nation	Columbia 86593
				TRAPT ★	
				Rock group from Los Gatos, California: Chris Brown (vocals, guitar), Simon Ormandy (guitar), Peter Charell (bass) and Aaron Montgomery (drums).	
2/8/03	42	61↑	▲	Trapt	Warner 48296
				TRAVIS	
11/1/03	41	3		12 Memories	Independiente 90672
				TRAVIS, Randy	
11/29/03	90	7		Worship & Faith	Word-Curb 86273
				TRIBE CALLED QUEST, A	
7/5/03	190	1		Hits, Rarities & Remixes .... [G]	Jive 41839
				TRICE, Obie ★	
				Born on 11/14/79 in Detroit, Michigan. Male rapper.	
10/11/03	5	22	●	Cheers	Shady 001105
				TRIUMPH THE INSULT COMIC DOG ★	
				Hand puppet dog created and voiced by writer/comedian Robert Smigel (born on 2/7/60 in Brooklyn, New York). Regular character on Conan O'Brien's *Late Night* TV show. Smigel is also a longtime writer for TV's *Saturday Night Live*.	
11/22/03	141	3		Come Poop With Me .... [C]	Warner 48328
				TURK	
11/8/03	193	1		Raw & Uncut	Koch 8661
				TURNER, Josh ★	
				Born in 1977 in Hannah, South Carolina. Country singer/songwriter/guitarist.	
11/1/03+	29	23↑	●	Long Black Train	MCA Nashville 000974
				TWIZTID	
7/19/03	52	2		The Green Book	Psychopathic 4014
				2PAC	
10/25/03	15	8		Nu-Mixx Klazzics .... [K]	Death Row 9530
11/29/03	2[1]	19↑	▲	Tupac: Resurrection [S]	Amaru 001533
				TYPE O NEGATIVE	
7/5/03	39	4		Life Is Killing Me...	Roadrunner 618438
				TYRELL, Steve ★	
				Born in Houston, Texas. Jazz-styled singer.	
1/18/03	7[X]	1		This Time Of The Year [X]	Columbia 86638
				TYRESE	
1/4/03	16	35	●	I Wanna Go There	J Records 20041
				UNWRITTEN LAW	
2/8/03	134	2		Music In High Places	Lava 83632
				USED, The	
8/2/03	84	2		Maybe Memories .... [K-L]	Reprise 48503
				VANDROSS, Luther	
6/28/03	❶[1]	41↑	▲	Dance With My Father	J Records 51885
6/28/03	154	1		The Essential Luther Vandross .... [G]	Legacy 89167 [2]
11/15/03	22	5		Luther Vandross Live: Radio City Music Hall 2003...... [L]	J Records 55711
11/15/03	57[X]	1		Home For Christmas .... [X]	Sony 52545
				VELASQUEZ, Jaci	
4/12/03	55	8		Unspoken..	Word/Curb 886223
				VENDETTA RED ★	
				Hard-rock group from Seattle, Washington: Zach Davidson (vocals, guitar), Justin Cronk (guitar), Erik Chapman (keyboards), Michael Vermillion (bass) and Joseph Lee Childres (drums).	
7/12/03	101	8		Between The Never And The Now	Epic 86415
				VERTICAL HORIZON	
10/11/03	61	3		Go	RCA 68121
				VICENTE ★	
				Born Vicente Fernandez in Jalisco, Mexico. Latin singer. Known as the "King of the Rancheros."	
11/8/03	196	1		En Vivo: Juntos Por Ultima Vez .... [F-L] VICENTE Y ALEJANDRO FERNANDEZ	Sony Discos 91088 [2]

DEBUT DATE	PEAK POS	WKS CHR	G L D	ARTIST / Title	Label & Number
				VICIOUS, Johnny ★	
				Born Jonathan Coles in Chicago, Illinois. Electronic producer/musician/remixer.	
3/22/03	162	3		Ultra.Dance 03	Ultra 1155 [2]
				VIOLENT J ★	
				Born Joseph Bruce on 4/27/72 in Detroit, Michigan. White male rapper. One-half of Insane Clown Posse.	
8/9/03	89	2		Wizard Of The Hood .... [M]	Psychopathic 4016
10/11/03	60	4		**WAINWRIGHT, Rufus** Want One	DreamWorks 000896
9/27/03	23	4		**WALKER, Clay** A Few Questions	RCA 67068
8/2/03	133	1		**WAR** The Very Best Of War .... [G]	Avenue 73895 [2]
				WATSON, Doc — see SCRUGGS, Earl	
				WAYNE, Jimmy ★	
				Born on 10/23/72 in Bessemer City, North Carolina; raised in Gastonia, North Carolina. Country singer/songwriter.	
7/12/03	64	9↑		Jimmy Wayne	DreamWorks 450355
8/23/03	81	2		**WEEN** Quebec	Sanctuary 84591
6/21/03	107	3		**WELCH, Gillian** Soul Journey	Acony 0305
11/8/03	176	1		**WESTERBERG, Paul** Come Feel Me Tremble	Vagrant 387
12/27/03	16	15↑	●	**WESTSIDE CONNECTION** Terrorist Threats	Hoo-Bangin' 24030
9/6/03	100	5		**WHITE, Barry** The Best Of Barry White: 20th Century Masters The Millennium Collection .... [G]	Island 000884
4/19/03	6	51↑	▲	**WHITE STRIPES, The** Elephant	Third Man 27148
5/3/03	61	4		**WIDESPREAD PANIC** Ball	Sanctuary 84606
				WILLIAMS, Bernie ★	
				Born on 9/13/68 in San Juan, Puerto Rico. Jazz guitarist. Better known as the all-star center fielder for baseball's New York Yankees.	
8/2/03	157	2		The Journey Within .... [I]	GRP 000725
3/8/03	120	5		**WILLIAMS, Dar** The Beauty Of The Rain	Razor & Tie 82886
12/6/03	166	1		**WILLIAMS, Hank Jr.** I'm One Of You	Curb 78830
4/26/03	18	17		**WILLIAMS, Lucinda** World Without Tears	Lost Highway 170355
4/19/03	43	7		**WILLIAMS, Robbie** Escapology	Chrysalis 81777
11/8/03	68	3		**WILLS, Mark** And The Crowd Goes Wild	Mercury 001012
9/27/03	32	18		**WINANS, CeCe** Throne Room..	Pure Springs 90361
				WINANS, Vickie ★	
				Born in Detroit, Michigan. Gospel singer. Member of the famous Winans family.	
5/24/03	110	9		Bringing It All Together	Verity 43214
7/5/03	126	2		**WINWOOD, Steve** About Time	Wincraft 0001
				WONDER, Wayne ★	
				Born VonWayne Charles in Jamaica. Reggae singer.	
3/22/03	29	18		No Holding Back	VP 83628
				WOODWARD, Lucy ★	
				Born in 1978 in England; raised in New York. Pop singer/songwriter.	
4/19/03	148	1		While You Can...	Atlantic 83637

POP ALBUMS

DEBUT DATE	PEAK POS	WKS CHR	GLD	ARTIST / Title	Label & Number
				WORLEY, Darryl	
5/3/03	4	22	●	Have You Forgotten?	DreamWorks 000064
				WYNONNA	
8/23/03	8	9		What The World Needs Now Is Love	Curb 78811
				YANKOVIC, "Weird Al"	
6/7/03	17	15		Poodle Hat .... [N]	Way Moby 31294
				YANNI	
2/8/03	74	5		Ultimate Yanni .... [I-K]	Windham Hill 18106 [2]
3/1/03	27	17		Ethnicity .... [I]	Virgin 81516
				YEAH YEAH YEAHS ★	
				Punk-rock trio from Long Island, New York: Karen O (vocals), Nick Zinner (guitar) and Brian Chase (drums).	
5/17/03+	55↑	11↑		Fever To Tell	Interscope 000349
				YELLOWCARD ★	
				Punk-rock group from Jacksonville, Florida: Ryan Key (vocals, guitar), Sean Mackin (violin, vocals), Benjamin Harper (guitar), Alex Lewis (bass) and Longineu Parsons (drums).	
8/9/03+	60↑	32↑	●	Ocean Avenue	Capitol 39844
				YING YANG TWINS	
10/4/03	11	27↑	●	Me & My Brother	Collipark 2480
				YOAKAM, Dwight	
7/12/03	75	7		Population: Me	Audium 8176
				YO LA TENGO	
4/26/03	115	2		Summer Sun	Matador 0548
				YORN, Pete	
5/3/03	18	10		Day I Forgot	Columbia 86922
				YOUNG, Neil	
9/6/03	22	6		Greendale	Reprise 48533
				NEIL YOUNG & CRAZY HORSE	
				YOUNGBLOODZ	
9/13/03	5	23	●	Drankin' Patnaz	So So Def 50155
				YUKMOUTH	
8/23/03	112	2		Godzilla	J Prince 42028
				ZEVON, Warren	
9/13/03	12	18		The Wind	Artemis 51156
9/27/03	168	1		Genius: The Best Of Warren Zevon .... [G]	Elektra 73771
				ZOEGIRL	
10/4/03	149	3		Different Kind Of Free	Sparrow 80666
				ZOMBIE, Rob	
10/11/03	11	21	●	Past, Present & Future .... [G]	Geffen 001041
				ZWAN ★	
				Rock group formed by former Smashing Pumpkins members Billy Corgan (vocals, guitar) and Jimmy Chamberlain (drums), with Matt Sweeney (guitar) and David Pajo (bass).	
2/15/03	3	11		Mary Star Of The Sea	Martha's Music 48436
				ZZ TOP	
9/27/03	57	3		Mescalero	RCA 51168
				MOVIE SOUNDTRACKS	
8/9/03	23	8		American Wedding .... [V]	Universal 000744
				Jason Biggs/Alyson Hannigan/January Jones/Fred Willard/Eugene Levy	
8/2/03	❶⁴	25	▲	Bad Boys II .... [V]	Bad Boy 000716
				Martin Lawrence/Will Smith/Peter Stormare/Theresa Randle/Joe Pantoliano	
3/22/03	111	6		Bringing Down The House .... [V]	Hollywood 162386
				Steve Martin/Queen Latifah/Eugene Levy/Jean Smart/Joan Plowright	
11/8/03	52	9		Brother Bear .... [V]	Walt Disney 860127
				animated movie, voices by: Joaquin Phoenix/Jeremy Suarez/Rick Moranis/Dave Thomas	
7/12/03	12	8	●	Charlie's Angels: Full Throttle .... [V]	Columbia 90132
				Cameron Diaz/Drew Barrymore/Lucy Liu/Bernie Mac/Crispin Glover	

DEBUT DATE	PEAK POS	WKS CHR	G L D	ARTIST Title	Label & Number
				MOVIE SOUNDTRACKS — Cont'd	
2/1/03	2¹	51	▲²	Chicago [M]	Epic 87018
				Catherine Zeta-Jones/Renée Zellweger/Richard Gere/Queen Latifah/John C. Reilly	
2/15/03	143	2		Coyote Ugly: More Music From Coyote Ugly [V]	Curb 78765
3/8/03	6	16	●	Cradle 2 The Grave [V]	Bloodline 063615
				Jet Li/DMX/Anthony Anderson/Kelly Hu/Tom Arnold	
2/22/03	9	24	●	Daredevil [V]	Wind-Up 13079
				Ben Affleck/Jennifer Garner/Michael Clarke Duncan/Colin Farrell/Joe Pantoliano	
1/25/03	88	8		Deliver Us From Eva [V]	Hollywood 162369
				LL Cool J/Gabrielle Union/Duane Martin/Essence Atkins/Megan Good	
12/27/03	114	6		Dirty Dancing: Ultimate Dirty Dancing [V]	RCA 55525
6/7/03	191	1		Down With Love [V]	Reprise 48480
				Renée Zellweger/Ewan McGregor/David Hyde Pierce/Sarah Paulson/Tony Randall	
1/11/03	133	8		Drumline [V]	Fox 41810
				Nick Cannon/Zoë Saldana/Orlando Jones/Leonard Roberts/Jason Weaver	
5/10/03	95	2		Dysfunktional Family [V]	Tha Row 63053
				movie is a stand-up performance by comedian Eddie Griffin	
11/29/03+	40ˣ	4		Elf [X-V]	New Line 39028
				Will Ferrell/James Caan/Zooey Deschanel/Edward Asner/Bob Newhart	
9/27/03	19	16↑		Fighting Temptations, The [V]	Music World 90286
				Cuba Gooding Jr./Beyoncé Knowles/Mike Epps/LaTanya Richardson/Faith Evans	
11/15/03	156	2		Finding Nemo: Ocean Favorites [V]	Walt Disney 861022
				animated movie, voices by: Alexander Gould/Albert Brooks/Ellen DeGeneres/Geoffrey Rush	
8/16/03	19	34↑	●	Freaky Friday [V]	Hollywood 162404
				Jamie Lee Curtis/Lindsay Lohan/Harold Gould/Chad Michael Murray/Mark Harmon	
8/30/03	25	6		Freddy vs. Jason [V]	Roadrunner 618347
				Robert Englund/Ken Kirzinger/Kelly Rowland/Monica Keena/Jason Ritter	
4/12/03	162	1		Frida [F-V]	Universal 474150
				Salma Hayek/Julie Taymor/Alfred Molina/Geoffrey Rush/Roger Rees	
2/22/03	196	1		Gods And Generals [I]	Sony Classical 87891
				Jeff Daniels/Stephen Lang/Robert Duvall; cp/cd: John Frizzell and Randy Edelman	
5/10/03	80	16		Holes [V]	Walt Disney 860092
				Sigourney Weaver/Jon Voight/Patricia Arquette/Tim Blake Nelson/Shia LaBeouf	
12/13/03	105	7		Honey [V]	Elektra 62925
				Jessica Alba/Mekhi Phifer/Joy Bryant/Lil' Romeo/Missy Elliott	
4/19/03	53	4		House Of 1000 Corpses [V]	Geffen 49364
				Sid Haig/Bill Moseley/Sheri Moon/Karen Black/Tom Towles	
2/22/03	96	15		How To Lose A Guy In 10 Days [V]	Virgin 81522
				Kate Hudson/Matthew McConaughey/Adam Goldberg/Michael Michele/Thomas Lennon	
10/25/03	45	7		Kill Bill Vol. 1 [V]	A Band Apart 48570
				Uma Thurman/Lucy Liu/Vivica Fox/Michael Madsen/Darryl Hannah	
8/9/03	177	2		Lara Croft Tomb Raider: The Cradle Of Life [V]	Hollywood 162417
				Angelina Jolie/Gerard Butler/Noah Taylor/Djimon Hounsou/Chris Barrie	
5/10/03	6	46	▲	Lizzie McGuire Movie, The [V]	Walt Disney 860080
				Hilary Duff/Adam Lamberg/Robert Carradine/Hallie Todd/Jake Thomas	
12/13/03+	36	17↑	●	Lord Of The Rings: The Return Of The King, The [I]	Reprise 48521
				Elijah Wood/Ian McKellen/Liv Tyler/Viggo Mortensen/Sean Astin; cp/cd: Howard Shore	
11/29/03	39	14	●	Love Actually [V]	J Records 56760
				Alan Rickman/Colin Firth/Emma Thompson/Hugh Grant/Rowan Atkinson	
8/9/03	94	2		Masked And Anonymous [V]	Columbia 90536
				Jeff Bridges/Penelope Cruz/Bob Dylan/John Goodman/Jessica Lange	
5/24/03	5	15	●	Matrix Reloaded, The [V]	Warner Sunset 48411 [2]
				Keanu Reeves/Laurence Fishburne/Carrie-Anne Moss/Jada Pinkett Smith	
11/22/03	69	2		Matrix Revolutions, The [I]	Warner Sunset 48412
				Keanu Reeves/Laurence Fishburne/Carrie-Anne Moss/Jada Pinkett Smith; cp/cd: Don Davis	
10/4/03	174	1		Once Upon A Time In Mexico [F-V]	Milan 36038
				Antonio Banderas/Salma Hayek/Johnny Depp/Mickey Rourke/Enrique Iglesias	
8/9/03	75	15		Pirates Of The Caribbean: The Curse Of The Black Pearl [I]	Walt Disney 860089
				Johnny Depp/Geoffrey Rush/Orlando Bloom/Keira Knightley; cp: Klaus Badelt; cd: Hans Zimmer	
7/5/03	198	1		RugRats Go Wild [V]	Nickelodeon 162399
				animated movie, voices by: Bruce Willis/Tim Curry/E.G. Dailey/Cheryl Chase	
10/18/03	95	8↑		School Of Rock [V]	Atlantic 83694
				Jack Black/Joan Cusack/Mike White/Sarah Silverman/Adam Pascal	
6/14/03	5	22	●	2 Fast 2 Furious [V]	Def Jam 000426
				Paul Walker/Tyrese/Eva Mendes/Cole Hauser/Ludacris	
9/20/03	55	5		Underworld [V]	Lakeshore 33781
				Kate Beckinsale/Scott Speedman/Michael Sheen/Shane Brolly/Erwin Leder	
4/19/03	106	8		What A Girl Wants [V]	Atlantic 83641
				Amanda Bynes/Colin Firth/Eileen Atkins/Anna Chancellor/Jonathan Pryce	
1/18/03	167	4		Wild Thornberrys Movie, The [V]	Nick/Jive 48503
				animated movie, voices by: Lacey Chabert/Tim Curry/Lynn Redgrave/Flea/Alfre Woodard	

POP ALBUMS

DEBUT DATE	PEAK POS	WKS CHR	G L D	ARTIST Title	Label & Number
				ORIGINAL CAST	
9/6/03	175	1		Gypsy	Broadway Angel 83858
				Bernadette Peters/David Burtka/Heather Lee; mu: Jule Styne; ly: Stephen Sondheim	
				TELEVISION SOUNDTRACKS	
5/24/03	48	5		American Dreams: 1963-1964.. [V]	Hip-O 000231
				Gail O'Grady/Tom Verica/Brittany Snow/Will Estes/Rachel Boston	
5/17/03	2¹	15	●	American Idol Season 2: All-Time Classic American Love Songs [L-V]	RCA 51169
11/1/03	28	11	●	American Idol: The Great Holiday Classics........... [X-L-V]	RCA 55424
				above 2 contain performaces by contestants such as Clay Aiken/Ruben Studdard/Kimberley Locke	
9/27/03	113	2		American Juniors: Kids In America............................ [L-V]	19/Jive 55973
				contains performances by contestants Morgan Burke/Lucy Hale/A.J. Melendez/Taylor Thompson	
10/11/03	177	1		Charmed .... [V]	Private Music 52130
				Alyssa Milano/Holly Marie Combs/Rose McGowan/Brian Krause	
8/30/03+	33	32↑	▲	Cheetah Girls, The .... [M]	Walt Disney 860126
				Raven-Symone/Adrienne Bailon/Kiely Williams/Sabrina Bryan/Lynn Whitfield	
8/9/03	125	5		Kim Possible .... [V]	Walt Disney 860097
				animated series, voices by: Christy Romano/Will Friedle/Nancy Cartwright/Gary Cole	
9/13/03	92	9		Martin Scorsese Presents The Best Of The Blues ...... [V]	UTV 000704
				music from the PBS-TV documentary series	
5/24/03	174	1		Nashville Star: The Finalists .... [L-V]	Columbia 87169
				contains performances by such contestants as Jamey Garner/Brandi Gibson/Buddy Jewell	
6/7/03	173	1		Queer As Folk: The Third Season .... [V]	Tommy Boy 1568 [2]
				Hal Sparks/Sharon Gless/Gale Harold/Randy Harrison/Scott Lowell	
3/15/03	31	5		Smallville .... [V]	Elektra 62792
				Tom Welling/Kristen Kreuk/Michael Rosenbaum/John Schneider/Annette O'Toole	
				CHRISTMAS (Various Artists)	
11/15/03	27ˣ	2		Christmas In Nashville	Warner 0496
				songs performed by Kenny Rogers, Randy Travis, Crystal Gayle and Travis Tritt	
12/20/03	133	2		Classic Country: Christmas	Time-Life 18927
				songs by Alabama, Johnny Cash, Vince Gill, Buck Owens, Elvis Presley, and others	
11/15/03	35ˣ	3		Disney's Family Christmas Collection	Walt Disney 860130
				contains songs performed by a studio group and several Disney characters	
12/6/03+	29ˣ	5		Heavenly Christmas...	Rhino 73958
				songs by Sarah Brightman, Michael Crawford, Linda Ronstadt, Carly Simon, and others	
12/6/03	182	2		iWorsh!p Christmas: A Total Worship Experience	Integrity 90365 [2]
				songs by Sara Groves, MercyMe, SonicFlood, and others	
1/4/03	38ˣ	1		Maybe This Christmas	Nettwerk 30295
				songs by Barenaked Ladies, Vanessa Carlton, Coldplay, Ben Folds, Jimmy Eat World, and others	
11/8/03	17	10	▲²	Now That's What I Call Christmas! 2: The Signature Collection................................	EMI 83098 [2]
				songs by Chuck Berry, Mariah Carey, Elton John, Norah Jones, Kenny Rogers, and others	
11/15/03+	32ˣ	3		Songs 4 Worship Kids Christmas	Time-Life 18952
				contains songs performed by a children's studio group	
11/15/03	22ˣ	4		Strawberry Shortcake: Berry, Merry Christmas	Koch 9502
				songs by Jay Hanson, Sandy Howell, Sarah Heinke, Jerry Longe and Rachel Ware	
12/13/03	162	3		Thomas Kinkade-St. Nicholas Circle: Treasury Of Christmas.............................. [I]	Music Of Light 2219
11/15/03	33ˣ	1		Thomas Kinkade-Silent Night: The Best Of Christmas.............................. [I]	Music Of Light 4425
11/15/03	40ˣ	1		Thomas Kinkade-Victorian Christmas: Christmas Favorites................................ [I]	Music Of Light 4460
11/15/03	24ˣ	2		Thomas Kinkade-Village Christmas: Home For Christmas.............................. [I]	Music Of Light 4459
				Thomas Kinkade is a famous painter; above 4 contain songs performed by the 101 Strings Orchestra	
12/20/03	144	2		Time-Life Treasury Of Christmas: Evergreen, The	Time-Life 18950
				songs by John Denver, Celine Dion, Gloria Estefan, Kenny Loggins, Donna Summer, and others	
12/20/03	159	2		Very Special Acoustic Christmas, A	Lost Highway 001038
				songs by Alan Jackson, Alison Krauss, Reba McEntire, Willie Nelson, Marty Stuart, and others	
11/15/03	11ˣ	5		Windham Hill Christmas II, A .... [I]	Windham Hill 53901
				songs by Philip Aaberg, Jim Brickman, Alex DeGrassi, Liz Story, George Winston, and others	
11/15/03	23ˣ	1		WNUA 95.5: Smooth Jazz Sampler, Volume 16..................	WNUA 9553 [2]
				songs by Rick Braun, Natalie Cole, Dave Koz, Ramsey Lewis, Brenda Russell, and others	

DEBUT DATE	PEAK POS	WKS CHR	G L D	ARTIST Title	Label & Number
				VARIOUS ARTIST COMPILATIONS	
4/5/03	51	8		Atticus: Dragging The Lake II	Side One Dummy 1236
				songs by Alkaline Trio, Blink-182, Box Car Racer, Lagwagon, Taking Back Sunday, and others	
2/15/03	73	6		Body + Soul: Absolute...	Time-Life 18882
				songs by Toni Braxton, Deborah Cox, Joe, Brian McKnight, Angie Stone, and others	
6/21/03	157	2		Church: Songs Of Soul & Inspiration............................	DMI 067763
				songs by Patti Austin, En Vogue, Jennifer Holliday, Stephanie Mills, Dionne Warwick, and others	
10/18/03	80	6		CMT Most Wanted Volume 1	Capitol 93166
				songs by Trace Adkins, Chris Cagle, Joe Nichols, Rascal Flatts, Keith Urban, and others	
4/5/03	134	2		Conception: An Interpretation Of Stevie Wonder's Songs ...	Motown 067314
				songs by Marc Anthony, Eric Clapton, Glenn Lewis, John Mellencamp, Musiq, and others	
12/6/03	97	6		Concert For George .... [L]	Warner 74546 [2]
				tribute to George Harrison; songs by Eric Clapton, Paul McCartney, Tom Petty, Ringo Starr, and others	
12/27/03	161	7		Crunk And Disorderly..	TVT 2500
				songs by David Banner, Bone Crusher, Killer Mike, Lil Flip, Lil Jon, and others	
10/4/03	83	4		Def Jam Recordings Presents Music Inspired By Scarface	Def Jam 001196
				songs by Joe Budden, Cam'ron, Jay-Z, Mobb Deep, Scarface, and others	
4/5/03	98	8		Dove Hits 2003	Reunion 10076
				songs by Jars Of Clay, MercyMe, Nicole C. Mullen, Point Of Grace, Third Day, and others	
9/6/03	187	1		Drive-Thru Invasion Tour Compilation............................	Drive-Thru 001028
				songs by Early November, New Found Glory, Senses Fail, Something Corporate, and others	
5/31/03	149	6		ESPN Presents Stadium Anthems: Music For The Fans...	Hollywood 162387
				songs by Baha Men, Fatboy Slim, Gary Glitter, Moby, Queen, Sister Sledge, and others	
2/15/03	12^C	1		Favorite Love Songs From The Slow Jams Collection	EMI-Capitol 24181
				songs by Enchantment, Al Green, Freddie Jackson, Minnie Riperton, Shalamar, and others	
4/26/03	73	8		Got Hits!..	Virgin 81922
				songs by Aaliyah, Nick Carter, Dirty Vegas, Kylie Minogue, Justin Timberlake, and others	
11/29/03	187	4		Gotta Have Gospel!	Integrity Gospel 90671 [2]
				songs by Yolanda Adams, Kurt Carr, Kirk Franklin, Mary Mary, CeCe Winans, and others	
3/1/03	6	16	●	**Grammy Nominees 2003**	Grammy 73843
				songs by Sheryl Crow, Craig David, Dixie Chicks, Nickelback, P!nk, Britney Spears, and others	
4/5/03	186	1		Heart Of Roadrunner Records, The...................................	Roadrunner 618387
				songs by Coal Chamber, Ill Nino, Machine Head, Slipknot, Soulfly, Spineshank, and others	
4/5/03	133	1		I Could Sing Of Your Love Forever: Kids	Worship Together 20371
				songs by Ben Byler, Brandon Harris, Graham Keen, Hannah Reddick, Sarah Valley, and others	
9/27/03	134	5		iWorsh!p: A Total Worship Experience Vol. 2	Integrity 90362 [2]
				songs by Delirious, Robin Mark, MercyMe, SonicFlood, Darlene Zschech, and others	
9/6/03	131	2		I've Always Been Crazy: A Tribute To Waylon Jennings ..	RCA 67064
				songs by Brooks & Dunn, Jessi Colter, Andy Griggs, John Mellencamp, Travis Tritt, and others	
11/1/03	55	9		Just Because I'm A Woman: Songs Of Dolly Parton........	Sugar Hill 3980
				songs by Kasey Chambers, Melissa Etheridge, Emmylou Harris, Shania Twain, and others	
5/3/03	154	2		Living The Gospel: Gospel Greats	Time-Life 606
				songs by Commodores, Aretha Franklin, Al Green, Mighty Clouds Of Joy, Staple Singers, and others	
10/25/03	34	6		MTV2: Headbangers Ball	Roadrunner 618327 [2]
				songs by Anthrax, Cold, Deftones, Godsmack, Marilyn Manson, Sevendust, and others	
9/6/03	❶^1	13	●	**Neptunes Present...Clones, The**	Star Trak 51295
				songs by Busta Rhymes, Clipse, Kelis, Ludacris, Pharrell, Snoop Dogg, and others	
4/12/03	3	26	▲	**Now 12**	EMI 82344
				songs by JC Chasez, Dru Hill, Jennifer Lopez, Amanda Perez, 3 Doors Down, and others	
8/9/03	2^3	23	▲	**Now 13**	Universal 000556
				songs by Daniel Bedingfield, Bowling For Soup, Counting Crows, Stacie Orrico, and others	
11/22/03	3	20↑	▲	**Now 14**	Columbia 90753
				songs by Black Eyed Peas, Chingy, Ginuwine, Good Charlotte, Liz Phair, and others	
3/8/03	187	1		Power, The	Razor & Tie 89061
				songs by Amber, Black Box, Nicki French, Real McCoy, Crystal Waters, and others	
6/7/03	79	6		Punk-O-Rama 8	Epitaph 86673 [2]
				songs by Atmosphere, Bad Religion, Distillers, Pennywise, Rancid, and others	
2/15/03	197	1		Pure 80's Love: The #1 Hits	UTV 069612
				songs by Air Supply, Cutting Crew, Cyndi Lauper, Lionel Richie, Simply Red, and others	
9/27/03	105	10		Radio Disney Jams Vol. 6	Walt Disney 860088
				songs by Atomic Kitten, Hilary Duff, Lil' Romeo, Play, S Club 7, and others	
6/7/03	137	4		Rasta Jamz	Razor & Tie 89062
				songs by Ini Kamoze, Diana King, Mad Lion, Shabba Ranks, Snow, and others	
11/1/03	143	3		Red Star Sounds Presents Def Jamaica	Def Jam 001195
				songs by Buju Banton, Capone-N-Noreaga, Method Man, 112, Scarface, and others	
7/5/03	43	12		Reggae Gold 2003	VP 83654
				songs by Beenie Man, Bounty Killer, Busta Rhymes, Elephant Man, Wayne Wonder, and others	
9/27/03	71	4		Remembering Patsy Cline	MCA 170297
				songs by Terri Clark, Natalie Cole, Amy Grant, Martina McBride, Lee Ann Womack, and others	
4/12/03	34	6		Rewind: The Hip-Hop DVD Magazine Issue 1	Shadyville 6101
				songs by Fat Joe, 50 Cent, Jadakiss, Nappy Roots, Nelly, Snoop Dogg, and others	
5/17/03	149	1		Songs 4 Worship En Español: Canta Al Señor .... [F]	Integrity 18629 [2]
				songs by Marco Barrientos, Don Moen, Ingrid Rosario, Paul Wilbur, and others	
1/4/03	35	15		Source Presents Hip Hop Hits - Volume 6, The	Def Jam 063546
				songs by Big Tymers, Foxy Brown, Eminem, Nelly, P. Diddy, Ying Yang Twins, and others	
12/27/03	89	13		Source Presents Hip Hop Hits - Volume 7, The.................	Def Jam 001614
				songs by Bone Crusher, Missy Elliott, Ja Rule, Ludacris, Snoop Dogg, 2Pac, and others	

DEBUT DATE	PEAK POS	WKS CHR	G L D	ARTIST Title	Label & Number
				VARIOUS ARTIST COMPILATIONS — Cont'd	
8/30/03	6	9		State Property Presents: The Chain Gang Vol. II	Roc-A-Fella 000971
				songs by Freeway, Peedi Crakk, Beanie Sigel, Young Gunz, and others	
10/11/03	37	14		Totally Country Vol. 3	Warner 73955
				songs by Diamond Rio, Faith Hill, Jo Dee Messina, Blake Shelton, Phil Vassar, and others	
7/19/03	48	10		Totally Hip Hop	Warner 52553
				songs by Christina Aguilera, Brandy, Fabolous, Sean Paul, Wayne Wonder, and others	
10/25/03	13	15	●	Totally Hits 2003	Warner 55777
				songs by Michelle Branch, Kelly Clarkson, Jewel, Avril Lavigne, Ruben Studdard, and others	
7/19/03	66	5		Totally R&B	Warner 52552
				songs by Jimmy Cozier, Craig David, R. Kelly, Gerald Levert, Tyrese, Usher, and others	
6/21/03	55	6		Ultimate Smash Hits	Arista 52522
				songs by Baby, Clipse, Whitney Houston, OutKast, P!nk, Santana, and others	
6/21/03	21	12	●	Vans Warped Tour 2003 Compilation .... [L]	Side One D. 71237 [2]
				songs by Bouncing Souls, Lagwagon, Less Than Jake, Simple Plan, Thrice, and others	
9/13/03	149	4		Verve//Remixed2	Verve 000598
				new remixes of old songs by Willie Bobo, Ella Fitzgerald, Nina Simone, Sarah Vaughan, and others	
3/1/03	43	5		We're A Happy Family: A Tribute To Ramones	DV8 86352
				songs by Garbage, Green Day, Kiss, Metallica, Tom Waits, Rob Zombie, and others	
6/7/03	103	8		Worship Together: Be Glorified	Time-Life 42011 [2]
				songs by Brenton Brown, Keith Green, Matt Redman, Chris Tomlin, and others	
2/1/03	39	48	▲	Worship Together: I Could Sing Of Your Love Forever	Time-Life 42010 [2]
				songs by Fusebox, Charlie Hall, Matt Redman, Rebecca St. James, Chris Tomlin, and others	
2/22/03	29	20	●	WOW Gospel 2003	EMI 43213 [2]
				songs by Shirley Caeser, Fred Hammond, Donald Lawrence, Aaron Neville, Smokie Norful, and others	
10/25/03	51	24↑		WOW Hits 2004	EMI 90652 [2]
				songs by Jeremy Camp, Steven Curtis Chapman, Amy Grant, Chris Rice, Michael W. Smith, and others	
4/5/03	44	30	▲	WOW Worship Yellow	EMI 80198 [2]
				songs by Caedmon's Call, Rich Mullins, Newsong, Nichole Nordeman, Third Day, and others	

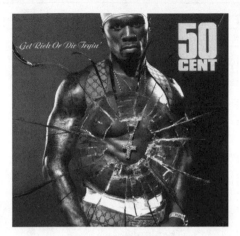

1. **50 CENT**
205

2. **NORAH JONES**
185

3. **EVANESCENCE**
124

4.	102	**DIXIE CHICKS**		13.	46	**LINKIN PARK**
5.	88	**BEYONCÉ**		14.	45	**LUTHER VANDROSS**
6.	72	**OUTKAST**		15.	44	**ALAN JACKSON**
7.	72	**AVRIL LAVIGNE**		16.	42	**METALLICA**
8.	56	**R. KELLY**		17.	39	**TOBY KEITH**
9.	54	**HILARY DUFF**		18.	38	**CHINGY**
10.	51	**JENNIFER LOPEZ**		19.	35	**CHER**
11.	49	**KELLY CLARKSON**		20.	33	**ASHANTI**
12.	47	**KID ROCK**				

PEAK DATE	WEEKS				RANK	RECORD TITLE	PEAK POSITION	ARTIST
	CH	40	10	PK				
						1		
10/11	26 +	26 +	24	7	1.	Speakerboxxx/The Love Below		OutKast
2/22	59 +	39	27	6	2.	Get Rich Or Die Tryin'		50 Cent
1/25	108 +	98 +	36	4	3.	Come Away With Me		Norah Jones
8/2	25	12	9	4	4.	Bad Boys II		Movie Soundtrack
12/20	16 +	16 +	8	2	5.	The Diary Of Alicia Keys		Alicia Keys
4/12	52 +	50 +	7	2	6.	Meteora		Linkin Park
11/29	19 +	19 +	7	2	7.	The Black Album		Jay-Z
7/19	30	15	6	2	8.	Chapter II		Ashanti
11/1	23 +	17	4	2	9.	Measure Of A Man		Clay Aiken
11/22	20 +	20 +	14	1	10.	Shock'n Y'all		Toby Keith
7/12	39 +	39 +	13	1	11.	Dangerously In Love		Beyoncé
9/20	30 +	30 +	12	1	12.	Metamorphosis		Hilary Duff
5/3	47	18	9	1	13.	Thankful		Kelly Clarkson
12/27	15 +	15 +	9	1	14.	Soulful		Ruben Studdard
3/8	57 +	22	7	1	15.	Chocolate Factory		R. Kelly
12/6	18 +	18 +	7	1	16.	In The Zone		Britney Spears
8/30	32 +	25	6	1	17.	Greatest Hits Volume II and Some Other Stuff		Alan Jackson
6/28	41 +	16	6	1	18.	Dance With My Father		Luther Vandross
6/21	23	11	6	1	19.	St. Anger		Metallica
10/25	24 +	24 +	5	1	20.	Chicken*N*Beer		Ludacris
9/6	13	6	4	1	21.	The Neptunes Present...Clones		Various Artists
9/27	28 +	9	3	1	22.	Heavier Things		John Mayer
7/5	24	7	3	1	23.	After The Storm		Monica
9/13	25	6	3	1	24.	Love & Life		Mary J. Blige
6/7	41	17	2	1	25.	14 Shades Of Grey		Staind
10/4	24	7	2	1	26.	Grand Champ		DMX
5/24	23	7	2	1	27.	Body Kiss		The Isley Brothers Featuring Ronald Isley
6/14	16	5	2	1	28.	How The West Was Won		Led Zeppelin
5/10	14	4	2	1	29.	American Life		Madonna
4/26	49 +	8	1	1	30.	Faceless		Godsmack

#1 BILLBOARD 200 ALBUMS

	Date Hit #1	Wks @ #1	Title	Artist
1.	1/4	5	Up!.. *Shania Twain* (includes 4 weeks at #1 in 2002)	
2.	1/11	4↕	8 Mile... *Movie Soundtrack* (includes 2 weeks at #1 in 2002)	
3.	1/25	4↕	Come Away With Me.......................................*Norah Jones*	
4.	2/15	4↕	Home .... *Dixie Chicks* (includes 3 weeks at #1 in 2002)	
5.	2/22	6↕	Get Rich Or Die Tryin' .... *50 Cent*	
6.	3/8	1	Chocolate Factory .... *R. Kelly*	
7.	4/12	2	Meteora .... *Linkin Park*	
8.	4/26	1	Faceless..*Godsmack*	
9.	5/3	1	Thankful .... *Kelly Clarkson*	
10.	5/10	1	American Life... *Madonna*	
11.	5/24	1	Body Kiss.......... *The Isley Brothers Featuring Ronald Isley AKA Mr. Biggs*	
12.	5/31	1	The Golden Age Of Grotesque .... *Marilyn Manson*	
13.	6/7	1	14 Shades Of Grey .... *Staind*	
14.	6/14	1	How The West Was Won................................. *Led Zeppelin*	
15.	6/21	1	St. Anger .... *Metallica*	
16.	6/28	1	Dance With My Father ....*Luther Vandross*	
17.	7/5	1	After The Storm .... *Monica*	
18.	7/12	1	Dangerously In Love.. *Beyoncé*	
19.	7/19	2	Chapter II.. *Ashanti*	
20.	8/2	4	Bad Boys II.. *Movie Soundtrack*	
21.	8/30	1	Greatest Hits Volume II And Some Other Stuff ....*Alan Jackson*	
22.	9/6	1	The Neptunes Present...Clones................... *Various Artists*	
23.	9/13	1	Love & Life .... *Mary J. Blige*	
24.	9/20	1	Metamorphosis ....*Hilary Duff*	
25.	9/27	1	Heavier Things.. *John Mayer*	
26.	10/4	1	Grand Champ .... *DMX*	
27.	10/11	7↕	Speakerboxxx/The Love Below .... *OutKast* (includes 4 weeks at #1 in 2004)	
28.	10/25	1	Chicken*N*Beer .... *Ludacris*	
29.	11/1	2	Measure Of A Man .... *Clay Aiken*	
30.	11/22	1	Shock'n Y'all .... *Toby Keith*	
31.	11/29	2↕	The Black Album...*Jay-Z*	
32.	12/6	1	In The Zone .... *Britney Spears*	
33.	12/20	2↕	The Diary Of Alicia Keys .... *Alicia Keys* (includes 1 week at #1 in 2004)	
34.	12/27	1	Soulful.. *Ruben Studdard*	

#1 TOP POP CATALOG ALBUMS

	Date Hit #1	Wks @ #1	Title	Artist
1.	1/4	11 ↕	**Now That's What I Call Christmas!** .... *Various Artists* (includes 7 weeks at #1 in 2002)	
2.	1/11	2 ↕	**Christmas Extraordinaire** .... *Mannheim Steamroller* (includes 1 week at #1 in 2004)	
3.	1/18	2 ↕	**Greatest Hits**................................... *Bob Seger & The Silver Bullet Band* (includes 1 week at #1 in 2004)	
4.	1/25	8 ↕	**1** .... *The Beatles* (includes 4 weeks at #1 in 2004)	
5.	2/1	2 ↕	**One Night Only** .... *Bee Gees*	
6.	2/8	1	**O Brother, Where Art Thou?** .... *Movie Soundtrack*	
7.	2/15	8 ↕	**Wide Open Spaces** .... *Dixie Chicks* (includes 1 week at #1 in 2000)	
8.	4/5	2 ↕	**The Marshall Mathers LP**....................................... *Eminem* (includes 1 week at #1 in 2002)	
9.	4/12	1	**Dark Side Of The Moon (SACD)** .... *Pink Floyd*	
10.	5/10	92 ↕	**Legend**.. *Bob Marley* (includes 19 weeks at #1 in 1993, 7 weeks in 1994, 11 weeks in 1995, 27 weeks in 1996, 9 weeks in 1999, and 8 weeks in 2002)	
11.	5/31	40 ↕	**Metallica**... *Metallica* (includes 11 week at #1 in 1998 and 22 weeks in 1999)	
12.	9/20	1	**Parachutes**... *Coldplay*	
13.	9/27	6 ↕	**16 Biggest Hits** .... *Johnny Cash*	
14.	10/25	1	**The Lion King** .... *Movie Soundtrack*	
14.	11/8	1	**Room For Squares**... *John Mayer*	
14.	11/15	1	**Greatest Hits**... *Tim McGraw*	
14.	11/29	1	**Santa Claus Lane**... *Hilary Duff*	
15.	12/27	2	**Christmas Eve And Other Stories**................*Trans-Siberian Orchestra* (includes 1 week at #1 in 2004)	

CHANGES IN HIGHEST POSITION/TOTAL WEEKS DATA

The following albums were listed in our *Top Pop Albums 1955-2001*, our *2001 Music Yearbook* and/or our *2002 Music* Yearbook. They were still charted or returned to the charts in late 2003 and/or early 2004. This list updates these albums' peak position and weeks charted data through the *Billboard's* 4/3/04 *Top Pop Albums* chart.

The superior number next to an album that peaked at #1 or #2 indicates the total number of weeks that album topped the chart.

A '+' symbol next to the weeks indicates that an album was still charted as of the 4/3/04 cut-off date.

POS	WKS	Album Title
AALIYAH		
3	26	I Care 4 U
ADKINS, Trace		
59	20	Chrome
AGUILERA, Christina		
2^1	73+	Stripped
ALLAN, Gary		
39	42	Alright Guy
AMOS, Tori		
7	22	Scarlet's Walk
ASHANTI		
1^3	55	Ashanti
AUDIOSLAVE		
7	70+	Audioslave
BABY		
24	20	Birdman
BECK		
8	26	Sea Change
BEDINGFIELD, Daniel		
41	35	Gotta Get Thru This
BEE GEES		
49	40	Their Greatest Hits – The Record
BENNETT, Tony/lang, k.d.		
41	18	A Wonderful World
BOCELLI, Andrea		
12	20	Sentimento
BOND		
61	6	Shine
BONE THUGS-N-HARMONY		
12	16	Thug World Order
BON JOVI		
2^1	29	Bounce
BOWIE, David		
70	16	Best Of Bowie
BRANCH, Michelle		
28	86	The Spirit Room
B2K		
10	35	Pandemonium!
BUSTA RHYMES		
43	34	It Ain't Safe No More...
CAREY, Mariah		
3	22	Charmbracelet
CARLTON, Vanessa		
5	51	Be Not Nobody
CASH, Johnny		
45	60	American IV: The Man Comes Around
CHESNEY, Kenny		
1^1	100+	No Shoes, No Shirt, No Problems
CHEVELLE		
14	49	Wonder What's Next
CHICAGO		
38	25	The Very Best Of: Only The Beginning
CLIPSE		
4	31	Lord Willin'
COLDPLAY		
5	82+	A Rush Of Blood To The Head
COUNTING CROWS		
5	34	Hard Candy
CREED		
1^8	74	Weathered
CROW, Sheryl		
2^1	61	C'mon, C'mon
DIAMOND RIO		
23	40	Completely
DION, Celine		
1^1	60	A New Day Has Come
DISTURBED		
1^1	53	Believe
DIXIE CHICKS		
1^4	56	Home
DONNAS, The		
62	26	Spend The Night
DRU HILL		
21	26	Dru World Order
ELLIOTT, Missy		
3	35	Under Construction
EMINEM		
1^6	96+	The Eminem Show
FIELD MOB		
33	21	From Tha Roota To Tha Toota
FINCH		
99	21	What It Is To Burn
FLEETWOOD MAC		
12	42	The Very Best Of Fleetwood Mac
FLOETRY		
19	47	Floetic
FOO FIGHTERS		
3	50	One By One
FRANKLIN, Kirk		
4	47	The Rebirth Of Kirk Franklin
GAITHER VOCAL BAND, The		
159	5	Everything Good
GOOD CHARLOTTE		
7	77+	The Young And The Hopeless
GRAY, David		
17	23	A New Day At Midnight
GREEN, Vivian		
51	27	A Love Story
GROBAN, Josh		
8	101	Josh Groban
34	17	Josh Groban In Concert

HEADLEY, Heather
38   44   This Is Who I Am

HILL, Faith
1 [1]   39   Cry

HOUSTON, Whitney
9   24   Just Whitney...

INDIA.ARIE
6   32   Voyage To India

JACKSON, Alan
1 [4]   76   Drive

JACKSON, Michael
85   25   Greatest Hits:
HIStory – Volume 1

JAHEIM
8   41   Still Ghetto

JA RULE
4   26   The Last Temptation

JAY-Z
1 [1]   26   The Blueprint 2: The
Gift And The Curse

JOHN, Elton
12   53+   Greatest Hits
1970-2002

JOHNSON, Jack
34   59   Brushfire Fairytales

JOHNSON, Syleena
104   19   Chapter 2: The Voice

JONES, Norah
1 [4]   108+   Come Away With Me

JUANES
110   21   Un Dia Normal

KEITH, Toby
1 [1]   87+   Unleashed

KIDZ BOP KIDS
76   34   Kidz Bop
37   35   Kidz Bop 2

KRALL, Diana
18   30   Live In Paris

KRAUSS, Alison, + Union Station
36   52+   Live

KWELI, Talib
21   29   Quality

lang, k.d. — see BENNETT, Tony

LAVIGNE, Avril
2 [2]   90   Let Go

LED ZEPPELIN
116   38+   Early Days & Latter
Days: The Best Of
Led Zeppelin Vol.
One And Two

LIL JON & THE EAST SIDE BOYZ
15   73+   Kings Of Crunk

LINKIN PARK
2 [1]   33   Reanimation

LL COOL J
2 [1]   29   10

LOPEZ, Jennifer
2 [1]   40   This Is Me...Then

MATCHBOX TWENTY
6   70+   More Than You Think
You Are

MATTHEWS, Dave, Band
1 [1]   37   Busted Stuff

MAYER, John
8   95   Room For Squares

McBRIDE, Martina
5   104   Greatest Hits

McGRAW, Tim
2 [2]   69+   Tim McGraw And The
Dancehall Doctors

MERCYME
37   96   Almost There
41   29   Spoken For

MONTGOMERY GENTRY
26   68+   My Town

MUDVAYNE
17   41   The End Of All
Things To Come

NAS
12   28   God's Son

NELLY
1 [4]   71   Nellyville

NEW FOUND GLORY
4   39   Sticks And Stones

NICKELBACK
2 [1]   80   Silver Side Up

NICHOLS, Joe
72   52   Man With A Memory

NIRVANA
3   28   Nirvana

NIVEA
80   18   Nivea

NO DOUBT
9   76   Rock Steady

NORDEMAN, Nichole
136   8   Woven & Spun

PAUL, Sean
9   71+   Dutty Rock

P!NK
6   90   M!ssundaztood

PRESLEY, Elvis
1 [3]   73+   Elv1s: 30 #1 Hits

PUDDLE OF MUDD
9   88   Come Clean

QUEENS OF THE STONE AGE
17   50   Songs For The Deaf

RASCAL FLATTS
5   73+   Melt

RED HOT CHILI PEPPERS
2 [1]   60   By The Way

ROLLING STONES, The
2 [1]   47   Forty Licks

ROOTS, The
28   38   Phrenology

SALIVA
19   29   Back Into Your System

SANTANA
1 [1]   56   Shaman

SEETHER
92   41   Disclaimer

SIMPLE PLAN
36   68+   No Pads, No
Helmets...Just Balls

SINATRA, Frank
22 [C]   57+   Classic Sinatra:
His Greatest
Performances
1953-1960

SMILEZ & SOUTHSTAR
91   15   Crash The Party

SMITH, Michael W.
20   83   Worship
14   34   Worship Again

SNOOP DOGG
12   36   Paid Tha Cost To Be
Da Bo$$

SPRINGSTEEN, Bruce
1 [2]   37   The Rising

STARTING LINE, The
109   5   Say It Like You
Mean It

STEWART, Rod
40   49   The Very Best Of
Rod Stewart
4   74+   It Had To Be You...
The Great American
Songbook

SUM 41
32   27   Does This Look
Infected?

SYSTEM OF A DOWN
1 [1]   91   Toxicity
15   22   Steal This Album!

POS	WKS	Album Title	POS	WKS	Album Title	POS	WKS	Album Title

THEORY OF A DEADMAN
85   6   Theory Of A Deadman

3 DOORS DOWN
8   71 +   Away From The Sun

TIMBERLAKE, Justin
2 [1]   72 +   Justified

TLC
6   20   3D

TRAVIS, Randy
73   23   Rise And Shine

TRINA
14   24   Diamond Princess

TWAIN, Shania
1 [5]   70 +   Up!

2PAC
5   25   Better Dayz

UNCLE KRACKER
43   41   No Stranger To
Shame

URBAN, Keith
11   76 +   Golden Road

USED, The
63   34   The Used

WHITE STRIPES, The
61   52   White Blood Cells

WONDER, Stevie
35   23   The Definitive
Collection

MOVIE SOUNDTRACKS
1 [4]   43   8 Mile
11   40   Lilo & Stitch
43   18   Lord Of The Rings:
The Two Towers,
The
3   80   Moulin Rouge
46   22   Sweet Home Alabama
34   47   Walk To Remember, A

TELEVISION SOUNDTRACK
31   54   Lizzie McGuire

VARIOUS ARTIST COMPILATIONS
52   36   Disneymania:
Superstar Artists
Sing Disney...Their
Way!
60   37   iWorship: A Total
Worship Experience
2 [1]   25   Now 11
122   13   Radio Disney Jams
Vol. 5
34   30   WOW Hits 2003

COUNTRY ALBUMS

This section lists, by artist, every album that debuted in 2003 on *Billboard's* weekly **Top Country Albums** chart (a top 75 listing).

DEBUT DATE	PEAK POS	WKS CHR	G L D	ARTIST / Title	Label & Number
				ADKINS, Trace	
7/26/03	❶[1]	37↑	●	Greatest Hits Collection, Volume I [G]	Capitol 81512
12/20/03	3	16↑	●	Comin' On Strong	Capitol 40517
				ALABAMA	
2/8/03	4	33		In The Mood: Love Songs [K]	RCA 67052 [2]
10/25/03	6	24↑		The American Farewell Tour [K]	RCA 54371
				ALLAN, Gary	
10/18/03	2[1]	25↑	●	See If I Care	MCA Nashville 000111
				ANDREWS, Jessica	
5/3/03	4	24		Now	DreamWorks 450356
				ATKINS, Rodney ★	
				Born on 3/28/69 in Knoxville, Tennessee. Singer/songwriter.	
11/1/03	50	9		Honesty	Curb 78745
				AUSTIN, Sherrié	
8/30/03	22	22		Streets Of Heaven	Broken Bow 75872
				BATES, Jeff ★	
6/7/03	14	13		Rainbow Man	RCA 67071
				BENTLEY, Dierks ★	
9/6/03	4	31↑	●	Dierks Bentley	Capitol 39814
				BERING STRAIT ★	
2/22/03	17	22		Bering Strait	Universal South 170218
				BLACK, Clint	
2/8/03	53	11		Super Hits [G]	RCA 67075
10/11/03	39	9↑		Ultimate Clint Black [G]	RCA 52551
				BOGGUSS, Suzy	
7/19/03	66	2		Swing	Compadre 925151
				BROOKS & DUNN	
8/2/03	❶[1]	36↑	●	Red Dirt Road	Arista Nashville 67070
				BYRD, Tracy	
7/19/03	5	38↑		The Truth About Men	RCA 67073
				CAGLE, Chris	
4/19/03	❶[1]	51↑	●	Chris Cagle	Capitol 40516
				CAMPBELL, Glen	
2/15/03	12	15		All The Best [G]	Capitol 41816
				CARPENTER, Mary-Chapin	
11/22/03	70	2		The Essential Mary Chapin Carpenter [G]	Legacy 90772
				CARRINGTON, Rodney	
3/1/03	14	50		Nut Sack [C]	Capitol 36579
				CARTER, Deana	
4/5/03	6	19		I'm Just A Girl	Arista Nashville 67054
				CARTER, June ★	
				Born Valerie June Carter on 6/23/29 in Maces Springs, Virginia. Died of heart failure on 5/15/2003 (age 73). Member of the legendary Carter Family. Married to Carl Smith from 1952-56; their daughter is Carlene Carter. Married Johnny Cash on 3/1/68.	
9/27/03	33	7		Wildwood Flower JUNE CARTER CASH	Dualtone 01142
				CASH, Johnny	
9/27/03	47	4		The Best Of Johnny Cash: 20th Century Masters The Millennium Collection [G]	Mercury 170217
9/27/03	49	2		The Heart Of A Legend [K]	Madacy 6494
9/27/03	66	2		The Legend Of Johnny Cash: First Original Hits [K]	K-Tel 3515
9/27/03	71	1		Johnny Cash Sings His Best: 40 Original Hits [G]	TeeVee 7430
12/13/03	33	12		Cash Unearthed [K]	American 001679
12/13/03	58	4		Christmas With Johnny Cash [X]	Legacy 90701
				CASH, Rosanne	
4/12/03	16	17		Rules Of Travel	Capitol 37757

COUNTRY ALBUMS

DEBUT DATE	PEAK POS	WKS CHR	G L D	ARTIST Title	Label & Number
				CHESNEY, Kenny	
10/25/03	4	13	●	All I Want For Christmas Is A Real Good Tan .... [X]	BNA 51808
				CHIEFTAINS, The	
9/27/03	28	8		Further Down The Old Plank Road....................................	Victor 52897
				CLARK, Terri	
1/25/03	5	52↑		Pain To Kill	Mercury 170325
				COE, David Allan	
5/17/03	71	1		Live At Billy Bob's Texas .... [L]	Image 5017
				COUNTDOWN SINGERS, The ★	
				Studio group from Canada.	
3/22/03	58	9		Today's Country...	Madacy 6816 [2]
				CREAGER, Roger ★	
				Born in Houston, Texas. Singer/songwriter/guitarist.	
9/27/03	63	2		Long Way To Mexico	Dualtone 01148
				CROSS CANADIAN RAGWEED ★	
				Group from Stillwater, Oklahoma: Cody Canada (vocals, guitar), Grady Cross (guitar), Jeremy Plato (bass) and Randy Ragsdale (drums).	
2/8/03	70	3		Cross Canadian Ragweed	Universal South 064414
				CROWELL, Rodney	
9/13/03	29	16		Fate's Right Hand	DMZ/Epic 89082
				CURRINGTON, Billy ★	
10/18/03	17	20↑		Billy Currington	Mercury 000164
				CYRUS, Billy Ray	
5/10/03	59	10		The Best Of Billy Ray Cyrus: 20th Century Masters The Millennium Collection .... [G]	Mercury 170165
7/5/03	56	7		Time Flies	SMCMG 4114
11/15/03	18	20↑		The Other Side	Word-Curb 886274
				DANIELS, Charlie, Band	
8/9/03	55	6		Freedom And Justice For All	Blue Hat 8188
				DENVER, John	
2/15/03	75	1		Songs For America... [K]	BMG 47533
				DERAILERS, The	
4/12/03	44	5		Genuine..	Lucky Dog 86873
				DIXIE CHICKS	
12/6/03	3	18↑	●	Top Of The World Tour Live .... [L]	Monument 90794 [2]
				DODD, Deryl	
8/30/03	61	1		Live At Billy Bob's Texas .... [L]	Smith Music Group 5021
				DRAKE, Dusty ★	
				Born in Monaca, Pennsylvania. Singer/songwriter/guitarist.	
6/21/03	30	8		Dusty Drake	Warner 48051
				EARLE, Steve	
10/11/03	43	3		Just An American Boy: The Audio Documentary	E-Squared 51256
				ELY, Joe	
8/2/03	51	2		Streets Of Sin	Rounder 613181
				ENGVALL, Bill	
11/29/03	37	19↑		Here's Your Sign: Reloaded .... [C]	Warner 48534
				EVANS, Sara	
9/6/03	3	31↑		Restless	RCA 67074
				FOXWORTHY, Jeff	
9/20/03	10	29↑		The Best Of Jeff Foxworthy: Double Wide, Single Minded .... [C-K]	Warner 73903

DEBUT DATE	PEAK POS	WKS CHR	G L D	ARTIST Title	Label & Number
				GILL, Vince	
3/1/03	4	34		Next Big Thing	MCA Nashville 170286
				GILMAN, Billy	
5/3/03	15	15		Music Through Heartsongs: Songs Based On The Poems Of Mattie J.T. Stepanek	Epic 86954
				GREEN, Pat	
8/2/03	2[1]	36↑	●	Wave On Wave	Republic 000562
				GRIFFITH, Andy ★	
				Born on 6/1/26 in Mount Airy, North Carolina. Actor/comedian. Starred in several movies and Broadway shows. Star of TV's *The Andy Griffith Show* and *Matlock*.	
11/22/03	21	4		The Christmas Guest: Stories And Songs Of Christmas	[X] Sparrow 51815
				produced by Marty Stuart	
				HAGGARD, Merle	
10/18/03	40	5		Haggard Like Never Before	Hag 0005
				HANSON, Jennifer ★	
3/8/03	20	10		Jennifer Hanson	Capitol 35247
				HARRIS, Emmylou	
10/11/03	6	26↑		Stumble Into Grace	Nonesuch 79805
				HAYSEED DIXIE	
3/8/03	52	3		Kiss My Grass: A Hillbilly Tribute To Kiss	Dualtone 01136
				IVES, Burl ★	
				Born on 6/14/09 in Huntington Township, Illinois. Died of cancer on 4/14/95 (age 85). Actor/author/folk singer. Starred in several movies and narrated the animated TV classic *Rudolph The Red-Nosed Reindeer*.	
12/20/03	64	2		The Best Of Burl Ives: 20th Century Masters The Christmas Collection	[X] MCA Nashville 000519
				JACKSON, Alan	
8/23/03	❶[11]	33↑	▲[3]	Greatest Hits Volume II and Some Other Stuff	[G] Arista Nashville 53097 [2]
				JENNINGS, Waylon	
6/7/03	64	1		Waylon Live: The Expanded Edition	[L] RCA 51855 [2]
				JEWELL, Buddy	
7/19/03	❶[1]	38↑	●	Buddy Jewell	Columbia 90131
				JONES, George	
4/19/03	19	26		The Gospel Collection: George Jones Sings The Greatest Stories Ever Told	Bandit 67063 [2]
				JUDD, Cledus T.	
5/17/03	19	10		A Six Pack Of Judd	[M-N] Monument 89223
11/29/03	62	2		The Original Dixie Hick	[M-N] Audium 8194
				KEEN, Robert Earl	
10/25/03	24	4		Farm Fresh Onions	Audium 8191
11/1/03	68	3		The Party Never Ends: Songs You Know From The Times You Can't Remember	[K] Sugar Hill 1080
				KEITH, Toby	
5/3/03	5	49↑		The Best Of Toby Keith: 20th Century Masters The Millennium Collection	[G] Mercury 170351
11/22/03	❶[13]	20↑	▲[3]	Shock'n Y'all	DreamWorks 450435
				KERSHAW, Sammy	
4/12/03	39	5		I Want My Money Back	Audium 8167
				KNIGHT, Chris ★	
				Born in Slaughters, Kentucky. Singer/songwriter/guitarist.	
10/11/03	67	1		The Jealous Kind	Dualtone 01139
				LANE, Cristy	
7/12/03	62	13		One Day At A Time: 22 All Time Favorites Vol. I & II	[G] LS 11980 [2]

DEBUT DATE	PEAK POS	WKS CHR	G L D	ARTIST Title	Label & Number
				LARRY THE CABLE GUY ★	
				Born in Pawnee City, Nebraska. Stand-up comedian.	
6/21/03	53	21		Lord, I Apologize .... [C]	Ark 21 810076
				LeDOUX, Chris	
8/9/03	24	13		Horsepower	Capitol 81580
				LINES, Aaron ★	
1/25/03	9	19		Living Out Loud	RCA 67057
				LONESTAR	
6/21/03	❶²	42↑	▲	From There To Here: Greatest Hits [G]	BNA 67076
				LOVELESS, Patty	
10/4/03	7	21		On Your Way Home	Epic 86620
				LOVETT, Lyle	
10/18/03	7	25↑		My Baby Don't Tolerate	Curb 001162
				MARCEL ★	
				Born Marcel Chagnon in Grosse Pointe, Michigan. Singer/songwriter/guitarist.	
5/31/03	48	4		You, Me And The Windshield...............................	Mercury 170303
				MARSHALL, Mike, & Chris Thile ★	
				Bluegrass mandolin duo: Mike Marhsall (from Florida) and Chris Thile (from California; member of Nickel Creek).	
5/31/03	71	1		Into The Cauldron .... [I]	Sugar Hill 3967
				MATTEA, Kathy	
12/27/03	69	1		Joy For Christmas Day .... [X]	Narada 90506
				MAVERICKS, The	
10/11/03	32	7		The Mavericks	Sanctuary 84612
				McBRIDE, Martina	
10/18/03	❶¹	25↑	▲	Martina	RCA 54207
				McCLINTON, Delbert	
11/8/03	44	5		Delbert McClinton Live .... [L]	New West 6048
				McCOMAS, Brian ★	
8/9/03	21	11↑		Brian McComas	Lyric Street 165025
				McCOURY, Del, Band	
8/30/03	47	5		It's Just The Night	McCoury Music 0001
				McENTIRE, Reba	
12/6/03	4	18↑	●	Room To Breathe	MCA Nashville 000451
12/6/03	67	4		The Best Of Reba: 20th Century Masters The Christmas Collection .... [X]	MCA Nashville 000648
				MERCER, Roy D.	
6/28/03	31	14		Roy D. Mercer Hits The Road .... [C]	Capitol 38088
				MESSINA, Jo Dee	
6/7/03	❶¹	44↑		Greatest Hits [G]	Curb 78790
				MONTGOMERY, John Michael	
9/13/03	11	29↑		The Very Best Of John Michael Montgomery .... [G]	Warner 73918
				MOORER, Allison	
7/12/03	49	3		Show	Universal South 000097
				MORGAN, Craig	
3/29/03	16	41		I Love It	Broken Bow 75672
				MORROW, Cory	
8/9/03	40	4		Full Exposure	Write On 6000
				NELSON, Willie	
3/1/03	32	16		Crazy: The Demo Sessions .... [K]	Sugar Hill 1073
4/19/03	24	50↑		The Essential Willie Nelson........................... [G]	Legacy 86740 [2]
7/12/03	4	27		Live And Kickin' [L]	Lost Highway 000453
				WILLIE NELSON & FRIENDS	
7/19/03	62	2		Run That By Me One More Time	Lost Highway 000616
				WILLIE NELSON and RAY PRICE	

DEBUT DATE	PEAK POS	WKS CHR	G L D	ARTIST / Title	Label & Number
6/7/03	53	8		**OAK RIDGE BOYS**	
				Colors..	Spring Hill 21042
				O'BRIEN, Tim ★	
				Born on 3/16/54 in Wheeling, West Virginia. Bluegrass singer/songwriter/guitarist.	
8/30/03	74	1		Traveler	Howdy Skies 3978
				PAISLEY, Brad	
8/9/03	❶²	35↑	●	Mud On The Tires	Arista Nashville 50605
				PARTON, Dolly	
6/21/03	20	31↑		Ultimate Dolly Parton .... [G]	RCA 52008
7/12/03	74	1		Ultimate Dolly Parton .... [G]	RCA 50389 [2]
11/29/03	23	7		For God And Country	Blue Eye 79756
				PRESLEY, Elvis	
7/19/03	41	3		Elvis: Close Up .... [K]	RCA 50537
11/22/03	30	8		Elvis: Christmas Peace .... [X-K]	RCA 52393 [2]
				PRICE, Ray — see NELSON, Willie	
				PRIDE, Charley	
7/5/03	64	8		22 All-Time Greatest Hits............................. [G]	TeeVee 0708
				RECKLESS KELLY ★	
				Alternative group from Bend, Oregon: brothers Willy Braun (vocals, guitar) and Cody Braun (vocals, fiddle), with David Abeyta (guitar), Jimmy McFeeley (bass) and Jay Nazz (drums).	
5/31/03	67	1		Under The Table & Above The Sun	Sugar Hill 3968
				RIMES, LeAnn	
12/6/03	3	18↑	●	Greatest Hits [G]	Curb 78829
				ROBISON, Charlie	
5/24/03	51	4		Live... [L]	Columbia 86787
				ROGERS, Kenny	
10/11/03	52	3		Back To The Well	DreamCatcher 008
				SCRUGGS, Earl	
8/2/03	24	16		The Three Pickers	Rounder 610526
				EARL SCRUGGS / DOC WATSON / RICKY SKAGGS	
				SHELTON, Blake	
2/22/03	2¹	45		The Dreamer	Warner 48237
				SKAGGS, Ricky	
4/12/03	32	19		Live At The Charleston Music Hall .... [L]	Skaggs Family 901004
				RICKY SKAGGS & KENTUCKY THUNDER	
8/2/03	24	16		The Three Pickers	Rounder 610526
				EARL SCRUGGS / DOC WATSON / RICKY SKAGGS	
				STRAIT, George	
3/1/03	2¹	55↑	●	For The Last Time: Live From The Astrodome [L]	MCA Nashville 170319
6/28/03	❶²	41↑	●	Honkytonkville	MCA Nashville 000114
11/29/03	60	5		The Best Of George Strait: 20th Century Masters The Christmas Collection........................... [X]	MCA Nashville 000912
				STUART, Marty	
7/19/03	40	8		Country Music	Columbia 87063
				MARTY STUART And His Fabulous Superlatives	
				TRAVIS, Randy	
11/29/03	9	19↑		Worship & Faith	Word-Curb 86273
				TREVINO, Rick	
9/27/03	58	2		In My Dreams...	Warner 48484
				TURNER, Josh ★	
11/1/03+	4	23↑	●	Long Black Train	MCA Nashville 000974
				VINCENT, Rhonda	
5/17/03	30	18		One Step Ahead	Rounder 610497

COUNTRY ALBUMS

DEBUT DATE	PEAK POS	WKS CHR	G L D	ARTIST / Title	Label & Number
				WALKER, Clay	
9/27/03	3	23↑		A Few Questions	RCA 67068
				WARINER, Steve	
2/22/03	31	5		Steal Another Day	Selectone 11955
				WATSON, Doc — see SCRUGGS, Earl	
				WAYNE, Jimmy ★	
7/12/03	7	39↑		Jimmy Wayne	DreamWorks 450355
				WILLIAMS, Hank Jr.	
12/6/03	24	15		I'm One Of You	Curb 78830
				WILLS, Mark	
11/8/03	5	15		And The Crowd Goes Wild	Mercury 001012
				WILSON, Tim	
6/7/03	57	4		Super Bad Sounds Of The '70s .... [N]	Capitol 37886
				WORLEY, Darryl	
5/3/03	❶⁴	42	●	Have You Forgotten?	DreamWorks 000064
				WYNONNA	
8/23/03	❶¹	33↑		What The World Needs Now Is Love	Curb 78811
				YOAKAM, Dwight	
7/12/03	8	19		Population: Me	Audium 8176
10/11/03	59	3		In Other's Words	Reprise 48342
				YONDER MOUNTAIN STRING BAND & BENNY GALLOWAY ★	
				Bluegrass group from Nederland, Colorado: Dave Johnston (banjo), Jeff Austin (mandolin), Adam Aijala (guitar) and Ben Kauffman (bass). Benny Galloway is a solo singer/songwriter/guitarist.	
7/5/03	54	1		Old Hands	Frog Pad 0103

MOVIE SOUNDTRACKS

DEBUT DATE	PEAK POS	WKS CHR	G L D	Title	Label & Number
4/12/03+	16	49↑		Blue Collar Comedy Tour: The Movie .... [L]	Warner 48424
				Jeff Foxworthy/Bill Engvall/Larry The Cable Guy/Ron White	
4/5/03	63	2		View From The Top .... [V]	Curb 78763
				Gwyneth Paltrow/Christina Applegate/Mark Ruffalo/Candice Bergen/Kelly Preston	

TELEVISION SOUNDTRACK

DEBUT DATE	PEAK POS	WKS CHR	G L D	Title	Label & Number
4/12/03	25	13		Nashville Star: The Finalists .... [L-V]	Columbia 87169
				contains performances by such contestants as Jamey Garner/Brandi Gibson/Buddy Jewell	

CHRISTMAS (Various Artists)

DEBUT DATE	PEAK POS	WKS CHR	G L D	Title	Label & Number
11/22/03	20	8		Classic Country: Christmas	Time-Life 18927
				songs by Alabama, Johnny Cash, Vince Gill, Buck Owens, Elvis Presley, and others	
11/15/03	24	9		Very Special Acoustic Christmas, A	Lost Highway 001038
				songs by Alan Jackson, Alison Krauss, Reba McEntire, Willie Nelson, Marty Stuart, and others	

DEBUT DATE	PEAK POS	WKS CHR	G L D	ARTIST Title	Label & Number
				VARIOUS ARTIST COMPILATIONS	
6/28/03	57	3↑		**Best Of Bluegrass Gospel** .... Madacy Christian 3241 [3]	
				songs by Richard Bailey, Jesse Campbell, Charlie Chadwick, Steve Ivey, and others	
2/15/03	63	7		**Best Of Country** .... Madacy 1424 [3]	
				songs by Lynn Anderson, Dave Dudley, Donna Fargo, Nat Stuckey, Faron Young, and others	
7/12/03	48	11		**Bluegrass Today** .... Warner 18890	
				songs by Steve Earle, Vince Gill, Patty Loveless, Nickel Creek, Rhonda Vincent, and others	
11/15/03+	55	8		**Classic Country: Queens Of Country** .... Time-Life 18949	
				songs by Patsy Cline, Loretta Lynn, Tanya Tucker, Kitty Wells, Dottie West, and others	
5/24/03	72	3		**Classic Country: Road Songs** .... Time-Life 18900	
				songs by John Anderson, Alan Jackson, Waylon Jennings, Ronnie Milsap, Don Williams, and others	
8/16/03	45	11		**Classic Country: The '80s** .... Warner 18905	
				songs by Alabama, Merle Haggard, George Jones, Willie Nelson, Jerry Reed, and others	
10/18/03	11	25↑		**CMT Most Wanted Volume 1** .... Capitol 93166	
				songs by Trace Adkins, Chris Cagle, Joe Nichols, Rascal Flatts, Keith Urban, and others	
5/24/03	56	8		**Country Gospel** .... Madacy Christian 1423 [3]	
				songs by Wilma Burgess, Ferlin Huskey, Mac Wiseman, and others	
11/22/03+	37	20↑		**Gospel Bluegrass Homecoming Volume One, A** .... [L] Gaither Music 42459	
				songs by Gaither Vocal Band, Marty Raybon, Ricky Skaggs, Marty Stuart, and others	
11/22/03+	42	14		**Gospel Bluegrass Homecoming Volume Two, A** .... [L] Gaither Music 42460	
				songs by Gaither Vocal Band, Ralph Stanley, Marty Stuart, Vestal Goodman, and others	
3/1/03	46	1		**Heart Full Of Country** .... Capitol 43305	
				songs by Freddie Hart, Jean Shepard, Wynn Stewart, Gene Watson, Slim Whitman, and others	
8/23/03	66	5		**Heaven Bound: The Best Of Bluegrass Gospel** .... Time Life 18940	
				songs by Flatt & Scruggs, Emmylou Harris, Bill Monroe, Osborne Brothers, Ralph Stanley, and others	
9/6/03	19	10		**I've Always Been Crazy: A Tribute To Waylon Jennings** .. RCA 67064	
				songs by Brooks & Dunn, Jessi Colter, Andy Griggs, John Mellencamp, Travis Tritt, and others	
5/31/03	37	6		**It'll Come To You...The Songs Of John Hiatt** .... Vanguard 79735	
				songs by Rosanne Cash, Rodney Crowell, Freddy Fender, Patty Griffin, Linda Ronstadt, and others	
11/1/03	6	23↑		**Just Because I'm A Woman: Songs Of Dolly Parton**	Sugar Hill 3980
				songs by Kasey Chambers, Melissa Etheridge, Emmylou Harris, Shania Twain, and others	
12/6/03+	44	17↑		**Livin', Lovin', Losin' - Songs Of The Louvin Brothers**....... Universal South 000458	
				songs by Terri Clark, Vince Gill, Joe Nichols, Dolly Parton, Pam Tillis, and others	
5/3/03	47	6		**Lonesome, On'ry And Mean: A Tribute To Waylon Jennings** .... Dualtone 01137	
				songs by Dave Alvin, Junior Brown, Carlene Carter, Guy Clark, Allison Moorer, and others	
4/19/03	51	9		**O Mickey, Where Art Thou?: The Voices Of Bluegrass Sing The Best of Disney**................................. Walt Disney 860083	
				songs by Sonya Isaacs, Stonewall Jackson, Charlie Louvin, Ronnie Milsap, Collin Raye, and others	
3/15/03	37	16		**Pure Country Classics: The #1 Hits** .... UTV 064091	
				songs by Eddy Arnold, Jimmy Dean, Sonny James, Loretta Lynn, Hank Williams, and others	
9/27/03	8	16		**Remembering Patsy Cline**	MCA 170297
				songs by Terri Clark, Natalie Cole, Amy Grant, Martina McBride, Lee Ann Womack, and others	
3/1/03	37	5		**Songs Of Hank Williams Jr.: A Bochepus Celebration, The** . Curb/Warner 48233	
				songs by Chad Brock, Andy Griggs, Montgomery Gentry, Blake Shelton, Trick Pony, and others	
1/25/03	45	11		**Time-Life Treasury Of Bluegrass: America's Music, The**.. Time-Life 18861 [2]	
				songs by Jim & Jesse, Bill Monroe, Reno & Smiley, Stonemans, Mac Wiseman, and others	
10/11/03	2¹	26↑		**Totally Country Vol. 3**	Warner 73955
				songs by Diamond Rio, Faith Hill, Jo Dee Messina, Blake Shelton, Phil Vassar, and others	

1. TOBY KEITH
410

2. SHANIA TWAIN
366

3. DIXIE CHICKS
257

4.	198	KENNY CHESNEY		13.	63	BROOKS & DUNN
5.	180	ALAN JACKSON		14.	62	FAITH HILL
6.	178	TIM MCGRAW		15.	56	ELVIS PRESLEY
7.	124	JOHNNY CASH		16.	33	GARY ALLAN
8.	121	MARTINA MCBRIDE		17.	32	JO DEE MESSINA
9.	112	LONESTAR		18.	31	TRACE ADKINS
10.	99	GEORGE STRAIT		19.	29	BRAD PAISLEY
11.	96	RASCAL FLATTS		20.	28	BLAKE SHELTON
12.	79	DARRYL WORLEY				

TOP 30 COUNTRY ALBUMS

PEAK DATE	CH	40	10	PK	RANK	RECORD TITLE / PEAK POSITION	ARTIST
					1		
11/22	20 +	20 +	20 +	13	1.	Shock'n Y'all	Toby Keith
8/30	33 +	32 +	25	11	2.	Greatest Hits Volume II and Some Other Stuff	Alan Jackson
5/3	42	24	10	4	3.	Have You Forgotten?	Darryl Worley
6/21	42 +	42 +	20	2	4.	From There To Here: Greatest Hits	Lonestar
6/28	41 +	41 +	7	2	5.	Honkytonkville	George Strait
8/9	35 +	35 +	4	2	6.	Mud On The Tires	Brad Paisley
10/18	25 +	25 +	25 +	1	7.	Martina	Martina McBride
8/2	36 +	36 +	13	1	8.	Red Dirt Road	Brooks & Dunn
7/26	37 +	37 +	5	1	9.	Greatest Hits Collection, Volume I	Trace Adkins
6/7	44 +	34	5	1	10.	Greatest Hits	Jo Dee Messina
4/19	51 +	51 +	4	1	11.	Chris Cagle	Chris Cagle
7/19	38 +	38 +	3	1	12.	Buddy Jewell	Buddy Jewell
8/23	33 +	12	2	1	13.	What The World Needs Now Is Love	Wynonna
					2		
9/27	72 +	72 +	24	2	14.	American IV: The Man Comes Around	Johnny Cash
10/18	25 +	25 +	10 +	1	15.	See If I Care	Gary Allan
3/1	55 +	29	9	1	16.	For The Last Time: Live From The Astrodome	George Strait
2/22	45	24	6	1	17.	The Dreamer	Blake Shelton
10/11	26 +	16	5	1	18.	Totally Country Vol. 3	Various Artists
8/2	36 +	31	4	1	19.	Wave On Wave	Pat Green
					3		
12/13	18 +	18 +	10	2	20.	Top Of The World Tour Live	Dixie Chicks
12/6	18 +	18 +	9	1	21.	Greatest Hits	LeAnn Rimes
12/20	16 +	16 +	6	1	22.	Comin' On Strong	Trace Adkins
9/6	31 +	28 +	2	1	23.	Restless	Sara Evans
9/27	23 +	6	1	1	24.	A Few Questions	Clay Walker
					4		
5/3	24	16	3	2	25.	Now	Jessica Andrews
12/13	13	12	7	1	26.	All I Want For Christmas Is A Real Good Tan	Kenny Chesney
9/6	31 +	31 +	4	1	27.	Dierks Bentley	Dierks Bentley
12/6	18 +	18 +	3	1	28.	Room To Breathe	Reba
7/12	27	12	3	1	29.	Live And Kickin'	Willie Nelson & Friends
2/22	33	21	2	1	30.	In The Mood: Love Songs	Alabama

#1 COUNTRY ALBUMS

	Date Hit #1	Wks @ #1	Title	Artist
1.	1/4	6	Up! .... Shania Twain (includes 4 weeks at #1 in 2002)	
2.	1/25	19↕	Home .... Dixie Chicks (includes 5 weeks at #1 in 2002)	
3.	4/19	1	Chris Cagle .... Chris Cagle	
4.	5/3	4	Have You Forgotten? .... Darryl Worley	
5.	5/31	7↕	Unleashed .... Toby Keith (includes 5 weeks at #1 in 2002)	
6.	6/7	1	Greatest Hits .... Jo Dee Messina	
7.	6/21	2↕	From There To Here: Greatest Hits .... Lonestar	
8.	6/28	2	Honkytonkville .... George Strait	
9.	7/19	1	Buddy Jewell .... Buddy Jewell	
10.	7/26	1	Greatest Hits Collection, Volume I .... Trace Adkins	
11.	8/2	1	Red Dirt Road .... Brooks & Dunn	
12.	8/9	2	Mud On The Tires .... Brad Paisley	
13.	8/23	1	What The World Needs Now Is Love .... Wynonna	
14.	8/30	11↕	Greatest Hits Volume II And Some Other Stuff .... Alan Jackson	
15.	10/18	1	Martina .... Martina McBride	
16.	11/22	13	Shock'n Y'all .... Toby Keith (includes 7 weeks at #1 in 2004)	

#1 COUNTRY CATALOG ALBUMS

	Date Hit #1	Wks @ #1	Title	Artist
1.	1/4	10↕	O Brother, Where Art Thou? .... Movie Soundtrack (includes 2 weeks at #1 in 2002)	
2.	2/15	51↕	Wide Open Spaces .... Dixie Chicks (includes 14 weeks at #1 in 2000, 21 weeks at #1 in 2001 and 8 weeks at #1 in 2002)	
3.	4/19	14↕	Greatest Hits .... Tim McGraw (includes 1 week at #1 in 2002 and 5 weeks at #1 in 2004)	
4.	5/3	13↕	Greatest Hits .... Kenny Chesney (includes 2 weeks at #1 in 2004)	
5.	5/24	16↕	Rascal Flatts .... Rascal Flatts (includes 13 weeks at #1 in 2002)	
6.	9/6	24↕	Come On Over .... Shania Twain (includes 2 weeks at #1 in 2000, 17 weeks at #1 in 2001, and 4 weeks at #1 in 2002)	
7.	9/27	10↕	16 Biggest Hits .... Johnny Cash	
8.	12/13	4	Let It Be Christmas .... Alan Jackson (includes 1 week at #1 in 2004)	

TOP COUNTRY ALBUMS
CHANGES IN HIGHEST POSITION/TOTAL WEEKS DATA

The following albums were listed in our *Top Country Albums 1964-1997,* our *1997 Music Yearbook,* our *1998 Music Yearbook,* our *1999 Music Yearbook,* our *2000 Music Yearbook,* our *2001 Music Yearbook* and/or our *2002 Music Yearbook.* They were still charted or returned to the charts in 2003 and/or early 2004. This list updates these albums' peak position and weeks charted data through *Billboard's* 4/3/04 *Top Country Albums* chart.

The superior number next to an album that peaked at #1 or #2 indicates the total number of weeks that album topped the chart.

A '+' symbol next to the weeks indicates that an album was still charted as of the 4/3/04 cut-off date.

POS	WKS	Album Title
ADKINS, Trace		
4	93	Chrome
ALLAN, Gary		
4	104	Alright Guy
BLACK, Clint		
8	51	Greatest Hits II
BROOKS, Garth		
1^7	84	Scarecrow
BROOKS & DUNN		
1^1	104	Steers & Stripes
BYRD, Tracy		
12	85	Ten Rounds
CASH, Johnny		
16	62	The Essential Johnny Cash
39	8	Johnny Cash At Madison Square Garden
2^2	72+	American IV: The Man Comes Around
CHESNEY, Kenny		
1^{11}	100+	No Shoes, No Shirt, No Problems
CHIEFTAINS, The		
21	29	Down The Old Plank Road/The Nashville Sessions
COFFEY, Kellie		
5	55	When You Lie Next To Me

POS	WKS	Album Title
DANIELS, Charlie, Band		
40	21	How Sweet The Sound: 25 Favorite Hymns And Gospel Greats
DIAMOND RIO		
3	79+	Completely
DIXIE CHICKS		
1^{16}	82+	Home
EARLE, Steve		
7	24	Jerusalem
EMERSON DRIVE		
13	70	Emerson Drive
ENGVALL, Bill		
37	28	Cheap Drunk: An Autobiography
GREEN, Pat		
7	68	Three Days
HILL, Faith		
1^3	63	Cry
HOWARD, Rebecca Lynn		
5	27	Forgive
JACKSON, Alan		
1^6	103	Drive
JENNINGS, Waylon		
19	55	RCA Country Legends: Waylon Jennings
JUDD, Cledus T.		
19	42	Cledus Envy

POS	WKS	Album Title
KEITH, Toby		
1^1	104	Pull My Chain
1^7	87+	Unleashed
KRAUSS, Alison/Union Station		
3	104	New Favorite
9	72+	Live
LONESTAR		
1^1	103	I'm Already There
McBRIDE, Martina		
1^3	104	Greatest Hits
McCLINTON, Delbert		
12	27	Room To Breathe
McENTIRE, Reba		
1^1	79	Greatest Hits Volume III – I'm A Survivor
McGRAW, Tim		
1^6	104	Set This Circus Down
2^2	69+	Tim McGraw And The Dancehall Doctors
MONTGOMERY GENTRY		
6	87	Carrying On
3	82+	My Town
MURRAY, Anne		
13	36	Country Croonin'
NELSON, Willie		
5	64	The Great Divide
18	39	Stars & Guitars
NICHOLS, Joe		
9	87+	Man Wirh A Memory
NICKEL CREEK		
2^1	84+	This Side

POS	WKS	Album Title
NITTY GRITTY DIRT BAND		
18	28	Will The Circle Be Unbroken, Vol III
PAISLEY, Brad		
3	104	Part II
PARTON, Dolly		
4	38	Halos & Horns
PRESLEY, Elvis		
1 [3]	78+	Elv1s: 30 #1 Hits
RASCAL FLATTS		
1 [1]	73+	Melt
RIMES, LeAnn		
3	46	Twisted Angel
RONSTADT, Linda		
19	51+	The Very Best Of Linda Ronstadt
SHELTON, Blake		
3	99	Blake Shelton

POS	WKS	Album Title
STRAIT, George		
1 [1]	92	The Road Less Traveled
8	104+	The Best Of George Strait: 20th Century Masters The Millennium Collection
TIPPIN, Aaron		
10	21	Stars & Stripes
TRAVIS, Randy		
8	75+	Rise And Shine
TRICK PONY		
12	104	On A Mission
TRITT, Travis		
4	34	Strong Enough
TWAIN, Shania		
1 [6]	70+	Up!
URBAN, Keith		
3	76+	Golden Road

POS	WKS	Album Title
VASSAR, Phil		
4	43	American Child
WILLS, Mark		
16	44	Greatest Hits
WOMACK, Lee Ann		
2 [1]	30	Something Worth Leaving Behind
WORLEY, Darryl		
1 [1]	40	I Miss My Friend
VARIOUS ARTIST COMPILATIONS		
21	15	Best Of America, The
17	19	Kindred Spirits: A Tribute To The Songs Of Johnny Cash
27	56	Time-Life's Treasury Of Bluegrass
2 [1]	80	Totally Country
5	49	Totally Country Vol. 2

R&B/ HIP-HOP ALBUMS

This section lists, by artist, every album that debuted in 2003 on *Billboard's* weekly **Top R&B/Hip-Hop Albums** chart (a top 100 listing).

DEBUT DATE	PEAK POS	WKS CHR	G L D	ARTIST Title	Label & Number
				ABK ★	
4/26/03	42	1		Hatchet Warrior	Psychopathic 4012
				ADAMS, Yolanda	
5/24/03	65	3		The Praise And Worship Songs Of Yolanda Adams ... [K]	Verity 43222
				AESOP ROCK ★	
10/11/03	44	2		Bazooka Tooth	Definitive Jux 68
				ASHANTI	
6/21/03	87	1		Ashanti: The 7 Series .... [K-M]	Murder Inc. 000494
				contains seven songs from her *Ashanti* album	
7/12/03	❶²	38↑	▲	Chapter II	Murder Inc. 000143
12/6/03+	43	6		Ashanti's Christmas .... [X]	The Inc. 001612
				ATMOSPHERE	
10/11/03	58	3		Seven's Travels	Rhymesayers 86690
				AVANT	
12/27/03	4	15↑	●	Private Room	Magic Johnson 001567
				BABY BASH ★	
10/11/03	32	26↑	●	Tha Smokin' Nephew	Universal 001258
				BACHARACH, Burt — see ISLEY BROTHERS	
				BAD AZZ	
5/10/03	85	5		Money Run...................................	Out Of Bounds 2010
				BAD BOY'S DA BAND ★	
10/18/03	❶¹	22↑	●	Too Hot For T.V.	Bad Boy 001118
				BADU, Erykah	
10/4/03	2¹	27↑	●	World Wide Underground	Motown 000739
				BANNER, David ★	
6/7/03	❶¹	36		Mississippi: The Album	SRC 000312
9/27/03	50	9		Mississippi: The Screwed & Chopped Album.......... [K]	SRC 000576
				BANTON, Buju	
3/29/03	44	11		Friends For Life.............................	VP 83634
				BENSON, George	
7/26/03	74	4		The Greatest Hits Of All .... [G]	Rhino 78284
				BENSON, Rhian ★	
				Born in Ghana, West Africa (mother from Wales; father from West Africa); raised in New Dehli, India. Female singer/songwriter.	
10/25/03	45	10		Gold Coast..................................	DKG 71007
				BENZINO	
2/1/03	31	6		Redemption	Surrender 62827
				BEYONCÉ ★	
7/5/03	❶¹	40↑	▲³	Dangerously In Love	Columbia 86386
				B.G.	
3/15/03	4	22		Livin' Legend	Koch 8465
				BIG GIPP ★	
8/30/03	20	9		Mutant Mindframe	Koch 8481
				BIG MOE	
6/21/03	33	4		Moe Life	Wreckshop 4040
				BIG NOYD	
11/8/03	45	3		Only The Strong	Noyd 9223
				BIG REN ★	
				Born in New Orleans, Louisiana. Male rapper.	
3/1/03	81	7		The Streets Won't Let Me Go	Corrupt Inmate 2111
				BIG TYMERS	
12/27/03	6	15↑	●	Big Money Heavyweight	Cash Money 000815
				BIRMINGHAM J ★	
10/18/03	75	3		Da Neighborhood Superstars	Kottage Boy 3903
				BISHOP, Kalvin ★	
				Born in Atlanta, Georgia. Male singer/songwriter.	
10/25/03	70	12		Do What I Gotta Do	Numillennium 13001

R&B/HIP-HOP ALBUMS

DEBUT DATE	PEAK POS	WKS CHR	G L D	ARTIST / Title	Label & Number
				BLACK EYED PEAS	
7/12/03	23	39↑	▲	Elephunk..	A&M 000699
				BLACK MOON	
10/25/03	47	3		Total Eclipse..	Duck Down 2005
				BLACKstreet	
3/29/03	8	10		Level II	DreamWorks 450392
				BLIGE, Mary J.	
9/6/03	❶²	31↑	▲	Love & Life	Geffen 000956
				BMD ★	
1/25/03	96	1		Summertime	Music Vibe 1200
				BONE CRUSHER ★	
5/17/03	❶¹	25		AttenCHUN!	Break-Em-Off 50995
				BOO & GOTTI ★	
9/13/03	32	6		Perfect Timing	Cash Money 000542
				BOOBE & THE YOUNG FARMERS ★	
10/11/03	78	2↑		One Way Up	One Way 12345
				BOO-YAA T.R.I.B.E.	
10/25/03	85	1		West Koasta Nostra	Sarinjay 82024
				BOYZ II MEN	
10/25/03	84	1		The Best Of Boyz II Men: 20th Century Masters The Millennium Collection .... [G]	Motown 001098
12/20/03	87	2		The Best Of Boyz II Men: 20th Century Masters The Christmas Collection .... [X]	Motown 000611
				BRADSHAW, Jeff ★ Born in Philadelphia, Pennsylvania. Trombone player.	
11/15/03	85	3		Bone Deep	Hidden Beach 90698
				BRAXTON, Toni	
11/22/03	43	6		Ultimate Toni Braxton .... [G]	Arista 51699
				BROTHA LYNCH HUNG	
6/28/03	21	13		Lynch By Inch: Suicide Note	Siccmade 70132 [2]
				B2K	
7/19/03	38	9		B2K: The Remixes - Vol. 2 .... [K]	Epic 86885
				BUDDEN, Joe ★	
6/28/03	2¹	21		Joe Budden	Def Jam 000505
				CANIBUS	
8/9/03	34	7		Rip The Jacker	Babygrande 5
				CANNON, Nick ★	
12/27/03	15	13		Nick Cannon	Nick 48500
				CANTRELL, Blu	
7/12/03	8	14		Bittersweet	Arista 52728
				CAREY, Mariah	
11/1/03	25	5		The Remixes .... [K]	Columbia 87154 [2]
				CARIBBEAN PULSE ★ Reggae group from Belize: brothers William (guitar) and Jason (bass) Smith, Ezzy Judah (male vocals, percussion) and LaNiece McKay (female vocals).	
3/15/03	81	10		Stand Up	Irie 1002
				CASH KOLA ★	
10/11/03	51	11		Life In General	Wonderboy 8001
				C-BO	
6/28/03	46	3		West Side Ryders...	West Coast Mafia 2009
8/9/03	37	5		The Mobfather	West Coast Mafia 2010
				CHINGY ★	
8/2/03	2³	36↑	▲²	Jackpot	Disturbing Tha P. 82976
				CHOPPA ★	
3/8/03	99	1		Choppa Style	Take Fo' 1901
3/22/03	17	14		Straight From The N.O..	New No Limit 075007
				CLARK SHEARD, Karen	
11/22/03	44	6		The Heavens Are Telling	Elektra 62894

DEBUT DATE	PEAK POS	WKS CHR	G L D	ARTIST / Title	Label & Number
				CLAYTON, Willie ★	
				Born on 3/29/55 in Indianola, Mississippi. Blues singer/songwriter.	
6/21/03	89	1		The Last Man Standing............................	End Zone 2056
				COX, Deborah	
8/9/03	85	1		Deborah Cox Remixed .... [K]	J Records 53717
				CRAIG-G	
6/7/03	99	1		This Is Now!!!	Overnight Sen. 641251
				CRUSADERS, The	
4/19/03	73	9		Rural Renewal	PRA 060077
				CULBERTSON, Brian ★	
7/12/03	36	5		Come On Up	Warner 48300
				CUNNINGHAM, Omar ★	
				Born in Jacksonville, Florida. Blues singer/songwriter.	
7/19/03	53	6		Hell At The House	On Top 4904
				DA BRAT	
8/2/03	6	13		Limelite, Luv & Niteclubz	So So Def 51586
				DA HOL '9 ★	
				Male rap duo from St. Louis, Missouri: Kaos and Kemo.	
4/5/03	43	1		That Hella Thurl Sh!#	Hella Thurl 40263
				DAVIS, Tyrone	
8/23/03	42	16		Come To Daddy..	Future 1005
				DEAD PREZ	
11/8/03	32	5		Turn Off The Radio The Mixtape Vol. 2: Get Free Or Die Tryin'..	Boss Up 9228
				DeBARGE, Chico	
4/12/03	79	5		Free	Alove 8620
				DF DUB ★	
4/5/03	78	1		Country Girl	3Sixty 89089
				DILLINGER, Daz	
7/19/03	35	9		DPGC-U Know What I'm Throwin' Up................ DAZ	Gangsta Advisory 164
				DIPLOMATS, The ★	
4/12/03	❶¹	39↑	●	Diplomatic Immunity	Roc-A-Fella 063211 [2]
				DIRTY	
3/15/03	13	14		Keep It Pimp & Gangsta	Universal 018415
10/25/03	22	14		Love Us Or Hate Us	Nfinity 42030
				DJ ENVY ★	
3/1/03	8	9		The Desert Storm Mixtape: Blok Party Vol. 1	Desert Storm 86737
				DJ KAYSLAY ★	
6/7/03	4	14		The Streetsweeper Vol. 1	Columbia 87048
				DJ KUT ★	
				Born in St. Louis, Missouri. Male DJ/rapper.	
7/5/03	79	1		Sequence Hip Hop Vol. 1.........................	Sequence 8013
				DJ WHOOKID ★	
				Born in Queens, New York. Male DJ/rapper.	
3/15/03	63	9		Hood Radio V. 1	Full Clip 2005
				DMX	
10/4/03	❶¹	27↑	▲	Grand Champ	Ruff Ryders 063369
				D.O.C., The	
3/15/03	57	3		Deuce	Silverback 2113
				DONNIE ★	
				Born in Lexington, Kentucky; raised in Atlanta, Georgia. Singer/songwriter.	
6/7/03	31	12		The Colored Section	Giant Step 000324
				DO OR DIE	
9/6/03	17	14		Pimpin' Ain't Dead..................................	J Prince 42029
				DOWNING, Will	
11/1/03	9	23↑		Emotions	GRP 000529
				DWELE ★	
6/7/03	20	44↑		Subject	Virgin 80919

R&B/HIP-HOP ALBUMS

DEBUT DATE	PEAK POS	WKS CHR	G L D	ARTIST Title	Label & Number
				EARTH, WIND & FIRE	
6/7/03	19	9		The Promise	Kalimba 973002
				E-40	
9/27/03	4	11		Breakin News	Sick Wid' It 41857
				ELEPHANT MAN ★	
12/20/03	14	11		Good 2 Go..	VP 83681
				ELLIOTT, Missy	
12/13/03	3	17↑	▲	This Is Not A Test!	Gold Mind 62905
				ESHAM	
12/6/03	71	1		Repentance..	Psychopathic 4021
				FABOLOUS	
3/22/03	3	38	▲	Street Dreams	Desert Storm 62791
11/22/03	9	12		More Street Dreams Pt. 2: The Mixtape	Desert Storm 62924
				FATHER MC	
4/5/03	59	7		My	Empire 39048
				FIEND	
5/31/03	55	6		Fiend Presents: Can I Burn? 2.............................	Fiend 2002
				50 CENT	
2/22/03	❶[8]	59↑	▲[6]	Get Rich Or Die Tryin'	Shady 493544
5/3/03	❶[1]	21		The New Breed	Shady 000108
				54TH PLATOON ★	
5/24/03	21	12		All Or N.O.thin	Fubu 9001
				FLOETRY	
12/6/03	11	16		Floacism "Live" .... [L]	DreamWorks 001438
				40 GLOCC ★ Born Tory Gasaway on 12/16/79 in Galveston, Texas; raised in Colton, California. Male rapper.	
1/25/03	65	8		The Jakal..	Empire 39056
				FOXXX, Freddie	
6/28/03	95	1		Konexion... FREDDIE FOXXX (BUMPY KNUCKLES)	BBE 9014
				FRANKIE J ★	
6/14/03	33	18		What's A Man To Do?	Columbia 90073
				FRANKLIN, Aretha	
10/4/03	11	27↑		So Damn Happy	Arista 50174
				FRAYSER BOY ★	
9/13/03	23	11		Gone On That Bay...	Hypnotize Minds 3606
				FREEWAY ★	
3/8/03	3	31		Philadelphia Freeway	Roc-A-Fella 586920
				FRUKWAN ★ Born Arnold Hamilton in Brooklyn, New York. Male rapper. Member of Stetsasonic and Gravediggaz.	
3/1/03	83	5		Life..	Empire 39034
				GANGSTA BOO	
11/1/03	53	4		Enquiring Minds 2: The Soap Opera	RTE 300
				GANG STARR	
7/12/03	5	14		The Ownerz	Virgin 80247
				GINUWINE	
4/26/03	❶[1]	44	●	The Senior	Epic 86960
				GOAPELE ★ Born Goapele Mohlabane on 7/11/77 in Oakland, California (African father/American mother). Female singer/songwriter. Name pronounced: gwa-pa-lay.	
8/30/03	63	14↑		Even Closer	Skyblaze 230108
				GRAY, Macy	
8/2/03	29	5		The Trouble With Being Myself............................	Epic 86535
				GREEN, Al	
2/15/03	64	5		The Love Song Collection .... [K]	Right Stuff 80327
12/6/03	9	17		I Can't Stop	Blue Note 93556

DEBUT DATE	PEAK POS	WKS CHR	G L D	ARTIST / Title	Label & Number
				G-UNIT ★	
11/29/03	2³	19↑	▲²	Beg For Mercy	G-Unit 001593
				HAMILTON, Anthony ★	
10/11/03	6	26↑		Comin' Where I Come From	So So Def 52107
				HARGROVE, Roy ★	
6/7/03	32	13		Hard Groove .... [I]	Verve 065192
				ROY HARGROVE PRESENTS THE RH FACTOR	
				HIEROGLYPHICS	
10/25/03	53	3		Full Circle..	Hiero Imperium 230109
				HITMAN SAMMY SAM ★	
5/17/03	27	8		The Step Daddy	ColliPark 000380
				HOLLISTER, Dave	
12/6/03	23	11		Real Talk	DreamWorks 450500
				HOT BOY$	
4/12/03	3	13		Let 'Em Burn	Cash Money 860966
				HOUSTON, Marques ★	
11/8/03	5	20		MH	T.U.G. 62935
				HOUSTON, Whitney	
12/6/03	14	6		One Wish: The Holiday Album .... [X]	Arista 50996
				INCOGNITO	
10/18/03	74	2		Who Needs Love	Narada 91627
				INSPECTAH DECK	
6/28/03	29	3		The Movement.......................................	Koch 8660
				ISLEY BROTHERS, The	
5/24/03	❶³	45↑	●	Body Kiss	DreamWorks 450409
11/29/03	22	14		Here I Am: Isley Meets Bacharach	DreamWorks 001005
				RONALD ISLEY/BURT BACHARACH	
				JACKSON, Michael	
12/6/03	6	18↑	●	Number Ones [G]	Epic 88998
				JACKSON 5, The	
12/20/03	96	2		The Best Of The Jackson 5: 20th Century Masters The Christmas Collection............................ [X]	Motown 000706
				JAGGED EDGE	
11/1/03	❶¹	23↑	●	Hard	Columbia 87017
				JA RULE	
11/22/03	❶¹	16		Blood In My Eye	Murder Inc. 001577
				JAVIER ★	
8/23/03	18	19		Javier..	Capitol 39843
				JAYLIB ★	
				Collarboration of rappers/producers James "Jay Dilla" Yancey (from Detroit, Michigan) and Otis "Madlib" Jackson (from Oxnard, California).	
10/25/03	92	1		Champion Sound	Fat Beats 2062
				JAY-Z	
4/26/03	6	17		Blueprint 2.1	Roc-A-Fella 000297
11/29/03	❶³	19↑	▲²	The Black Album	Roc-A-Fella 001528
				JEAN, Wyclef	
11/22/03	5	16		The Preacher's Son	Yclef 55425
				JEDI MIND TRICKS ★	
				Male rap duo from Brooklyn, New York: Vinnie Paz (rapper) and Stoupe (producer).	
9/13/03	61	4		Visions Of Gandhi..	Babygrande 006
				JORDAN, Montell	
11/8/03	54	5		Life After Def	Enterprise 5702
				JS ★	
8/16/03	11	30		Ice Cream...	DreamWorks 450332

DEBUT DATE	PEAK POS	WKS CHR	G L D	ARTIST Title	Label & Number
				KANE & ABEL	
10/4/03	100	2		Welcome Home	Most Wanted 1001
				KANE & ABEL WITH THE MOST WANTED BOYS	
				KEAK DA SNEAK	
11/8/03	87	3		Counting Other People's Money..	Moe Doe 104
				KELIS	
12/27/03	7	15↑	●	Tasty	Star Trak 52132
				KELLY, R.	
3/1/03	❶¹	58↑	▲²	Chocolate Factory	Jive 41849
10/4/03	2¹	27↑	▲	The R. In R&B Collection Volume One [G]	Jive 55214
11/8/03	31	13	●	The R. In R&B: The Video Collection.................... [G]	Jive 53709
				KEM ★	
3/15/03	14	56↑		Kemistry..	Motown 067516
				KEYS, Alicia	
12/13/03	❶⁶	17↑	▲²	The Diary Of Alicia Keys	J Records 55712
				KHADAFI, Tragedy ★	
				Born Percy Chapman on 8/13/71 in Queens, New York. Male rapper.	
11/8/03	53	2		Still Reportin...	25 To Life 1006
				KILLER MIKE ★	
3/29/03	4	18		Monster	Aquemini 86862
				KINDRED THE FAMILY SOUL ★	
4/12/03	29	52↑		Surrender To Love	Hidden Beach 86491
				KOOL G RAP	
11/8/03	99	1		Click Of Respect	Igloo 101
				KRS-ONE	
7/12/03	30	5		Kristyles..	Koch 8342
				LAST MR. BIGG, The	
8/2/03	44	7		The Mask Is Off	Warlock 2894
				LATIF ★	
				Boprn Corey Williams in 1983 in Philadelphia, Pennsylvania. Siner/songwriter.	
10/11/03	67	3		Love In The First	Motown 000517
				LATTIMORE, Kenny	
3/1/03	3	22		Things That Lovers Do	Arista 14751
				KENNY LATTIMORE & CHANTÉ MOORE	
				LEE, Murphy ★	
10/11/03	5	26↑	●	Murphy's Law	Fo' Reel 001132
				LES NUBIANS	
4/12/03	16	22		One Step Forward	Omtown 82569
				LEVERT, Gerald	
11/15/03	❶¹	21↑		Stroke Of Genius	Elektra 62903
				LIL' BOOSIE AND WEBBIE ★	
8/23/03	56	9		Pimp C Presents...Ghetto Stories..	Trill 6310
				LIL BOW WOW	
9/6/03	4	25	●	Unleashed	Columbia 87103
				BOW WOW	
				LIL' FLIP	
4/19/03	35	14		Lil' Flip And Sucka Free Present 7-1-3 And The Undaground Legend: Remixed	Sucka Free 89228 [?]
				LIL JON & THE EAST SIDE BOYZ	
11/22/03	40	6		Certified Crunk	Ichiban 01037
12/13/03	7	17↑		Part II	BME 2378
				LIL' KEKE	
7/26/03	37	3		The Big Unit...	Nod Factor 42025
				LIL' KEKE / SLIM THUG	
				LIL' KIM	
3/15/03	4	34	▲	La Bella Mafia	Queen Bee 83572

DEBUT DATE	PEAK POS	WKS CHR	G L D	ARTIST Title	Label & Number
				LIL' MO	
5/17/03	4	18		Meet The Girl Next Door	Elektra 62835
				LIL' ROMEO	
1/4/03	10	17		Game Time	New No Limit 060055
				LIL WYTE ★	
3/22/03	44	25		Doubt Me Now	Hypnotize Minds 3604
				LIL' ZANE	
9/6/03	39	4		The Big Zane Theory	Priority 50191
				ZANE	
				LOON ★	
11/8/03	2¹	15		Loon	Bad Boy 000892
				LSG	
8/16/03	3	14		LSG2	Elektra 62851
				LUDACRIS	
10/25/03	❶²	24↑	▲	Chicken*N*Beer	Disturb. Tha P. 000930
				LUMIDEE ★	
7/12/03	11	13		Almost Famous	Straight Face 000681
				MACK 10	
8/9/03	28	7		Ghetto, Gutter & Gangsta	Hoo-Bangin' 970028
				MAGIC	
4/5/03	37	9		White Eyes	New No Limit 860993
9/13/03	54	4		On My Own	Da Vault 5701
				MANHATTANS, The	
9/6/03	83	2		...Even Now...	Beemark 107
				MARIA ★	
				Born in Denmark (Danish father/African mother); raised in Spain. Female singer/songwriter.	
10/18/03	84	1		My Soul	DreamWorks 000890
				MARLEY, Ziggy, And The Melody Makers	
5/3/03	84	8		Dragonfly	Tuff Gong 11636
				MC LYTE	
5/24/03	95	1		MC Lyte Is Lytro: Da Undaground Heat Vol. 1	CMM 01094
				McCLURKIN, Donnie	
3/22/03	12	33↑		Donnie McClurkin...Again	Verity 43199
				McDONALD, Michael	
7/12/03+	17	34↑	▲	Motown	Motown 000651
				McKNIGHT, Brian	
4/12/03	4	26	●	U Turn	Motown 067315
				MENACE TO SOCIETY ★	
3/8/03	92	1		Bring It On	I.T.P. 232
				MR. CHEEKS	
4/5/03	25	9		Back Again!	Universal 067615
				MOBB DEEP	
5/3/03	4	19		Free Agents: The Murda Mix Tape	Landspeed 9222
				MONICA	
6/28/03	2¹	38	●	After The Storm	J Records 20031
				MOORE, Chanté — see LATTIMORE, Kenny	
				M.O.P.	
4/19/03	67	2		10 Years And Gunnin'	Loud 89095
				MOSLEY, Lou ★	
				Born in Compton, California. Singer/songwriter/guitarist.	
5/10/03	69	19		Finally	Jenstar 1379
				MO THUGS FAMILY	
6/28/03	25	10		The Movement	D3 9918
				MS. DYNAMITE ★	
3/29/03	80	1		A Little Deeper	Polydor 076043
				MUL-TY ★	
				Born in Vidalia, Georgia. Male singer/songwriter.	
3/1/03	80	3		Made 4 Love	Superkala 066794

R&B/HIP-HOP ALBUMS

DEBUT DATE	PEAK POS	WKS CHR	GLD	ARTIST / Title	Label & Number
				MURRAY, Keith	
8/2/03	11	8		He's Keith Murray..	Def Jam 000316
				MUSIQ	
12/27/03	3	15↑	●	soulstar	Def Soul 001616
				MYA	
8/9/03	2[1]	32	●	Moodring	A&M 000734
				NAIJA, T. ★	
				Born in Brooklyn, New York. Female singer/songwriter.	
6/14/03	58	20		Rhythm Of Love	NOK 0537
				NAJEE	
10/25/03	67	3		Embrace .... [I]	N-Coded 4248
				NAPPY ROOTS	
9/13/03	9	15		Wooden Leather	Atlantic 83646
				NDEGÉOCELLO, Me'Shell	
11/1/03	43	5		Comfort Woman	Maverick 48547
				NELLY	
12/13/03	6	17↑	▲	Da Derrty Versions - The Reinvention [K]	Fo' Reel 001665
				NEVILLE, Aaron	
9/13/03	78	2		Nature Boy: The Standards Album.......................................	Verve 065633
				NEXT	
1/4/03	27	17		The Next Episode	J Records 20016
				NORFUL, Smokie ★	
8/9/03	26	34		I Need You Now	EMI Gospel 20374
11/8/03	24	22↑		Smokie Norful: Limited Edition..	EMI Gospel 95086
				ONE TWELVE	
12/6/03	4	18↑		Hot & Wet	Bad Boy 000927
				ONYX	
9/27/03	66	3		Triggernometry	In The Paint 9923
				OSBORNE, Jeffrey	
6/28/03	50	8		Music Is Life	Jay Oz 8452
				OUTKAST	
10/4/03	❶[1]	27↑	▲[9]	Speakerboxxx/The Love Below	Arista 50133 [2]
				PEREZ, Amanda ★	
3/8/03	36	20		Angel	Powerhouse 82131
				PRICE, Kelly	
5/17/03	2[1]	21		Priceless	Def Soul 586777
				PRINCE PAUL	
5/24/03	58	3		Politics Of The Business...	Razor & Tie 82888
				PROJECT PAT	
11/22/03	37	10		The Appeal Mix Tape	Hypnotize Minds 3609
				RARE ESSENCE	
8/16/03	97	1		Live At Club U: Old School Volume 2 .... [L]	Rare One 2004
				RICHARDSON, Calvin ★	
9/27/03	8	28↑		2:35 PM	Hollywood 162351
				RICHIE, Lionel	
2/22/03	31	21	●	The Definitive Collection .... [G]	Motown 068140
				RONSON, Mark ★	
				Born in 1978 in London, England; raised in New York. White DJ/producer/remixer.	
9/27/03	84	1		Here Comes The Fuzz...	Elektra 62839
				ROSCOE ★	
6/28/03	22	13		Young Roscoe Philaphornia	Priority 28291
				RUN-D.M.C.	
11/15/03	62	2		Ultimate Run-DMC... [G]	BMG Heritage 54628

DEBUT DATE	PEAK POS	WKS CHR	G L D	ARTIST / Title	Label & Number
				RZA	
10/25/03	20	7		Birth Of A Prince	Wu-Records 84652
				SAADIQ, Raphael	
11/1/03	40	3		All Hits At The House Of Blues	[L] Pookie 1001 [2]
				SANDMAN ★	
				Born in Detroit, Michigan. Male rapper.	
5/10/03	66	7		Face Value	Lo End 0615
				SANTANA, Juelz ★	
9/6/03	3	22		From Me To U	Roc-A-Fella 000142
				SCARFACE	
4/26/03	3	26		Balls And My Word	Rap-A-Lot 42024
				702	
4/12/03	22	10		Star	Motown 066130
				SHEEK LOUCH ★	
10/4/03	3	10		Walk Witt Me	D-Block 001042
				SILK	
10/11/03	30	11		Silktime	Silk 12147
				SOLANGE ★	
2/8/03	23	19		Solo Star	Music World 86354
				SOMMERS, Jimmy	
8/30/03	82	1		Lovelife	Gemini 90445
				SOULJA SLIM	
1/25/03	72	5		Years Later	Cut Throat 5819
9/13/03	44	9		Years Later...A Few Months After	Cut Throat 5703
				SOUL POSITION ★	
				Male rap duo from Columbus, Ohio: Blueprint (vocals) and RJD2 (producer).	
11/15/03	91	1		8 Million Stories	Rhymesayers 35107
				SPARXXX, Bubba	
10/4/03	9	16		Deliverance	Beat Club 001147
				STARR, Fredro	
6/14/03	99	1		Don't Get Mad Get Money	D3 9917
				STICKY FINGAZ	
5/3/03	37	10		Decade	D3 9916
				STONE, Joss ★	
10/4/03+	48	24↑		The Soul Sessions	[M] S-Curve 42234
				STUDDARD, Ruben ★	
12/27/03+	❶²	15↑	▲	Soulful	J Records 54639
				SUMMER, Donna	
10/18/03	65	2		The Journey: The Very Best Of Donna Summer	[G] Mercury 001009
				SWEAT, Keith	
2/22/03	34	6		Keith Sweat Live	[L] Elektra 62855
				TAYLOR, Gary	
11/1/03	100	1		Eclectic Bohemian	Morning Crew 1857
				TAYLOR, Johnnie	
7/19/03	30	10		There's No Good In Goodbye	Malaco 7515
				TEMPTATIONS, The	
12/13/03	55	4		The Best Of The Temptations: 20th Century Masters The Christmas Collection	[X] Motown 000620
				THREE 6 MAFIA	
7/12/03	2¹	20		Da Unbreakables	Hypnotize Minds 89030
				T.I.	
9/6/03	2¹	31↑	●	Trap Muzik	Grand Hustle 83650
				TIMBALAND AND MAGOO	
12/6/03	16	9		Under Construction Part II	Blackground 001185
				TOO $HORT	
11/22/03	7	20↑		Married To The Game	$hort 53722

DEBUT DATE	PEAK POS	WKS CHR	G L D	ARTIST Title	Label & Number
				TRIBE CALLED QUEST, A	
7/5/03	51	2		Hits, Rarities & Remixes .... [G]	Jive 41839
				TRICE, Obie ★	
10/11/03	3	26↑	●	Cheers	Shady 001105
				T-ROCK ★	
				Born in Atlanta, Georgia. Male rapper.	
3/15/03	77	2		Rock Solid/4:20	Hypnotize Minds 3603
				TURK	
11/8/03	22	5		Raw & Uncut..	Koch 8661
				2PAC	
10/25/03	5	14		Nu-Mixx Klazzics [K]	Death Row 9530
11/22/03	3	20↑	▲	Tupac: Resurrection [S]	Amaru 001533
				TYRESE	
1/4/03	2²	44	●	I Wanna Go There	J Records 20041
				UGK	
7/5/03	22	13		Best Of .... [G]	Jive 41866
				VANDROSS, Luther	
6/21/03	❶²	42↑	▲	Dance With My Father	J Records 51885
7/5/03	49	7		The Essential Luther Vandross .... [G]	Legacy 89167 [2]
11/15/03	6	16		Luther Vandross Live: Radio City Music Hall 2003 [L]	J Records 55711
				VAUGHN, Viktor ★	
				Born Daniel Dumile in Long Island, New York. Male rapper.	
10/11/03	99	1		Vaudeville Villain	Traffic 2409
				VIKTOR VAUGHN AKA MF DOOM	
				VIOLENT J ★	
8/9/03	31	4		Wizard Of The Hood...................................... [M]	Psychopathic 4016
				WAITERS, Mel	
10/18/03	98	1		Nite Out	Waldoxy 2835
				WESTSIDE CONNECTION	
12/27/03+	3	15↑	●	Terrorist Threats	Hoo-Bangin' 24030
				WHALUM, Kirk	
8/9/03	44	8		Into My Soul.. [I]	Warner 48446
				WHITE, Barry	
9/6/03	54	5		The Best Of Barry White: 20th Century Masters The Millennium Collection .... [G]	Island 000884
				WILLIAMS, Bernie ★	
8/16/03	72	5		The Journey Within... [I]	GRP 000725
				WILSON, Natalie, and The S.O.P. Chorale	
11/8/03	75	5		The Good Life..	Gospo Centric 70053
				WINANS, BeBe	
12/20/03	77	3		My Christmas Prayer... [X]	Hidden Beach 90788
				WINANS, CeCe	
9/27/03	21	28↑		Throne Room..	Pure Springs 90361
				WINANS, Vickie ★	
10/4/03	38	27↑		Bringing It All Together	Verity 43214
				WONDER, Wayne ★	
3/22/03	10	22		No Holding Back	VP 83628
				WYATT, Gary L. ★	
				Born in Seattle, Washington. Singer/songwriter.	
10/4/03	63	13		I Do Love You	HR 9198
				YAHZARAH ★	
				Born Dana Williams in Los Angeles, California. Female singer/songwriter.	
10/11/03	44	12		Blackstar..	Three Keys 22256

DEBUT DATE	PEAK POS	WKS CHR	G L D	ARTIST Title	Label & Number
				YING YANG TWINS	
10/4/03	4	27↑	●	Me & My Brother	Collipark 2480
				YO GOTTI ★	
				Born in Memphis, Tennessee. Male rapper.	
5/31/03	59	3		Life	Rap Hustlaz 2490
				YOUNGBLOODZ	
9/13/03	❶¹	30↑	●	Drankin' Patnaz	So So Def 50155
				YOUNG HUSTLAZ ★	
				Male rap group from Dallas, Texas: Cal, Dub, Ralo and Snaps.	
7/5/03	67	7		Where's My Money?	Power Houze 4639
				YUKMOUTH	
8/23/03	21	9		Godzilla	J Prince 42028
				MOVIE SOUNDTRACKS	
8/2/03	❶⁴	26	▲	Bad Boys II [V]	Bad Boy 000716
				Martin Lawrence/Will Smith/Peter Stormare/Theresa Randle/Joe Pantoliano	
2/22/03	98	1		Biker Boyz [V]	DreamWorks 450415
				Laurence Fishburne/Derek Luke/Orlando Jones/Lisa Bonet/Larenz Tate	
3/22/03	23	12		Bringing Down The House [V]	Hollywood 162386
				Steve Martin/Queen Latifah/Eugene Levy/Jean Smart/Joan Plowright	
3/8/03	3	26	●	Cradle 2 The Grave [V]	Bloodline 063615
				Jet Li/DMX/Anthony Anderson/Kelly Hu/Tom Arnold	
1/18/03	19	17		Deliver Us From Eva [V]	Hollywood 162369
				LL Cool J/Gabrielle Union/Duane Martin/Essence Atkins/Megan Good	
5/10/03	14	9		Dysfunktional Family [V]	Tha Row 63053
				movie is a stand-up performance by comedian Eddie Griffin	
9/27/03	14	20↑		Fighting Temptations, The [V]	Music World 90286
				Cuba Gooding Jr./Beyoncé Knowles/Mike Epps/LaTanya Richardson/Faith Evans	
10/11/03	69	5		Hip Hop Story: Tha Movie, A [V]	Raprock 691015
				movie is a documentary about rap stars	
12/13/03	47	6		Honey [V]	Elektra 62925
				Jessica Alba/Mekhi Phifer/Joy Bryant/Lil' Romeo/Missy Elliott	
12/27/03	22	11		Love Don't Cost A Thing [V]	Hollywood 162396
				Nick Cannon/Christina Milian/Nichole Robinson/Al Thompson	
5/10/03	75	1		Standing In The Shadows Of Motown [V]	Hip-O 064691
				movie is a documentary about the 1960s Motown studio musicians known as the Funk Brothers	
6/14/03	❶¹	20	●	2 Fast 2 Furious [V]	Def Jam 000426
				Paul Walker/Tyrese/Eva Mendes/Cole Hauser/Ludacris	
				TELEVISION SOUNDTRACK	
11/29/03	100	1		True Crime: Streets Of LA [V]	Vybe Squad 5709
				animated video game, voices by: Russell Wong/Christopher Walken/Gary Oldman	
				VARIOUS ARTIST COMPILATIONS	
2/15/03	64	5		Body + Soul: Absolute	Time-Life 18882
				songs by Toni Braxton, Deborah Cox, Joe, Brian McKnight, Angie Stone, and others	
6/21/03	41	6		Church: Songs Of Soul & Inspiration	DMI 067763
				songs by Patti Austin, En Vogue, Jennifer Holliday, Stephanie Mills, Dionne Warwick, and others	
4/5/03	44	6		Conception: An Interpretation Of Stevie Wonder's Songs	Motown 067314
				songs by Marc Anthony, Eric Clapton, Glenn Lewis, John Mellencamp, Musiq, and others	
12/27/03	25	14		Crunk And Disorderly	TVT 2500
				songs by David Banner, Bone Crusher, Killer Mike, Lil Flip, Lil Jon, and others	
10/4/03	32	7		Def Jam Recordings Presents Music Inspired By Scarface	Def Jam 001196
				songs by Joe Budden, Cam'ron, Jay-Z, Mobb Deep, Scarface, and others	
8/30/03	❶¹	23	●	Neptunes Present Clones, The	Star Trak 51295
				songs by Busta Rhymes, Clipse, Kelis, Ludacris, Pharrell, Snoop Dogg, and others	
4/12/03	10	17	▲	Now 12	EMI 82344
				songs by JC Chasez, Dru Hill, Jennifer Lopez, Amanda Perez, 3 Doors Down, and others	
11/22/03	11	20↑	▲	Now 14	Columbia 90753
				songs by Black Eyed Peas, Chingy, Ginuwine, Good Charlotte, Liz Phair, and others	

DEBUT DATE	PEAK POS	WKS CHR	G L D	ARTIST Title	Label & Number
				VARIOUS ARTIST COMPILATIONS — Cont'd	
6/7/03	65	4		**Rasta Jamz**	Razor & Tie 89062
				songs by Ini Kamoze, Diana King, Mad Lion, Shabba Ranks, Snow, and others	
11/1/03	30	6		**Red Star Sounds Presents Def Jamaica**	Def Jam 001195
				songs by Buju Banton, Capone-N-Noreaga, Method Man, 112, Scarface, and others	
7/5/03	14	22		**Reggae Gold 2003**	VP 83654
				songs by Beenie Man, Bounty Killer, Busta Rhymes, Elephant Man, Wayne Wonder, and others	
4/12/03	11	10		**Rewind: The Hip-Hop DVD Magazine Issue 1**	Shadyville 6101
				songs by Fat Joe, 50 Cent, Jadakiss, Nappy Roots, Nelly, Snoop Dogg, and others	
1/4/03	31	14		**Source Presents Hip Hop Hits - Volume 6, The**	Def Jam 063546
				songs by Big Tymers, Foxy Brown, Eminem, Nelly, P. Diddy, Ying Yang Twins, and others	
12/27/03	46	12		**Source Presents Hip Hop Hits - Volume 7, The**	Def Jam 001614
				songs by Bone Crusher, Missy Elliott, Ja Rule, Ludacris, Snoop Dogg, 2Pac, and others	
8/30/03	❶[1]	15		Source Presents: The Chain Gang Vol. II	Roc-A-Fella 000971
				songs by Freeway, Peedi Crakk, Beanie Sigel, Young Gunz, and others	
4/26/03	44	7		**Streetwize: Work It!**	Shanachie 5100
				songs by Randy Brecker, Chuck Loeb, David Mann, Maysa, Nestor Torres, and others	
7/19/03	30	12		**Totally Hip Hop**	Warner 52553
				songs by Christina Aguilera, Brandy, Fabolous, Sean Paul, Wayne Wonder, and others	
7/19/03	36	7		**Totally R&B**	Warner 52552
				songs by Jimmy Cozier, Craig David, R. Kelly, Gerald Levert, Tyrese, Usher, and others	
10/11/03	72	2		**Twist Of Motown, A**	GRP 000115
				songs by Gerald Albright, George Benson, Will Downing, Lee Ritenour, Brenda Russell, and others	
6/21/03	78	1		**Ultimate Smash Hits**	Arista 52522
				songs by Baby, Clipse, Whitney Houston, OutKast, P!nk, Santana, and others	
12/20/03	100	1		**WDAS 105.3FM: Classic Soul Hits Volume 8**	Collectables 7626
				songs by Peabo Bryson, Commodores, Manhattans, Teena Marie, Deniece Williams, and others	

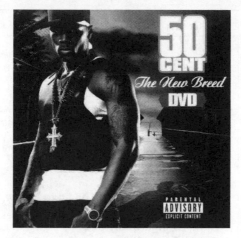

1. **50 CENT**
230

2. **R. KELLY**
183

3. **CHINGY**
91

4.	90	OUTKAST		12.	60	LUDACRIS
5.	88	BEYONCÉ		13.	60	NAS
6.	87	AALIYAH		14.	60	TYRESE
7.	85	MISSY ELLIOTT		15.	56	JAY-Z
8.	76	LUTHER VANDROSS		16.	56	THE ISLEY BROTHERS
9.	61	JA RULE		17.	52	2PAC
10.	61	LIL JON & THE EAST SIDE		18.	51	LIL' KIM
		BOYZ		19.	47	ASHANTI
11.	61	SEAN PAUL		20.	43	BONE CRUSHER

TOP 30 R&B/HIP-HOP ALBUMS

PEAK DATE	WEEKS				RANK	RECORD TITLE	PEAK POSITION	ARTIST
	CH	40	10	PK				
						1		
2/22	59+	55	28	8	1.	Get Rich Or Die Tryin'..		50 Cent
12/20	17+	16+	14+	6	2.	The Diary Of Alicia Keys		Alicia Keys
8/2	26	13	8	4	3.	Bad Boys II..		Movie Soundtrack
11/29	19+	19+	19+	3	4.	The Black Album		Jay-Z
5/24	44	23	7	3	5.	Body Kiss	The Isley Brothers Featuring Ronald Isley	
10/25	24+	24+	18+	2	6.	Chicken*N*Beer..		Ludacris
6/28	42+	41+	12	2	7.	Dance With My Father..............................		Luther Vandross
7/19	37	24	7	2	8.	Chapter II...		Ashanti
9/13	31+	12	4	2	9.	Love & Life..		Mary J. Blige
10/11	27+	26+	24	1	10.	Speakerboxxx/The Love Below		OutKast
3/8	58+	57	22	1	11.	Chocolate Factory..		R. Kelly
7/12	40+	39+	18	1	12.	Dangerously In Love..		Beyoncé
1/4	36	22	9	1	13.	God's Son		Nas
4/26	44	24	8	1	14.	The Senior		Ginuwine
5/17	25	18	7	1	15.	AttenCHUN!..		Bone Crusher
6/21	20	11	7	1	16.	2 Fast 2 Furious..		Movie Soundtrack
6/7	36	20	6	1	17.	Mississippi: The Album..............................		David Banner
10/4	27+	13	6	1	18.	Grand Champ..		DMX
11/1	23+	23+	5	1	19.	Hard		Jagged Edge
4/12	39+	22	5	1	20.	Diplomatic Immunity.........	Cam'ron Presents The Diplomats	
9/27	30+	12	5	1	21.	Drankin' Patnaz		Youngbloodz
9/6	23	10	5	1	22.	The Neptunes Present...Clones		Various Artists
5/3	21	10	5	1	23.	The New Breed		50 Cent
10/18	22+	9	5	1	24.	Too Hot For T.V.		Bad Boy's Da Band
11/15	21+	12	3	1	25.	Stroke Of Genius..		Gerald Levert
11/22	16	6	3	1	26.	Blood In My Eye		Ja Rule
8/30	15	8	2	1	27.	State Property Presents: The Chain Gang Vol. II...		Various Artists
						2		
8/2	36+	36+	21	3	28.	Jackpot..		Chingy
11/29	19+	19+	13	3	29.	Beg For Mercy		G Unit
2/22	44	35	10	2	30.	I Wanna Go There..		Tyrese

#1 R&B/HIP-HOP ALBUMS

	Date Hit #1	Wks @ #1	Title	Artist
1.	1/4	1	God's Son	Nas
2.	1/11	7 ↕	I Care 4 U (includes 1 week at #1 in 2002)	Aaliyah
3.	2/22	8 ↕	Get Rich Or Die Tryin'	50 Cent
4.	3/8	1	Chocolate Factory	R. Kelly
5.	4/12	1	Diplomatic Immunity	Cam'ron Presents The Diplomats
6.	4/26	1	The Senior	Ginuwine
7.	5/3	1	The New Breed	50 Cent
8.	5/17	1	AttenCHUN!	Bone Crusher
9.	5/24	3 ↕	Body Kiss	The Isley Brothers Featuring Ronald Isley AKA Mr. Biggs
10.	6/7	1	Mississippi: The Album	David Banner
11.	6/21	1	2 Fast 2 Furious	Movie Soundtrack
12.	6/28	2	Dance With My Father	Luther Vandross
13.	7/12	1	Dangerously In Love	Beyoncé
14.	7/19	2	Chapter II	Ashanti
15.	8/2	4	Bad Boys II	Movie Soundtrack
16.	8/30	1	State Property Presents: The Chain Gang Vol. II	Various Artists
17.	9/6	1	The Neptunes Present...Clones	Various Artists
18.	9/13	2	Love & Life	Mary J. Blige
19.	9/27	1	Drankin' Patnaz	Youngbloodz
20.	10/4	1	Grand Champ	DMX
21.	10/11	1	Speakerboxxx/The Love Below	OutKast
22.	10/18	1	Too Hot For T.V.	Bad Boy's Da Band
23.	10/25	2 ↕	Chicken*N*Beer	Ludacris
24.	11/1	1	Hard	Jagged Edge
25.	11/15	1	Stroke Of Genius	Gerald Levert
26.	11/22	1	Blood In My Eye	Ja Rule
27.	11/29	3	The Black Album	Jay-Z
28.	12/20	6	The Diary Of Alicia Keys (includes 4 weeks at #1 in 2004)	Alicia Keys

#1 R&B/HIP-HOP CATALOG ALBUMS

	Date Hit #1	Wks @ #1	Title	Artist
1.	1/4	13 ↕	**Give Love At Christmas** .... *The Temptations*	
			<small>(includes 3 weeks at #1 in 2001, 4 weeks at #1 in 2002 and 2 weeks at #1 in 2004)</small>	
2.	1/11	24 ↕	**The Marshall Mathers LP** .... *Eminem*	
			<small>(includes 12 weeks at #1 in 2002)</small>	
3.	2/1	3 ↕	**The Don Killuminati: The 7 Day Theory** .... *Makaveli*	
			<small>(includes 2 weeks at #1 in 2002)</small>	
4.	2/15	14 ↕	**Greatest Hits** *2Pac*	
			<small>(includes 11 weeks at #1 in 2002)</small>	
5.	2/22	15 ↕	**All Eyez On Me** *2Pac*	
			<small>(includes 3 weeks at #1 in 2001 and 9 weeks at #1 in 2002)</small>	
6.	3/1	3	**[Ghetto Love]** .... *Jaheim*	
7.	4/19	1	**The Slim Shady LP** .... *Eminem*	
8.	4/26	21 ↕	**Legend** .... *Bob Marley And The Wailers*	
			<small>(includes 8 weeks at #1 in 2002 and 1 week at #1 in 2004)</small>	
9.	5/17	2 ↕	**E. 1999 Eternal** .... *Bone Thungs-N-Harmony*	
9.	7/19	6 ↕	**All Time Greatest Hits** .... *Barry White*	
			<small>(includes 1 week at #1 in 2004)</small>	
9.	7/26	2 ↕	**Barry White's Greatest Hits Vol. 1** .... *Barry White*	
			<small>(includes 1 week at #1 in 2001)</small>	
9.	9/27	6 ↕+	**Life After Death** .... *The Notorious B.I.G.*	
			<small>(includes 3 weeks at #1 in 2002 and 2+ weeks at #1 in 2004)</small>	
9.	11/8	1	**The Best Of Sade** .... *Sade*	
10.	11/15	4 ↕	**Thriller** ....*Michael Jackson*	
			<small>(includes 2 weeks at #1 in 2001 and 1 week at #1 in 2002)</small>	
11.	11/29	12 ↕	**Reasonable Doubt** ....*Jay-Z*	
			<small>(includes 3 weeks at #1 in 2001 and 7 weeks at #1 in 2004)</small>	

TOP R&B/HIP-HOP ALBUMS
CHANGES IN HIGHEST POSITION/TOTAL WEEKS DATA

The following albums were listed in our *Top R&B Albums 1965-1998,* our *1999 Music Yearbook,* our *2000 Music Yearbook,* our *2001 Music Yearbook* and/or our *2002 Music Yearbook.* They were still charted or returned to the charts in 2003 and/or early 2004. This list updates these albums' peak position and weeks charted data through *Billboard's* 4/3/04 *Top R&B/Hip-Hop Albums* chart.

The superior number next to an album that peaked at #1 or #2 indicates the total number of weeks that album topped the chart.

A '+' symbol next to the weeks indicates that an album was still charted as of the 4/3/04 cut-off date.

POS	WKS	Album Title
AALIYAH		
1[7]	40	I Care 4 U
ADAMS, Yolanda		
7	67	Believe
AMERIE		
2[1]	35	All I Have
ASHANTI		
1[4]	64	Ashanti
BABY		
4	28	Birdman
BAKER, Anita		
29	81+	The Best Of Anita Baker
BLIGE, Mary J.		
3	37	No More Drama
BONE THUGS-N-HARMONY		
3	31	Thug World Order
BRANDY		
1[1]	34	Full Moon
BRAXTON, Toni		
5	20	More Than A Woman
B2K		
3	43	Pandemonium!
BUSTA RHYMES		
10	38	It Ain't Safe No More...
CAREY, Mariah		
2[1]	25	Charmbracelet
CLIPSE		
1[2]	52	Lord Willin'
COMMON		
9	19	Electric Circus

POS	WKS	Album Title
DA HEADBUSSAZ		
15	26	Dat's How It Happen To'm
DRU HILL		
2[1]	32	Dru World Order
ELLIOTT, Missy		
2[3]	43	Under Construction
EMINEM		
1[6]	96+	The Eminem Show
EVE		
1[1]	30	Eve-olution
FAT JOE		
11	24	Loyalty
FIELD MOB		
4	35	From Tha Roota To Tha Toota
50 CENT		
13	41	Guess Who's Back?
504 BOYZ		
13	18	Ballers
FLOETRY		
4	77+	Floetic
FRANKLIN, Kirk		
1[2]	80	The Rebirth Of Kirk Franklin
GREEN, Vivian		
14	49	A Love Story
HAMMOND, Fred		
13	13	Speak Those Things: POL Chapter 3
HEADLEY, Heather		
14	55	This Is Who I Am

POS	WKS	Album Title
HOUSTON, Whitney		
3	31	Just Whitney...
INDIA.ARIE		
3	86	Acoustic Soul
1[1]	56	Voyage To India
JACKSON, Michael		
45	14	Greatest Hits: HIStory – Volume 1
JAHEIM		
3	72+	Still Ghetto
JA RULE		
2[2]	29	The Last Temptation
JAY-Z		
1[3]	49	The Blueprint
1[2]	41	The Blueprint 2: The Gift And The Curse
JOHNSON, Syleena		
19	39	Chapter 2: The Voice
JONES, Donell		
2[2]	32	Life Goes On
JONES, Sir Charles		
28	57	Love Machine
K-CI & JOJO		
18	20	Emotional
KEYS, Alicia		
1[6]	68	Songs In A Minor
KWELI, Talib		
6	42	Quality
LEVERT, Gerald		
2[2]	33	The G Spot
LIL' FLIP		
4	55+	Undaground Legend

257

POS	WKS	Album Title
		LIL JON & THE EAST SIDE BOYZ
2[1]	74 +	Kings Of Crunk
		LL COOL J
1[2]	32	10
		LOPEZ, Jennifer
5	32	This Is Me...Then
		LUDACRIS
1[3]	72	Word Of Mouf
		MARY MARY
10	34	Incredible
		McKNIGHT, Brian
21	17	1989-2002: From There To Here
		MUSIQ
1[1]	48	JUSLISEN (Just Listen)
		NAAM BRIGADE
37	16	Early In The Game
		NAPPY ROOTS
3	55	Watermelon, Chicken & Gritz
		NAS
1[1]	36	God's Son
		NELLY
1[5]	74	Nellyville
		NIVEA
35	26	Nivea
		PAUL, Sean
5	71 +	Dutty Rock
		PEOPLES, Dottie
68	56	Churchin' With Dottie

POS	WKS	Album Title
		PRINCE
72	8	The Very Best Of Prince
		ROOTS, The
11	41	Phrenology
		ROWLAND, Kelly
3	21	Simply Deep
		SCARFACE
10	35	Greatest Hits
		SMILEZ & SOUTHSTAR
24	54	Crash The Party
		SNOOP DOGG
3	42	Paid Tha Cost To Be Da Bo$$
		STONE, Angie
4	56	Mahogany Soul
		TECH N9NE
28	4	Absolute Power
		T.I.
27	36	I'm Serious
		TIMBERLAKE, Justin
2[1]	68	Justified
		TLC
4	23	3D
		TRICK DADDY
2[1]	34	Thug Holiday
		TRINA
5	34	Diamond Princess
		2PAC
1[2]	43	Better Dayz

POS	WKS	Album Title
		VANDROSS, Luther
2[1]	82	Luther Vandross
		WALKER, Hezekiah
37	53	Family Affair II: Live At Radio City Music Hall
		WC
7	15	Ghetto Heisman
		WONDER, Stevie
28	16	The Definitive Collection
		Z-RO
57	3	Life
		MOVIE SOUNDTRACKS
2[1]	27	Brown Sugar
61	9	Drumline
1[2]	41	8 Mile
64	6	8 Mile: More Music From 8 Mile
10	25	Paid In Full
		VARIOUS ARTIST COMPILATIONS
30	17	Hidden Beach Recordings Presents: Unwrapped Vol. 2
67	18	Slow Jams Vol. 1 & 2
10	19	Swizz Beatz Presents G.H.E.T.T.O. Stories

BEST-SELLING ALBUMS OF 2003

Compiled from a national sample of retail store, mass merchant and internet sales reports collected, compiled and provided by Nielsen SoundScan. Includes U.S. sales of albums for the period December 30, 2002 through December 28, 2003.

TITLE...ARTIST	SALES
Get Rich Or Die Tryin'...*50 Cent*	6,536,000
Come Away With Me...*Norah Jones*	5,137,000
Meteora...*Linkin Park*	3,478,000
Fallen...*Evanescence*	3,365,000
Speakerboxxx/The Love Below...*OutKast*	3,090,000
Dangerously In Love...*Beyoncé*	2,527,000
Chocolate Factory...*R. Kelly*	2,440,000
Metamorphosis...*Hilary Duff*	2,406,000
Shock'n Y'all...*Toby Keith*	2,324,000
A Rush Of Blood To The Head...*Coldplay*	2,184,000
Measure Of A Man...*Clay Aiken*	2,101,000
Greatest Hits Volume II And Some Other Stuff ...*Alan Jackson*	2,052,000
Now 14...*Various Artists*	2,016,000
Home...*Dixie Chicks*	2,005,000
Away From The Sun...*3 Doors Down*	1,984,000
Cocky...*Kid Rock*	1,953,000
Chicago...*Movie Soundtrack*	1,922,000
Dutty Rock...*Sean Paul*	1,912,000
The Very Best Of Cher...*Cher*	1,852,000
Thankful...*Kelly Clarkson*	1,843,000
Let Go...*Avril Lavigne*	1,835,000
The Young And The Hopeless...*Good Charlotte*	1,827,000
Up!...*Shania Twain*	1,821,000
Jackpot...*Chingy*	1,810,000
Closer...*Josh Groban*	1,769,000
Stripped...*Christina Aguilera*	1,736,000
The Diary Of Alicia Keys...*Alicia Keys*	1,707,000
Unleashed...*Toby Keith*	1,698,000
Dance With My Father...*Luther Vandross*	1,662,000
One Heart...*Celine Dion*	1,661,000
The Lizzie McGuire Movie...*Movie Soundtrack*	1,635,000
Chicken*N*Beer...*Ludacris*	1,586,000
The Black Album...*Jay-Z*	1,585,000
In The Zone...*Britney Spears*	1,580,000
Audioslave...*Audioslave*	1,567,000
Justified...*Justin Timberlake*	1,566,000
St. Anger...*Metallica*	1,548,000
Bad Boys II...*Movie Soundtrack*	1,516,000
The Very Best Of Sheryl Crow...*Sheryl Crow*	1,489,000
As Time Goes By...The Great American Songbook Vol. II...*Rod Stewart*	1,485,000
Now 12...*Various Artists*	1,481,000
Beg For Mercy...*G-Unit*	1,470,000
Afterglow...*Sarah McLachlan*	1,457,000
Room For Squares...*John Mayer*	1,370,000
Kings Of Crunk...*Lil Jon & The East Side Boyz*	1,367,000
The Eminem Show...*Eminem*	1,355,000
Chapter II...*Ashanti*	1,343,000
Heavier Things...*John Mayer*	1,296,000
Elephant...*The White Stripes*	1,296,000
More Than You Think You Are...*Matchbox Twenty*	1,272,000
Life For Rent...*Dido*	1,267,000
Some Devil...*Dave Matthews*	1,232,000
The Long Road...*Nickelback*	1,222,000
This Is Me...Then...*Jennifer Lopez*	1,201,000
Street Dreams...*Fabolous*	1,194,000
It Had To Be You...The Great American Songbook ...*Rod Stewart*	1,191,000
Tupac: Resurrection...*2Pac*	1,189,000
No Pads, No Helmets...Just Balls...*Simple Plan*	1,172,000
14 Shades Of Grey...*Staind*	1,163,000
Nellyville...*Nelly*	1,102,000
8 Mile...*Movie Soundtrack*	1,083,000
No Shoes, No Shirt, No Problems...*Kenny Chesney*	1,080,000
Josh Groban...*Josh Groban*	1,068,000
Tim McGraw And The Dancehall Doctors...*Tim McGraw*	1,049,000
Faceless...*Godsmack*	1,039,000
Results May Vary...*Limp Bizkit*	1,022,000
The Singles 1992-2003...*No Doubt*	1,010,000
La Bella Mafia...*Lil' Kim*	1,007,000
Blink-182...*Blink-182*	1,007,000

#1 ALBUMS
ON VARIOUS OTHER BILLBOARD CHARTS

Blues Albums

Independent Albums

Classical:
  Classical Albums
  Classical Crossover

Religious Albums:
  Christian Albums
  Gospel Albums

Electronic Albums

Latin Albums

Heatseekers

Internet Album Sales

Jazz Albums:
  Jazz Albums
  Contemporary Jazz Albums

Bluegrass Albums

New Age Albums

Reggae Albums

World Albums

Soundtracks

Eurochart — Albums

Hits Of The United Kingdom — Albums

EXPLANATION OF COLUMNAR HEADINGS

DATE HIT #1: Date title first peaked at the #1 position in <u>2003</u>

WKS @ #1: Total weeks title held the #1 position

LABEL: Original label

$\updownarrow$: Indicates title hit #1, dropped down, and then returned to the #1 spot

+: Indicates title is still #1 as of the 4/3/04 cut-off date

A note below some titles indicates the title also held the #1 position in years other than 2003.

#1 BLUES ALBUMS

	Date Hit #1	Wks. @ #1	Title	Artist...Label
1.	1/4	24	**Wait For Me**...*Susan Tedeschi*...Tone-Cool (includes 4 weeks at #1 in 2002)	
2.	5/24	3	**Let's Roll**... *Etta James*...Private Music	
3.	6/14	1	**Have Love Will Travel**..........................*Jim Belushi & Dan Aykroyd*...Have Love	
4.	6/21	11 ↕	**Trouble No More**...*John Mellencamp*...Columbia	
5.	7/26	1	**New York City** .... *The Peter Malick Group Featuring Norah Jones*...Koch	
6.	9/13	23 ↕	**Martin Scorsese Presents The Best Of The Blues** ...*Various Artists*...UTV (includes 8 weeks at #1 in 2004)	
12.	11/1	1	**Long Time Coming**... *Jonny Lang*...A&M	

#1 INDEPENDENT ALBUMS

	Date Hit #1	Wks. @ #1	Title	Artist...Label
1.	1/4	1	**MTV Unplugged V 2.0** ....*Dashboard Confessional*...Vagrant	
2.	1/11	31 ↕	**Kings Of Crunk**....................................... *Lil Jon & The East Side Boyz*...BME (includes 1 week at #1 in 2002 and 4 weeks at #1 in 2004)	
3.	2/8	3	**Guess Who's Back?** .... *50 Cent*...Full Clip	
4.	3/1	1	**Romantic Melodies** .... *Mannheim Steamroller*...American Gramaphone	
5.	3/15	2	**Livin' Legend**.. *B.G.* ...Choppa City	
6.	3/29	1	**Evolve**.. *Ani DiFranco*...Righteous Babe	
7.	4/5	1	**Atticus: Dragging The Lake II** .... *Various Artists*...Side One Dummy	
8.	4/12	3	**Rewind: The Hip-Hop DVD Magazine Issue 1** . *Various Artists*...Shadyville	
9.	5/10	2	**Free Agents: The Murda Mix Tape** .... *Mobb Deep*...Landspeed	
10.	5/24	1	**The War On Errorism**.. *NOFX*...Fat Wreck Chords	
11.	5/31	2	**Good Mourning** .... *Alkaline Trio*...Vagrant	
12.	6/21	1	**Vans Warped Tour 2003 Compilation** .... *Various Artists*...Side One Dummy	
13.	8/30	2	**A Mark, A Mission, A Brand, A Scar** ....*Dashboard Confessional*...Vagrant	
14.	9/13	2 ↕	**The Wind**... *Warren Zevon*...Artemis	
15.	10/4	9 ↕+	**Me & My Brother** .... *Ying Yang Twins*...Collipark (includes 8+ weeks at #1 in 2004)	
16.	10/25	1	**Seasons** .... *Sevendust*...TVT	
17.	12/13	2	**Part II** .... *Lil Jon & The East Side Boyz*...BME	

#1 CLASSICAL ALBUMS

	Date Hit #1	Wks. @ #1	Title	Artist...Label
1.	1/4	35 ↕	**Sentimento** .... *Andrea Bocelli*...Philips (includes 6 weeks at #1 in 2002)	
2.	4/12	6 ↕	**The Pianist**... *Movie Soundtrack*...Sony Classical	
3.	8/2	2	**Duetto** .... *Marcelo Alvarez/Salvatore Licitra*...Sony Classical	
4.	8/16	3	**Tchaikovsky/Mendelssohn: Piano Concertos** ....*Lang Lang*...DG	
5.	10/11	1	**Bach: Violin Concertos** .... *Hilary Hahn*...DG	
6.	10/18	1	**The Salieri Album** ....*Cecilia Bartoli*...Decca	
7.	10/25	1	**By Request**... *Renee Fleming*...Decca	
8.	11/1	9 ↕	**Sacred Arias: Special Edition**................................ *Andrea Bocelli*...Philips (includes 2 weeks at #1 in 2004)	
9.	12/6	2	**Master And Commander** ....*Movie Soundtrack*...Decca	

#1 CLASSICAL CROSSOVER ALBUMS

	Date Hit #1	Wks. @ #1	Title	Artist...Label
1.	1/4	32 ↕	**Josh Groban**.. *Josh Groban*...143 Records (includes 2 weeks at #1 in 2002)	
2.	6/28	7	**Harem**.. *Sarah Brightman*...Angel	
3.	8/16	10 ↕	**Obrigado Brazil** .... *Yo-Yo Ma*...Sony Classical	
4.	11/29	19 +	**Closer**.. *Josh Groban*...143 Records (includes 14+ weeks at #1 in 2004)	

#1 CHRISTIAN ALBUMS

	Date Hit #1	Wks. @ #1	Title	Artist...Label
1.	1/4	8	WOW Hits 2003 .... *Various Artists*...EMI (includes 4 weeks at #1 in 2002)	
2.	2/1	16 ↕	Worship Together: I Could Sing Of Your Love Forever ...*Various Artists*...Time-Life	
3.	2/15	3	All About Love .... *Steven Curtis Chapman*...Sparrow	
4.	3/22	5	Fallen..*Evanescence*...Wind-Up	
5.	4/26	1	Adoration: The Worship Album .... *Newsboys*...Sparrow	
6.	5/24	1	WOW Worship Yellow .... *Various Artists*...EMI	
7.	6/7	3	Stacie Orrico... *Stacie Orrico*...ForeFront	
8.	6/28	1	Rise And Shine .... *Randy Travis*...Word-Curb	
9.	8/23	9 ↕	Almost There ....*MercyMe*...Ino	
10.	9/6	1	Simple Things.. *Amy Grant*...A&M	
11.	9/27	1	Throne Room.. *CeCe Winans*...Pure Springs	
12.	10/25	1	The Second Decade: 1993-2003 .... *Michael W. Smith*...Reunion	
13.	11/22	5 ↕	Payable On Death.. *P.O.D.* ...Atlantic (includes 1 week at #1 in 2004)	
14.	12/20	3	WOW Hits 2004... *Various Artists*...Provident (includes 1 week at #1 in 2004)	

#1 GOSPEL ALBUMS

	Date Hit #1	Wks. @ #1	Title	Artist...Label
1.	1/4	13 ↕	Incredible ....*Mary Mary*...Columbia (includes 11 weeks at #1 in 2002)	
2.	1/18	29 ↕	The Rebirth Of Kirk Franklin .... *Kirk Franklin*...Gospo Centric (includes 24 weeks at #1 in 2002)	
3.	2/22	5 ↕	WOW Gospel 2003 .... *Various Artists*...EMI Christian	
4.	3/22	10 ↕	Donnie McClurkin...Again.................................... *Donnie McClurkin*...Verity	
5.	4/19	1	A Wing And A Prayer .... *Bishop T.D. Jakes*...Dexterity Sounds	
6.	5/24	8 ↕	Bringing It All Together .... *Vickie Winans*...Verity	
7.	6/21	1	Church: Songs Of Soul & Inspiration....................... *Various Artists*...DMI	
8.	8/9	1	Let It Rain... *Bishop Paul S. Morton*...Tehillah	
9.	8/23	5	I Need You Now .... *Smokie Norful*...EMI Gospel	
10.	9/27	6 ↕	Throne Room..*CeCe Winans*...Pure Springs (includes 3 weeks at #1 in 2004)	
11.	10/4	6 ↕	The Fighting Temptations ....*Movie Soundtrack*...Music World	
12.	11/8	1	Smokie Norful: Limited Edition........................ *Smokie Norful*...EMI Gospel	
13.	12/6	1	Live...This Is Your House ....*The Brooklyn Tabernacle Choir*...Word-Curb	
14.	12/13	2 ↕	Gotta Have Gospel!................................... *Various Artists*...Integrity Gospel (includes 1 week at #1 in 2004)	
15.	12/20	4	Go Tell It On The Mountain .... *The Blind Boys Of Alabama*...Real World (includes 2 weeks at #1 in 2004)	

#1 ELECTRONIC ALBUMS

	Date Hit #1	Wks. @ #1	Title	Artist...Label
1.	1/4	12	New York City Underground Party Volume 5 .... Louie DeVito...Dee Vee (includes 6 weeks at #1 in 2002)	
2.	2/15	1	Other People's Songs .... Erasure...Mute	
3.	2/22	1	Disco 3 .... Pet Shop Boys...Sanctuary	
4.	3/1	7	100th Window.. Massive Attack...Virgin	
5.	4/19	2	Ultra.Dance 03...Johnny Vicious...Ultra	
6.	5/3	5	Dance Divas .... Louie DeVito...Dee Vee	
7.	6/7	3	Queer As Folk: The Third Season.................. TV Soundtrack...Tommy Boy	
8.	6/28	1	Global Underground: Toronto.................... Deep Dish...Global Underground	
9.	7/5	5	Louie DeVito's Dance Factory Level 2.................... Louie DeVito...Dee Vee	
10.	8/9	2	Lara Croft: Tomb Raider: The Cradle Of Life .... Movie Soundtrack ...Hollywood	
11.	8/23	3	Emotional Technology .... BT...Nettwerk	
12.	9/13	5	Ultra.Dance 04... Louie DeVito...Ultra	
13.	10/18	2	Voyageur .... Enigma...Virgin	
14.	11/1	8↕	The Remixes... Mariah Carey...Columbia	
15.	12/6	1	New York City Underground Party Volume 6 .... Louie DeVito...Dee Vee	

#1 LATIN ALBUMS

	Date Hit #1	Wks. @ #1	Title	Artist...Label
1.	1/4	10↕	Las Ketchup ....Las Ketchup...Columbia (includes 6 weeks at #1 in 2002)	
2.	2/1	2	30 Inolvidables .... Los Bukis...Fonovisa	
3.	2/15	2	Mambo Sinuendo.......................... Ry Cooder & Manuel Galbán...Perro Verde	
4.	3/1	3↕	La Historia .... Intocable...EMI Latin	
5.	3/15	4	4...Kumbia Kings...EMI Latin	
6.	4/19	1	Y Tenerte Otra Vez... Pepe Aguilar...Univision	
7.	4/26	5	20 Inolvidables ....Los Bukis/Los Temerarios...Fonovisa	
8.	5/31	1	Tu Amor O Tu Desprecio .... Marco Antonio Solís...Fonovisa	
9.	6/7	6	Almas Del Silencio .... Ricky Martin...Sony Discos	
10.	7/19	3	Herencia Musical: 20 Corridos Inolvidables .... Los Tigres Del Norte ...Fonovisa	
11.	8/9	1	Siempre Arriba...Bronco...Fonovisa	
12.	8/16	3	Regalo Del Alma ....Celia Cruz...Sony Discos	
13.	9/6	1	Nuestro Destino Estaba Escrito................................. Intocable...EMI Latin	
14.	9/13	1	Sincero .... Chayanne...Sony Discos	
15.	9/20	4	Un Dia Normal ....Juanes...Surco	
16.	10/18	3	33 .... Luis Miguel...Warner Latina	
17.	11/8	3↕	La Historia .... A.B. Quintanilla III & Kumbia Kings...EMI Latin (includes 1 week at #1 in 2004)	
18.	11/22	5↕	La Historia Continua... .... Marco Antonio Solís...Fonovisa (includes 3 weeks at #1 in 2004)	
19.	12/6	1	Por Ti...Ednita Nazario...Sony Discos	
20.	12/13	6↕	Tributo Al Amor ....Los Temerarios...Fonovisa (includes 3 weeks at #1 in 2004)	

#1 HEATSEEKERS

	Date Hit #1	Wks. @ #1	Title / Artist...Label
1.	1/4	1	**MTV Unplugged V 2.0** .... *Dashboard Confessional*...Vagrant
2.	1/11	2↕	**Nivea**... *Nivea*....Jive
			(includes 1 week at #1 in 2002)
3.	1/18	2↕	**The Used** .... *The Used*...Reprise
			(includes 1 week at #1 in 2002)
4.	1/25	1	**Inertia** .... *The Exies*...Melisma
5.	2/1	1	**200 KM/H In The Wrong Lane**.. *t.A.T.u.* ...Interscope
6.	2/8	1	**Man With A Memory**.. *Joe Nichols*...Universal South
7.	2/15	3↕	**Chapter 2: The Voice** .... *Syleena Johnson*....Jive
8.	3/1	1	**How To Start A Fire**................................ *Further Seems Forever*...Tooth & Nail
9.	3/8	1	**You Are Free**.. *Cat Power*...Matador
10.	3/15	1	**Trapt** .... *Trapt*...Warner
11.	3/29	1	**Angel** .... *Amanda Perez*...Powerhouse
12.	4/5	5	**What It Is To Burn** ....*Finch*...Drive-Thru
13.	5/10	1	**Peter Cincotti**... *Peter Cincotti*...Concord
14.	5/17	1	**The Step Daddy** .... *Hitman Sammy Sam*...ColliPark
15.	5/24	2	**Bringing It All Together** .... *Vickie Winans*...Verity
16.	6/7	1	**Places For Breathing** .... *Revis*...Epic
17.	6/14	2↕	**I Love It**... *Craig Morgan*...Broken Bow
18.	6/21	1	**Soul Journey** .... *Gillian Welch*...Acony
19.	7/5	1	**Kemistry**.. *Kem*...Motown
20.	7/12	1	**Between The Never And The Now** ....*Vendetta Red*...Epic
21.	7/19	1	**Take A Break** .... *Me First And The Gimme Gimmes*...Fat Wreck Chords
22.	7/26	3	**Songs About Jane**... *Maroon5*...Octone
23.	8/16	2	**Smile Empty Soul**................................... *Smile Empty Soul*...Throback
24.	8/30	1	**25 Joyas Musicales**.. *Los Bukis*...Fonovisa
25.	9/6	1	**Youth & Young Manhood** .... *Kings Of Leon*...RCA
26.	9/13	1	**Decide Tú**... *Conjunto Primavera*...Fonovisa
27.	9/20	2	**Un Dia Normal** .... *Juanes*...Surco
28.	10/4	2↕	**Page Avenue**..*Story Of The Year*...Maverick
			(includes 1 week at #1 in 2004)
29.	10/11	1	**Bazooka Tooth** .... *Aesop Rock*...Definitive Jux
30.	10/18	1	**Billy Currington** .... *Billy Currington*...Mercury
31.	10/25	1	**The Room's Too Cold** .... *The Early November*...Drive-Thru
32.	11/1	3	**Welcome Interstate Managers** .... *Fountains Of Wayne*...S-Curve
33.	11/22	3↕	**Three Days Grace**... *Three Days Grace*...Jive
			(includes 1 week at #1 in 2004)
34.	12/6	1	**Por Ti**... *Ednita Nazario*...Sony Discos
35.	12/13	1	**3 Sides**... *Bob Guiney*...Wind-Up
36.	12/20	2↕	**Long Black Train** .... *Josh Turner*...MCA Nashville
			(includes 1 week at #1 in 2004)
37.	12/27	3↕	**Fefe Dobson** .... *Fefe Dobson*...Island
			(includes 2 weeks at #1 in 2004)

#1 INTERNET ALBUM SALES

	Date Hit #1	Wks. @ #1	Title	Artist...Label
1.	1/4	19↕	**Come Away With Me** .... (includes 3 weeks at #1 in 2002)	*Norah Jones*...Blue Note
2.	2/1	1	**Chasing Daylight**	*Sister Hazel*...Sixthman
3.	2/15	1	**Chicago**...	*Movie Soundtrack*...Epic
4.	4/12	1	**Meteora**	*Linkin Park*...Warner
5.	4/26	1	**World Without Tears**	*Lucinda Williams*...Lost Highway
6.	5/3	3	**The Very Best Of Cher**	*Cher*...Geffen
7.	5/24	1	**On And On**...	*Jack Johnson*...Moonshine Conspiracy
8.	6/14	1	**How The West Was Won**...	*Led Zeppelin*...Atlantic
9.	6/21	1	**Vans Warped Tour 2003 Compilation**..........	*Various Artists*...Side One Dummy
10.	6/28	1	**Hail To The Thief**..	*Radiohead*...Capitol
11.	7/5	3	**Bare**...	*Annie Lennox*...J Records
12.	8/2	1	**Wave On Wave**	*Pat Green*...Republic
13.	8/9	1	**The Artist In The Ambulance**...................................	*Thrice*...Island
14.	8/16	1	**Pirates Of The Caribbean: The Curse Of The Black Pearl**	*...Movie Soundtrack*...Walt Disney
15.	8/23	1	**Speed Graphic**	*Ben Folds*...Epic
16.	8/30	1	**Greatest Hits Volume II And Some Other Stuff**..................	*Alan Jackson* ...Arista Nashville
17.	9/6	1	**On The Beach**..	*Neil Young*...Reprise
18.	9/13	3↕	**The Wind**...	*Warren Zevon*...Artemis
19.	9/27	1	**Heavier Things**	*John Mayer*...Aware
20.	10/11	1	**Some Devil**	*Dave Matthews*...RCA
21.	10/18	1	**Life For Rent**...	*Dido*...Arista
22.	10/25	1	**Sacred Love**	*Sting*...A&M
23.	11/1	1	**Measure Of A Man**	*Clay Aiken*...RCA
24.	11/8	1	**The Very Best Of**..	*Eagles*...Warner
25.	11/15	2↕	**As Time Goes By...The Great American Songbook Vol. II**	*...Rod Stewart*...J Records
26.	11/22	1	**Afterglow**	*Sarah McLachlan*...Arista
27.	11/29	2↕	**Closer**.. (includes 1 week at #1 in 2004)	*Josh Groban*...143 Records
28.	12/6	1	**The Central Park Concert**	*Dave Matthews Band*...Bama Rags
29.	12/13	4	**Let It Be...Naked**... (includes 2 weeks at #1 in 2004)	*The Beatles*...Apple

#1 JAZZ ALBUMS

	Date Hit #1	Wks. @ #1	Title	Artist...Label
1.	1/4	15 ↕	**A Wonderful World** .... *Tony Bennett & k.d. lang*...RPM (includes 6 weeks at #1 in 2002)	
2.	1/18	18 ↕	**Live In Paris**..*Diana Krall*...Verve (includes 5 weeks at #1 in 2002 and 3 weeks at #1 in 2004)	
3.	5/10	3 ↕	**Peter Cincotti**... *Peter Cincotti*...Concord	
4.	5/24	1	**But Beautiful**.. *Boz Scaggs*...Gray Cat	
5.	5/31	1	**Paganini: After A Dream**................................ *Regina Carter*...Verve	
6.	6/14	1	**One Quiet Night**.. *Pat Metheny*...Warner	
7.	6/21	11 ↕	**timeagain** .... *David Sanborn*...Verve	
8.	9/13	3 ↕	**Nature Boy: The Standards Album** .... *Aaron Neville*...Verve	
9.	9/27	1	**Remembering Patsy Cline**........................... *Various Artists*...MCA	
10.	10/11	5	**North**.......................................*Elvis Costello*...Deutsche Grammophon	
11.	11/15	10	**Harry For The Holidays** .... *Harry Connick, Jr.* ...Columbia (includes 3 weeks at #1 in 2004)	

#1 CONTEMPORARY JAZZ ALBUMS

	Date Hit #1	Wks. @ #1	Title	Artist...Label
1.	1/4	108+	**Come Away With Me**... *Norah Jones*...Blue Note (includes 42 weeks at #1 in 2002 and 14+ weeks at #1 in 2004)	

#1 BLUEGRASS ALBUMS

	Date Hit #1	Wks @ #1	Title	Artist...Label
1.	1/4	69 ↕+	**Live**.. *Alison Krauss + Union Station*...Rounder (includes 6 weeks at #1 in 2002 and 14 weeks at #1 in 2004)	
2.	12/6	3 ↕	**A Very Special Acoustic Christmas**............ *Various Artists*...Lost Highway	

#1 NEW AGE ALBUMS

	Date Hit #1	Wks. @ #1	Title	Artist...Label
1.	1/4	6	**A Windham Hill Christmas**............................. *Various Artists*...Windham Hill (includes 5 weeks at #1 in 2002)	
2.	1/11	1	**A Peaceful Christmas**... *Various Artists*...Time-Life	
3.	1/18	5↕	**Pure Moods IV**.. *Various Artists*...Virgin (includes 2 weeks at #1 in 2002)	
4.	2/8	7↕	**Romantic Melodies**.................. *Mannheim Steamroller*...American Gramaphone (includes 5 weeks at #1 in 2004)	
5.	2/15	3↕	**Ultimate Yanni**.. *Yanni*...Windham Hill (includes 2 weeks at #1 in 2004)	
6.	3/1	14	**Ethnicity**.. *Yanni*...Virgin	
7.	6/7	9	**American Spirit** ...... *Mannheim Steamroller/C.W. McCall*...American Gramaphone	
8.	8/9	8↕	**Chimera** .... *Delerium*...Nettwerk	
9.	8/16	1	**Back 2 Back** ....*Estéban & Eugene Fodor*...Daystar	
10.	10/11	6	**Halloween** .... *Mannheim Steamroller*...American Gramaphone	
11.	11/22	9	**Peace** .... *Jim Brickman*...Windham Hill (includes 3 weeks at #1 in 2004)	

#1 REGGAE ALBUMS

	Date Hit #1	Wks. @ #1	Title	Artist...Label
1.	1/4	64↕	**Dutty Rock**.. *Sean Paul*...2 Hard (includes 5 weeks at #1 in 2002 and 8 weeks at #1 in 2004)	
2.	12/20	1	**Good 2 Go** ....*Elephant Man*...VP	

#1 WORLD MUSIC ALBUMS

	Date Hit #1	Wks. @ #1	Title	Artist...Label
1.	1/4	5	**Greatest Movie Hits** .... *Baha Men*...S-Curve (includes 2 weeks at #1 in 2002)	
2.	1/25	19↕	**Frida**.. *Movie Soundtrack*...Universal (includes 2 weeks at #1 in 2002)	
3.	2/15	8	**Mambo Sinuendo**........................... *Ry Cooder & Manuel Galbán*...Perro Verde	
4.	4/19	7	**Buenos Hermanos**..*Ibrahim Ferrer*...World Circuit	
5.	6/7	3	**Bend It Like Beckham** ....*Movie Soundtrack*...Milan	
6.	9/27	4	**Further Down The Old Plank Road** .... *The Chieftains*...Victor	
7.	10/25	9↕	**Celtic Circle**... *Various Artists*...Windham Hill (includes 4 weeks at #1 in 2004)	
8.	11/29	7	**We Three Kings**... *The Irish Tenors*...Razor & Tie (includes 2 weeks at #1 in 2004)	

#1 SOUNDTRACKS

	Date Hit #1	Wks. @ #1	Title	Label
1.	1/4	11	**8 Mile** .... Shady (includes 7 weeks at #1 in 2002)	
2.	2/1	12↕	**Chicago** ....Epic	
3.	3/8	2	**Cradle 2 The Grave** ....Bloodline	
4.	5/10	2↕	**The Lizzie McGuire Movie** .... Walt Disney	
5.	5/17	1	**American Idol Season 2: All-Time Classic American Love Songs** .. RCA	
6.	5/24	3	**The Matrix Reloaded** ....Warner Sunset	
7.	6/21	4	**2 Fast 2 Furious**... Disturbing Tha Peace	
8.	7/19	2	**Charlie's Angels: Full Throttle** .... Columbia	
9.	8/2	10	**Bad Boys II**...Bad Boy	
10.	10/11	3	**The Fighting Temptations** .... Music World	
11.	11/1	3	**Kill Bill Vol. 1** ....A Band Apart	
12.	11/22	4↕	**The Cheetah Girls** .... Walt Disney (includes 3 weeks at #1 in 2004)	
13.	11/29	9	**Tupac: Resurrection** .... Amaru (includes 4 weeks at #1 in 2004)	

#1 EUROCHART — ALBUMS

	Date Hit #1	Wks. @ #1	Title	Artist...Label
1.	1/4	12	**Escapology** .... Robbie Williams...Chrysalis (includes 4 weeks at #1 in 2002)	
2.	3/1	2	**100th Window** .... Massive Attack...Virgin	
3.	3/15	4	**Come Away With Me** ....Norah Jones...Blue Note	
4.	4/12	4	**Meteora** ....Linkin Park...Warner	
5.	5/10	3	**American Life** ....Madonna...Maverick	
6.	5/31	1	**The Golden Age Of Grotesque**......................... Marilyn Manson...Interscope	
7.	6/7	7↕	**Fallen**...Evanescence...Wind-Up	
8.	6/21	6	**St. Anger** .... Metallica...Vertigo	
9.	8/2	3	**Dangerously In Love** .... Beyoncé...Columbia	
10.	9/27	1	**Dance Of Death** .... Iron Maiden...Capitol	
11.	10/4	1	**Reality** .... David Bowie...Columbia	
12.	10/11	1	**Sacred Love** .... Sting...A&M	
16.	10/18	18↕	**Life For Rent** .... Dido...Arista (includes 7 weeks at #1 in 2004)	

#1 HITS OF THE UNITED KINGDOM — ALBUMS

	Date Hit #1	Wks. @ #1	Title	Artist...Label
1.	1/4	7 ↕	**Escapology**......................................Robbie Williams...Chrysalis (includes 4 weeks at #1 in 2002)	
2.	1/18	3	**Let Go** ....Avril Lavigne...Arista	
3.	2/8	7 ↕	**Justified**..Justin Timberlake....Jive	
4.	2/22	1	**Simply Deep** .... Kelly Rowland...Columbia	
5.	3/1	1	**100th Window**...................................... Massive Attack...Virgin	
6.	3/15	4	**Come Away With Me** ....Norah Jones...Blue Note	
7.	4/12	1	**Meteora**... Linkin Park...Warner	
8.	4/19	2	**Elephant**... The White Stripes...XL	
9.	5/3	1	**A Rush Of Blood To The Head** .... Coldplay...Parlophone	
10.	5/10	1	**American Life**......................................Madonna...Maverick	
11.	5/24	1	**Think Tank**... Blur...Parlophone	
12.	6/21	1	**You Gotta Go There To Come Back**...........................Stereophonics...V2	
13.	6/28	1	**Hail To The Thief**.......................................Radiohead...Parlophone	
14.	7/5	1	**Fallen** .... Evanescence...Epic	
15.	7/12	5	**Dangerously In Love** ....Beyoncé...Columbia	
16.	8/16	1	**Magic And Medicine** .... The Coral...Deltasonic	
17.	8/30	2	**American Tune**......................................Eva Cassidy...Blix Street	
18.	9/13	4	**Permission To Land** ....The Darkness...Must Destroy	
19.	10/11	1	**Absolution** .... Muse...EastWest	
20.	10/18	10 ↕	**Life For Rent**... Dido...Arista (includes 4 weeks at #1 in 2004)	
21.	11/15	1	**In Time 1988-2003: The Best Of R.E.M.** .........................R.E.M. ...Warner	
22.	11/22	1	**Guilty**...Blue...Innocent	
23.	12/6	1	**Number Ones** ....Michael Jackson...Epic	
24.	12/13	1	**Turnaround**.. Westlife...BMG	
25.	12/20	2 ↕	**Friday's Child** .... Will Young...BMG (includes 1 week at #1 in 2004)	

LABEL ABBREVIATIONS

American Gram. .... American Gramaphone
Cheap Trick Unlim. .... Cheap Trick Unlimited
Chocolate Ind. .... Chocolate Industries
Def Jam S. .... Def Jam South
Deutsche Gr. .... Deutsche Grammaphone
Disturb. Tha P. .... Disturbing Tha Peace
Disturbing Tha P. .... Disturbing Tha Peace
Eastern Conf. .... Eastern Conference
1972 Ent. .... 1972 Entertainment
Overnight Sen. .... Overnight Sensation

ALLEN, Rosalie
Country singer (known as "The Prairie Star" and "Queen of the Yodelers")...9/23...Age 79...Heart failure

APPLEGATE, Ross
Character actor (played "Dutch Doogan" in the movie *Seabiscuit*)...1/1...Age 63...House fire

BALLARD, Hank
R&B singer (recorded the original version of "The Twist")...3/2...Age 75...Throat cancer

BANKS, Homer
R&B songwriter (co-wrote "(If Loving You Is Wrong) I Don't Want To Be Right")...4/3...Age 61...Cancer

BATES, Alan
British actor (such movies as *Georgy Girl* and *The Rose*)...12/27...Age 69...Pancreatic cancer

BATTIN, Skip
One-half of Skip & Flip duo (1959 hit "It Was I")...7/6...Age 69...Alzheimer's disease

BERRY, Fred
Black actor (played "Rerun" on TV's *What's Happening*)...10/21...Age 52...Heart failure

BIG DS
Member of the rap group Onyx (1993 hit "Slam")...5/22...Age 30...Cancer

BLOOM, David
News reporter/co-anchor of *Weekend Today*...4/6...Age 39...Pulmonary embolism while covering the war in Iraq

BOYD, Eva — see LITTLE EVA

BRANDIS, Jonathan
Actor (played "Lucas Wolenczek" on TV's *SeaQuest DSV*)...11/12...Age 27...Suicide

BRAUNN, Erik
Lead guitarist for Iron Butterfly (1968 hit "In-A-Gadda-Da-Vida")...7/25...Age 52...Heart failure

BRINKLEY, David
Veteran news broadcaster...6/11...Age 82...Complications from a fall

BRONSON, Charles
Prolific actor (starred in the *Death Wish* series of movies)...8/30...Age 81...Pneumonia

BROOKS, Rand
Character actor (played "Charles Hamilton" in the movie *Gone With The Wind*)...9/1...Age 84...Cancer

BRYANT, Felice
Prolific songwriter (co-wrote several Everly Brothers' hits with husband Boudleaux)...4/22...Age 77...Cancer

BUCK, Gary
Country singer (1963 hit "Happy To Be Unhappy")...10/14...Age 63...Cancer

BURGESS, Wilma
Country singer (1966 hit "Misty Blue")...8/26...Age 64...Heart attack

CARLISLE, Bill
Lead singer of The Carlisles (1953 hit "No Help Wanted")...3/17...Age 94...Stroke

CARNEY, Art
Comic actor (played "Ed Norton" on TV's *The Honeymooners*)...11/9...Age 85...Heart failure

CARTER, Benny
R&B saxophonist (1944 hit "Hurry, Hurry!")...7/12...Age 95...Bronchitis

CARTER, Nell
R&B actress/singer (starred in the 1980s sitcom *Gimme A Break*)...1/23...Age 54...Diabetes

CARTER CASH, June
Country singer (wife of Johnny Cash)...5/15...Age 73...Heart failure

CASH, Johnny
Legendary singer/songwriter/guitarist (known as "The Man In Black")...9/12...Age 71...Respiratory failure due to diabetes

CONLEY, Arthur
R&B singer (1967 hit "Sweet Soul Music")...11/17...Age 57...Intestinal cancer

CONNOR, Keven "Dino"
Member of R&B group H-Town (1993 hit "Knockin' Da Boots")...1/28...Age 28...Car crash

CRAIN, Jeanne
Actress (played "Letty Page" in the 1957 movie *The Joker Is Wild*)...12/14...Age 78...Heart attack

CRENNA, Richard
Actor (played "Colonel Trautman" in the *Rambo* movie trilogy and "Luke McCoy" in the TV series *The Real McCoys*)...1/17...Age 76...Pancreatic cancer

CRONYN, Hume
Actor (played "Joe Finley" in the 1985 movie *Cocoon*)...6/15...Age 91...Prostate cancer

CRUZ, Celia
Latin singer (known as "The Queen of Salsa")...7/16...Age 77...Brain cancer

DEAL, Bill
Lead singer/organist of The Rhondels (1969 hit "What Kind Of Fool Do You Think I Am")...12/10...Age 59...Heart attack

DEANE, Buddy
Hosted popular music TV show in Baltimore (inspiration for the movie *Hairspray*)...7/16...Age 78...Stroke

DRAPER, Rusty
Singer/songwriter/guitarist (1955 hit "The Shifting, Whispering Sands")...3/28...Age 80...Pneumonia

DUDLEY, Dave
Country singer (1963 hit "Six Days On The Road")...
12/22...Age 75...Heart attack

EBSEN, Buddy
Beloved actor (starred on TV's *The Beverly Hillbillies* and *Barnaby Jones*)...7/6...Age 95...Pneumonia

ELAM, Jack
Veteran character actor (appeared in several westerns)...10/20...Age 84...Heart failure

EPSTEIN, Howie
Bassist for Tom Petty's Heartbreakers...2/23...
Age 47...Drug overdose

EVANS, Jerome
Member of The Furys (1963 hit "Zing! Went The Strings Of My Heart")...11/30...Age 65...Heart attack

FAFARA, Stanley
Child actor (played "Whitey Whitney" on TV's *Leave It To Beaver*)...9/20...Age 54...Complications following surgery

FAITH, Adam
British singer (1965 hit "It's Alright")...3/7...Age 62...
Heart attack

FARRAN, Edward
Member of The Arbors (1969 hit "The Letter")...
1/12...Age 64...Kidney failure

FINN, Mickey
Lead guitarist of T-Rex (1972 hit "Bang A Gong")...
1/11...Age 55...Liver failure

FLETCHER, Marlon — see BIG DS

FOREST, Earl
R&B singer/drummer (1953 hit "Whoopin' And Hollerin'")...2/26...Age 76...Cancer

GEORGE, Wally
Conservative TV talk show host (father of actress Rebecca De Mornay)...10/7...Age 71...Pneumonia

GIBB, Maurice
Member of the Bee Gees (twin brother of Robin Gibb)...1/12...Age 53...Heart attack during emergency surgery

GIBSON, Don
Country singer/songwriter (1958 hit "Oh Lonesome Me")...11/17...Age 75...Heart failure

GLAZER, Tom
Folk singer (1963 novelty hit "On Top Of Spaghetti)...
2/21...Age 88...Heart failure

GODDARD, Trevor
Actor (played recurring role of "Lt. Commander Michael 'Mic' Brumby" on TV's *JAG*)....6/7...Age 40...
Apparent drug overdose

GONZALEZ, Ruben
Cuban pianist (member of Buena Vista Social Club)...12/8...Age 84...Heart failure

GOODMAN, Vestal
Gospel singer (matriarch of the Happy Goodman Family)...12/27...Age 74...Flu complications

GOODWIN, Ron
British composer/conductor (1957 hit "Swinging Sweethearts")...1/8...Age 77...Heart failure

GOSTING, Dick
One half of Dick & DeeDee duo (1961 hit "The Mountain's High")...12/27...Age 63...Injuries suffered in a fall

GREAN, Charles Randolph
Conductor/arranger (1969 hit "Quentin's Theme")...
12/20...Age 90...Heart failure

GUIDRY, Greg
Pop singer/songwriter (1982 hit "Goin' Down")...
7/28...Age 53...Car fire

HACKETT, Buddy
Popular comedian (1956 novelty hit "Chinese Rock And Egg Roll")...6/30...Age 78...Heart failure

HATFIELD, Bobby
One-half of The Righteous Brothers (1966 hit "Soul And Inspiration")...11/5...Age 63...Cocaine-induced heart failure

HEMMINGS, David
British actor (such movies as *Blowup* and *Gladiator*)...12/3...Age 62...Heart attack

HEPBURN, Katharine
Legendary movie actress (such movies as *Bringing Up Baby*, *The Lion In Winter* and *On Golden Pond*)...6/29...Age 96...Heart failure

HILLER, Wendy
British actress (played "Mothershead" in the 1980 movie *The Elephant Man*)...5/14...Age 90...
Heart failure

HINDMAN, Earl
Character actor (played the neighbor "Wilson" on TV's *Home Improvement*)...12/29...Age 61...Lung cancer

HINES, Gregory
Dancer/actor (starred in such movies as *The Cotton Club* and *Running Scared*)...8/9...Age 57...Liver cancer

HOPE, Bob
Legendary comedian (one of the most popular entertainers of the 20th Century)...7/27...Age 100...
Pneumonia

HOVIS, Larry
Actor (played "Sgt. Carter" on TV's *Hogan's Heroes*)...9/9...Age 67...Esophagial cancer

JACKSON, Tony
Bassist for The Searchers (1965 hit "Love Potion Number Nine")...8/18...Age 63...Liver failure

JETER, Michael
Character actor (played "Herman Stiles" on TV's *Evening Shade* and "Eduard Delacroix" in the movie *The Green Mile*)...3/30...Age 50...AIDS

JUMP, Gordon
Character actor (played "Arthur Carlson" on TV's *WKRP In Cincinnati*) ...9/22...Age 71...Heart failure

KAMEN, Michael
Conductor/arranger (recorded a live album with Metallica)...11/18...Age 55...Heart attack

KAZAN, Elia
Legendary movie director (*A Streetcar Named Desire*, *On The Waterfront* and *East Of Eden*)...9/28...Age 94...Heart failure

KEIKO
Killer whale (star of movie *Free Willy*)...12/12... Age 27...Pneumonia

KING, Earl
R&B singer/guitarist (1955 hit "Those Lonely, Lonely Nights")...4/17...Age 69...Diabetes

KING, Robbie
Keyboardist for Bobby Taylor & The Vancouvers (1968 hit "Does Your Mama Know About Me")... 9/17...Age 56...Throat cancer

KING BISCUIT BOY — see NEWELL, Richard

KNUST, Michael
Lead guitarist of Fever Tree (1968 hit "San Francisco Girls")...9/15...Age 54...Heart failure

LANGE, Hope
Actress (starred in the TV series *The Ghost & Mrs. Muir*)...12/19...Age 72...Intestinal disorder

LITTLE EVA
R&B singer (1962 hit "The Loco-Motion")...4/10... Age 57...Cancer

MacKENZIE, Gisele
Star of TV's *Your Hit Parade* (1955 hit "Hard To Get")...9/5...Age 76...Colon cancer

MANN, Herbie
Jazz flutist (1975 hit "Hijack")...7/1...Age 73... Prostate cancer

MILLER, Stephen
Keyboardist for the rock group Grinder Switch (1977 album *Redwing*)...8/17...Age 60...Liver failure

MOST, Mickie
British record producer (such groups as Herman's Hermits)...5/30...Age 64...Cancer

NEWELL, Richard
Recorded under the name "King Biscuit Boy"...1/5... Age 58...Heart failure

N!XAU
African Bushman turned actor (starred in the movie *The Gods Must Be Crazy*)...7/5...Age 59...Heart failure

O'CONNOR, Donald
Actor/dancer (starred in the *Frances The Talking Mule* movie series)...9/27...Age 78...Heart failure

PALMER, Robert
British singer (1986 hit "Addicted To Love")...9/26... Age 54...Heart attack

PAONE, Nicola
Novelty singer (1959 hit "Blah, Blah, Blah")...12/25... Age 64...Pneumonia

PAYCHECK, Johnny
Country singer (1978 hit "Take This Job And Shove It")...2/18...Age 64...Emphysema

PECK, Gregory
Legendary actor (such movies as *Roman Holiday*, *To Kill A Mockingbird* and *The Omen*)...6/12...Age 87... Heart failure

PHILLIPS, Sam
Record executive (founder of the legendary Sun label)...7/30...Age 80...Respiratory failure

PLIMPTON, George
Author/actor (wrote *Paper Lion*)...9/26...Age 76... Heart failure

RANDAZZO, Teddy
Pop singer (1960 hit "The Way Of A Clown")... 11/21...Age 66...Heart attack

RAY, Gene Anthony
Actor (played "Leroy Johnson" on TV's *Fame*)...11/14 ...Age 41...Stroke

REDDING, Noel
Bassist for the Jimi Hendrix Experience (1968 hit "All Along The Watchtower")...5/12...Age 57... Heart failure

RIDGEWAY, Esther
Member of R&B group The Ridgeways (performed vocals for drummer Gene Dunlap)...2/22...Age 43... Heart attack

RIEFENSTAHL, Leni
Female movie director (made Nazi propaganda films during World War II)...9/8...Age 101...Heart failure

RITTER, John
Comic actor (played "Jack Tripper" on TV's *Three's Company*)/son of the late country singer Tex Ritter... 9/11...Age 54...Heart defect

ROBERTS, Malcolm
British singer (1970 hit "Love Is All")...2/7...Age 58... Heart attack

RODDY, Rod
TV announcer (*The Price Is Right*)...10/27...Age 66... Colon and breast cancer

ROGERS, Fred
Host of classic children's TV series *Mister Rogers' Neighborhood*...2/27...Age 74...Stomach cancer

ROWBERRY, Dave
Keyboardist for The Animals (replaced original member Alan Price)...6/6...Age 62...Heart failure

SAIN, Oliver
R&B saxophonist (1976 hit "Party Hearty")...10/28... Age 71...Bone and bladder cancer

SANTAMARIA, Mongo
Cuban conga player (1963 hit "Watermelon Man")... 2/1...Age 80...Stroke

SCARBOROUGH, Skip
R&B songwriter (wrote "Love Ballad" for George Benson)...7/3...Age 58...Cancer

SCHLESINGER, John
Movie director (1969's *Midnight Cowboy*)...7/25...
Age 77...Heart failure

SCOTT, Martha
Actress (played "Miriam" in the movie *The Ten Commandments*)...5/28...Age 90...Heart failure

SEGUNDO, Company
Cuban singer (member of Buena Vista Social Club)...
7/13...Age 95...Kidney failure

SHEPHERD, Gerry
Bassist for The Glitter Band (1976 hit "Makes You Blind")...5/6...Age 51...Heart failure

SILVETTI, Bebu
Argentinian disco producer (1977 hit "Spring Rain")...
7/5...Age 59...Lung cancer

SIMONE, Nina
Jazz-styled singer (1959 hit "I Loves You, Porgy")...
4/21...Age 70...Cancer

SINCLAIR, Ken
Member of The Six Teens (1956 hit "A Casual Look")...3/16...Age 63...Cancer

SINGLETON, Penny
Actress (starred in the popular *Blondie* series of movies)...11/12...Age 95...Stroke

SMITH, Elliott
Singer/songwriter (2000 album *Figure 8*)...10/21...
Age 34...Suicide

SOULJA SLIM
Male rapper (1998 album *Give It To 'Em Raw*)...
11/26...Age 25...Shot to death

STACK, Robert
Actor (played "Eliot Ness" on TV's *The Untouchables*)...5/14...Age 84...Heart attack

STARR, Edwin
R&B singer (1970 hit "War")...4/2...Age 61...
Heart attack

STEWART, Gary
Country singer (1975 hit "She's Actin' Single (I'm Drinkin' Doubles)")...12/16...Age 59...Suicide

STEWART, Redd
Country songwriter (co-wrote "The Tennessee Waltz")...8/2...Age 80...Injuries suffered in a fall

STONE, Philip
Character actor (played "Delbert Grady" in the movie *The Shining*)...6/15...Age 79...Cancer

TAPP, James — SOULJA SLIM

THIGPEN, Lynne
Singer/actress (played "Ella Mae Farmer" on TV's *The District*)...3/12...Age 54...Cerebral hemorrhage

THOMAS, Dick
Country singer (1945 hit "Sioux City Sue")...11/22...
Age 88...Heart attack

THOMPSON, Tony
Drummer for Chic (1978 hit "Le Freak")...11/12...
Age 48...Renal cell cancer

TILLMAN, Floyd
Country singer (1944 hit "They Took The Stars Out Of Heaven")...8/22...Age 88...Leukemia

TIM TAM — see WIESEND, Rick

TOWNSEND, Ed
R&B singer/songwriter (1958 hit "For Your Love")...
8/13...Age 74...Heart failure

TUTTLE, Wesley
Country singer/actor (1945 hit "With Tears In My Eyes")...9/29...Age 85...Heart failure

VANCE, Al
Member of Harvey Scales & The Seven Sounds (1967 hit "Get Down")...6/15...Age 59...Heart attack

VANDIS, Tito
Character actor (played "Karras' Uncle" in the movie *The Exorcist*)...2/23...Age 86...Cancer

VOUDOURIS, Roger
Pop singer (1979 hit "Get Used To It")...8/3...
Age 48...Heart failure

WAIBEL, Bruce
Rock bassist (member of Gregg Allman's band)...
9/2...Age 45...Suicide

WEBBER, Charlie
Member of the Swingin' Medallions (1966 hit "Double Shot (Of My Baby's Love)")...1/17...Age 57...Cancer

WELLS, Brandi
Lead singer of R&B group Slick (1980 hit "Sunrise")...
3/25...Age 48...Heart failure

WEST, Speedy
Country guitarist (one-half of Orville & Ivy duo)...
11/15...Age 79...Heart failure

WHISKEY, Nancy
British singer (sang lead on Chas McDevitt's 1957 hit "Freight Train")...2/1...Age 67...Heart attack

WHITE, Barry
R&B singer/songwriter/producer (1974 hit "Can't Get Enough Of Your Love, Babe")...7/4...Age 58...
Kidney failure

WIESEND, Rick
Leader of Tim Tam & The Turn-Ons (1966 hit "Wait A Minute")...10/22...Age 60...Leukemia

WILBURN, Teddy
One-half of the Wilburn Brothers duo (1967 hit "Hurt Her Once For Me")...11/24...Age 71...
Parkinson's disease

WOOLEY, Sheb
Singer/actor (1958 novelty hit "The Purple People Eater")...9/16...Age 82...Leukemia

ZEVON, Warren
Singer/songwriter (1978 hit "Werewolves Of London")
...9/7...Age 56...Lung cancer

The Charts From

When the talk turns to music, more people turn to Joel Whitburn's Record Research Collection than to any other reference source.

That's because these are the **only** books that get right to the bottom of *Billboard's* major charts, with **complete, fully accurate chart data on every record ever charted**. So they're quoted with confidence by DJ's, music show hosts, program directors, collectors and other music enthusiasts worldwide.

Each book lists every record's significant chart data, such as peak position, debut date, peak date, weeks charted, label, record number and much more, all conveniently arranged for fast, easy reference. Most books also feature artist biographies, record notes, RIAA Platinum/Gold Record certifications, top artist and record achievements, all-time artist and record rankings, a chronological listing of all #1 hits, and additional in-depth chart information.

TOP POP SINGLES 1955-2002
Over 25,000 pop singles — every "Hot 100" hit — arranged by artist. First-time ever feature.key information now highlighted **in red type**. Includes thousands of artist biographies and countless titles notes. Shows the B-side title of every "Hot 100" hit. 1,024 pages. Hardcover. $79.95

POP ANNUAL 1955-1999
A year-by-year ranking, based on chart performance, of over 23,000 pop hits. Also includes, for the first time, the songwriters for every "Hot 100" hit. 912 pages. $79.95 Hardcover / $69.95 Softcover.

HIT LIST 1955-1999
An accurate checklist of every title that appears in both our new Top Pop Singles 1955-1999 and new Pop Annual 1955-1999. Features an ample 11″ x 8½″ page format and includes a check box for each record and picture sleeve (where applicable). 304 pages. Spiral-bound softcover. $39.95.

POP HITS SINGLES & ALBUMS 1940-1954
Four big books in one: an artist-by-artist anthology of early pop classics, a year-by-year ranking of Pop's early hits, the complete story of the early pop albums and the Top 10 singles charts of every *Billboard* "Best Selling Singles" chart. Filled with artist bios, title notes, and many special sections. 576 pages. Hardcover. $69.95.

POP MEMORIES 1890-1954
Unprecedented in depth and dimension. An artist-by-artist, title-by-title chronicle of the 65 formative years of recorded popular music. Fascinating facts and statistics on over 1,600 artists and 12,000 recordings, compiled directly from America's popular music charts, surveys and record listings. 660 pages. Hardcover. $59.95.

A CENTURY OF POP MUSIC
This unique book chronicles the biggest Pop hits of the past 100 years, in yearly rankings of the Top 40 songs of every year from 1900 to 1999. Includes complete artist and title sections, pictures of the top artists, top hits and top artists by decade, and more. 256 pages. Softcover. $39.95.

TOP POP ALBUMS 1955-2001
An artist-by-artist history of the over 22,000 albums that ever appeared on *Billboard's* pop albums charts, with a complete A-Z listing below each artist of every track from every charted album by that artist. 1,208 pages. Hardcover. $99.95.

ALBUM CUTS 1955-2001
An all-inclusive, alphabetical index of every song track from every charted music album listed in the *Top Pop Albums 1955-2001* book, with the artist's name and the album's chart debut year. 720 pages. Hardcover. $44.95.

Top To Bottom

BILLBOARD HOT 100/POP SINGLES CHARTS:

THE NINETIES 1990-1999 **THE EIGHTIES 1980-1989** **THE SEVENTIES 1970-1979** **THE SIXTIES 1960-1969** **POP CHARTS 1955-1959**	Four complete collections of the actual weekly "Hot 100" charts from each decade; black-and-white reproductions at 70% of original size. Over 550 pages each. Deluxe Hardcover. $79.95 each. Reproductions of every weekly pop singles chart *Billboard* published from 1955 through 1959 ("Best Sellers," "Jockeys," "Juke Box," "Top 100" and "Hot 100"). 496 pages. Deluxe Hardcover. $59.95.

BILLBOARD POP ALBUM CHARTS 1965-1969
The greatest of all album eras...straight off the pages of *Billboard*! Every weekly pop albums chart, shown in its entirety, from 1965 through 1969. Black-and-white reproductions at 70% of original size. 496 pages. Deluxe Hardcover. $59.95.

TOP COUNTRY SINGLES 1944-2001
The complete history of the most genuine of American musical genres, with an artist-by-artist listing of every "Country" single ever charted. 608 pages. Hardcover. $69.95.

COUNTRY ANNUAL 1944-1997
A year-by-year ranking, based on chart performance, of over 16,000 Country hits. 704 pages. Hardcover. $64.95.

TOP COUNTRY ALBUMS 1964-1997
An artist-by-artist listing of every album to appear on *Billboard's* "Top Country Albums" chart from its beginning in 1964 through September, 1997. Includes complete listings of all tracks from every Top 10 Country album. 304 pages. Hardcover. $49.95.

TOP R&B SINGLES 1942-1999
Revised edition of our R&B bestseller — loaded with new features! Every "Soul," "Black," "Urban Contemporary" and "Rhythm & Blues" charted single, listed by artist. 688 pages. Hardcover. $69.95.

TOP R&B ALBUMS 1965-1998
First edition! An artist-by-artist listing of each of the 2,177 artists and 6,940 albums to appear on *Billboard's* "Top R&B Albums" chart. Includes complete listings of all tracks from every Top 10 R&B album. 360 pages. Hardcover. $49.95.

TOP ADULT CONTEMPORARY 1961-2001
An Artist-by-artist listing of the nearly 8,000 singles and over 1,900 artists that appeared on *Billboard's* "Easy Listening" and "Hot Adult Contemporary" singles charts from July 17, 1961 through December 29, 2001. 352 pages. Hardcover. $44.95.

#1 POP PIX 1953-2003
A Record Research first! Full-color pictures of nearly 1,000 Billboard Pop/Hot 100 #1 hits of the past 51 years in chronological sequence. 112 pages. Softcover. $24.95.

#1 ALBUM PIX 1945-2004
A Record Research first! Full-color pictures of every #1 Pop, Country and R&B album, in chronological sequence. 176 pages. Softcover. $29.95.

HOT DANCE/DISCO 1974-2003

First edition! Lists every one of the over 3,800 artists and over 8,000 hits that appeared on *Billboard's* national "Dance/Disco Club Play" chart from its inception. 368 pages. Hardcover. $49.95.

ROCK TRACKS 1981-2002

Two artist-by-artist listings of the over 4,800 titles that appeared on *Billboard's* "Album Rock Tracks" chart from March, 1981 through October, 2002 and the over 2,200 titles that appeared on *Billboard's* "Modern Rock Tracks" chart from September, 1988 through October, 2002. 336 pages. Hardcover. $49.95.

BILLBOARD TOP 10 SINGLES CHARTS 1955-2000

A complete listing of each weekly Top 10 singles chart from *Billboard's* "Best Sellers" chart (1955-July 28, 1958) and "Hot 100" chart from its inception (August 4, 1958) through 2000. Each chart shows each single's current and previous week's positions, total weeks charted on the entire chart, original label & number, and more. 712 pages. Hardcover. $49.95.

BILLBOARD TOP 10 ALBUM CHARTS 1963-1998

This books contains more than 1,800 individual Top 10 charts from over 35 years of *Billboard's* weekly Top Albums chart (currently titled The Billboard 200). Each chart shows each album's current and previous week's positions, total weeks charted on the entire Top Albums chart, original label & number, and more. 536 pages. Hardcover. $39.95.

BUBBLING UNDER SINGLES AND ALBUMS 1998 Edition

All "Bubbling Under The Hot 100" (1959-1997) and "Bubbling Under The Top Pop Albums" (1970-1985) charts covered in full and organized artist by artist. Also features a photo section of every EP that hit *Billboard's* "Best Selling Pop EP's" chart (1957-1960). 416 pages. Softcover. $49.95.

BILLBOARD SINGLES REVIEWS 1958

Reproductions of every weekly 1958 record review *Billboard* published for 1958. Reviews of nearly 10,000 record sides by 3,465 artists. 280 pages. Softcover. $29.95.

BILLBOARD TOP 1000 x 5 1996 Edition

Includes five complete separate rankings — from #1 through #1000 — of the all-time top charted hits of Pop & Hot 100 Singles 1955-1996, Pop Singles 1940-1954, Adult Contemporary Singles 1961-1996, R&B Singles 1942-1996, and Country Singles 1944-1996. 288 pages. Softcover. $29.95.

DAILY #1 HITS 1940-1992

A desktop calendar of a half-century of #1 pop records. Lists one day of the year per page of every record that held the #1 position on the pop singles charts on that day for each of the past 53+ years. 392 pages. Spiral-bound softcover. $24.95.

BILLBOARD #1s 1950-1991

A week-by-week listing of every #1 single and album from *Billboard's* Pop, R&B, Country and Adult Contemporary charts. 336 pages. Softcover. $24.95.

MUSIC YEARBOOKS 2003/2002/2001/2000/1999/1998/1997/1996/1995/1994/1993/1992/1991

A complete review of each year's charted music — as well as a superb supplemental update of our Record Research Pop Singles and Albums, Country Singles, R&B Singles, Adult Contemporary Singles, and Bubbling Under Singles books. Various page lengths. Softcover. 1999 thru 2003 editions $39.95 / 1995 thru 1998 editions $34.95 each / 1991 thru 1994 editions $29.95 each.